50

YEARS OF SINGAPORE'S

PRODUCTIVITY DRIVE

50 YEARS OF SINGAPORE'S PRODUCTIVITY DRIVE

Woon Kin Chung • Loo Ya Lee

 World Scientific

NEW JERSEY · LONDON · SINGAPORE · BEIJING · SHANGHAI · HONG KONG · TAIPEI · CHENNAI · TOKYO

Published by

World Scientific Publishing Co. Pte. Ltd.

5 Toh Tuck Link, Singapore 596224

USA office: 27 Warren Street, Suite 401-402, Hackensack, NJ 07601

UK office: 57 Shelton Street, Covent Garden, London WC2H 9HE

Library of Congress Cataloging-in-Publication Data
Names: Woon, Kin Chung, author. | Loo, Ya Lee, author.
Title: 50 years of Singapore's productivity drive / Kin Chung Woon, Ya Lee Loo.
Other titles: Fifty years of Singapore's productivity drive
Description: 1 Edition. | New Jersey : World Scientific, [2017] |
    Includes bibliographical references and index.
Identifiers: LCCN 2017045433 | ISBN 9789813141179
Subjects: LCSH: Industrial productivity--Singapore--History. | Singapore--Economic conditions. |
    Singapore--Economic policy.
Classification: LCC HC445.8.Z9 I5288 2017 | DDC 338.4/5095957--dc23
LC record available at https://lccn.loc.gov/2017045433

British Library Cataloguing-in-Publication Data
A catalogue record for this book is available from the British Library.

For any available supplementary material, please visit
http://www.worldscientific.com/worldscibooks/10.1142/10065#t=suppl

Desk Editor: Shreya Gopi

Typeset by Stallion Press
Email: enquiries@stallionpress.com

Printed in Singapore

*"Before you discuss your future, remember how we got here —
the past."*

Prime Minister Lee Kuan Yew
Opening Address at Seminar on 'Modernization of the
Labour Movement'
16-19 November 1969

Contents

Foreword

My first encounter with productivity was in 1976 when I started work as a young officer in the Economic Development Board (EDB) and saw how important productivity was to our investors.

Years later, I became deeply involved in Singapore's Productivity Movement when I was Chief Executive of the national productivity organisation — National Productivity Board (NPB) and its successors, Singapore Productivity and Standards Board (PSB) and Standards, Productivity and Innovation Board (SPRING Singapore). This spanned the period 1 February 1995–14 October 2003.

My personal experience in the Productivity Movement has taught me that there are certain constants that are important. The fact that the national productivity organisation that I helmed was transformed twice in less than nine years reflected the vast changes that took place during that period. Nevertheless, there were certain things that did not change. These are the constants which are just as important today.

First, productivity is vital to Singapore. It is in fact a subject that is of concern to all countries. During my stint as Chief Executive of the national productivity organisation, we received many requests from all over the world for us to share our success story on productivity. The Botswana National Productivity Centre, for instance, was established with our assistance. Whether a country is developing or whether it has reached a developed stage, it needs to address the central question of productivity: how can maximum value be derived from the goods and services produced in relation to the resources used? The answer matters because the rate of productivity growth determines how fast the country can grow and how high the standard of living can be. For Singapore, a small economy with very limited resources, productivity is absolutely critical. Similarly, at the enterprise or company level, productivity is of utmost importance. The rate of productivity growth in a company determines how fast it can grow and how competitive its goods and services are. This has a bearing on the amount of profit that can be generated and the level of wages that can be paid to the employees.

Second, the productivity message bears repeating. Productivity is a five-syllable word which does not roll off the tongue easily. It is also not a term that endears itself to all companies and individuals. For most companies, productivity does not matter as much as profit, even though the two are related. For some individuals, productivity has the negative connotation of working harder or, worse still, layoff. These misconceptions about productivity arise because of lack of understanding of what the term really means. We therefore need to de-mystify productivity and give it a human face. Promoting the productivity message has to be done continuously regardless of the ups and downs of the economy. Every generation of the workforce needs to be educated on the meaning of productivity and its significance, and be reminded of it all the time. The pursuit of productivity is akin to running a marathon with no finish line.

Third, productivity cannot be left to chance or even to market forces, since the market mechanism may not always function well. Even if the importance of productivity is well understood, not everyone knows how to be productive. A systematic approach is required to understand the determinants of productivity, formulate the policies and plans to improve productivity, and implement the programmes appropriately. Productivity must therefore be high on the Government's agenda at all times. Tackling productivity is not just a matter of trying to be more efficient in the use of resources — that is, doing things right. It is also about being effective in the choice of the goods and services produced and allocating the requisite resources accordingly — that is, doing the right things. These dual aspects of productivity need to be given focused attention.

It is important to keep these three constants in mind as one examines the efforts taken to improve productivity in the past, and sets sight on the future. Singapore's productivity drive has a 50-year history now, stretching all the way back to 1967 when the National Productivity Centre was set up in EDB to support the industrialisation programme. Over the course of the past five decades, the productivity drive has evolved in various ways to meet the economic priorities of the day.

This book traces the major developments that have taken place in the last 50 years and, more importantly, the raison d'etre for these developments. It provides the information that is required for good understanding of the past and for planning the directions ahead. The book is unique in terms of its extensive and yet in-depth coverage. Besides listing out the major programmes implemented in each decade, it lays bare the prevailing circumstances and the thinking underpinning the policies and plans adopted.

The contents of the book are the outcome of the direct experiences of the authors in Singapore's productivity drive over a period of many years. Dr Woon Kin Chung joined NPB in 1984 when the Productivity Movement was on the cusp of acceleration. For the next three decades, he was directly engaged in various aspects of the Movement. Ms Loo Ya Lee began her involvement in the Productivity Movement from 2010 when she joined SPRING's Productivity Programme Office, headed by Dr Woon.

This book should be useful to anyone who is interested to know details about the policies, plans and programmes undertaken by the Government in Singapore's productivity drive in the last 50 years. Its target audience includes policy-makers, companies, trainers, consultants and students of the Singapore economy. The contents of the book should provide food for thought, contribute to policy-making, and spur discussions and writings on the directions of the productivity drive in the future.

Lee Suan Hiang
President
The EDB Society

Abbreviations[1]

Amp-Box	Amplification-Box
APO	Asian Productivity Organization
A*STAR	Agency for Science, Technology and Research
CET	Continuing education and training
CFE	Committee on the Future Economy
COP	Committee on Productivity
CPSC	Central Productivity Steering Committee
CSC	Committee on Singapore's Competitiveness
CSIP	Council for Skills, Innovation and Productivity
EDB	Economic Development Board
EPC	Economic Planning Committee
EPTA	United Nations Expanded Programme of Technical Assistance
ERC	Economic Review Committee
ESC	Economic Strategies Committee
FDI	Foreign direct investment
GDP	Gross domestic product
GLC	Government-linked company
IDA	Info-communications Development Authority of Singapore

---

[1] The list covers only the core abbreviations used in the book.

ILO	International Labour Organization
ITE	Institute of Technical Education
JICA	Japan International Cooperation Agency
JPC	Japan Productivity Center
MFP	Multifactor productivity
MNC	Multinational corporation
MOF	Ministry of Finance
MOL	Ministry of Labour
MOM	Ministry of Manpower
MTI	Ministry of Trade and Industry
NPA*	National Productivity Association
NPA	National Productivity Award
NPB	National Productivity Board
NPC	National Productivity Council
NPC*	National Productivity Centre
NPCEC	National Productivity and Continuing Education Council
NPQC	National Productivity and Quality Council
NRF	National Research Foundation
NTU	Nanyang Technological University
NTUC	National Trades Union Congress
NUS	National University of Singapore
NWC	National Wages Council
PDP	Singapore Productivity Development Project
PSB	Singapore Productivity and Standards Board
RIEC	Research, Innovation and Enterprise Council
SCCCI	Singapore Chinese Chamber of Commerce & Industry
SDF	Skills Development Fund
SISIR	Singapore Institute of Standards and Industrial Research

SME	Small and medium enterprise
SMF	Singapore Manufacturing Federation
SNEF	Singapore National Employers Federation
SPA	Singapore Productivity Association
SPC	Singapore Productivity Centre
SPRING	Standards, Productivity and Innovation Board
SSG	SkillsFuture Singapore
STB	Singapore Tourism Board
TFP	Total factor productivity
UNDP	United Nations Development Programme
WDA	Singapore Workforce Development Agency
WSG	Workforce Singapore

About the Authors

Woon Kin Chung has had more than 30 years of experience working in the areas of productivity and organisational excellence. His most recent appointments are Chief Executive Officer of the Singapore Productivity Centre and Executive Director of the Productivity Programme Office in SPRING Singapore.

Dr Woon joined the National Productivity Board, which later evolved into SPRING Singapore, in 1984. He was among the pioneer batch of Singaporeans who were trained by Japanese experts in the 1980s under the Japan-Singapore Productivity Development Project. Subsequently, he was involved in various regional productivity programmes under the Asian Productivity Organization. In 2015, he was conferred the title of APO Honorary Fellow in recognition of his contributions to the work of the organisation.

In Singapore, Dr Woon led the formulation of national productivity plans, carried out research studies and implemented many productivity initiatives. Significant initiatives include the integrated management of productivity activities (IMPACT) framework, business excellence, service excellence and innovation excellence programmes; productivity measurement methodology; and national benchmarking programme. He also produced numerous publications and promotional materials to support Singapore's national productivity drive.

Dr Woon holds the degrees of Doctor of Business Administration (University of South Australia), Master of Social Sciences in Economics (National University of Singapore) and Bachelor of

Social Sciences with Honours [First Class in Economics] (University of Singapore).

Loo Ya Lee graduated with a Bachelor of Accountancy with Honours degree from Nanyang Technological University. She started her career as an auditor in Deloitte Singapore, and subsequently held positions in various sectors, including social services, healthcare, enterprise development and the arts.

Ms Loo's most recent appointments are Director (Planning and Corporate Development) in the Singapore Productivity Centre and Head (Productivity Programme Office) in SPRING Singapore. In these capacities, she developed many publications and tools, carried out benchmarking studies and undertook applied research on productivity improvement at the enterprise and industry levels.

I
Prologue

Chapter 1

Overview of 50-Year Productivity Journey

"To understand the present and anticipate the future, one must know enough of the past, enough to have a sense of the history of a people. One must appreciate not merely what took place but more especially why it took place and in that particular way."

Prime Minister Lee Kuan Yew[1]
PAP 25th Anniversary Rally
20 January 1980

Scope of Coverage

Productivity is a subject that is of great interest to every country because of its importance. An oft-quoted statement that bears repeating sums up what is at stake:

"Productivity isn't everything, but in the long run it is almost everything. A country's ability to improve its standard of living over time depends almost entirely on its ability to raise its output per worker."

---

[1]Throughout the book, the title associated with an individual reflects the title at a particular point in time. For example, the titles of 'Prime Minister' and 'Senior Minister' are used for Lee Kuan Yew in different parts of the book. The word 'then,' as in 'then Prime Minister,' is omitted to avoid its repetitious use.

This statement, made by Nobel laureate Paul Krugman (1997), applies to every country, big or small. The Amp-Box[2] on *Productivity Primer* dissects the meaning of productivity and its measurement, and explains why productivity is so important.

Productivity Primer[3]

What is Productivity?

At the most basic level, productivity is defined as the relationship between output and input. This can be expressed as an output-input ratio:

$$\text{Productivity} = \frac{\text{Output}}{\text{Input}} = \frac{\text{Products}}{\text{Resources}}$$

Output can be in the form of goods produced or services delivered, both of which are collectively known as products. Input comprises the resources used in producing the products. The main resources are labour (workforce or no. of workers) and capital (machinery and equipment).

Productivity is an indication of the amount or value of the products that can be obtained from the resources used in the production process (to convert resources to products). Put differently, productivity is an indication of how well the resources are used to produce the products. The higher the ratio, the higher is the productivity.

How is Productivity Measured?

Value Added

Output is usually expressed in monetary terms. A common measure is value added, which is obtained as follows:

Value added = Revenue − Bought-in materials and services
required for production

(Continued)

---

[2]This term is used as a short form for 'Amplification-Box'. An Amp-Box amplifies or provides more details on a particular point. Readers who are already familiar with the details or who do not need them can skip the Amp-Box.

[3]As the aim is to explain the basic concepts, measurement and importance of productivity simply, technical rigour and precision are dispensed with.

(Continued)

Revenue is not an appropriate output measure since materials and services may need to be bought to produce the products, which can then be sold. The amount that is bought-in should be subtracted from revenue to give the appropriate output measure of value added. This measure is applicable at the enterprise, sector and economy levels. At the economy level, it is known as gross domestic product (GDP). The growth of GDP from one year to another or over a period of time is known as economic growth.

Labour Productivity

When labour is used as the input in the output-input ratio, the productivity measure is known as labour productivity. This can be expressed as:

$$\text{Labour productivity} = \frac{\text{Value added}}{\text{Labour}} = \frac{\text{Value added}}{\text{No. of workers}} \text{ or } \frac{\text{Value added}}{\text{No. of hours worked}}$$

The most appropriate measure of labour is no. of hours worked but it is not often used because of difficulty in getting the data. In place of this, no. of workers is used. At the economy level, the labour productivity measure is GDP per worker or GDP per hour worked, depending on the labour measure used. The growth of GDP per worker or GDP per hour worked from one year to another or over a period of time is known as labour productivity growth.

Labour productivity is the most common measure of productivity. When the terms 'productivity' and 'productivity growth' are used by the Singapore Government, they refer to 'labour productivity' and 'labour productivity growth' respectively, unless specified otherwise.

Total Factor Productivity

A more refined measure of productivity is total factor productivity (TFP), or what is sometimes known as multifactor productivity (MFP). As the name implies, the input measure is now more than just labour. Most commonly, it refers to a combination of labour and capital. TFP measures how well labour and capital are used to produce the products. This can be expressed simplistically as:

$$\text{Total factor productivity} = \frac{\text{Value Added}}{\text{Workers} + \text{capital}}$$

(Continued)

(*Continued*)

What Determines Productivity Growth?

Short Run: Demand-side Factors

In the short run, typically from one year to another, the labour productivity growth rates may fluctuate because of cyclical changes or unexpected jolts to the demand-side factors. These are the factors that determine the size of demand for an economy's products, and which thus have an impact on GDP and the capacity utilisation of resources. A regional financial crisis, for example, may curtail the demand for an economy's products during the year. This will have a negative impact on GDP. At the same time, the economy may not be able to reduce its resources fast enough, or it may not want to do so if it expects the lower demand to be temporary. The capacity utilisation of the resources is thus sub-optimal. The combined result is a decrease in productivity growth. Conversely, in a situation when the demand goes up in a particular year, the impact on GDP is positive. However, the economy may not be able to increase its resources fast enough, which means that the existing resources will have to be stretched. The result is an increase in productivity growth. Thus, productivity growth is said to be pro-cyclical in the short run. For small, open economies like Singapore, the demand-side factors depend much on the state of the global economy.

Long Run: Supply-side Factors

In the long run, the labour productivity growth that can be sustained depends on the supply-side factors affecting it. These are the factors that determine the productive capacity of the economy. Broadly, they fall under two categories, viz. capital intensity and TFP. The relationship can be expressed as:

$$\text{Labour productivity growth} = \frac{\text{Value Added}}{\text{Labour}} \text{ growth}$$

$$= \underbrace{\frac{\text{Capital}}{\text{Workers}} \text{ growth}}_{\text{(capital intensity)}} + \underbrace{\frac{\text{Value added}}{\text{Workers + capital}} \text{ growth}}_{\text{(TFP)}}$$

Capital intensity reflects the capital resources that are available for the workers to use in the production process to produce products. The higher the capital intensity, the better it is for labour productivity. On the other hand, labour productivity will be adversely affected if the capital intensity is low. This can happen if there is not enough investment in capital or if the rate of increase

(*Continued*)

(*Continued*)

in the number of workers exceeds that of capital — e.g. when there is a liberal inflow of foreign workers to complement the limited local manpower pool.

Increasing capital intensity is a common way of raising labour productivity. This takes place on a large scale when there is a shift from labour-intensive industrialisation to capital-intensive industrialisation as an economy develops. However, there is a limit to how much capital intensity can be increased — either because of finite supplies of capital or diminishing returns to capital over time.

In the long run, labour productivity can be sustained only through higher TFP growth. TFP reflects both effectiveness and efficiency in the use of the labour and capital resources. Comparatively, effectiveness has a bigger impact on TFP growth.

Effectiveness means doing the right things — ensuring that the right products are produced and brought to market to maximise value added, and that resources are channelled into the production of these products. This requires priority to be given to some sectors or industries, and engagement of certain markets, domestic or international, to sell the products. Over time, the right products for the economy could change for various reasons, such as competition from lower-cost producers, emergence of new industry needs, and change in consumer profiles and preferences. To sustain effectiveness, there must minimally be improvements to the existing products so that there is continued demand for them. More importantly, new products or new business models should be created to serve the existing markets, new markets, or both. Correspondingly, resources need to be shifted from the sectors or industries that are declining to the new growth areas. This is, in a nutshell, what economic restructuring is about.

To increase effectiveness continually, technical progress or innovation has to be prevalent — to spur product improvement and new product creation (product innovation) and new business models of existing products (business model innovation). Hence, innovation is often considered the key driver of TFP growth. Factors that boost innovation include intense competition, high research & development (R&D) investments and availability of mechanisms to diffuse the technological and scientific discoveries for applications in the industry, large and sophisticated market, high-quality workforce, good management systems in enterprises, and an innovation culture.

(*Continued*)

(*Continued*)

Efficiency means doing things right — ensuring that the production of products is done right by making optimal use of the resources. This has largely to do with the processes used for the production. Whether the processes are cumbersome or streamlined will make a big difference to efficiency, which ultimately impacts costs. To increase efficiency continually, process improvements (also known as process innovation) are critical. Lean production systems, based on the lean management philosophy of maximising value for customers and minimising wastes and non-value added steps in all the production processes, are thus important. Factors that boost process improvements include intense competition, large and sophisticated market, increased scale of operation, high-quality workforce, and a culture of continuous improvement.

Why is Productivity Important?

Productivity, Economic Growth and Standard of Living

The usual measure of economic growth, GDP growth, can be broken down as follows:

GDP growth = Labour growth + Labour productivity growth
(capital intensity growth + TFP growth)

GDP growth is determined by labour growth and labour productivity growth. Since there is a limit to which labour (no. of workers) can grow, labour productivity is critical to GDP growth in the long run. And because of the constraints to capital intensity growth, it is TFP growth that matters most to GDP growth when an economy develops and reaches its limit in the use of physical resources. As opposed to GDP growth through an increase in the inputs of labour and capital (known as 'extensive growth'), TFP is a summary measure of the qualitative, non-input factors affecting economic growth.

The broad measure of standard of living is GDP per capita, which can be expressed as:

$$\text{GDP per capita} = \frac{\text{GDP}}{\text{Population}}$$

(*Continued*)

(*Continued*)

This measure provides an indication of the average income per person in the country. No doubt, it is a crude measure of standard of living. Nevertheless, it is a useful 1st-level measure that can be used to gauge a country's progress over time and to make cross-country comparisons. Since GDP is the numerator, it means that all the determinants of GDP growth, particularly labour productivity and TFP in the long run, affect the standard of living. This is the basis for Paul Krugman's statement on the importance of productivity.

Productivity, Competitiveness and Wages in Enterprises

The determinants of productivity and the reasons for its importance apply as much at the enterprise level as they do at the economy level. High productivity growth enables an enterprise to price its products competitively, sell more and enlarge its market share. As a result, its wealth (value added) will increase over time, which means that higher profit can be made and higher wages can be paid at the same time without compromising profit.

To have a better grasp of the determinants of productivity at the enterprise level, lower level-measures, including physical measures, can be used to complement the value added per worker or hour worked measure. Examples are sales per square foot, check size per person and table turns in a restaurant. All these ultimately affect the amount of value added per worker or hour worked that can be achieved.

Source: Woon and Loo (2017).

In small countries with very limited resources, productivity is absolutely critical. It is therefore high on the Singapore Government's economic agenda. Over the years, the Government has articulated policies and plans and implemented many programmes to raise the country's productivity. This has not gone unnoticed by others. Within the Asian Productivity Organization (APO), Singapore is regarded as one of the forerunners in driving national productivity. Many countries organise study visits to Singapore to learn and emulate what has been done. Singapore's experience in productivity development has also been the subject of study by institutions such as the Harvard Business School and the National Graduate Institute for Policy Studies (GRIPS) in Japan.

Nevertheless, in terms of outcomes achieved, Singapore's productivity performance has not been outstanding.[4] First, the productivity growth is significantly lower than that of the other Newly Industrialised Economies (NIEs) of Hong Kong, Taiwan and South Korea, which are at a similar stage of development as Singapore. While these NIEs' productivity grew by 2–3 per cent a year in the 2000s, Singapore managed to grow by only 1 per cent. Second, the productivity level is much lower than that of the developed countries such as the United States, Japan and many of the European countries. Depending on what countries are used for comparison, the difference ranges from 20 to 40 per cent. Third, the contribution of productivity growth to GDP growth is far below that in the NIEs and the developed countries. In these countries, the contribution is typically between 40–80 per cent. This is much higher than the 10 per cent in Singapore in the 2000s.

Singapore's productivity performance seems to be incongruous with the efforts expended and stands in stark contrast to its economic growth performance which is often hailed as a model. The situation is akin to the statement famously made by Nobel laureate Robert Solow (1987):

"You can see the computer age everywhere but in the productivity statistics."

In a similar vein, you can see the productivity drive everywhere in Singapore but in the productivity statistics. Besides problems with statistics, reasons that have been advanced for the lacklustre performance include the Government's overwhelming concern with economic growth, the over-reliance on multinational corporations (MNCs) for the export-oriented industrialisation model, the liberal import of foreign workers to support the economic growth strategy,

---

[4]A wide range of conclusions has been reached by different analysts, depending on the data used for the analysis. There are some studies that conclude that Singapore's productivity performance is not as dismal as that shown by other studies. Nevertheless, there is general agreement that the record has not been sterling.

and the consequent stifling of efforts to restructure the economy and upgrade the operations of companies.

These various aspects of Singapore's productivity drive and performance have been well-researched and published. Broadly, the studies fall into three categories. The first category focuses on quantitative analyses of Singapore's productivity performance, trend-wise and in comparison with other countries. The second category is qualitative in nature, covering specific aspects of the subject such as productivity practices in companies, skills upgrading programmes and government incentive schemes. The third category describes different aspects of Singapore's productivity policies and initiatives.

The problem is that the information from such studies, as well as other sources, is literally everywhere — scattered in different publications, speeches and other media — and is often patchy. What is not available is a comprehensive account of the productivity policies, plans and programmes undertaken by the Government. Consequently, there may be lack of awareness of, or even disagreement on, certain facts or events that have transpired. Even if the facts are known, the rationale and the contexts for the programmes may be shrouded in mystery. This makes it difficult to do detailed research and analysis — including assessing the adequacy and efficacy of the programmes implemented and drawing lessons for the future. It is also a bane for policy formulation. Without adequate knowledge of the past, much time and resources could be expended on solving issues that have been addressed before, recreating initiatives which might not be new but thought to be new, and, worse still, repeating mistakes made in the past.

This book aims to plug the gap in the current body of writings by providing a detailed historical account and the underlying thinking of the Government's productivity policies, plans and programmes over a 50-year period, stretching from 1967 to 2017.[5] The details are

---

[5]The cut-off date is 2 March 2017, the date of the round-up of the debate on Budget 2017. This allows inclusion of the salient points of the *Report of the Committee on the Future Economy* and the Government's response to it, while giving sufficient time to meet the publishing deadline.

culled from the Government's official statements and economic development plans, the productivity plans and initiatives of the national council overseeing the productivity drive, and the programmes implemented by the national productivity organisation. The main programmes carried out by the national productivity organisation — either by itself or in partnership with other agencies — are listed out comprehensively, as they reflect the priorities of the Government and the national productivity council at both the national and sectoral levels.[6]

Throughout the book, productivity statistics are cited.[7] However, the intent is not to analyse Singapore's productivity growth and its determinants per se. Rather, the statistics are included to provide the context for the actions taken by the Government and the outcomes achieved.

Approach Taken

To reveal the thinking behind the policies, plans and programmes, primary sources of data and information, including extracts from writings and speeches, are used profusely. This approach minimises the risk of misinterpretation or misrepresentation of historical facts when secondary or, even worse, tertiary information is used and when original sources are paraphrased. The well-known fact of how a point can get distorted as it is transmitted from one source to another is illustrated in the Amp-Box on *The Project.*

---

[6]While it could be argued that many other organisations carry out their own productivity programmes, the main programmes, from the national perspective, are those undertaken by the national productivity organisation, as mandated by the Government and the national productivity council. As the focus of the book is on the Singapore economy, productivity-related programmes undertaken by the Government to assist other countries are excluded.

[7]All the productivity growth statistics, as well as economic growth statistics, are based on GDP at 2010 market prices.

The Project

In the beginning was the Project, and then arose the Assumptions. And the Project was without form and the Assumptions were void. And darkness was upon the faces of the Implementers. And they spake unto their manager, and their voices said,

> "It is a crock of shit, and it stinketh."

And the manager went to the second level manager, and he spake unto him saying,

> "It is a crock of excrement, and none may abide the odor thereof."

And the second level manager went to the third level manager, and he spake unto him saying,

> "It is a container of excrement, and it is so strong that none may abide before it."

And the third level manager went to the headquarters director, and he spake unto him saying,

> "It is a vessel of fertilizer, and none may abide its strength."

And the director went to the divisional vice president, and he spake unto him saying,

> "It contains that which aids plant growth, and is very strong."

And the vice president went to the division president, and he spake unto him saying,

> "It promoteth growth, and it is very powerful."

And the division president went before the executive board, and he spake unto them saying,

> "This powerful new project will promote the growth of the company."

And the executive board looked upon the project, and saw that it was GOOD.

Source: Author unknown.

The prevalence of information distortion is obvious when one examines what is said about productivity policies, plans and programmes in Singapore. Many of the writings and statements are generalisations of the original sources, paraphrases of what has been written before, or regurgitations of party lines which then become the accepted wisdom. When these are compared with the original sources, vast disparities are observed. The approach taken in this book avoids this predicament by going back to the original sources as much as possible.

Singapore's Productivity Drive: A 50-Year History

It may be surprising that the history of Singapore's productivity drive can be traced all the way back to the nation's early post-independence years. What is fairly well known is the highly-publicised Productivity Movement fronted by Teamy the Bee, which began in the early 1980s. The exact date for the launch of that Movement is 25 September 1981, which therefore might seem to be the logical start date for Singapore's productivity drive. However, this is inaccurate.

Fourteen years before that, in 1967, a deliberate decision was taken by the Government to set up Singapore's own national productivity organisation to spearhead the nation's productivity drive. Many other countries had established similar organisations earlier, but the Government felt that the political situation and the industrial relations climate were not conducive to productivity improvement then. After Singapore's independence on 9 August 1965, the ground for productivity improvement was ready to be tilled following the strong measures taken by the Government on the political front and in improving industrial relations. The National Productivity Centre (NPC*)[8] was thus set up in May 1967.

An examination of NPC*'s achievements shows that they were at best modest. The organisation was constrained by limited resources

---

[8]* is placed against NPC when it is used as the acronym for National Productivity Centre to differentiate it from the same acronym used for National Productivity Council.

and by the fact that it was a Division, albeit autonomously-run, in the Economic Development Board (EDB) which had the primary task of leading Singapore's industrialisation drive. Nonetheless, the establishment of NPC* in May 1967 marked the start of Singapore's productivity drive since it was the first time that a concerted effort had been made to improve productivity in the nation. Subsequently, NPC* morphed into the National Productivity Board (NPB) in May 1972, Singapore Productivity and Standards Board (PSB) in April 1996, and Standards, Productivity and Innovation Board (SPRING Singapore, or SPRING in short) in April 2002.

Structure of Book

The 50-year history of Singapore's productivity drive can be analysed in various ways. One convenient way is to divide it into the periods associated with the terms of NPC*, NPB, PSB and SPRING. The second way is to divide it into periods corresponding to Singapore's economic growth performance, such as high growth, moderate growth and low growth. The third way is to divide it according to the decades.

There is no right or wrong way to decide the basis for the analysis. For the purpose of this book, the third way is used. There are two reasons for this. First, the productivity priorities and plans were determined by the economic priorities, which panned out largely according to the decades. Second, the division by decades makes it possible to compare the productivity achievements for equal periods of time. Figure 1.1 shows the structure of the book.

Chapter 1 serves as an overview. Besides giving a synopsis of the subsequent chapters, it synthesises the pertinent points that provide the context for understanding the efforts undertaken in the last five decades.

Chapters 2 to 13 are organised according to five broad periods. For each period, the economic priorities and the policy intent on productivity are stated, the major programmes are listed in detail, and a summary of the productivity drive in retrospect is given. This structure enables conclusions to be drawn on not just what took

Chapter	Title
	Prologue
1	Overview of 50-Year Productivity Journey
	1960s–1970s
2	1960s: Sowing Seeds of Productivity to Support Industrialisation
3	1970s: Ramping Up the Productivity Drive
4	Role of United Nations Development Programme: 1967–1982
	1980s
5	Laying Foundation for the Productivity Push in the 1980s
6	1980s: Decade of Intense Productivity Drive
7	Singapore Productivity Development Project: 1983–1990
	1990s
8	Establishing Framework to Address Total Factor Productivity in the 1990s
9	1990s: Intensification of Total Approach to Productivity
	2000s
10	Shifting Productivity Gears in the 2000s
11	2000s: Turning Point in the Productivity Drive
	2010s
12	Renewing the Productivity Drive in the 2010s
13	2010s: The Big Challenge to Raise Productivity
	Epilogue
14	Back to the Future

Figure 1.1:   Structure of Book

place but, more importantly, why they took place and why they took place in a particular manner. Lessons can then be drawn for the future.

The first period of the *1960s–1970s* is covered in Chapters 2 to 4. **Chapter 2** gives a snapshot of the Singapore economy in the 1960s, following its attainment of a self-governing State in 1959 and leading to its status as an independent Republic in 1965. Starting with an environment that was fraught with political and economic uncertainties in the early 1960s, Singapore evolved into a state that was fairly conducive to productivity improvement in the second half of the decade. The establishment of NPC* in May 1967 marked an important milestone. However, its achievements in the first three years were limited. **Chapter 3** recounts the steps taken to restructure NPC* to improve its performance. This culminated in the establishment of NPB as an independent national productivity organisation in May 1972. With this development, the productivity drive was ramped up as NPB intensified its training, consultancy, promotion and research activities to assist the industry and the workforce. NPB's own competencies were strengthened significantly through the assistance of the United Nations Development Programme (UNDP), which was rendered from 1967 in conjunction with the set-up of NPC.* The background, details and assessment of the impact of UNDP's assistance are given in **Chapter 4**.

The decade of the *1980s* spans Chapters 5 to 7. From its nascent years in the late 1960s and fledgling years in the 1970s, Singapore's productivity drive became sturdy in the 1980s. **Chapter 5** provides the background to this development. The overriding concern then was with the human aspects of productivity and drawing lessons from Japan to improve the prevailing less-than-desired situation. This led to the formation of the Committee on Productivity (COP) and the National Productivity Council (NPC), as well as a restructured NPB with a strong mandate to drive the nation's productivity. A highly visible and visceral outcome was the launch of the nationwide Productivity Movement in September 1981. **Chapter 6** presents the details of the numerous activities carried out during the 1980s under the umbrella of the Productivity Movement to address, in the main, the human aspects of productivity. This decade marked the start of many activities, including the annual productivity campaign, that stayed the course for another 15–20 years. In spearheading the Productivity Movement, NPB was very much influenced by the Japanese experience and it had its competencies built through what was known as the Singapore Productivity Development Project (PDP). **Chapter 7** describes the details of PDP, a vehicle through which Japanese productivity technology and knowledge were transferred to Singapore.

The *1990s* encompasses Chapters 8 and 9. From the human aspects of productivity in the 1980s, attention turned to a total approach to productivity in the 1990s. In fact, NPB began to promote this approach in 1986. This stepped up in the early 1990s when the economists' concept of TFP was popularised and Singapore's poor performance on this measure was brought to the open. **Chapter 8** explains the concern with Singapore's TFP performance, which ultimately led to the formation of PSB. Formed through the merger of NPB and the Singapore Institute of Standards and Industrial Research (SISIR), PSB was charged with the responsibility for raising TFP. In terms of institutional capabilities for driving Singapore's productivity, PSB was in a much stronger position than NPB. **Chapter 9** outlines the various programmes implemented by PSB through a combination of the 'soft power' of NPB and the 'hard power' of SISIR to offer a holistic approach to productivity improvement.

The next period of the *2000s* extends over Chapters 10 and 11. Looking back, the crossing from the old millennium to the new in 2000, including the so-called Y2K Millennium Bug, was a non-event for Singapore. However, it marked a turning point in Singapore's productivity drive. A confluence of factors, including a preoccupation with innovation and the divestment of certain PSB functions, contributed to a muted productivity drive in the 2000s. The details of these developments are given in **Chapter 10**. Institution-wise, a major change during this decade was the formation of SPRING in April 2002, succeeding PSB after its corporatisation and subsequent divestment of certain core functions. It was more than a name change. In 2004, SPRING's role shifted from the national productivity champion to an enterprise development agency. **Chapter 11** highlights the activities undertaken in the 2000s, as well as those that were discontinued. The conclusion is a shift in emphasis of programmes from productivity per se to enterprise development during the decade.

The final period of the *2010s* covers Chapters 12 and 13. After the hiatus in the 2000s, the productivity drive was given renewed emphasis in 2010. **Chapter 12** elaborates the reason for this, which had largely to do with the need to tighten the inflow of foreign workers. It also describes the formation of the National Productivity and

Continuing Education Council (NPCEC), the sectoral approach taken and the supporting infrastructure that was put in place. **Chapter 13** gives an account of the main initiatives rolled out in the first half of the 2010s, presents the report card at the halfway mark, and highlights the abrupt halt to the high-profile productivity drive in the second half. The picture that emerges is a decade that is saddled with the big challenge to raise productivity from the doldrums.

Chapter 14 concludes the book. From the preceding chapters, the fundamentals that have served Singapore's productivity drive well and the key issues for reflection are identified. For each of the issues, certain views are presented to facilitate and stimulate discussion on what needs to be done for the future.

Productivity Plans in Relation to Economic Plans

Throughout the book, the various productivity plans and economic plans are introduced. In the last 50 years, the productivity drive was guided by the productivity plans, even if the actual course taken subsequently deviated from the plans because of the prevailing circumstances. The productivity plans were, in turn, broadly aligned with the national economic plans although the latter were not always developed according to the decades. For most of the economic plans and productivity plans, quantitative targets for economic growth, measured by GDP growth, and productivity growth, measured by labour productivity growth,[9] were set.

Figure 1.2 summarises the economic plans, productivity plans, targets and achievements in the last five decades.

In the 1960s, there were two economic plans. The *State of Singapore Development Plan 1961–1964* was the first official blueprint

---

[9]The labour productivity figures in this book are based on the traditional measure of value added per worker. In November 2015, the Ministry of Trade and Industry announced that it would start taking into account the actual hours worked, instead of just the number of workers, in its labour productivity measure. Hence, the measure of value added per hour worked would be used as well. For the purpose of intertemporal comparison, the measure of value added per worker is used in the book. In any case, the targets set by the Government were based on this measure.

Period	Economic plan	Date of release/ publication	Time horizon (years)	Goal / vision	GDP growth		Productivity growth		Productivity plan
					Target	Actual	Target	Actual	
1960s	State of Singapore Development Plan 1961–1964	April 1961	4	To create more jobs for Singapore's growing population, as well as expand the economy, through industrialisation	—	8.7% p.a.	—	5.0% p. a.	—
	A Proposed Industrialisation Programme for the State of Singapore (The Winsemius Report)	June 1961	10	To examine the opportunities and measures for rapid industrial expansion in Singapore					
1970s	—	—	—	—	—	9.0% p.a.	—	3.5% p.a.	—
1980s	Economic Development Plan for the Eighties	March 1981	10	To develop Singapore into a modern industrial economy based on science, technology, skills and knowledge	8–10% p.a. for 1980s	7.5% p.a.	6–8% p.a. for 1980s	4.4% p.a.	Report of Committee on Productivity

Figure 1.2: Economic Plans, Productivity Plans, Targets and Achievements, 1960s–2010s

Source: Various economic plans and productivity plans.

1990s	Report/Committee	Date	No. of years	Objective	Growth target		Productivity target		
1990s	Report of the Economic Committee	February 1986	10	To be a developed nation by the 1990s	4–6% p.a. over next 10 years	6.9% p.a.	3–4% p.a. over next 10 years	3.0% p.a.	Productivity 2000
	The Strategic Economic Plan	December 1991	30 to 40	To attain the status and characteristics of a first league developed country within the next 30 to 40 years	*Projected GNP growth (see table below)*		—		
	Committee on Singapore's Competitiveness	November 1998	10	Singapore as an advanced and globally competitive knowledge economy within the next decade, with manufacturing and services as its twin engines of growth	No quantitative target set. 4–6% p.a. (from Report of the Economic Committee)		No quantitative target set. 3–4 % p.a. (from Report of the Economic Committee)		

Projected GNP growth:

	4 mil. population by 2030		4.4 mil. population by 2030	
	Pessimistic (%)	Optimistic (%)	Pessimistic (%)	Optimistic (%)
'90–95	6.1	7.1	6.3	7.3
'95–00	5.0	6.0	5.2	6.2
'00–10	3.9	4.8	4.1	5.0
'10–20	3.4	4.3	3.6	4.5
'20–30	3.1	4.0	3.3	4.3

Figure 1.2:   (*Continued*)

Period	Economic plan	Date of release/ publication	Time horizon (years)	Goal / vision	GDP growth		Productivity growth		Productivity plan
					Target	Actual	Target	Actual	
2000s	Report of the Economic Review Committee	February 2003	15	Singapore as a leading global city, a hub of talent, enterprise and innovation	3–5% p.a. (sustainable growth rate)	4.8% p.a.	2–3% p.a.	1.0% p.a.	ProAct 21
2010s	Report of the Economic Strategies Committee	February 2010	10	High-skilled people, innovative economy, distinctive global city	3–5% p.a. over next 10 years	4.0% p.a. (for 2010–2015)	2–3% p.a. over next 10 years	0.4% p.a. (for 2010–2015)	—
	Report of the Committee on the Future Economy	February 2017	10	Singaporeans of today being pioneers of the next generation, making progress by embracing new realities and creating new opportunities. In the future economy:	2–3% p.a. over next 10 years	—	—	—	—

*people: deep skills and inspired to learn throughout their lives

*businesses: innovative and nimble

*city: connected and vibrant, continually renewing itself

*Government: coordinated, inclusive and responsive

Figure 1.2: *(Continued)*

for the economic and social development of Singapore, following its attainment of self-governance in 1959. It was formulated with the primary aim of solving the high unemployment rate, as well as expanding the economy, through industrialisation. However, it was the report by the United Nations Industrial Survey Mission, *A Proposed Industrialisation Programme for the State of Singapore*, or *The Winsemius Report* in short, that became the de facto economic plan for Singapore in the 1960s. The industrialisation of the economy that took place was largely in accordance with this 10-year plan. As the emphasis on productivity was in its nascent stage, there was no corresponding productivity plan during this period. The productivity growth achieved averaged 5 per cent a year, contributing 57 per cent to the GDP growth of 8.7 per cent a year. This signalled a developing economy that was beginning to grow rapidly.

The 1970s was unusual compared with the other decades. There was neither an economic plan nor a productivity plan. Essentially, the economic strategies during the decade continued to be guided by the directions spelt out in *The Winsemius Report*. In the area of productivity, NPB carried out various activities and started to have a 5-year plan in 1978 but there were no formal productivity plans. For the entire decade, the productivity growth averaged 3.5 per cent a year, contributing 39 per cent to the high GDP growth of 9 per cent a year.

In the 1980s, there were two economic plans. The 10-year *Economic Development Plan for the Eighties* was developed to guide the transition from labour-intensive to capital-intensive industrialisation during the decade. A mid-term stock-take was done in 1986 with the release of the 10-year *Report of the Economic Committee,* which reviewed the economic plan for the 1980s and defined new strategies for promoting further growth. There was no formal productivity plan during this decade. Nevertheless, the *Report of Committee on Productivity,* released in June 1981, served as the de facto productivity plan. Many of the activities carried out to boost the human aspects of productivity in the 1980s were in accordance with the report. The productivity growth during this period averaged 4.4 per cent a year, contributing 59 per cent to the GDP growth of 7.5 per cent a year.

In the 1990s, there were again two economic plans. Unlike the other plans, *The Strategic Economic Plan* was more in the nature of scenario planning with a 30 to 40-year time frame. In contrast, the *Committee on Singapore's Competitiveness* assessed Singapore's economic competitiveness over a 10-year horizon and proposed strategies to strengthen it. *Productivity 2000*, the first formal productivity plan, was prepared by NPC and released in March 1990. The plan focused on the qualitative aspects of productivity and guided activities in the first half of the 1990s. In the second half of the decade, the directions changed, following the formation of PSB. For the whole 10-year period, the productivity growth averaged 3 per cent a year, contributing 43 per cent to the GDP growth of 6.9 per cent a year.

For the next decade of the 2000s, there was one economic plan. The *Report of the Economic Review Committee* reviewed the prevailing policies and proposed strategies to promote the further growth and development of the economy over the next 15 years. In the sphere of productivity, the *ProAct 21* plan was released by the National Productivity and Quality Council (NPQC) in December 1999 to guide activities in the 2000s. However, this was somewhat derailed by the reduced emphasis on productivity soon after. The average annual productivity growth during this period was a mere 1 per cent, contributing a low 21 per cent to the GDP growth of 4.8 per cent a year.

For the 2010s, two economic plans have been formulated. The *Report of the Economic Strategies Committee* was released in February 2010. It spelt out strategies for Singapore to maximise its opportunities in a new world environment with the aim of achieving sustained and inclusive growth over a 10-year period. This led to the revival of the national productivity drive. However, no national productivity plan was drawn up. Instead, sectoral productivity plans were formulated because of the sectoral approach taken. In February 2017, the *Report of the Committee on the Future Economy* was released. Building on the work of the previous plan and taking into account the new challenges facing Singapore, the latest plan developed broad economic strategies for the decade ahead. Unlike the previous plan, there was no explicit strategy for productivity.

There was also no corresponding national productivity plan. At the mid-point of the 10-year period, the productivity growth was close to stagnant. For the period 2010–2015, it averaged 0.4 per cent a year, contributing only 10 per cent to the GDP growth of 4 per cent a year.

Role of National Productivity Organisation

The role of the national productivity organisation at any point in time is spelt out in the list of functions in the relevant Act of Parliament. Figure 1.3 lists out the functions of NPC*, NPB, PSB and SPRING over the years.

The first formal Act for the national productivity organisation was enacted on 12 May 1972 with the establishment of NPB. Compared with NPC*, the role of NPB, as reflected in the National Productivity Board Act 1972, was wider in scope. This was the result of NPB being an independent full-fledged national productivity organisation, unlike NPC* which was a Division in EDB.

On 7 May 1991, the Act was amended for the first time. The purpose of the amendment was to include NPB's additional responsibility for post-employment training and administration of the Skills Development Fund (SDF), which was transferred from EDB.

The next milestone was 1 April 1996, when PSB was formed through the merger of NPB and SISIR. Compared with NPB, the functions of PSB, as reflected in the Singapore Productivity and Standards Board Act 1995, were considerably expanded to enable a holistic approach to managing TFP. Instead of 'to promote productivity consciousness,' the more quantifiable function of 'to raise productivity and improve competitiveness' was included.

On 1 April 2002, this Act was replaced by the Standards, Productivity and Innovation Board Act 2002 when SPRING was formed in place of PSB after the corporatisation and subsequent divestment of certain PSB functions. Instead of 'to raise productivity,' the more technical and amorphous function of 'to raise total factor productivity' was included. This was in fact a tall order since TFP was not only difficult to measure, it was also a factor that was influenced by a whole host of factors, many of which were beyond what an individual agency could control.

Since then, the Act has remained unchanged except for some minor changes in SPRING's functions. This is an incongruity as SPRING has become an enterprise development agency, rather than the national productivity organisation, since 2004.

Mission of National Productivity Organisation

As the Act is intended to spell out the roles and responsibilities of the national productivity organisation unambiguously, it is detailed in its coverage and written in legalistic language. As such, it is not a document that one can easily identify with. In contrast, the mission statement is concise and is intended to rally everyone for a common purpose.

Figure 1.4 shows the mission statements of the national productivity organisation over the years. Logically, the mission statement at any point in time should be consistent with the set of functions spelt out in the Act. But this was not always the case.

From 1972–1988, the mission statement was in congruence with NPB's role as the national productivity organisation.

For the period 1989–1991, the mission emphasised the importance of labour-management cooperation, involving employers, unions and the workforce, in improving productivity. This was a time when NPB began to pay attention to the Labour Force Evaluation Measure (LFEM) by the US-based Business Environment Risk Intelligence (BERI). Singapore's workforce had been rated highly by BERI and the importance of labour-management cooperation was emphasised by BERI. The inclusion of labour-management cooperation in NPB's mission was intended to remind everyone not to take it for granted.

Thereafter, for the next period of 1992–1995, the mission switched to a focus on the workforce, as interest in LFEM and the Quality of Workforce Index (QWI), newly developed by BERI, intensified. This focus on the workforce was, however, incongruous with NPB's role as the national productivity organisation.

Act of Parliament and effective date	With effect from May 1967	National Productivity Board Act 1972 (with effect from 12 May 1972)	National Productivity Board (Amendment) Act 1991 (with effect from 7 May 1991)	Singapore Productivity and Standards Board Act 1995 (with effect from 1 April 1996)	Standards, Productivity and Innovation Board Act 2002 (with effect from 1 April 2002)	Standards, Productivity and Innovation Board Act 2002 (as at 31 December 2016)
National productivity organisation	NPC*	NPB	NPB	PSB	SPRING	SPRING
Functions in Act	a) To promote productivity consciousness in management, trade union leaders and workers. b) To provide training facilities for management and trade union personnel in all productivity techniques, including general management, personnel management, supervisory training,	Section 6 (1) The objects of the Board shall be a) to promote productivity consciousness in managements, trade union leaders and workers; b) to provide training facilities for managerial and supervisory personnel in all relevant aspects of modern management including general management, personnel management, management accounting, industrial engineering, achievement motivation and supervisory training;	Section 6 (1) The objects of the Board shall be a) to promote productivity consciousness in managements, trade union leaders and workers; b) to provide training facilities for managerial and supervisory personnel in all relevant aspects of modern management including general management, personnel management, management	Section 6 (1) The functions of the Board shall be a) to raise productivity and improve competitiveness through manpower development, economic restructuring, technical progress, standardisation and any other activity considered necessary or desirable; b) to promote, facilitate and assist in the development and management	Section 6 (1) The functions of the Board shall be a) to raise total factor productivity and improve Singapore's competitiveness through productivity and innovation promotion, domestic sector development, standards, conformance, metrology and any other activity	Section 6 (1) The functions of the Board shall be a) to raise total factor productivity and improve Singapore's competitiveness through productivity and innovation promotion, domestic sector development, standards, conformance and any other activity considered

Figure 1.3: Functions of National Productivity Organisation

Note. The functions of NPC* were not formally in an Act of Parliament since NPC* was not a separate entity but a Division in EDB. They are included here for the purpose of comparison.

Source. Various Acts of Parliament.

management accounting, and industrial engineering. c) To foster the further development of good industrial relations by training. d) To render management consultancy services in the fields of general management, personnel management, supervisory development, management accounting, and industrial engineering with a view to assisting industrial enterprises to achieve a general raising of productivity. e) To assist industrial establishments in	c) to train workers' representatives in measures for raising labour productivity, and to relate wages and productivity to competitiveness in export markets and industrial relations; d) to foster and promote good industrial relations by training and by promoting the formation of joint consultative councils; e) to render management consultancy services in the same fields in which training activities are undertaken with a view to assisting industrial enterprises to achieve a general raising of productivity; f) to assist industrial establishments and trade unions in formulating and rationalising wage policies and wage systems;	accounting, industrial engineering, achievement motivation and supervisory training; c) to train workers' representatives in measures for raising labour productivity, and to relate wages and productivity to competitiveness in export markets and industrial relations; (ca) to promote the development and upgrading of skills and expertise of persons in employment; (cb) to control and administer the Skills Development Fund in accordance with the Skills Development Levy Act[10] (Cap 306); d) to foster and promote good industrial relations by training and	upgrading of skills and expertise of persons preparing to join the workforce, persons in the workforce and persons rejoining the workforce; c) to administer the Skills Development Fund in accordance with the Skills Development Levy Act [Cap. 306]; d) to promote, facilitate and assist in the development and upgrading of industry and enterprises and support the growth of small and medium enterprises; e) to serve as the national standards body and to promote and facilitate the national standardisation programme and the participation of	considered necessary or desirable; b) to promote, facilitate and assist in the development and upgrading of skills and expertise of persons preparing to join the workforce, persons in the workforce and persons rejoining the workforce, and to support the growth of small and medium enterprises and any other enterprise requiring its assistance; c) to administer the Skills Development Fund in accordance with	necessary or desirable; b) to promote, facilitate and assist in the development and upgrading of skills and expertise of persons preparing to join the workforce, persons in the workforce and persons rejoining the workforce, and to support the growth of small and medium enterprises and any other enterprise requiring its assistance; c) [Deleted by Act 14/2003 wef 01/09/2003] d) to assess and certify persons for achievements in

Figure 1.3: (*Continued*)

[10]Skills Development Levy (Amendment) Bill — Section 9-(1) The Board shall control and administer the Skills Development Fund established under Section 6, including the collection of the skills development levy and the disbursement of grants and loans from the Fund for the purposes of this Act; Section 9-(2) The Board shall have power to do all things necessary or convenient to be done for or in connection with the performance of its functions under this Act.

formulating and rationalising the wage policy and wage systems.	g) to assist the Government from time to time in shaping a national wage policy; h) to undertake manpower and wage studies; and i) to provide a library of books, files and other information material to all interested parties.	by promoting the formation of joint consultative councils; e) to render management consultancy services in the same fields in which training activities are undertaken with a view to assisting industrial enterprises to achieve a general raising of productivity; f) to assist industrial establishments and trade unions in formulating and rationalising wage policies and wage systems; g) to assist the Government from time to time in shaping a national wage policy; h) to undertake manpower and wage studies; and i) to provide a library of books, files and other information material to all interested parties.	Singapore in international standardisation activities; f) to promote and facilitate the adoption of practices that enhance the safety, efficiency and quality of products, processes and technology in industry; g) to promote, facilitate and assist in the development, application and diffusion of technology in industry; h) to advise the Government and industrial, commercial, trading and other organisations in respect of matters relating to productivity and standards; i) to represent the Government internationally in respect of matters relating to productivity, standards and conformity assessment; and	the Skills Development Levy Act [Cap. 306]; d) to assess and certify persons for achievements in productivity, innovation, skills or standards; (*da*) to register management systems personnel; e) to promote and facilitate the national standardisation programme and the participation of Singapore in international standardisation activities; f) to be the accreditation body for the assessment and accreditation of bodies and institutions whose activities include sampling, testing, calibration, inspection or certification;	productivity, innovation, skills or standards; e) to register management systems personnel; f) to promote and facilitate the national standard-isation programme and the participation of Singapore in international standardisation activities; g) to be the accreditation body for the assessment and accreditation of bodies and institutions whose activities include sampling, testing, calibration, inspection or certification; h) to designate, appoint, authorise or recognise for any purpose any person who performs conformity

j) to perform such other functions as are conferred on the Board by any other written law.	g) to designate, appoint, authorise or recognise for any purpose any person who performs conformity assessment and any person who performs any test relating to conformity assessment, and to perform all functions necessary or incidental thereto, including (i) determining the qualifications of such persons; (ii) controlling and regulating the practice of such persons; (iii) suspending, lifting the suspension of or withdrawing the designation,	assessment and any person who performs any test relating to conformity assessment, and to perform all functions necessary or incidental thereto, including (i) determining the qualifications of such persons; (ii) controlling and regulating the practice of such persons; (iii) suspending, lifting the suspension of or withdrawing the designation, appointment, authorisation or recognition of such persons; and (iv) establishing, maintaining and developing the

Figure 1.3: (*Continued*)

appointment, authorisation or recognition of such persons; and (iv) establishing, maintaining and developing the standards of practice, and professional conduct and ethics, of such persons; h) to serve as the national productivity, innovation and standards body, and to advise the Government and industrial, commercial, trading and other organisations in respect of matters relating to productivity, innovation and standards; i) to represent the Government internationally in	standards of practice, and professional conduct and ethics, of such persons; i) to serve as the national productivity, innovation and standards body, and to advise the Government and industrial, commercial, trading and other organisations in respect of matters relating to productivity, innovation and standards; j) to represent the Government internationally in respect of matters relating to productivity, innovation, standards and conformity assessment;

respect of matters relating to productivity, innovation, standards and conformity assessment; (*ia*) to administer the Weights and Measures Act (Cap.349); and j) to perform such other functions as are conferred on the Board by any other written law.

k) to administer the Weights and Measures Act (Cap. 349); ka) to promote fair trading among suppliers and consumers and to promote measures to enable consumers to make informed purchasing decisions in Singapore; kb) to prevent suppliers in Singapore from engaging in unfair practices; kc) to advise the Government, any public authority or any consumer protection organisation on consumer protection matters generally;

Figure 1.3: (*Continued*)

kd) to administer and enforce the Consumer Protection (Fair Trading) Act (Cap. 52A); and
l) to perform such other functions as are conferred on the Board by any other written law.
(1A) In carrying out its functions, the Board shall have regard to the policies and directions of the Research, Innovation and Enterprise Council established under the National Research Fund Act 2006.

Figure 1.3:   (*Continued*)

Year	Organisation	Mission Statement
1972–1988	NPB	To make Singapore a highly productive nation
1989–1990	NPB	To improve productivity through the cooperative actions of employers, unions and workers
1991	NPB	To have highly productive organisations through the cooperation and actions of employers, unions and the workforce
1992–1995	NPB	To develop a world-class quality workforce with a rewarding worklife
1996	PSB	To raise productivity so as to enhance Singapore's competitiveness and economic growth
1997–2001	PSB	To raise productivity so as to enhance Singapore's competitiveness and economic growth for a better quality of life for our people
2002–2003	SPRING	To raise productivity so as to enhance Singapore's competitiveness and economic growth for a better quality of life for our people
2004–2009	SPRING	To enhance the competitiveness of enterprises for a vibrant Singapore economy
2010–present	SPRING	To help Singapore enterprises grow and to build trust in Singapore products and services

Figure 1.4:   Mission of National Productivity Organisation

Note: NPC* did not have an explicit mission statement.
Source: Annual report of national productivity organisation, various years.

For the subsequent period of 1996–2003, beginning from the formation of PSB, the mission focused explicitly on raising productivity. This was in line with the organisation's responsibility for implementing a total approach to productivity.

From 2004–2009, 'productivity' was dropped from the mission statement while 'competitiveness of enterprises' was included.

From 2010, the focus on enterprises remained. In addition, the organisation's role as the national standards body was incorporated in the mission statement.

The changes from 2004 were in line with SPRING's switch in role from the national productivity organisation to an enterprise

Organisation	Term	Chairman
NPC*	May 1967–August 1971	Tang See Chim
NPC*	September 1971–11 May 1972	Dr Augustine H. H. Tan
NPB	12 May 1972–15 June 1975	Dr Augustine H. H. Tan
NPB	16 June 1975–30 September 1975	Hwang Peng Yuan
NPB	1 October 1975–31 December 1977	Thio Gek Choo
NPB	13 January 1978–12 January 1981	Dr Lee Chiaw Meng
NPB	13 January 1981–31 December 1985	Dr Wong Kwei Cheong
NPB	1 January 1986–30 September 1991	Mah Bow Tan
NPB	1 October 1991–31 March 1996	Lim Boon Heng
PSB	1 April 1996–31 March 2002	
SPRING	1 April 2002–31 March 2003	
SPRING	1 April 2003–31 March 2007	Cedric Foo
SPRING	1 April 2007–Present	Philip Yeo
Organisation	Term	Chief Executive
NPC*	May 1967–January 1971	Lee Ong Pong
NPC*	February 1971–11 May 1972	Dr David Chew Chin Eng
NPB	12 May 1972–1978	Loo Heng Shuen
NPB	16 April 1980–31 May 1981	Dr Goh Keng Leng
NPB	1 June 1981–30 September 1983	Lim Jit Poh
NPB	1 October 1983–30 September 1987	Ng Kiat Chong
NPB	1 October 1987–31 January 1995	Koh Juan Kiat
NPB	1 February 1995–31 March 1996	Lee Suan Hiang
PSB	1 April 1996–31 March 2002	
SPRING	1 April 2002–14 October 2003	
SPRING	15 October 2003–30 April 2008	Loh Khum Yean
SPRING	1 May 2008–30 April 2013	Png Cheong Boon
SPRING	1 May 2013–31 July 2015	Tan Kai Hoe
SPRING	1 November 2015–Present	Poon Hong Yuen

Figure 1.5: Leadership of National Productivity Organisation

Notes:

1. As NPC* was a Division in EDB, there was no Board of Directors. Tang See Chim was Chairman of the NPC* Advisory Council; and Dr Augustine H. H. Tan was Chairman of the NPC* Management Committee before it became the NPB Board on 12 May 1972.
2. The title of 'Chief Executive' was first used when Lee Suan Hiang took over the helm of NPB from 1 February 1995. Before that, 'Executive Director' was used in NPB, and 'Director' in NPC*.
3. Loo Heng Shuen left for a 2-year MBA programme at Harvard Business School from September 1972–June 1974. During his absence, Ow Chin Cheow covered his duties.
4. Douglas Chua covered the Executive Director's duties in his position as Deputy Executive Director before Dr Goh Keng Leng came on board on 16 April 1980.
5. Ted Tan Teck Koon was Acting Chief Executive of SPRING from 1 August–31 October 2015.

Source: Annual report of national productivity organisation, various years.

development agency. This took place even though the Act continued to spell out the organisation's responsibility for raising TFP.

Leadership of National Productivity Organisation

Over the decades, the roles and responsibilities of the national productivity organisation were determined largely by the priorities of the productivity drive, as well as the economic priorities. The leadership of the organisation played an important part in planning the exact directions to take, and in steering the organisation to execute the specific programmes.

Figure 1.5 shows the leadership of the national productivity organisation, comprising the Chairman and the Chief Executive, over the years. In the last 50 years, 10 individuals have served as Chairman and another 12 as Chief Executive of the national productivity organisation. The caveat is that since 2004, SPRING has become an enterprise development agency rather than the national productivity organisation.

Moving On to the Rest of the Book

In trying to understand or in attempting to analyse the myriad of productivity activities in Singapore in the last 50 years, it is important to have a sense of perspective and the context to place these activities. Without this helicopter view, there is the danger of missing the forest for the trees and of getting lost in a seemingly complicated maze. This is where the synthesis of the key points in this chapter comes in useful as the subsequent chapters are read.

II
1960s–1970s

Chapter 2

1960s: Sowing Seeds of Productivity to Support Industrialisation

"For us in Singapore, it was a turbulent decade during which momentous changes took place. Singapore entered the 1960s as a British colony with self-governing powers in domestic affairs. We later achieved independence as part of independent Malaysia, only to be expelled from the Federation after two years. On August 9ᵗʰ, 1965, the independent Republic of Singapore was created."

Dr Goh Keng Swee
Minister for Finance
Annual Budget Statement
9 March 1970

Economic Priorities in the 1960s

For 140 years since its founding in 1819 by Stamford Raffles, Singapore was under British rule. On 3 June 1959, it achieved full internal self-governance, with the People's Action Party (PAP) forming the Government of the new State of Singapore.

The Government had to address two pressing issues. The first issue was housing, which had to be tackled quickly as a large part of the population was living in overcrowded and unsanitary conditions. The second issue was the high unemployment rate, which had reached a dizzying 13.5 per cent. Both of these were

41

compounded by the population growth of 4.5 per cent, one of the highest in the world. These issues could not be solved by the hitherto reliance on entrepot trade, which was declining. Hence, the Government decided on the course of industrialisation and set up the Economic Development Board (EDB) on 1 August 1961 to lead the industrialisation programme. These priorities were summed up in the Government's *State of Singapore Development Plan 1961–1964,* the first official blueprint for the economic and social development of Singapore following its attainment of self-governance in 1959.[1]

To accelerate the industrialisation programme, the Government sought assistance from the United Nations Expanded Programme of Technical Assistance (EPTA), the details of which are elaborated in Chapter 4. The immediate output from the assistance was a report called *A Proposed Industrialisation Programme for the State of Singapore (The Winsemius Report,* in short). This report became the de facto economic plan for Singapore in the 1960s, as it closely guided the course of the industrialisation programme. However, the road to industrialisation and economic development in the 1960s was anything but smooth.

During the pre-Malaysia period of 3 June 1959–15 September 1963, the Government had to deal with political issues arising from the divide between the democratic social faction and the communist faction in the PAP. When the pro-communists broke off from the PAP, the resulting communist united front instigated strikes to cause unrest and dissension with the ultimate aim of seizing power. The number of man-days lost in strikes rose from 152,995 in 1960 to 388,219 in 1963. Industrial peace was restored to some extent only after security action had been taken against the pro-communists. In 1964, the number of man-days lost in strikes plunged to 35,908.

---

[1]The Plan was subsequently extended to 1965. This was followed by the Second Development Plan for 1966–1970, which was formulated in the context of the formation of Malaysia and the expected common market. As the Plan was later overtaken by Singapore's independence from Malaysia, it was not implemented.

The next tumultuous period was the time when Singapore was part of Malaysia during 16 September 1963–8 August 1965. When the Federation of Malaysia was proclaimed, there was an unexpected strong reaction from Indonesia. This led to the Confrontation of 1963–1966, which adversely affected Singapore's entrepot trade with Indonesia, a key trading partner. The hope of a large common market was also dashed. For the period 1959–1965, the Government had adopted an import-substitution strategy to grow the domestic manufacturing industries to supply products to the larger common market of Malaysia. The ultimate aim was to generate growth and employment for Singapore. This hope was dented even when Singapore was part of Malaysia because of the onerous terms of the financial arrangement between Singapore and the Federal Government, and disagreements on the structure of the common market. It was completely dashed when Singapore separated from Malaysia and gained full independence on 9 August 1965.

Upon separation from Malaysia, Singapore began a new phase of industrial development based on an export-oriented strategy. The rationale for this was put forth by Lim Kim San, Minister for Finance, in his 1967 Budget Speech delivered in Parliament on 5 December 1966. He said:

"As in the case of all countries which strive for industrial development, we have initially only a limited number of industries directed entirely towards exports. The majority of our existing industries still depend to a great extent on the domestic market. This is inevitable in the early stages of our industrial development. We must now move to a new phase of the industrial programme, namely, the development of export-oriented industries. In order to achieve early full employment and to ensure long-term economic stability and growth, we need specially to encourage manufacturers with established markets and which can draw their raw material supply on a world-wide basis."

The export-oriented strategy entailed attracting foreign multinational corporations (MNCs) to establish their manufacturing operations in Singapore. The Government's position on the preconditions that must be in place had been articulated even before the export-oriented strategy was actively pursued. At the Legislative

Assembly Debate on *State of Singapore Development Plan 1961–1964* on 12 April 1961, Dr Goh Keng Swee, Minister for Finance, said:

"Certain things are necessary for rapid industrialisation ... Our local industrialists will be encouraged to the maximum extent to take advantage of these opportunities. But in the first phase, at any rate, it is certain that we shall require manufacturers from abroad to invest in industries in Singapore ... It is, therefore, vital for our survival that we made the conditions attractive. There are the economic inducements such as the Pioneer Industry Legislation ... We can create favourable conditions for new industries if we are prepared to set up import duties, which must have the effect of raising prices and increasing the cost of living. We may try to extend our overseas markets by various kinds of trade agreements with our neighbours. These all help to make investments in Singapore attractive both to the domestic as well as the overseas manufacturer. But more important than these matters is to create a climate of economic stability and confidence so that people who make the decisions whether to invest in Singapore or not know for certain that the calculations which they now make have a reasonable chance of fulfilment. One of the most important elements in this climate of confidence is stability in labour-management relations. The responsibility for maintaining good labour-management relations rests not merely with labour, not merely with management; nor is it the entire responsibility of the Government. It is necessary to have all three parties working towards an agreed objective and agreeing also on the means whereby inevitable differences must be resolved."

This was one of the earliest statements made by the Government on the absolute importance of good labour-management relations and tripartism (collaboration between unions, employers and the Government) to the economy.

In line with this conviction, two labour laws were passed in 1968. These were the Employment Act, which standardised the terms and conditions of employment; and the Industrial Relations (Amendment) Act, which excluded certain issues, such as recruitment, dismissal and retrenchment, from collective bargaining, and specified new procedures for labour negotiation and conflict resolution.

The strategy proved to be successful. MNCs with labour-intensive factories were soon attracted to Singapore, with the first wave of foreign direct investment (FDI) streaming in from 1967.

An unexpected impetus for accelerating the industrialisation drive came in early 1968 when the British announced the withdrawal of their troops from Singapore by March 1971.[2] The pull-out meant an impending loss of employment and revenue for Singapore. The British military bases then employed about 10 per cent of the local labour force and accounted for about 20 per cent of the nation's gross domestic product (GDP). To counter this setback, the pace of export-oriented industrialisation was stepped up.

Despite all the challenges, Singapore's GDP grew by a high average of 8.7 per cent a year from 1960 to 1969. This came from the double-digit growth of 13.2 per cent during 1966–1969 (roughly the post-Malaysia period), together with the high growth of 8.4 per cent during 1960–1963 (roughly the pre-Malaysia period) and the lower growth of 7.6 per cent during 1964–1965 (roughly the Malaysia period).

Policy Intent on Productivity in the 1960s

As the Government's focus in the 1960s was on economic growth through industrialisation, explicit policy statements on productivity per se were scant. Nonetheless, high productivity was recognised as a critical factor for Singapore's industrialisation drive. This point was emphasised strongly in *The Winsemius Report*, the details of which are given in Chapter 4.

The Government's position on productivity was stated clearly by Dr Goh Keng Swee, Minister for Finance, in his speech at the Third Anniversary Celebration of Shell Refinery Company (Singapore) Limited on 12 August 1964. He said:

"During 1960/61, a proposal was made by the Ministry of Labour to establish a Productivity Centre. The International Labour Office[3] itself was willing, and indeed anxious, to provide experts and other services for the establishment of the Centre. I decided then not to proceed with this project because at that time, the Communists were in full cry, and nothing worthwhile would have been achieved. For the raising of productivity is not merely

---

[2]This was later extended to December 1971.

[3]The International Labour Office is the permanent secretariat of the International Labour Organization.

a responsibility of management, it is a joint responsibility of both labour and management. Unless there is a strong trade union movement which supports a productivity drive, the effort of the Productivity Centre will come to nought.

Now we have a situation under which organised labour and organised management can work together for the common good of all. We can therefore pay attention to the question of productivity. It is a crucial element in industrialisation, particularly with regard to our ability to compete successfully in the export market. As we raise productivity, so we would extend the range of possible industries and increase the scope of existing ones. If we succeed, we may, for the first time, have in sight the possibility of banishing the spectre of unemployment which has been haunting the island for so long."

With the precondition of stable labour-management relations satisfied, the first step towards setting up a Productivity Centre was taken in 1964. This took the form of the establishment of a Productivity Unit within the Technical Consultant Services Division in EDB. The Unit provided training and technical consulting services to upgrade the skills of the workforce and to meet the demands of the manufacturing sector. It was supported by EDB's Light Industries Unit and the Industrial Research Unit.

The setting up of the EDB Productivity Unit was soon followed by a joint declaration of *The Charter for Industrial Progress and the Productivity Code of Practice* by the National Trades Union Congress (NTUC), the Singapore Manufacturers' Association (SMA) and the Singapore Employers Federation (SEF) in January 1965.

Charter for Industrial Progress and Productivity Code of Practice

The Charter for Industrial Progress and the Productivity Code of Practice was prepared in conjunction with the establishment of the State Economic Consultative Council, announced by Dr Goh Keng Swee at the Shell Refinery Company event. The aim of the Council was to secure cooperation between labour, management and the Government in all fields of economic endeavour.

The Charter for Industrial Progress and the Productivity Code of Practice was signed by the tripartite partners at the first meeting of the Council on 15 January 1965. The event was witnessed by Dr Goh Keng Swee and Jek Yeun Thong, Minister for Labour. Figure 2.1 shows the contents of the joint declaration made by the three parties.

THE CHARTER FOR INDUSTRIAL PROGRESS

A Joint Declaration
Made this 15th day of January 1965
by
The National Trades Union Congress
and
The Singapore Manufacturers' Association
and
The Singapore Employers Federation

1. The National Trades Union Congress, the Singapore Manufacturers' Association and the Singapore Employers Federation share the common conviction that the future economic and social well-being of the people of the State depends primarily on the continuing expansion of its economy through accelerated industrial growth. While the industrialisation programme is still in its infant stage, the Nation and the State are being confronted with a serious outside threat. In the circumstances, every citizen of the country is duty-bound to intensify his contribution to all national development efforts.

2. The need for concerted effort is especially important for the continuing expansion of the industrialisation programme of Singapore. Young industries take time to mature and, yet, have to face a highly competitive international market from the start. To overcome these initial difficulties, all partners in the industrialisation programme — workers, employers and Government — must pool their efforts and strive for a continuing increase in productivity and output in all enterprises.

3. Higher productivity brings better wages and working conditions, lower prices for consumers at home and a wider market abroad, and, finally,

---

Figure 2.1: Charter for Industrial Progress and Productivity Code of Practice

Source: National Trades Union Congress, Singapore Manufacturers' Association and Singapore Employers Federation (1965).

adequate investment returns, continuing expansion of production capacities and full employment. All these, however, can only be achieved through the closest collaboration between workers and employers on a common understanding of "Industrial Progress through Industrial Partnership, Justice and Peace."

4. With this objective in view, the National Trades Union Congress, the Singapore Manufacturers' Association and the Singapore Employers Federation support wholeheartedly the action of the Government in forming a State Economic Consultative Council. The Council, with equal representation from workers, employers and Government, will be kept apprised of current economic and business conditions of the State and should serve as the main vehicle for fostering the spirit of partnership in the formulation as well as the implementation of the economic and social development policies.

5. In the industrial field, the translation of these policies into concrete action and practical results has to be initiated, obviously, from plant level in each enterprise. In order to improve the competitive position of Singapore-made products in the world market and to raise the operational efficiency of industrial enterprises up to international standards, the National Trades Union Congress, the Singapore Manufacturers' Association and the Singapore Employers Federation jointly pledge to strive through mutual cooperation to increase the industrial productivity in the State. With a view to fulfilling this objective, the three Organisations have agreed to subscribe to a Productivity Code of Practice as detailed in the attached Annex.

6. It is recognised that the implementation of this Productivity Code of Practice will require considerable promotional effort as well as technical assistance especially in the application of work study, quality control, cost analysis and other modern industrial engineering techniques. To assist in these purposes, there will be established a Singapore Productivity Centre governed by a Board with equal representation from workers, employers and Government. The Centre will be responsible for promoting and coordinating the productivity movement in the State. Initially, the Productivity Unit of the Singapore Economic Development Board will serve as the technical secretariat of the Centre.

In witness whereof, the parties to this Declaration have hereunto set their hands and seals the year and date first above written.

Figure 2.1: (*Continued*)

(1) The Common Seal of the National Trades Union Congress is hereunto affixed in the presence of
Ho See Beng,
President

G. Kandasamy,
Acting Secretary-General

(2) The Common Seal of the Singapore Manufacturers' Association is hereunto affixed in the presence of
Whang Tar Liang,
Chairman

(3) The Common Seal of the Singapore Employers Federation is hereunto affixed in the presence of
M. Lewis,
President

The execution of the above Declaration is hereby witnessed by:
Goh Keng Swee,
Minister for Finance
Jek Yeun Thong,
Minister for Labour

A PRODUCTIVITY CODE OF PRACTICE
for
TRADE UNIONS AND MANUFACTURING INDUSTRIES IN SINGAPORE

COVERAGE AND SCOPE

1. This Productivity Code of Practice has been adopted jointly by the National Trades Union Congress (NTUC), the Singapore Manufacturers' Association (SMA) and the Singapore Employers Federation (SEF). It applies to all manufacturing industries being members of SMA and/or SEF and to all trade unions affiliated to NTUC. It is hoped that this Code of Practice will be subscribed to by all trade unions and manufacturing industries in the State of Singapore, Malaysia. It is agreed that the operation of this Code will be without prejudice to the rights of workers or employers under the

Figure 2.1: (*Continued*)

provisions of any collective agreement and/or awards of the Industrial Arbitration Court or of the Industrial Relations Ordinance, 1960.

NEGOTIATIONS AND ARBITRATION

2. The trade unions and the employers will endeavour to conclude long-term collective agreements of up to three years on the basis of fairness and justice.
3. In case of disputes, both the trade union and the employer will refrain from taking any industrial action and will endeavour to refer jointly to arbitration any dispute which cannot be settled through direct negotiation or conciliation.
4. For the purpose of negotiations or conciliations or arbitration, should there be any unsettled disputes of a technical nature which require independent work study, cost analysis or other industrial engineering or economic appraisals, the trade union and the employer concerned may jointly request the Singapore Productivity Centre or other mutually agreed independent technical organisation to undertake the necessary technical studies. The results of such studies may be used as a guide in negotiations, but shall be regarded as confidential and not divulged by the persons conducting the studies to other than the union and the employer concerned.

COOPERATION MACHINERY

5. Industrial establishments employing more than fifty workers will try to set up, within the next three years, Joint Productivity Consultative Councils which will serve as consultative bodies for guiding and promoting productivity in the respective enterprises.
6. Each Council, which will be composed of not more than four representatives of workers and management respectively, will be chaired by the head of the enterprise or a representative designated by him. The employees' representatives to the Council will be appointed from among the employees by the trade union recognised by the enterprise.
7. The functions of the Council are to advise on measures necessary to promote productivity and rationalise production, for example, improving methods, layouts and processes, uplifting staff morale, eliminating waste, effecting economies with a view to lowering costs, eliminating defective work

Figure 2.1: (*Continued*)

and improving the upkeep and care of machinery, tools and instruments, promoting efficient use of safety precautions and devices, encouraging suggestions, promoting vocational training schemes, improving physical working conditions and suggesting ways and means of improving the operational efficiency of various production units of the enterprise.

8. The Council will not interfere with the authority of management nor with that of the trade union and will not discuss wages and conditions of service which are matters for negotiations between trade union and management.

9. Members of the Council on both sides are bound to maintain absolute secrecy regarding confidential information of the enterprise which may come to their knowledge.

10. The Council may seek the advice of specialists of the Singapore Productivity Centre or of other organisations who will not be members of the Council.

11. All agreed decisions reached by the Council are considered recommendations to the management who may accept them or reject them. In the latter case, the management should give the Council the reasons for rejection.

INCENTIVE SCHEMES

12. Recognising the possible contributions of incentive schemes to a productivity movement, trade unions and management will encourage, subject to mutual agreement in specific cases, the introduction of such schemes whenever applicable, on the understanding that the benefits of higher productivity will be shared equitably between workers, employers and consumers.

EMPLOYMENT PRACTICES

13. The employers will ensure that there shall be no retrenchment as a result of increase in productivity from the improvement of labour efficiency.

14. Trade unions and employers will establish on a mutually agreed basis the appropriate procedures for recruitment and termination of employment which would protect the interests of workers and employers.

PROMOTION PROGRAMME

15. The employers will undertake to train and orientate their supervisory personnel at all levels on measures for promoting workers-management cooperation.

Figure 2.1: (*Continued*)

---

16. The trade unions will undertake to promote "Productivity Consciousness" among their members, thereby minimising absenteeism and practising economy in using raw materials and other production facilities.

17 Copies of the Joint Declaration together with this Code of Practice in the appropriate languages will be displayed in a conspicuous place in all industrial establishments concerned.

Figure 2.1:   (*Continued*)

One of the important points in the joint declaration was the setting up of the Singapore Productivity Centre to assist the implementation of the Productivity Code of Practice. Subsequently, the specific plan for setting up the Centre was stated by Finance Minister Lim Kim San in his Budget Speech for 1967. The statement was made in conjunction with the national productivity drive which was identified as a key area of action, together with specialised skills training and incentives for exports and investments, to make the export-oriented strategy successful. He said:

> *"With the cooperation of the NTUC, the Singapore Manufacturers' Association and the Singapore Employers Federation, we have jointly drawn up in 1965 a Charter for Industrial Progress. It is recognised by all parties that high productivity brings better wages and working conditions, lower prices for consumers at home, and a wider market abroad and, finally adequate investment returns, continuing expansion of production capacities, and full employment. To translate this basic policy into concrete action, practical steps have been initiated. The Singapore Productivity Centre, under a Governing Council with representation of all parties concerned, will come into operation in January 1967. The Centre will be entrusted with the responsibility of launching a national movement directed to further labour-management cooperation, and to improve the operational efficiency of every enterprise in the Republic."*

Formation of National Productivity Centre

The proposed Singapore Productivity Centre came into operation in May 1967 through a re-organisation of the Productivity Unit into

---

a) To promote productivity consciousness in management, trade union leaders and workers.

b) To provide training facilities for management and trade union personnel in all productivity techniques, including general management, personnel management, supervisory training, management accounting, and industrial engineering.

c) To foster the further development of good industrial relations by training.

d) To render management consultancy services in the fields of general management, personnel management, supervisory development, management accounting, and industrial engineering with a view to assisting industrial enterprises to achieve a general raising of productivity.

e) To assist industrial establishments in formulating and rationalising the wage policy and wage systems.

Figure 2.2:   Objectives of National Productivity Centre

Source: National Productivity Board (1972).

an autonomously-run Division within EDB. However, it was named National Productivity Centre (NPC*) instead. The specific objectives of NPC* are given in Figure 2.2.

The setting up of NPC* marked the beginning of a national productivity organisation in Singapore, as well as the start of the national productivity drive. It was a humble beginning. As recounted by National Productivity Board (1972):

> "Then, the full complement of 9 local staff were accommodated in small blocks of JTC one-room flats which had been perfunctorily converted into a lecture room and office facilities."

Similarly, the following recollection was made by National Productivity Board (1987):

> "The Productivity Unit, first set up in 1964, was changed into an autonomously-run division under the purview of the EDB in May 1967. The division was re-named the National Productivity Centre and it set up its office in some ground floor units of a JTC block of flats - - Block 20 in Corporation Drive."

Chairman:

- Tang See Chim, Parliamentary Secretary of Ministry of Finance

Representing the employees:

- Seah Mui Kok
- Eric Cheong
- A. Ramanujan

National Trades Union Congress

Representing the employers:

- Thio Gek Choo, Singapore Employers Federation[4]
- Lim Cheng Hai, National Employers Council[4]
- Ong Leng Chuan, Singapore Manufacturers' Association
- Charlie Young Oon Chaw, Jurong Light Industries Association

Representing the Government:

- Hsu Tse Kwang, Ministry of Culture
- C. S. Nair, Ministry of Labour
- Ernest Wong, Economic Development Board
- Lee Ong Pong, National Productivity Centre

Experts from the International Labour Organization:

- J. R. Ivarson
- H. Pornschlegel
- S. Ramalingam

Figure 2.3:   Composition of 1st Advisory Council of National Productivity Centre
Source: National Productivity Board (1972).

NPC* was headed by a Director, Lee Ong Pong, who had a small team of 8 staff in charge of industrial relations, industrial engineering and clerical duties. Governing NPC* was an Advisory Council, the composition of which is shown in Figure 2.3.

---

[4]On 1 July 1980, the Singapore Employers Federation and the National Employers Council merged to form the current Singapore National Employers Federation.

Significantly, the composition of the Advisory Council was tripartite in composition, with representatives from NTUC, employers and the Government. In addition to the local representatives, three experts from the International Labour Organization (ILO), who helped in the set-up of NPC*, were roped in. The details of ILO's assistance in setting up NPC* are given in Chapter 4.

One year after its establishment, NPC* organised the first regional productivity conference at the Singapore Conference Hall on 20 May 1968. The conference was proposed by the Advisory Council in December 1967. It was held to facilitate the exchange of ideas and experiences on various productivity management matters. The 5-day event was attended by employees, employers, and local and regional government representatives.

Besides the conference, NPC* conducted courses and seminars in English and Mandarin to train management, workers and union members on productivity concepts and techniques. They covered areas such as office management, job evaluation, work simplification, and production planning and control. The courses included an 'in-plant training' component for participants to carry out projects in their own companies after attending classroom training. In addition to courses imparting technical knowledge, NPC* organised seminars on management-related topics such as marketing, collective bargaining and executive development.

NPC* also provided direct assistance to companies through consultancy services. The companies obtained help in implementing productivity improvement initiatives, particularly in industrial engineering; and the management and workers received advice on matters concerning industrial relations.

All of NPC*'s courses, seminars and consultancy services were rendered at nominal charges. The revenue received supplemented the funds from the Ministry of Finance.

On 14 October 1969, NPC* represented Singapore to join the Asian Productivity Organization (APO). Further details on APO are given in the Amp-Box on *Asian Productivity Organization*.

Asian Productivity Organization

The Asian Productivity Organization (APO) is a regional inter-governmental organisation established on 11 May 1961 and located in Tokyo, Japan. Its mission is to 'contribute to the sustainable socioeconomic development of Asia and the Pacific through enhancing productivity.'

APO started with eight founding member economies, namely, India, Japan, Nepal, Pakistan, Philippines, Republic of China, Republic of Korea and Thailand. Its membership is open to economies in Asia and the Pacific region which are members of the United Nations Economic and Social Commission for Asia and the Pacific. Currently, it has 20 members. Besides the eight founding members, the rest are Bangladesh, Cambodia, Fiji, Hong Kong, Indonesia, Islamic Republic of Iran, Lao PDR, Malaysia, Mongolia, Singapore, Sri Lanka and Vietnam. Each member pays an annual membership contribution to the APO according to the size of its gross national income.

APO is led by a Governing Body, comprising the APO Directors appointed by each member economy. The chairmanship of the Governing Body is rotated among the members on an annual basis. The APO Directors are supported by their respective national productivity organisations (NPOs), which are designated by the members' governments to drive productivity within their countries. The NPOs work with the Secretariat of APO, headed by a Secretary-General, to plan and execute the strategic directions decided by the Governing Body.

The APO programmes include:

- Observational study missions.
- Training courses, workshops and conferences.
- Technical expert services.
- Research projects.
- Bilateral Cooperation Between NPOs.

The programmes are hosted by the Secretariat and/or the NPOs.

Singapore joined APO on 14 October 1969 as its 14th member economy. NPC* represented Singapore on APO then, and the Chairman of NPC* was appointed the APO Director for Singapore. Currently, Singapore is represented on APO by SPRING, with one of its Assistant Chief Executives as the APO Director.

(Continued)

(*Continued*)

Over the years, especially in the early years of its economic development, Singapore has benefited from the APO membership through its participation in the various programmes. In September 1981, the Government launched the Productivity Movement after seeking the advice of Kohei Goshi, founder and Chairman of Japan Productivity Center, who had been deputed to Singapore through APO earlier in the year.

Singapore has also contributed to APO and the other NPOs through the deputation of experts to other countries. Some of the more notable contributions were made after APO's appointment of SPRING as the Center of Excellence for Business Excellence in 2009. As the Center of Excellence, SPRING assisted its fellow NPOs to build their expertise in business excellence, through best practice sharing sessions, research and development of resources.

Source: Ng, J. (2001); www.apo-tokyo.org.

Productivity Drive in the 1960s in Retrospect

The decade of the 1960s was a time when the seeds of productivity were being sown to support Singapore's industrialisation. High productivity was considered critical to economic growth, even at the start of the industrialisation programme. Nevertheless, it made sense to focus on productivity only when the state of labour-management relations was stable. This explains the timing for the formation of NPC* in May 1967.

For the remainder of the 1960s, the activities of NPC* were limited in scope and impact, as the organisation was constrained by its small size and the fact that it was not an independent entity with the full mandate for productivity. Hence, the productivity drive in the 1960s was at best nascent. The Government's priority was to attract FDI into Singapore to grow the economy through industrialisation. The strategy proved to be successful, with full employment reached by the turn of the decade. For the whole of the 1960s, the economy grew by an average of 8.7 per cent a year, while the productivity growth averaged 5.0 per cent a year, contributing 57 per cent to the economic growth. These growth rates were the outcomes of a developing economy that was beginning to grow rapidly.

Chapter 3

1970s: Ramping Up the Productivity Drive

"So all this hand wringing over the dependence of Singapore's economy on external factors is somewhat pointless. What is more pertinent is whether Singapore has inner resilience and strength to cope with adverse external developments and exploit them to advantage when they are favourable. This, in my view, is what distinguish a sound economic system from an unsound one ... I know that the term 'productivity' has become something of a cliché but nevertheless it holds the key to our economic future."

> *S. Rajaratnam*
> *Minister for Foreign Affairs*
> *Opening of National Productivity Campaign*
> *12 April 1975*

Economic Priorities in the 1970s

By the start of the 1970s, the industrialisation programme was in full steam as the Economic Development Board (EDB) aggressively marketed Singapore as an attractive location where factories could be built quickly and where a skilled workforce was readily available. Unlike in the 1960s, there was no formal economic plan in the 1970s. Essentially, the economic strategies during the decade continued to be guided by the directions spelt out in *The Winsemius Report*.

For the period 1965–1973, despite the sudden political independence and the British military withdrawal, Singapore achieved double-digit economic growth averaging 12.6 per cent a year. As the pursuit of export-oriented industrialisation had coincided with a rapid growth in world trade, Singapore was able to take advantage of easy access to the expanding markets in the United States, Europe and Japan. By 1970, the economy was in full employment situation. Labour shortage began to emerge, as foreign investments continued to pour in and create more jobs than people available. From a labour surplus economy in the beginning of the 1960s, Singapore had become a labour shortage economy.

To address the labour shortage, the Government relaxed the immigration rules in 1972 to import more foreign workers. At the same time, to check rising wages caused by the labour shortage, it set up a tripartite National Wages Council (NWC) in February 1972. NWC was tasked to provide recommendations to the Government on annual wage guidelines, wage structure and incentive schemes for promoting productivity in enterprises.

Against this economic backdrop, Hon Sui Sen, Minister for Finance, outlined the future directions for Singapore at the annual dinner of the Singapore Manufacturers' Association (SMA) on 18 June 1971. Five areas were identified as priorities for the 1970s:

a. Move from labour-intensive industries to more capital-intensive and highly skilled ones that pay higher wages;
b. Develop a pool of highly skilled workforce to meet the demands of the highly-skilled industries;
c. Address rising manpower costs due to a full employment situation;
d. Improve the quality and standard of products to increase competitiveness in overseas markets; and
e. Develop specialised industries and facilities to support the highly skilled and capital-intensive industries.

Clearly, the Government was aware of the need to shift the economy towards capital-intensive industries, thus reducing the reliance on foreign workers, even in the early 1970s. However, the subsequent successive external shocks to the economy caused the restructuring plans to be shelved. In 1973, Singapore was hit by the first oil crisis, marked by the price hikes for crude oil which led to a worldwide recession. In the same year, the stock market in the United States crashed. In 1974, global trade went into a recession, and the developed countries experienced stagflation. Because of its external orientation, Singapore could not be shielded against these developments. From the double-digit performance during 1965–1973, the gross domestic product (GDP) growth plunged to 6.5 per cent in 1974 and 4.6 per cent in 1975.

Faced with the prospect of slower growth and a large number of job losses, the Government responded by attracting even more foreign direct investment (FDI), including labour-intensive investments, into Singapore. This meant that more foreign workers had to be imported. At the same time, it undertook land reclamation and construction activities to lessen the impact of the recession. As a result of all the actions taken by the Government, the economy continued to grow, albeit at a slower rate. The growth rebounded to 7.4 per cent in 1976 and averaged 7.3 per cent for the period 1973–1979. Despite the second oil shock in 1979, which set off the longest and deepest recession in the developed countries since the Great Depression of the 1930s, the Singapore economy was not badly affected. For the whole of the 1970s, the growth rate averaged 9.0 per cent a year.

Policy Intent on Productivity in the 1970s

The importance of productivity to the success of the export-oriented industrialisation strategy had been established in the 1960s. This was reinforced further with the Government's plan in the early 1970s to promote capital-intensive industries, the success of which depended on high skills and high productivity.

The importance of productivity was re-emphasised by Dr Goh Keng Swee, Deputy Prime Minister and Defence Minister, who wrote an essay titled *A Socialist Economy that Works* in 1976. He said:

"Singapore's growing industries produced goods not for the domestic market, which was far too small, nor even for the regional market in Southeast Asia ... Our market was the world markets. A number of consequences follow from this.

First, the best vehicles for achieving this kind of industrial growth are large foreign manufacturing enterprises who wish to reduce costs in order to remain competitive in the world market ... They brought with them not only production and management know-how, but also the world market for their products.

The second consequence of this policy was the need to maintain a high degree of efficiency in Singapore. This, in turn, meant that services and facilities such as power and factory sites had to be made available at the lowest, but not subsidised, cost. Labour productivity had to be raised to the highest possible level by good work attitudes and keen management. Last, but by no means least, the credibility of government policies had to be maintained by rational and consistent application."

With the strong emphasis on productivity, there were high expectations of the National Productivity Centre (NPC*). Unfortunately, it did not live up to expectations. To strengthen NPC* and improve its performance, the Government stepped in to restructure the organisation in late 1970. This was an intermediate step towards creating a new statutory board from NPC* to spearhead the productivity drive. The final step took place in 1972 when the new statutory board, National Productivity Board (NPB), was established.

Restructuring of National Productivity Centre to Improve Performance

The establishment of NPC* in May 1967 marked an important milestone in the development of a full-fledged national productivity organisation in Singapore. However, despite the laudable efforts made, NPC* faced challenges in delivering what it was expected to achieve. Being a Division in EDB, it had no authority to mandate actions to be taken by companies and workers. It was also restricted by the small staff strength, and had difficulties in educating and convincing companies and employees of the need to improve productivity.

Because it had failed to live up to expectations, NPC* was lambasted by the labour leaders in the early 1970s. Seah Mui Kok, former secretary-general of the National Trades Union Congress (NTUC), criticised NPC* for its lack of achievement which had led to workers' disenchantment with productivity. N. Govindasamy, Member of Parliament and trade unionist, lamented in Parliament about the failure of NPC* to produce substantial results. In response, Finance Minister Dr Goh Keng Swee provided assurance that the Government would look into the issue of improving the efficiency of NPC*.

On 5 February 1971, C. V. Devan Nair, Secretary-General of NTUC, expressed similar views about NPC* at an Industrial Arbitration Court hearing.[1] Referring to *The Charter for Industrial Progress and the Productivity Code of Practice*, executed in 1965, Devan Nair said that it had been breached more than observed. He added:

> "*Management proved indifferent. Trade unions did not push hard enough. But probably a sizeable share of the blame belongs to the government itself, for it was blandly assumed that a resounding declaration about a productivity code of practice, which hit all the headlines, would by itself do the trick of ensuring actual implementation of the code in factory floors and plants without a close follow-up and sustained leadership ... Through no fault of its own, but through sheer lack of leadership on the part of the government organisations concerned, and of any kind of co-operative response and initiative on the part of the management and trade unions, the National Productivity Centre failed to obtain an opportunity to demonstrate what it really could do.*"

Nevertheless, Devan Nair was optimistic about the future in view of the Government's determination to get the productivity movement off the launching pad, and especially with assistance from the United Nations Development Programme (UNDP), the details of which are given in Chapter 4. He said:

> "*The Singapore Government has, in conjunction with the United Nations Development Programme, initiated a multi-million dollar project to rejuvenate and expand the productivity movement.*"

To improve its performance, NPC* started to revamp itself in October 1970, some four months before Devan Nair's comments

---

[1] The hearing concerned a dispute between the Sugar Industry of Singapore and the Pioneer Industries' Union over a productivity scheme recommended by NPC*.

In February 1971, Dr David Chew Chin Eng, a senior lecturer in economics at the University of Singapore, took over from Lee Ong Pong as the Director of NPC*. This was followed by a physical shift of the office premises in June 1971. From the small blocks of JTC one-room flats, NPC* moved to the 6th floor of Jurong Flatted Factory at Chia Ping Road, at the junction of Corporation Road and International Road. Occupying a total floor area of 22,000 sq ft, the new facility encompassed a sound-proof theatrette; three lecture rooms; a library with management and technical books, journals and periodicals; a technical laboratory stocked with audio visual equipment; and aluminium cast models of factory and office equipment and machinery, for industrial engineering training.

NPC* also set up a Research Unit and an Information Unit to provide research and information services to assist companies. The Research Unit carried out studies and undertook surveys to obtain up-to-date information covering a wide range of economic, industrial and labour fields. The results of the studies were compiled in the form of reports, and distributed to the relevant government authorities and interested institutions. The Information Unit, which included a Public Relations Section and a Library, produced and disseminated information resources to the various stakeholders. One of the key initiatives started by the Unit was a monthly productivity publication titled *Minimax*, an acronym for 'minimise input and maximise output'. The first issue of *Minimax* was published in April 1972. The free publication contained news related to NPC*, upcoming events, and articles on productivity concepts and tools contributed by local and overseas experts. It was subsequently issued on a bi-monthly basis from 1980 onwards, with Jan/Feb 1982 Vol. 3 No. 1 as the last issue.

Projects undertaken by NPC* were profiled by the media. An example is a productivity improvement project with the Postal Services Department that was highly publicised. In February 1971, NPC* conducted a preliminary assessment of the Department's productivity and recommended a 'reorganisation study' to improve its services. As a follow-up, it started work on a year-long project at the request of Yong Nyuk Lin, Minister for Communication. The project involved in-house training for the employees, studies of processes at the General Post Office and the branch offices, and development and implementation of recommendations.

In executing its projects and activities, NPC* partnered various organisations, such as NTUC, trade associations and tertiary institutions (e.g. University of Singapore). It also collaborated with the Singapore Institute of Standards and Industrial Research (SISIR) to run seminars on quality control, an area that was critical for the international competitiveness of Singapore-manufactured products.

In July 1971, NPC* was transferred from EDB to the Ministry of Labour (MOL). The aim was to forge a close link between productivity and wages, and to ensure widespread acceptance of the principle of higher productivity leading to higher wages. This principle was, in fact, not new as it had been stated explicitly in *The Charter for Industrial Progress and the Productivity Code of Practice*. What was needed now was to institutionalise the principle to give a boost to the productivity drive.

Establishment of National Productivity Board

On 28 August 1971, Hon Sui Sen, Minister for Finance, announced the Government's aim to strengthen NPC* even further by establishing it as a distinct organisation apart from EDB. In his speech at EDB's 10ᵗʰ Anniversary, focusing on the need for internationalisation and modernisation of Singapore's economic activities, he said:

> *"In stimulating an international outlook and promoting modernisation, Government will, of course, play its part in setting policy, and implementing it in the public sector. This, however, is not enough. A strong economy requires that every sector and every individual unit is modernised and built up to maximum capacity ... these changes towards internationalisation and modernisation must be supported by a broad base of diligent and easily trained workers, in which measures to upgrade skill and improve productiv-ity can be spread down to all levels ... As for productivity, I am taking this opportunity to inform you that steps have been taken to strengthen the National Productivity Centre. It should soon be established as a separate*

statutory board, the National Productivity Board, which would be adminis-
tered by the Ministry of Labour ... With the full support of all concerned, the
National Productivity Board can play a key role in the modernisation process
and will maximise the use of our most precious resources, human resources."

This statement provides the raison d'etre for establishing NPB as a separate statutory body under MOL, replacing NPC*.

A month later, in September, an interim Management Committee was set up to formulate policies and strategies for the further development of NPC* in the light of it being a separate statutory board in the near future. The Committee was chaired by Dr Augustine H. H. Tan, a Member of Parliament, senior economics lecturer in the University of Singapore and a Member of the EDB Board. The composition of the Committee, with equal representation from the Government, employers, unions and academic/professional institutions, is shown in Figure 3.1. On 8 October 1971, this same Committee was appointed the 1st NPB Board of Directors by the Ministry of Finance (MOF) in consultation with MOL.

On 12 May 1972, NPB was formally established as a statutory board under MOL. The objectives of NPB, as spelt out in the National Productivity Board Act (1972), are shown in Figure 3.2. Compared with the objectives of NPC* (Figure 2.2), objectives (a), (e) and (f) were largely the same; (b) was widened to 'modern management' instead of just 'productivity techniques'; (d) was expanded to cover 'promoting the formation of joint consultative councils' beyond training; and (c), (g), (h) and (i) were new.

The importance of tripartite cooperation between labour, employers and the Government, with support from academic/professional institutions, was reflected in the composition of the Board of Directors. As specified in the Act, the Board comprised:

a. a Chairman;
b. three directors representing the interests of the Government;
c. three directors representing the interests of employers;
d. three directors nominated by the National Trades Union Congress of Singapore;

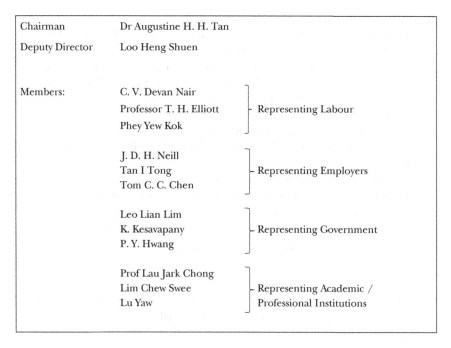

Figure 3.1: NPC* Management Committee and First NPB Board of Directors

Note: Loo Heng Shuen took over the responsibilities of Dr David Chew Chin Eng, who was appointed Advisor to the Ministry of Labour in the latter part of 1971.

Source: National Productivity Board (1972).

a. To promote productivity consciousness in managements, trade union leaders and workers.

b. To provide training facilities for managerial and supervisory personnel in all relevant aspects of modern management including general management, personnel management, management accounting, industrial engineering, achievement motivation and supervisory training.

c. To train workers' representatives in measures for raising labour productivity, and to relate wages and productivity to competitiveness in export markets and industrial relations.

Figure 3.2: Objectives of National Productivity Board from 12 May 1972

Source: National Productivity Board Act (1972).

---

d. To foster and promote good industrial relations by training and by promoting the formation of joint consultative councils.

e. To render management consultancy services in the same fields in which training activities are undertaken with a view to assisting industrial enterprises to achieve a general raising of productivity.

f. To assist industrial establishments and trade unions in formulating and rationalising wage policies and wage systems.

g. To assist the Government from time to time in shaping a national wage policy.

h. To undertake manpower and wage studies.

i. To provide a library of books, files and other information material to all interested parties.

Figure 3.2: (*Continued*)

e. three directors representing the professional and academic interests associated with productivity; and

f. the Executive Director of NPB.

In addition to Dr Augustine H. H. Tan (12 May 1972–15 June 1975), Hwang Peng Yuan (16 June 1975–30 September 1975), Thio Gek Choo (1 October 1975–31 December 1977) and Dr Lee Chiaw Meng[2] (13 January 1978–12 January 1981) served as the Chairman of NPB in the 1970s. Loo Heng Shuen (12 May 1972–1978) was the only Executive Director during that decade.

NPB's Programmes in the 1970s

NPB started off with a staff strength of 69, considerably more than the 9 in NPC* when it was set up in 1967. For the first five years, a large part of its time was spent on institution-building in addition to the programmes that it ran for the industry. Staff were sent for overseas training and fellowships mainly through the sponsorships of UNDP, as well as the Asia Foundation and the Asian Productivity Organization (APO).

---

[2] Dr Lee Chiaw Meng was also a Member of Parliament.

Assistance to companies focused on four key areas, namely, training, consultancy, promotion and research. The services centred on the topics of industrial engineering, general management, personnel management, and automation and technology.

To better cater to the needs of the workforce and the industry, NPB laid out a plan to do the following for the first five years:

a. Conduct more courses and seminars in Mandarin and in the evenings;
b. Establish a Panel of Consultants to bring together expertise from the industry and academic institutions to service companies;
c. Promote low cost automation, management information systems and electronic data processing as means to further drive the productivity of enterprises;
d. Carry out more in-depth research studies and annual surveys to allow NPB to improve its services, and to provide recommendations to policy-makers to better assist enterprises;
e. Promote formation of work councils to encourage greater cooperation between management and labour; and
f. Establish an affiliate body called the National Productivity Association to reach out to the workforce and enterprises, and create more awareness of the need to improve productivity.

In February 1978, NPB announced its 5-year plan for the period 1977–1981. The plan was formulated with the long-term goal of making NPB the leading centre for training managers, supervisors, workers and trade unionists on productivity and management techniques; providing technical assistance and consultancy; and conducting research and disseminating information on productivity-related issues.

Training to Impart Skills and Knowledge

First 5 Years: 1972–1977

The training programmes conducted by NPB were in four main areas: industrial engineering and management, industrial health and safety, training-within-industry and low-cost automation.

The emphasis for industrial engineering and management was on skills-based training to meet the needs of the growing economy. The training covered industrial engineering and production, personnel management and industrial relations, and general and financial management.

The importance of industrial health and safety came to light as the number of accidents and fatalities from the industrial activities increased. Industrial health and safety was promoted through seminars and courses, with the assistance of experts from the International Labour Organization (ILO). The first Safety Officer's Course was conducted by NPB in January 1973 in collaboration with MOL. Separate training programmes were also customised for individual companies and sectors with high rates of industrial accidents.

Training-within-industry (TWI) courses dominated the training scene, covering about 70 per cent of the participants trained. TWI was first promoted in Singapore in 1955 by F. G. Tyson, Chief Employment Officer from the Labour Department, with assistance from ILO. It was seen as a useful programme to train supervisors to increase productivity and improve industrial relations. Post-independence, MOL continued with the promotion of TWI; and, in 1971, it began to train external trainers to meet the increasing demand from supervisors in the public and private sectors. In July 1973, the TWI Section in MOL was transferred to NPB and expanded into a Supervisory Development Unit. The Unit conducted various courses to train supervisors on job relations, job instruction and communications, and job methods and job safety (TWI-RIMS); and supplementary programmes on job discussion, job action, job control, and job orientation (TWI-DACO). A Certificate in Supervision course was also launched to accelerate the training of supervisors.

Low Cost Automation (LCA), involving the use of standard equipment or devices to automate parts of the manufacturing process, was another key initiative of NPB. It was deemed to be especially useful for small and medium enterprises (SMEs), and in helping companies to transit from labour-intensive to capital-intensive operations. On 19 February 1974, a LCA Unit was officially opened in NPB to help companies implement LCA. The services of the Unit included a training laboratory to showcase, develop and simulate LCA applications; a library on LCA; consultancy services; and training seminars and courses. On the same day, a LCA Week was launched. The Week included an exhibition and seminars showcasing various LCA devices and their applications.

In its first five years, NPB conducted more than 1,500 courses and trained over 25,000 participants at all levels of the workforce. The training programmes were delivered in the form of in-centre courses (i.e. courses delivered in NPB), in-company courses (i.e. courses customised and delivered in companies), and seminars and conferences. To cater to the increased number of courses and training participants, NPB launched a new training centre at Hotel Royal Ramada on 29 October 1976. Located at Newton Road, the training centre supplemented the facilities in Jurong and was more convenient for participants attending night classes after work.

Beyond First 5 Years: 1978–1979

Beyond the first five years, NPB's training activities continued to focus on meeting the needs of SMEs. Besides TWI, the key areas of training included LCA, industrial engineering, business management and management information system. In addition to these courses, management and supervisory development was emphasised. To bcef up the quality of programmes offered, NPB partnered foreign institutions and increased its collaboration with APO to facilitate the transfer of overseas best practices to the industry. Activities jointly organised with APO included a symposium on productivity measurement, multi-country study missions and workshops conducted by international experts.

NPB also started to offer training programmes in a more integrated manner to provide trainees with a holistic perspective of their work and responsibilities. Modules that had been delivered as individual workshops in the past were now offered as a package. An example is the Supervisory Development programme, comprising four modules, viz. the supervisor and his role, elements of industrial engineering, personnel management for supervisors, and cost accounting and control. Upon completing the four modules, the trainees received the NPB Certificate in Supervision. Another example is the Business Management programme, comprising six modules, viz. business management, managerial accounting and finance, marketing management, personnel management, productivity and management, and legal and information services.

Consultancy to Help Companies Improve their Operations

First 5 Years: 1972–1977

Similar to the areas of focus for training, consultancy services were rendered to assist companies in LCA, industrial engineering, management accounting and personnel management.

For the initial years, the consultancy projects covered mainly specific techniques in industrial engineering (e.g. production planning and quality control) and personnel management (e.g. job evaluation and incentive schemes). Subsequently, the projects were more multi-disciplinary in nature. The number of projects for automation and technology services also increased over the years as NPB promoted the concept of LCA.

In late 1975, NPB's focus shifted to assisting SMEs. This change resulted in a higher proportion of SMEs in consultancy projects, as well as training programmes. For the period 1972–1975, 46 per cent of the projects were carried out for SMEs. This increased to 67 per cent in 1976. Similarly, for training programmes, the percentage of participants from SMEs increased from 27 per cent in 1972 to 34 per cent in 1975.

Beyond First 5 Years: 1978–1979

Beyond 1977, NPB intensified its consultancy assistance to companies, especially SMEs, in the areas of automation and technology adoption, and business management (e.g. management accounting and personnel management). Besides an increase in the demand for consultancy services, there was a shift towards more advanced areas such as management information systems, computer processing and energy management.

In addition to assisting companies, NPB helped the Public Utilities Board (PUB) to secure expert services in energy management. In 1979, amidst the oil crisis, PUB initiated a national 'save electricity' campaign targeted at consumers. Factories were also urged to conserve energy and manage their energy consumption. To support this initiative, NPB started courses on energy management, and introduced a new Energy Conservation System for Hotels programme with expert help from UNDP.

Promotion to Increase Awareness and Understanding of Productivity

First 5 Years: 1972–1977

The third pillar of promotion was intended to increase awareness and understanding of productivity and its related concepts among workers and companies. The key initiatives carried out included the formation of the National Productivity Association (NPA*)[3], promotion of work councils and productivity committees, and launch of a 6-month national productivity campaign.

National Productivity Association

NPA* was registered with the Registry of Societies on 19 February 1973. It was set up as an affiliated body of NPB to support the productivity promotion effort, by facilitating the involvement of companies and the workforce in the various productivity programmes. More details are given in the Amp-Box on *Singapore Productivity Association*.

---

[3]* is placed against NPA when it is used as the acronym for National Productivity Association to differentiate it from the same acronym used for National Productivity Award.

Singapore Productivity Association

Background to Formation and Changes Over the Years

Soon after its formation in May 1972, NPB started a membership scheme to promote productivity to individuals and institutions. On 19 February 1973, it set up the National Productivity Association (NPA*) as an affiliated body, registered as a society, to take over the membership scheme and to help promote productivity.

The objectives set for NPA* were:

a. To actively involve all sectors of the economy with the Productivity Movement and to facilitate the spread of productivity concepts and techniques; and
b. To acquaint individuals, interested groups and organisations with the role and activities of NPB.

With these objectives, NPA*'s activities were closely aligned with the strategic directions and priorities of NPB.

The Chairman of NPB, Dr Augustine H. H. Tan, was appointed the first Chairman of NPA*'s Management Committee, in accordance with the NPA* Constitution. A Working Committee assisted the Management Committee to develop and execute a programme of activities. On 17 October 1977, the Constitution was amended to replace the Management Committee with a Governing Council; and the Working Committee was replaced with an Executive Committee, which was subsequently renamed Management Committee. In October 1982, a full-time Secretariat for NPA* was formed.

The establishment of Singapore Productivity and Standards Board (PSB) in April 1996 to succeed NPB led to a series of changes for NPA*. For better alignment with PSB, the name of the Association was changed to Singapore Productivity Association (SPA) on 6 February 1997. To support PSB's mission, SPA took on the mission of 'To help raise the level of productivity in Singapore by being the preferred provider of productivity enhancement programmes and related services so as to increase individual and corporate competitiveness'. It also developed a new corporate identity with a new logo to symbolise the objective of nurturing growth in productivity. The logo is still being used currently.

Today, the stated objective of SPA is 'To promote the active involvement of organisations and individuals in the Productivity Movement, and to expedite

(Continued)

(*Continued*)

the spread of productivity and its techniques.' This is a variant of its first objective in 1973. Its mission is 'To raise the productivity of organisations and individuals in Singapore', and its vision is 'To be the world-class productivity association in Singapore.'

Governing Structure and Membership Scheme

The governing structure for SPA has remained unchanged since 1977. However, instead of the Chairman of SPRING (successor of PSB), the Chief Executive of SPRING is now the Chairman of the Governing Council. Members of the Governing Council comprise the President and Vice-Presidents of the Management Committee, senior management staff of SPRING and the Executive Director of SPA.

The Management Committee is headed by the President, who is assisted by two Vice-Presidents, all of whom are from the private sector. Members of the Management Committee comprise elected members from the private and public sectors and senior management staff of SPRING. The SPA Secretariat is headed by the Executive Director and is manned by full-time employees.

SPA offers two types of membership, viz. Institutional and Individual. The fee for Individual membership is a flat rate per year, while the fee structure for Institutional membership varies by company size (according to number of employees). Membership is open to 'individuals and organisations that have interest and conviction in the objectives of the Productivity Movement.'

The members enjoy certain benefits. These include access to skills training, participation in study missions, networking sessions, participation in Asian Productivity Organization (APO) programmes, membership talks, and regular news and email alerts.

Priorities and Activities

1970s to 1990s

During its initial years, NPA* functioned very much like the marketing arm of NPB. It focused on creating awareness of productivity and increasing membership. Its activities were subsidised by NPB and were reported in NPB's annual reports from FY72/73 to FY84/85.

(*Continued*)

(Continued)

With the launch of the Productivity Movement in 1981, NPA* expanded its activities. Promotional and educational activities, ranging from publications, training programmes and study missions, were carried out to support NPB in the national productivity drive.

Publications

The first *NPA* Year Book* was published for FY78/79. It included a compilation of articles related to productivity and management practices. Similar publications were produced subsequently to commemorate NPA*'s 10th, 15th, 20th and 25th anniversaries but were discontinued thereafter. On 1 November 1983, NPA* launched its own *NPA* Times* in conjunction with the Productivity Month in 1983. The magazine covered a mix of productivity-related articles targeted at individuals and enterprises. It was subsequently renamed *SPA Times*, with the change in name of the Association, and was published until January 2002. Besides its own publications, SPA published *Productivity Digest* jointly with NPB from March 1982 to December 1985.

Networking Activities, Training Programmes and Study Missions

To facilitate networking and interaction among its members, NPA* organised many activities with a social element. These included luncheon and dinner talks, film shows, and members' nights to welcome new members.

In 1983, NPA* started a PROREC programme to promote the setting up of productivity recreation clubs in companies. The aim was to encourage teamwork and engage employees, by introducing fun activities at the workplace. In the same year, in December, an inaugural Productivity Cruise was organised to soft-sell productivity concepts and strengthen worker-management relationship through a mix of training and recreational activities. The Cruise, targeted at management and employees, was modelled on the annual cruises organised by the Japan Productivity Center.

As NPA* expanded its operations, special interest groups and chapters were formed to drive various initiatives and to cater to specific groups of members. They covered areas such as training, Quality Control Circles (QCCs) and human resource management, and targeted specific segments such as productivity managers and SME entrepreneurs. For example, a Production

---

(Continued)

(*Continued*)

Managers Chapter was formed in April 1987 to increase productivity in the manufacturing sector.

NPA* also extended its services to include formal training programmes. The first training programme, on production management, was launched in November 1982. This was followed by other training courses and seminars on a wide range of topics, including office management, project management, finance, marketing and communication. By the mid-1990s, NPA* had introduced degree and post-graduate programmes to help members advance their careers. For example, a Master in Business Administration (MBA) programme with the Oklahoma City University was launched in 1989, and a MBA programme in Information Systems with the Netherlands International Institute for Management was launched in 1991.

Besides bringing in international experts to complement the local experts in assisting members, NPA* invited members to participate in training courses and other activities organised by foreign organisations. Overseas study missions were also organised for members to learn best practices in countries such as China, Japan and South Korea.

2000s–2010s

In the 2000s, besides its core programmes, SPA took over the productivity promotion programmes from SPRING after the latter had changed its role from the national productivity champion to an enterprise development agency. One of these was the Innovation and Quality Circle (IQC) programme, which was transferred from SPRING to SPA in 2008. Correspondingly, the International Exposition of Innovation and Quality Circles (IEIQC), which was subsequently renamed International Exposition of Team Excellence (IETEX), was also transferred to SPA. Another programme was the International Management Action Award (IMAA), administered by the Chartered Management Institute. SPA now serves as its Secretariat.

Today, SPA is a self-financing organisation. Its programmes fall into four categories, viz. Productivity Programmes, Team Excellence, Membership and International Programmes. Two of its established programmes are the Enhanced Certified Productivity Practitioner Programme (eCPP) and the Toyota Production System Study Mission to Japan. On 1 May 2016, SPA was appointed a Lean Enterprise Development Multiplier by the Singapore

(*Continued*)

(Continued)

Workforce Development Agency (WDA) to help SMEs be more manpower-lean, develop a strong Singapore core and build a quality workforce.

Besides its own activities, SPA set up a wholly-owned subsidiary called the Singapore Productivity Centre (SPC) in 2013. SPC is the productivity competency centre for the services sectors, established under the aegis of the National Productivity and Continuing Education Council (NPCEC). Its initial focus is on the retail, food services and hotel sectors. SPC's activities for the retail and food services sectors are funded largely by SPRING; and those for the hotel sector, by Singapore Tourism Board (STB).

Role of SPA in Relation to SPRING's Directions and the National Productivity Drive

SPA's activities today are not as closely aligned with SPRING's directions as in the past. While SPA continues to run productivity-related programmes, SPRING has evolved into an enterprise development agency. Hence, it is not surprising that the original second objective of NPA* in 1973 has been dropped.

With respect to the national productivity drive, SPA has not been given the specific role of productivity promotion. This is a contrast to the past when it was used directly by NPB/PSB to promote productivity. Instead, SPA assists organisations and individuals directly through various productivity improvement programmes.

Source: National Productivity Association/Singapore Productivity Association, *Commemorative Publication,* various issues; National Productivity Board, *Annual Report,* various years; National Productivity Board, *Productivity Digest,* various issues; www.spa.org.sg.

Work Councils and Productivity Committees

Joint consultation, aimed at improving worker-management relations and facilitating collaboration in productivity activities, was first highlighted in *The Charter for Industrial Progress and the Productivity Code of Practice.* From the formation of NPC* in 1967 till 1974, the platform for joint consultation was promoted in the form of work councils. Following a review by senior members of unions and management at a NPB seminar in June 1974, 'productivity committee' replaced 'work council' to emphasise the importance of productivity.

In February 1975, NPB convened a National Industrial Relations Committee (NIRC)[4] to drive the promotion of productivity committees and discuss the link between wages and productivity performance. The objectives of productivity committees, as well as the guidelines for their establishment, were spelt out by NIRC. These objectives are shown in Figure 3.3. To help the attainment of the objectives, an instruction manual was published by NPB to train the committee members.

National Productivity Campaign

The first national productivity campaign in Singapore was launched on 12 April 1975 by S. Rajaratnam, Minister for Foreign Affairs, at the Victoria Memorial Hall. Stretching over six months from April to September 1975, the campaign aimed to instil greater awareness of the importance of productivity to Singapore. The theme used was 'increasing productivity by reducing costs, wastage of materials and time; improving quality and efficiency; and promoting an ethos of mutual co-operation and trust between management and labour.' Joint consultation, productivity committees and automation were the key areas promoted. The campaign was backed by the slogan 'Productivity is Our Business'; and the productivity message was disseminated through various channels including television and radio, seminars, and paraphernalia such as pamphlets, key chains, posters and car decals. Figure 3.4 shows the main activities held during the campaign.

---

[4]NIRC was appointed by the Minister for Labour and placed under the aegis of NPB to provide a forum to deliberate and provide advice on matters related to industrial relations in Singapore. It was chaired by the Chairman of NPB and comprised members from NPB, MOL, NTUC, National Employers Council, Singapore Employers Federation and Singapore Institute of Personnel Management.

- Devote a large part of deliberation to management-workers co-operation to increase productivity.
- Discuss problems connected with more efficient use of existing machines and equipment and the rational re-arrangement of work processes, where necessary.
- Recommend ways and means of reducing the proportion of unproductive time to productive time.
- Recommend means of increasing the quality of products, reducing rejects, errors and customer dissatisfaction.
- Recommend measures for increasing efficiency and saving manpower, materials and expenses.
- Eliminate restrictive and protective practices which may hinder productivity.
- Encourage employees' suggestions and introduce suggestion schemes, or upgrade existing schemes.
- Recommend measures to re-train and re-allocate workers to upgrade skills and improve productivity.
- Recommend measures for improving working conditions and health and hygiene in the enterprise, such as clean and good canteens, showers, suitable lighting and ventilation.
- Evaluate and consult on a system of fair work standards and, where feasible, consider wage or other incentives based on measured standards and, where agreed upon by management and incorporated in a Collective Agreement, monitoring the operation of the system.
- Serve as a consultative machinery through which changes and innovations can be discussed.
- Provide a positive channel of communication between workers and management so as to provide an industrial climate conducive to the growth of productivity.
- Recommend methods to improve morale, general working attitude, motivation, and an identification with belonging to the company.
- Recommend general disciplinary codes affecting productivity.

Figure 3.3: Objectives of Productivity Committees

Source: National Productivity Board (1975b).

Beyond First 5 Years: 1978–1979

Beyond the first five years, NPB began to adopt a more organised approach to promoting productivity consciousness by focusing on the significance and benefits of higher productivity. Efforts were

Month	Activity
April	• Opening ceremony of National Productivity Campaign. • 5-day Gala Exhibition of Automated Office and Industrial Equipment held in conjunction with the ceremony. • 5-page special feature on the National Productivity Campaign in *The Straits Times* on 12 April 1975.
May	• Seminar on 'Modern Automatic Production Techniques & Processes' to examine the economic viability of applying automatic techniques and systems in production and control. • National management essay contest on role and issues faced by management in raising productivity. • National workers' essay contest on role and issues faced by workers in raising productivity.
June	• Talks and exhibitions at community centres at Bukit Panjang, Kim Tian, Kuo Chuan and Keppel Harbour. Activities at the community centres were opened by the respective Members of Parliament.
July	• Seminar on 'The Right Data Processing System for Your Business' to examine a cross-section of the major computer-based data processing methods and types of equipment available on the local market. • Poster competition for students and undergraduates on various productivity themes. • Talks and exhibitions at community centres at River Valley, Kallang, Changi, Kampong Ubi, Katong, Taman Jurong, Kampong Glam and Kampong Chai Chee.
August	• Seminar on 'Wage Incentive Schemes'. • Seminar on 'Energy Management and Efficiency for Industry and Commerce' to provide management and technical personnel with better knowledge of heat management and technology. • Talks for the general public at community centres. • Talks for unions and employers' organisations.
September	• Management game for industrial sector. • Talks for the general public at community centres. • Talks for unions and employers' organisations.

Figure 3.4: National Productivity Campaign Activities, April-September 1975
Source: National Productivity Board, *Minimax*, various issues.

directed at developing and disseminating publications and promotional collaterals; and promoting specific initiatives, such as productivity committees, and productivity solutions, such as automation. Besides reaching out to workers and employers, NPB extended its promotional efforts to new entrants to the workforce.

Examples of publications produced are *Productivity Audit*, a guide for productivity committees to diagnose and address their productivity problems at the workplace; *Productivity Review*, a collection of productivity-related articles and speeches; and *Productivity and Our Daily Life*, an informational booklet written in both English and Chinese. NPB also produced slides, tapes and films; and conducted talks on productivity concepts and productivity improvement techniques at community centres, libraries and schools.

The promotion of productivity committees was intensified. In April 1978, NPB organised a 2-day National Conference of Productivity Committees, together with National Employers Council (NEC), Singapore Employers Federation (SEF), SMA, NTUC and representatives of productivity committees. The aim was to promote the benefits of productivity committees and discuss the challenges in forming and sustaining them.

Research to Support Productivity Drive

First 5 Years: 1972–1977

For the first five years, NPB carried out mainly economic research related to productivity and wages, studies to assess the effectiveness of its programmes, and studies requested by NWC, NIRC and other government-related bodies. Examples of the research carried out during the five years are *Surveys on NPB's Programmes, Management Attitudes, and Training Provided by Manufacturing Firms; Study on Labour Turnover in the Private Sector; An in-depth Study into Blue and White Collar Workers in Singapore;* and *Productivity Survey of Firms in the Jurong Industrial Estate.* The research findings were published as separate reports or in NPB's publications and newsletters, and shared with the industry, policy-makers and relevant institutions.

Beyond First 5 Years: 1978–1979

Beyond the first five years, NPB continued to undertake research studies to support policy-making and to monitor and evaluate its programmes. Examples of the studies undertaken are *Comprehensive Study of Labour Productivity in Selected Asian Countries*, *The Measurement of Manufacturing Productivity in Singapore*, *Shiftwork in Industry*, and *Incentive Payment Schemes in the Manufacturing Industry*.

Productivity Drive in the 1970s in Retrospect

Compared with the nascent concern with productivity in the 1960s, the decade of the 1970s saw a ramping up of the productivity drive. High productivity was needed to fuel the intensified export-oriented industrialisation strategy, and the heavy dependence on foreign workers to meet the requirements of the growing manufacturing investments was becoming untenable. With the precondition of stable labour-management relations met, it was an appropriate time to lift productivity to a higher plane. The clearest sign of the Government's intention was the setting up of NPB as a distinct entity charged with the responsibility for spearheading the nation's productivity drive. The enlistment of UNDP to assist NPB, described in detail in Chapter 4, also underlined the Government's intent to give a boost to the fledgling national productivity drive.

However, at the same time, the external shocks to the economy caused the Government to focus more on growing the economy, even to the extent of being less discriminative against labour-intensive investments. This resulted in a further increase in the labour force to meet the demands of the industry. In 1970, the size of the labour force was 0.65 million, with a foreign labour share of 3.2 per cent. This increased to 1.07 million in 1980, with a foreign labour share that more than doubled to 7.3 per cent. For the 1970s as a whole, the average annual productivity growth was 3.5 per cent. This contributed 39 per cent to the average GDP growth of 9 per cent, a drop from the 57 per cent in the 1960s. Correspondingly, the contribution of labour to GDP growth increased from 43 per cent in the 1960s to 61 per cent in the 1970s.

Because of the prevailing circumstances in the 1970s, there was the tension to simultaneously pursue high productivity and high economic growth through dependence on foreign workers. This turned out to be the beginning of the tension found in the subsequent decades as well.

Chapter 4

Role of United Nations Development Programme: 1967–1982

"In retrospect, I can fairly describe Singapore's evolution since 1960, when the UN team on Economic Development led by Dr Winsemius first studied us, as the prototype of economic development promoted by international institutions such as the World Bank, IMF and GATT."

Hon Sui Sen
Finance Minister
1978 Budget Statement to Parliament

Catalytic Role of UNDP in Nascent Years of Singapore's Development

In its early years of development, Singapore received considerable assistance from the United Nations Expanded Programme of Technical Assistance (EPTA) and, subsequently, the United Nations Development Programme (UNDP).[1] Assistance, both in technical and financial forms, was provided based on UNDP's core principles of 'self-determination,' i.e. alignment of the projects with the country's needs and plans; and 'self-reliance,' i.e. commitment and contribution by the country (in the form of infrastructure, provision

---

[1] In 1966, EPTA merged with the UN Special Fund to become the United Nations Development Programme (UNDP).

and funding of local counterparts and recurrent expenses) to the success of the projects.

The first substantive assistance came soon after Singapore achieved full internal self-government in 1959 and had to address the pressing issues of unemployment and housing. Since there was no sizeable agriculture sector to absorb the unemployed, the Government turned its attention to the industrial sector. Thus, in its *State of Singapore Development Plan 1961–1964*, it set forth industrialisation as one of its basic economic policies. To speed up the industrialisation programme and to obtain a clear picture of the types of industries, particularly export industries which could be readily expanded or established, the Government approached the United Nations Bureau of Technical Assistance Operations for assistance. The specific request made was for an expert team to examine the opportunities and measures for rapid industrial expansion in Singapore.

Following the request, a United Nations Industrial Survey Mission, led by Dr Albert Winsemius, visited Singapore in October–December 1960 (first phase) and March–April 1961 (second phase). A preliminary report was submitted to the Government at the end of the first phase. During the second phase, the Mission examined the comments made by the Government and the results of the actions taken to implement the recommendations in the preliminary report. A final report titled *A Proposed Industrialization Programme for the State of Singapore* (commonly known as *The Winsemius Report*) was then submitted to the Government in June 1961.

The Winsemius Report documented an assessment of the economic situation and the magnitude of the unemployment and industrial relations problems. It noted that the quality of the workforce was high, and workers had the right aptitude to work in manufacturing industries. However, the deteriorating state of industrial relations was a major hindrance to the industrialisation programme. In 1960, the number of strikes totalled 44, more than double the 20 in 1958. The work stoppages led to lost man-days and a decline in productivity.

A 10-year plan was proposed in *The Winsemius Report* to turn Singapore from a port dependent on entrepot trade to a manufacturing and industrial centre. The report emphasised the importance of raising productivity as a means to increase the competitiveness of Singapore's manufactured goods in the global market. As stated in the report:

> *"Since the export industries will be producing quality products for the international market, the investment policy will have to aim at high productivity ... To create a competitive and dynamic export industry, it would be necessary to decrease the cost of production considerably. Generally speaking, productivity should be increased by 20–30%. In the case of smaller establishments with obsolete equipment and poor management, even a higher rate of increase would be necessary. This could be done either through the usually long process of increasing productivity or through the introduction of shift systems[2]."*

The Winsemius Report guided much of the development of Singapore in the 1960s and 1970s, beginning with the industrialisation programme and then progressing to programmes in other sectors of the economy. In the implementation of many of these programmes, UNDP rendered assistance as well. This included assistance in agriculture, urban renewal and development, education and vocational training, transport and communications, and productivity.

One of the key recommendations of *The Winsemius Report* was the establishment of an agency for implementing the industrialisation programme. Initially, the agency would have separate divisions for financing, industrial facilities, projects, and technical consulting and services; but ultimately, it would only have the core function of investment promotion, after the transfer of the other functions to separate organisations. This led to the establishment of the Economic Development Board (EDB) on 1 August 1961. To kick-start the development of services for the industry, the various EDB divisions received assistance from UNDP experts. Subsequently, some of these were spun off and established as distinct agencies, as recommended in *The Winsemius Report*. One of them was the Productivity Unit, which

---

[2]The Mission recommended that the manufacturing industries work in two or three shifts to lower costs and the capital required for expansion. This would help to make them competitive in the global markets.

was set up in EDB in 1964, expanded into the National Productivity Centre (NPC*) in May 1967 and finally spun off as a separate organisation, National Productivity Board (NPB), in May 1972.

In its final assessment, *The Winsemius Report* emphasised the importance of good labour-management cooperation for the industrialisation to succeed. As stated in the report:

> *"In our opinion Singapore has the basic assets for industrialization. With the resourcefulness of her people, an active industrial promotion programme by the Government, and — this is the main point — close co-operation between employers and labour, Singapore can successfully carry out the expansion programmes proposed in this report to achieve their basic objectives. Her greatest asset is the high aptitude of her people to work in manufacturing industries. They can rank among the best factory workers in the world. But for that they need expansion possibilities, jobs. The co-operation between employers and labour must come about.*
>
> *If not, labour will suffer for it. Capital can go to other countries. Enterprise can quiet down or escape. Labour has no escape possibilities. It needs employment here and has no time to wait."*

Dr Albert Winsemius himself continued as the Chief Economic Advisor to the Singapore Government for the next 24 years until 1984. Fittingly, on 19 June 1984, in a speech at the General Electric International Personnel Council Meeting in Singapore, he spoke on the topic of 'The Dynamics of a Developed Nation: Singapore.' His final verdict of the progress made by Singapore was:

> *"A real 'global' city. It still has a long way to go. But even today, when compared to other underdeveloped and developing countries, amidst negligence, failure and mediocrity, a shiny example of economic and social progress."*

ILO's Assistance in Setting Up National Productivity Centre: 1967–1969

When the industrialisation programme began in Singapore, assistance was sought from the International Labour Organization (ILO) to set up a productivity centre in EDB. ILO's track record in such assistance stretched back to the 1950s when it began to place greater emphasis in all fields related to labour and the training and development of managers, and in setting up productivity centres. Assistance was rendered in the form of international experts and management development programmes to build the capabilities of national productivity centres and management institutes. By the early 1960s, ILO had assisted about 50 countries in establishing productivity and management development centres.

The objective of setting up a productivity centre in Singapore was to raise productivity in companies so that they could compete in overseas markets. In response to the Government's request, a team from ILO was despatched to Singapore to provide advice on what should be done in conjunction with the set-up. However, the productivity centre did not materialise. As stated in Chapter 2, Finance Minister Dr Goh Keng Swee concluded that the industrial relations climate was not conducive to a concerted productivity drive then.

Subsequently, ILO's advice was sought again when the industrial relations climate became better and after a firm decision had been made in 1965 to set up a productivity centre, as spelt out in *The Charter for Industrial Progress and the Productivity Code of Practice*. Thereafter, three ILO advisors, who were specialists in industrial relations and industrial engineering — J. R. Ivarson, H. Pornschlegel and S. Ramalingam — were attached to EDB to help set up NPC*. Their attachment spanned the period October 1966–1969. During this period, the advisors helped to draw up the plans for NPC*'s programmes, conducted training courses, provided consultancy services, promoted joint consultative councils, trained the locals in running NPC*, and served as members on the Advisory Council of NPC*.

UNDP Project to Boost Capabilities of National Productivity Centre: 1970–1982

In February 1969, the Government sought UNDP's assistance to strengthen and expand NPC*. As described in Chapter 3, criticisms had been hurled at NPC*, as well as the tripartite partners of management, labour and the Government, for lack of progress and results in raising productivity. UNDP's assistance was intended to widen the scope of training and consultancy services by NPC* to provide a much needed push to the fledgling productivity drive.

On 22 September 1970, Singapore and UNDP signed an agreement for a 3-year Plan of Operation for a project to boost NPC*'s capabilities. Singapore was represented by Francis D' Costa, acting Permanent Secretary, Ministry of Finance; and UNDP was represented by Alexander F. Campbell, regional representative of UNDP for Singapore, Malaysia and Brunei. NPC* was appointed the Government Implementing Agency by Singapore, and ILO was designated the executing agency by the United Nations. UNDP committed a contribution of US$589,300 (around S$1.8 million then) in the form of experts, instructors, fellowships and equipment. The commitment from the Government totalled S$3.8 million for staff, buildings and supporting services. In contrast to the ad hoc deputation of individual ILO experts in the past, the Plan provided for a bigger team of experts, led by a project manager, to execute the project.

The Plan aimed to help NPC* achieve its five objectives: promote productivity consciousness in management, trade union leaders and workers; train management and trade union personnel in various productivity techniques; foster further development of good industrial relations by training; render management consultancy services to assist industrial enterprises to achieve higher productivity; and assist industrial establishments in formulating and rationalising the wage policy and wage systems.

During the course of the 3-year Plan, NPC* had been transformed into NPB, which was established as a distinct statutory board on 12 May 1972. To beef up the competencies of NPB, the Government requested that the assistance rendered by UNDP be extended beyond the three years and the budget planned initially. Following that, the Plan of Operation was revised to cover three phases: Phase I (from 1970 to 1975), Phase II (from 1976 to 1978) and Phase III (from 1979 to 1982).

Phase I of UNDP Project: 1970–1975

The assistance under Phase I was provided in the form of expert services, fellowships, and equipment and books. The focus was on specialised areas such as industrial engineering, management accounting, industrial relations, and industrial safety and health. Training programmes were also instituted to transfer knowledge to the local counterparts. ILO Expert S. Ramalingam, who had been attached to NPC* since December 1967, was the Project Manager.

Provision of Expert Services

The experts deputed during Phase I were engaged in three areas: training NPB officers, providing technical advice, and conducting training programmes and providing consultancy services to the industry together with NPB officers. Figure 4.1 summarises the specialisations and utilisation of the experts in Phase I.

Expert post	Original plan (1970)	Revised plan (1973)	Actual utilised
	No. of man-months		
Project manager	36	45	45
Personnel management	24	36	36
General management	24	37	37
Supervisory development/ Achievement motivation	24	24	24
Industrial engineering	36	42	42
Management accounting	36	42	42
Occupational safety and health	—	24	24
Consultants	24	2	2
Total	204	252	252

Figure 4.1: Specialisations and Utilisation of Experts, Phase I of UNDP Project

Source: National Productivity Board, *Annual Report*, various years.

Expert post	No. of man-months used
Industrial marketing	9
Low cost automation	10
Industrial maintenance	11
Management information systems / Electronic data processing	6
Total	36

Figure 4.2:   Despatch of Short-term Experts to Singapore by UNIDO
Source: National Productivity Board, *Annual Report FY1975/1976.*

In 1973, revisions were made to the original plan upon the request of NPB. Additional help was solicited to provide in-depth training for NPB's consultants on personnel management, general management, industrial engineering and management accounting. The provision for consultants was reduced in exchange for an expert in the area of occupational safety and health.

With the end of Phase I in March 1975, additional experts were despatched to Singapore for short-term assignments. This was done under the Special Industrial Services scheme, administered by the United Nations Industrial Development Organization (UNIDO). The details of the experts are shown in Figure 4.2.

Fellowships for NPB Officers

NPB was awarded a total of six and a half years of fellowships for its officers under Phase I. The fellowships were offered mainly in advanced training on management and technology, leading to Master's degrees from established institutions in the United States, the United Kingdom and Canada. Courses that were more than a year were co-sponsored by UNDP and NPB. After completing the respective courses, the officers were bonded to NPB.

Equipment and Books for NPB's Library and Training Facilities

The equipment, books and teaching aids contributed by UNDP amounted to about US$38,000. These were used in NPB's library and training facilities. The contributions included films, books, subscriptions to magazines, visual aid projectors and technical equipment.

Review of Project

In June 1974, NPB and ILO undertook a review of the Project to assess the achievements of Phase I and to determine the nature of assistance required in Phase II. The review also covered the high turnover rate of the NPB staff and included recommended measures to address it.

As shown in Figure 4.1, the achievements in Phase I, in terms of utilisation of experts, met or even exceeded what was planned. However, the review concluded that NPB would not be able to sustain its progress in the future without further external assistance in view of the high staff turnover. It was noted that the employees were dissatisfied with their jobs because they had a high proportion of training work compared with consultancy. The problem was more serious for the Management Accounting unit, whose employees were attracted by the higher salaries offered by the private sector. Recommendations on the measures to address the high turnover included improvement to the pay scales and use of more external trainers for training.

NPB also felt that even though the Project had exceeded the targets set for Phase I, it still lacked experience in certain core areas, such as consultancy services and some aspects of management. On ILO's part, it was concluded that further UNDP assistance was justified because of NPB's progressive growth and the fact that NPB was the main institution responsible for promoting productivity in all sectors of the economy.

Phase I ended in March 1975. Following that, ILO and NPB agreed to an interval of one year between Phase I and Phase II to allow NPB time to strengthen its leadership and stabilise the workforce with the return of officers from their fellowships. The one-year period also provided the NPB management sufficient time to plan for the next phase of the Project.

Phase II of UNDP Project: 1976–1978

The assistance rendered in Phase II continued in the form of expert services in new fields or areas in which NPB was still weak. These services were rendered by expert individuals instead of a team. According to ILO, the reason for the change in approach was that the previous large-scale international team approach had been somewhat overwhelming and even intimidating to the high-level executive staff in NPB.

Two ILO experts, one each in management consultancy and production & automation technology, were attached to NPB during this phase. The expert services covered the following areas:

a. training management accounting personnel;
b. establishing competency in the fields of production technology and automatic control instrumentation; and
c. strengthening NPB's competencies in integrated management consultancy making use of various techniques and advice, so that the consultants could provide a wider scope of services to the industries.

As a result of these expert services, NPB achieved a fairly high degree of professional competence in the various functional areas covered.

Phase III of UNDP Project: 1979–1982

Despite the good progress made, the Government felt that an extension of UNDP's assistance was required to broaden NPB's competencies to include the latest technologies and management techniques. As described in Chapter 3, NPB, in announcing its 5-year plan for 1977–1981, had stated its long-term goal of becoming the leading centre training managers, supervisors, workers and trade unionists on productivity and management techniques; providing technical assistance and consultancy; and conducting research and disseminating information on productivity-related issues. To realise this goal, a request was made for the extension of UNDP's assistance. Subsequently, approval was given by UNDP in May 1979, and a document on Phase III of the UNDP Project was officially signed on 21 August 1979.

Phase III provided for a Government contribution of S$3,784,170 to support the services of NPB's professional and administrative staff; accommodation; secretarial, clerical and administrative support services; operating costs; and travel and transport costs. The commitment from UNDP totalled US$638,200, covering expert services, fellowships, equipment and miscellaneous costs. When Phase III ended in December 1982, UNDP's final contribution amounted to US$639,281.

Objectives of Phase III

Phase III commenced in July 1979 with specific objectives.

Development Objective

a. To enhance productivity in private and public enterprises through more effective management and utilisation of cost-effective production technology.

Immediate Objectives

a. To strengthen the capacity of NPB to provide management consultancy and training services in specific technological areas (low cost automation, control and instrumentation, management information systems, and energy management) and in a multi-disciplinary context.
b. To build up the level of expertise and experience of the core staff of NPB so that it could further develop newly-recruited staff, and expand NPB's competence on a self-sustaining basis without recourse to further extended periods of international assistance.

   Towards these ends, the Project aimed in particular:
   (i) to develop a core of national counterpart staff to a level where they could participate in higher-level, multi-disciplinary management consultancy assignments;
   (ii) to develop this same group to direct and supervise the assignments of their subordinate staff and train new staff to an acceptable standard of competency and reliability;

(iii) to further train and provide practical experience to the management accounting personnel and other senior consultants of NPB in the areas of corporate strategy, financial management and advanced management accounting techniques, and including the design, organisation and implementation of training and consultancy programmes in these fields for private and public sector clients;

(iv) to develop NPB's professional staff in the wide range of expertise required to enable them to participate in multidisciplinary consultancy assignments covering the problems of medium and small-scale enterprises;

(v) to further develop NPB's expertise and experience in the field of low cost automation and aimed at increasing productivity through the use of automatic control and instrumentation technology, and in providing technical advisory and information services in a variety of process-engineering applications;

(vi) to develop NPB's capabilities in the field of management information systems/electronic data processing (MIS/EDP), including the provision of higher-level training and consultancy;

(vii) to help establish a computer centre to be used primarily for EDP-related training and its support of management consultancy assignments in systems design and development; and

(viii) to develop NPB's capabilities in the field of energy conservation and management.

The immediate objectives of the Project were intended to build NPB's capabilities considerably, particularly in consultancy, so that the development objective could be met.

Shift in NPB's Focus During Implementation

However, the plan to meet the immediate objectives was soon derailed because of a shift in NPB's focus during the implementation of the Project. Instead of consultancy, the original primary area to be addressed by Phase III, the focus shifted to productivity promotion and improving labour-management relations. The shift was due to the launch of the nation-wide Productivity Movement in September 1981. To spearhead the Movement, NPB restructured the organisation in 1982. Automation and technology services were transferred to the Singapore Institute of Standards and Industrial Research (SISIR), and industrial engineering was phased out. On the other hand, promotional activities and training services, including the area of occupational safety and health, were stepped up. Consultancy work was discontinued, except for areas related to the human aspects of productivity. General management guidance was provided as a follow-up to training. These new directions were a stark contrast to the priority given to management consultancy, especially in the areas of automation and industrial engineering, since the formation of NPB in 1972. The details of the restructuring of NPB as a result of the launch of the Productivity Movement are given in Chapter 5.

To align the Project with NPB's new directions, its immediate objectives were revised. Instead of capacity and competency-building in consultancy, the Project shifted to a focus on training trainers and developing training materials in areas of concern to the Productivity Movement. These areas were personnel management, supervision and motivation, labour-management relations, occupational safety and health, and other aspects of human relations in industry.

Altogether, four international experts were attached to NPB during this phase. The experts were I. G. Cummings, the Team Leader and Expert in Management Consultancy; O. Bar, Expert in Production and Automation Technology; T. J. King, Expert in Management Information Systems; and R. Takahashi, Expert in Energy Management. As these experts had been identified based on the original objectives of Phase III, their expertise was not fully tapped when NPB's directions shifted during the course of the Project.

Key Activities and Achievements in Phase III

In 1983, ILO, as the executing agency of the UNDP Project, submitted a report to the Government upon completion of Phase III in December 1982. The report assessed the achievements and effectiveness of Phase

III of the Project, and provided recommendations to NPB to consider for the future. Figure 4.3 summarises the contents of the report.

Assessment of Achievements in Phase III

In its report, ILO made an assessment of the achievements in Phase III vis-à-vis the immediate objectives of the Project. This is summarised in Figure 4.4.

Area	Key Activities and Achievements
Staff development and fellowships	One of the key objectives of the Project was to strengthen the competencies of NPB staff.
	— A consultant development programme was developed for four different levels of staff. It covered consultancy skills, training skills, administrative skills and professional attitudes. 22 officers went through a consultant orientation course under the programme, before the management consultancy function was suspended in NPB.
	— The other training courses conducted for the staff were:
	o Training course on industrial instrumentation, design for maintenance, microprocessors and managerial aspects of management consultancy for officers in the Automation and Technology Services Unit before it was transferred to SISIR.
	o ILO's Supervisory Development Modular Programme to develop trainers for the Supervisory Development Unit.
	o Orientation course on electronic data processing and software packages for non-computer staff.
	o Training course on energy management.
	— Some of the courses included consultancy assignments to provide practical exposure to the trainees.
	— Besides in-house training programmes, fellowships were awarded to five officers to complete programmes such as Master of Business Administration at the University of Pittsburg in the United States, and a course in Microprocessor Technology at Swansea University in the United Kingdom.

Figure 4.3:   Key Activities and Achievements in Phase III of UNDP Project

Source: International Labour Organization (1983).

Area	Key Activities and Achievements
Management consultancy	As the management consultancy role in NPB was de-emphasised in 1981, the assistance rendered by the UNDP experts was confined mainly to direct consultancy assignments with 14 companies. These were in the areas of automation, computer services and energy management.
Training	The development and presentation of new training programmes was considered as one of the major contributions of the Project. Several training programmes and train-the-trainer sessions were delivered under the Project. They included: — A 400-hour modular course on industrial automation and production technology, including microprocessors. — A 200-hour Supervisory Development Modular Training Programme, contextualised based on ILO's Supervisory Development Modular Programme, and a 25-hour Section Leader Course. — A 100-hour course on energy management for factory engineers. The course was the first of its kind in Singapore, and was conducted with the National University of Singapore. — A 180-hour course in systems analysis. The course was developed by the Computer Services Unit of NPB in association with the Polytechnic of Central London, with the assistance of the Project. — Courses and workshops on digital electronics, personnel selection and placement, ergonomics, electronic data processing and manpower planning. The Project also invited an international expert to carry out a series of workshops on case study development, to support NPB's strong emphasis on training.
Equipment	The Project provided microprocessors, computer equipment, automation equipment, typewriters and books to NPB. Some of the equipment were later transferred to SISIR upon the transfer of the automation and technology services from NPB.
Others	The UNDP experts contributed to other areas of NPB's work, such as writing articles for publications and participating in seminars and exhibitions.

Figure 4.3:   (*Continued*)

Immediate Objective (summarised)	Assessment of Achievements
a. To strengthen the capacity of NPB to provide management consultancy and training services in specific technological areas.	Because of the change in NPB's directions during the course of the Project, it was not possible to attain the immediate objectives related to management consultancy, i.e. a. and b. (i)-(iv).

b. To build up the level of expertise and experience of the core staff of NPB and expand its competence on a self-sustaining basis. The Project aimed in particular:
  (i) to develop a core of staff to undertake higher-level management consultancy assignments;
  (ii) to develop this same group to supervise their staff and train new staff;
  (iii) to further train and provide practical experience to the senior consultants in implementing training and consultancy programmes in various fields;
  (iv) to develop the professional staff to undertake consultancy for medium and small-scale enterprises;
  (v) to further develop NPB's expertise and experience in the field of low cost automation;
 	
  (vi) to develop NPB's capabilities in MIS and EDP;
	
	This was attained by the capabilities developed. Although responsibility for training and consultancy in this area had been transferred to another institution, the capabilities were still available to the industry.
	This was attained by the preparation of training materials; and strengthening of the training capabilities of NPB staff.

Figure 4.4: UNDP's Assessment of Achievements in Phase III

Source: International Labour Organization (1983).

Immediate Objective (summarised)	Assessment of Achievements
(vii) to help establish a computer centre to support EDP-related training and management consultancy in systems design and development; and	A computer centre was established, training materials were prepared, and training sessions on EDP and MIS were held. Because of NPB's withdrawal from consultancy, the computer equipment was not used to support consultancy assignments.
(viii) to develop NPB's capabilities in energy conservation and management.	This was attained by the capabilities developed. Although responsibility for training and consultancy in this area had been transferred to another institution, the capabilities were still available to the industry.
c. Others (not in original list) (i) To raise competence of trainers and prepare training materials in new areas of concerns to the Productivity Movement (once it became clear that this was now a core area of work for NPB).	The Project's achievements fell below expectations. With pressure to undertake more courses and promotion activities, the staff had little time to plan for NPB's new role and to formulate a professional development programme. The Project drafted a training philosophy and outlined a set of training guidelines. However, these were not developed further, and NPB mounted courses and seminars without establishing an overall framework. In addition, there was no structured programme to develop the capabilities of trainers.

Figure 4.4:   (*Continued*)

In its report, ILO also highlighted the continuing problem of high staff turnover that had bugged NPB in Phase I of the Project. In fact, the problem was exacerbated by three factors in Phase III: shift of some staff to SISIR together with the transfer of automation and technology services; termination of management consultancy and industrial engineering services; and insecurity, lack of clarity of career paths and dissatisfaction caused by changes in NPB's directions. The NPB management had little time to plan and facilitate change management because of their heavy involvement in promotion activities. The staff involved in the Project were also distracted by other duties. Consequently, they did not have the time for proper planning, professional development and building of their own competencies.

Recommendations

In anticipation of NPB's role as a major training institution in the future (with the construction of the new NPB Building and with funding support from Japan for training equipment and aids), ILO made the following recommendations to NPB:

a. To establish a task force of senior officers to formulate policies, set objectives and draw up plans that are aligned with the Government's directions. The task force should be freed from daily operations and the pressure to achieve short-term objectives.
b. To conduct research and surveys on the profiles of Singapore managers so as to develop programmes that meet their training needs and interests. Post-training reviews should also be conducted to evaluate the effectiveness of the programmes, and to improve them.
c. To develop and institutionalise a staff development plan to motivate employees and raise their training competencies. The plan should also include external part-time instructors. Sufficient numbers of staff should be employed to better deliver the planned training programmes.
d. To increase the effectiveness of training programmes by extending assistance to companies beyond the classroom, and through the use of other training methods (e.g. self-study). Further assistance could be in the form of consulting and advisory services to help companies apply what they have learnt in class.
e. To tap the assistance of overseas institutions to beef up its programmes and development.

Overall Impact of UNDP's Assistance

In contrast to Phase I and Phase II of the UNDP Project, ILO clearly had some misgivings about Phase III where several of the intended objectives were not met because of the change in NPB's directions. In its 1983 report, it stated:

> *"During the course of the project, the NPB found it necessary to forsake some of its former activities and undertake new ones, in order to align itself with government policies. The redirection of the NPB's efforts necessitated an adaptation of the project objectives. The most significant modification occurred in 1981, when the Government launched a continuing long-term productivity movement, and assigned the NPB a major role in spearheading the concept of productivity. To implement the Government's wishes, a new chairman assumed direction of the NPB and leadership of the project. In pursuance of his mandate, he restructured the NPB in order to divert resources away from management consulting towards support for the productivity movement and the promotion of better human relations in industry. To release further resources, he suspended activities in the field of industrial engineering, and transferred responsibility for automation and production technology, including energy management to the Singapore Institute of Standards and Industrial Research (SISIR). Conforming to these arrangements, the project reoriented its objectives towards the development of a new corporate plan, which would emphasise the productivity movement, and towards the adaptation of training programmes to accord with government policies and actions."*

Similar sentiments were expressed by Chow, Chew and Su (1989):

> *"It could be concluded that the last phase of UNDP project was launched at an inopportune time with the redirection of NPB emerging soon after the project began and with the Board's new leadership not party to the original project objectives … Apparently, NPB is aiming to go places. But it is important that it should remember not to lose its sense of direction or attempt to achieve too many objectives at the sacrifice of meaningful, indepth concentration and focus … Today, NPB may have changed partners;*

UNDP has come and gone, and the Japanese are here.[3] Whatever partner it has in its search for development potential and goals, NPB still has a long way to go."

From the perspective of the Government, UNDP's assistance in the area of productivity, spanning 15 years from 1967 to 1982, had been beneficial. In particular, the technical assistance rendered through UNDP had provided the boost for kick-starting Singapore's national productivity organisation, first NPC* and then NPB; building up its competencies; and launching various activities to spearhead the national productivity drive. As summarised by K. Shanmugam, Minister for Foreign Affairs and Minister for Law, regarding UNDP's assistance to Singapore in general:

"Singapore has benefitted in significant ways from technical assistance. When we attained self-rule in 1959, our government turned to the UNDP to develop an economic plan for Singapore. The UNDP led a survey headed by Dutch economist Dr Albert Winsemius. Dr Winsemius later became the Singapore government's Chief Economic Advisor. Among his early suggestions was the creation of a one-stop investor agency — what we now know as the EDB — the key to our success that has brought several billions every year. He advised that Singapore establish a financial hub. In our first decades we sought and received technical expertise in almost every sector."

This statement was made by K. Shanmugam in his speech at the Commemorative Event for the 20th Anniversary of the Singapore Cooperation Programme on 29 November 2012. It affirmed the significant benefits that Singapore had reaped from UNDP in its early years of development.

---

[3]This refers to the assistance received from Japan through the Singapore Productivity Development Project, the details of which are covered in Chapter 7.

III
1980s

Chapter 5

Laying Foundation for the Productivity Push in the 1980s

"In Singapore, we emulate Japan's bold response to domestic and external problems and constraints. We are not in the same league as Japan but our hard-nosed approach to problems is the same: restructure or fall flat on your nose."

Goh Chok Tong
Minister for Trade and Industry
Opening of the Third ASIA-FIET Ordinary Conference
17 July 1980

Economic Priorities in the 1980s

At the turn of the decade from the 1970s to the 1980s, the Singapore economy was characterised by low-value added, labour-intensive and low-productivity industries. As described in Chapter 3, this was the result of keeping wages low to attract foreign direct investment (FDI) into Singapore, and shelving the plan to restructure the economy towards capital-intensive industries in the early 1970s. The labour-intensive industries, led by foreign multinational corporations (MNCs), had propelled the economic growth of 9.0 per cent a year in the 1970s. Foreign workers had to be imported in large numbers to fill the jobs created. At the same time, wage growth had to be restrained by the National Wages Council (NWC) to attract investments into Singapore. The situation was untenable in the long term.

In its *Economic Development Plan for the Eighties*, the Government therefore put forward the position that future economic growth should come primarily from high productivity improvements rather than labour growth. It set a gross domestic product (GDP) growth target of 8–10 per cent a year, with 6–8 per cent coming from productivity growth. This high productivity growth target was necessary because of the full employment situation. Domestically, labour had become a severe constraint on growth, and job hopping was rampant. Accelerating the inflow of foreign workers was not practical because of the potential social problems. Externally, there was growing competition in labour-intensive products from other countries with abundant labour.

To achieve the productivity target required for the projected GDP growth, the Government pushed for a 2nd Industrial Revolution following the 1st Industrial Revolution in the 1960s. This involved restructuring the economy towards high-value added, high-skills and capital-intensive industries. In 1981, it announced the plan to phase out unskilled foreign workers by 1991. To step up the pace of restructuring, the Government decided to implement a 3-year high-wage policy (1979–1981) recommended by NWC.

The specific intent of the 'wage correction policy' was to break the vicious circle of low wages sustaining labour-intensive activities, which, in turn, led to low productivity growth, a tight labour market and slower economic growth and wage increases. The wage correction was expected to force the unproductive companies to close down, and provide the boost for the shift towards high-value added, high-skills and capital-intensive operations. In conjunction with the high-wage policy, the Skills Development Fund (SDF) was set up in October 1979 under the administration of the Economic Development Board (EDB). The aims were to finance training of workers, retrain retrenched workers and upgrade business operations and technology.

The pace of economic restructuring proceeded according to plan in the first half of the 1980s. However, this was disrupted by the first recession that hit post-independence Singapore in 1985. From an average annual GDP growth of 8.8 per cent from 1980–1984, the economy not only did not grow but shrank by 0.7 per cent in 1985.

Before the full impact of the recession was felt in Singapore, the Economic Committee had been formed in April 1985. Led by Minister of State for Defence and Trade and Industry Lee Hsien Loong, the Committee was set up to review the economic development plan for the 1980s and to define new strategies for promoting further growth. With the onslaught of the recession, the Committee addressed the immediate causes of the recession as well. Externally, Singapore was affected by decreased exports due to a slowdown in the United States, reduced regional trade and tourist arrivals arising from falling commodity prices which hit the Association of Southeast Asian Nations (ASEAN), and lower demand for shipbuilding and ship repair due to the reduced need for super tankers as a result of lower volumes of crude oil shipments. Domestically, a major cause identified was the loss of competitiveness due to the rise in business costs, including high wage cost. The high-wage policy was meant to last only three years, but wages continued to increase because the demand for labour remained high. Wage rigidities also hindered businesses from making the necessary adjustments in response to changing market conditions.

Following the recommendations of the *Report of the Economic Committee* in February 1986, a slew of measures was taken to restore Singapore's competitiveness. This included a temporary cut in the employers' Central Provident Fund (CPF) contribution from 25 per cent to 10 per cent, and a 2-year wage restraint to stem wage cost from rising further. A tripartite NWC Sub-committee on Wage Reform was also formed to propose a longer-term solution to the rising wage problem. The key recommendation made was the adoption of a flexible wage system with a variable year-end payment linked to company performance. On foreign workers, the Economic Committee stated that a realistic stance was to allow for a 'revolving pool' of foreign workers on work permit. Subsequently, the Government responded by easing employers' access to unskilled foreign workers, thus shelving the long-term plan to phase them out.

As a result of the various measures taken, the economy recovered quickly from the recession. The GDP growth bounced back to 1.3 per cent in 1986 and 10.8 per cent in 1987. In 1990, after three years of double-digit growth, the Government pronounced that Singapore was out of the recession.

Policy Intent on Productivity in the 1980s

In conjunction with the economic restructuring strategy, productivity was high on the Government's agenda. Even during the recession when short-term cost-cutting measures had to be taken immediately, the Economic Committee did not take its eyes off productivity. In fact, it stressed that higher productivity was critical to Singapore's future growth and a higher standard of living. In relation to this, the Committee emphasised the need for good work attitudes, including cooperative and cordial labour-management relations; and willingness to be flexible in meeting job requirements, such as working the third shift.

Beyond promoting productivity consciousness, the Economic Committee stressed the need to begin taking a total approach to productivity. Such an approach was considered necessary to achieve high productivity growth associated with economic restructuring. As stated in the *Report of the Economic Committee*:

"The 10-year Plan therefore boldly recommended, as the central strategy, a restructuring of our economy so that future economic growth would be based on high productivity improvements each year ... A concerted attempt to increase overall productivity levels was made through the tripartite Productivity Movement. This was launched in 1981, arising from the recommendations of the Committee on Productivity (COP). The COP recommended that the focus should initially be on the human aspects of productivity. Therefore, the National Productivity Board (NPB), which spearheaded the Movement, concentrated on promoting productivity 'consciousness' and 'will'. As this 'will' could not be expected to evolve overnight, the strategy was a long-term one. We should continue to promote positive productivity attitudes ... We should now move beyond productivity consciousness, to begin to take a total approach towards productivity, incorporating other elements of productivity improvement.

A total approach to productivity must be aimed at improving all levels of the business process. Some key areas are:

(i) Management skills and overall business efficiency;

(ii) Investments in technology (both in production processes and office automation);

(iii) *Education and training;*
(iv) *Labour-management relations;*
(v) *Positive work attitudes at all levels; and*
(vi) *Sectoral productivity strategies.*"

The Economic Committee laid out the long-term productivity growth target of 3–4 per cent a year to sustain the GDP growth target of 4–6 per cent a year. Although this was much lower than the 6-8 per cent set for the 1980s, it was considered a more sustainable target.

The Economic Committee's stance on productivity was, in fact, a reiteration and reinforcement of the Government's strong position on the issue since the late 1970s and early 1980s. This position rested on the following two pillars in the first half of the 1980s:

a. Promoting the human aspects of productivity — particularly good work attitudes, labour-management relations and skills — to support the restructuring of the economy; and
b. Learning from Japan on the human aspects of productivity.

In the second half of the 1980s, these two pillars continued to underpin the productivity drive strongly. At the same time, following the recommendation of the Economic Committee, the seeds of a total approach to productivity began to be sown.

Concern with Human Aspects of Productivity

The concern with the human aspects of productivity was linked to the economic restructuring strategy. Attracting more capital-intensive investments meant an increase in automated and computerised machines. For these machines to be operated optimally, certain conditions must be in place, namely, a better educated and skilled workforce, right work attitudes, good labour-management relations and teamwork.

However, the prevailing state of labour-management relations and work attitudes was not ideal for the implementation of productivity improvement programmes. Although it was much better than in the 1960s, the state of labour-management relations was still fragile. This was evidenced by the high average of 635 industrial disputes that the Ministry of Labour (MOL) had to conciliate each year from 1975 to 1980. Employers were also unhappy about the poor work attitudes of the workers which had adversely affected productivity. They complained that they would not get higher productivity for the higher wages that they had to pay as a result of the 3-year high wage policy. This prompted the Government to state its stance on the issue.

In his speech at the Opening of the Third ASIA-FIET Ordinary Conference on 17 July 1980, Goh Chok Tong, Minister for Trade and Industry, said:

> *"To improve productivity growth, we need to change gear, from a labour-intensive phase to a skill-intensive phase. There are four main policy measures to bring this about: wage pressures, education and training of manpower, fiscal incentives and improved work attitudes.*
>
> *... But in the ultimate, the success of our restructuring policy depends on the fourth leg — workers' attitude. There has been a lot of discussion in the press recently on this subject, following the National Wages Council's recommendation of a two-tiered wage increase, a rate for the average workers, and a higher rate for the better workers. ... It is healthy to discuss openly, frankly and objectively, the strengths and weaknesses of the Singapore worker so that there are no misimpressions. The weak points of the Singapore worker can then be corrected and the strong points enhanced."*

On 14 August 1980, Prime Minister Lee Kuan Yew made public the findings of two reports on workers' attitudes which had hitherto been classified as 'secret.' The reports were compiled based on views obtained from employers. One was a report by EDB and the other was a report by MOL. Lee Kuan Yew decided to release the findings because he wanted to put across the seriousness of the issue even though it might have an adverse effect on potential investors. Figure 5.1 summarises the consolidated findings of the two reports.

Following the release of the two reports on 14 August 1980, Lee Kuan Yew made work attitudes the theme of his speech at the National Day Celebration at Tanjong Pagar on 15 August. He said:

> *"To succeed in restructuring our economy, our workers must have the right work attitudes ... Both reports list the more vivid examples of the*

Category of complaint	Details
Job hopping	• Top complaint of companies. • Prevalent in all sectors of the economy. • Companies' operations adversely affected by high turnover of trained engineers, craftsmen and supervisors. • Managerial and supervisory authority undermined for fear of causing resignations as a result of disciplining workers.

Overtime and shift work	• Reluctance of workers to work overtime.
	• Difficulty of operating second and, even worse, third shift work as this is shunned by workers for the following reasons:
	  — Hazardous to health
	  — Cannot sleep in the day
	  — Missing out on favourite television programmes
	  — Do not need the extra money
	• Economically infeasible to invest in automated machinery if it is not operated continuously round the clock.

Attitudes	• Choosy attitudes — preferring to work in air-conditioned environment, company near home, single shift, job with light duties. • Self-centredness — Interested in personal well-being rather than interest of the group or the company; refusal to do anything more than what is perceived as the specifications of the job. • Fear of making suggestions for improvement — Generally undemonstrative, preferring not to speak up for fear of infringing on the interests of fellow workers. • Impatience — Generally restless, not willing to remain too long in a similar position; impatient to move up the job ladder before acquiring the necessary experience and skills. • Lack of pride in work — Easily contented after being acquainted with the general functions; attaching little value to jobs. • Lack of sense of responsibility — Lack of care and concern in the use of materials, which affects costs. • Money-mindedness — Expect to be paid for any activity (e.g. training and sports) outside working hours. • Reluctance to change — Not willing to adapt to new work methods. • Lack of discipline — coming late for work, going off early for lunch, coming back late after lunch, slowing down before the end of the day.

Figure 5.1: Findings of Two Reports on Workers' Attitudes

Source: Compiled from various reports, surveys and media articles.

shortcomings of our workers. If such attitudes were the norm and widespread, then we would be in grave trouble. Nevertheless, they disclose the beginnings of a lackadaisical approach to life and work which Singaporeans can ill afford ... These shortcomings threaten our restructuring policy ... Government, management and unions, together, must join in the campaign to change these bad practices."

Two days later, at the National Day Rally on 17 August, Lee Kuan Yew dwelt at length again on the need to improve workers' attitudes, as well as the launch of a campaign for this purpose. He said:

"We are restructuring our economy to be trimmer and so better able to meet the changed conditions in the 80's ... Before settling our vision of the 1980's, we must put right the work attitudes of our younger workers. And we shall. ... Each time we campaigned, the Western press pokes fun at our campaigns. We try to be polite, try to speak more Mandarin, less dialects, to keep our city clean. We punish the recalcitrant by having fines. But we do make progress. And we got to get it into the heads of our younger generation that life is not a bed of roses. This generation has never known unemployment but if we run into stormy weather, they will get a dose of it in the 80s. That may be good for their souls. But let's try to educate them. There must be reason and logic; a package of incentives and disincentives, and social pressure at home, in school and at work."

This statement is a clear precursor of the productivity campaign that was subsequently launched. The details are given in Chapter 6.

Learning from Japan

Like many other countries in the late 1970s and early 1980s, the Government turned to Japan for inspiration on what should be done to raise the nation's productivity and economic growth. This was a time when worldwide attention was focused on Japan. In a short span of just 30 years after World War II, Japan had accumulated a record trade surplus and foreign exchange reserves to become the world's second largest economy (just behind the United States). Many publications and articles thus proclaimed

Japan as an economic miracle. A prominent example is the book *Japan as Number One*, by Ezra Vogel, published in 1979. The need to learn from Japan was stressed continually by the Government, even though it was open to good management ideas from the rest of the world. Besides its economic supremacy, Japan was considered a more relevant model to Singapore than the Western models, as it had successfully absorbed the best of Western technology without losing its cultural identity.

In his Address at the Opening of the Parliament on 8 February 1977, President Benjamin Sheares said:

"Whilst we admire and must learn and acquire their science and technology, their management skills and marketing knowhow, we do not seek to model our lives on Western social mores and their contemporary lifestyles. We must learn the experience of the Japanese — how, in less than a hundred years since the Meiji Restoration of 1868, they have become a modern industrial state, without abandoning their own cultural traditions. Their experience is more relevant to us than those of the countries of Western Europe. The exceptions are perhaps West Germany and Switzerland."

A few months earlier, in his speech at the NTUC Second Triennial Delegates Conference on 29 April 1976, Deputy Prime Minister Dr Goh Keng Swee said:

"A Singaporean who is assured of lifetime employment, annual increments, regular annual bonuses, will find his eagerness for hard work and initiative greatly reduced. Why try to excel when this makes no difference to your pay? This apparently has not happened in Japanese enterprises. Why? The answer lies in Japanese management philosophy. They believe that the way to get the most out of employees is to secure their total commitment to their company. Such loyal employees can then be depended on to give of their best without costly and irksome supervision ... Total commitment of a work force can be sustained only if relations between them are harmonious ... the Japanese experience shows that one basic ingredient of their economic success is the ability of unions and management to work for the common good of the enterprise."

Subsequently, in a speech on 12 September 1980, at the Third Japan-ASEAN Symposium, Dr Goh Keng Swee said:

> *"The successful transformation of Japan from a nation defeated and devastated in World War II to the front rank of industrial nations is known to all of us. However, some of us may not be aware of how spectacular Japan's great leap forward had been. They have beaten the Swiss in watches, the Germans in cameras, the Americans in steel and motor cars. They have beaten everybody in consumer electronics. They are making great strides in computer hardware and it is widely believed that they will soon move into the aircraft manufacturing industry … Our interest in Japan's great leap forward is, in part, to find out how the Japanese did it. In this way, we can learn some useful lessons, thereby improving our economic performance."*

Lee Kuan Yew himself spoke strongly of the need to learn from Japan. In his memoirs, *From Third World To First — The Singapore Story: 1965–2000, Memoirs of LEE KUAN YEW,* he devoted a whole chapter to 'Lessons from Japan.' Drawing lessons from his own observations, conversations and experiences, he spoke highly of the Japanese worker — dedication to their job, pride in work, multi-skilled, desire to excel in their given roles, disciplined and hardworking, and united and efficient. He wrote:

> *"I learnt from the Japanese the importance of increasing productivity through worker-manager cooperation, the real meaning of human resource development. We had formed a National Productivity Board (NPB) in 1972. We made progress, especially after Wong Kwei Cheong, a PAP MP and the managing director of a joint venture Japanese electronics company, educated me on the virtues of Japanese-style management … In spite of my experiences during the Japanese occupation and the Japanese traits I had learnt to fear, I now respect and admire them. Their group solidarity, discipline, intelligence, industriousness and willingness to sacrifice for their nation make them a formidable and productive force. Conscious of the poverty of their resources, they will continue to make that extra effort to achieve the unachievable."*

In his New Year message in 1981, Lee Kuan Yew said:

> *"If, like Japanese and Germans, our workers are industrious, eager to learn and to improve themselves, if like Japanese workers, we increase productivity*

by ceaselessly thinking up ingenious ways of co-operating to get more out of their machines and to improve the machines themselves, so that more goods are produced by the same people and with less defective items coming off the production line, then Singapore will attract those multi-nationals with efficient management and keen marketing techniques. This is the way to ride over recessionary times."

When Japan's Prime Minister Zenko Suzuki visited Singapore on 13 January 1981, Lee Kuan Yew said in a speech in honour of his visit:

"It is the unique Japanese ethos or team spirit, the work attitudes of Japanese workers, constantly seeking new ways to achieve perfection or zero defect in their work, the close and special relationships between management and labour, between government planners and private sector entrepreneurs, these are special factors for the high growth rates in Japanese productivity. Singaporeans have much to learn from the Japanese, especially in work attitudes, and in cooperative, not adversary, relationships between workers and management."

In line with the Government's stance on learning from Japan, organisations such as NPB and EDB invited Japanese experts and academics to give numerous talks and seminars to Singapore managers and government officials. Study missions were also organised to Japan to learn about the Japanese management system, which was believed to be the key reason for Japan's sterling productivity and economic performance.

Opinions were sought from experts, including Ezra Vogel, who visited Singapore in 1981 and appeared in three televised forums by the Singapore Broadcasting Corporation (SBC). Radio commentaries were also run by SBC to teach the public about the Japanese management system. Figure 5.2 summarises the programmes run by SBC in 1981.

Events Leading to Formation of Committee on Productivity and National Productivity Council

Following the Government's emphasis on the need to improve work attitudes and to learn from Japan, a number of successive events

Title	Details
1. An interview with Kohei Goshi (founder and Chairman of Japan Productivity Center)	Telecast on 'Friday Background' on 16 April 1981 Interviewer: Chan Heng Wing
2. Personnel management — Japanese style	Telecast on 24 April 1981 Interviewers: Dr Hong Hai, Director, Applied Research Corporation; Dr Lee Soo Ann, Dean, Business Administration and Accounting, National University of Singapore (NUS) Speakers: Zenjiro Isogai, Director, Training Consultants Group, Japan Management Association; Hajime Inoue, Vice-Chairman, Textile Union of Japan; Akira Takanaka, Executive Director, Central Japan Industries Association; Jiro Tokuyama, Adviser, Nomura Research Institute
3. The company union system in Japan	Radio commentary on Daily Digest, SBC, 4 May 1981 Commentator: Pauline Keng (writer/commentator with SBC)
4. How Japanese firms motivate their workers	Radio commentary on Daily Digest, SBC, 6 May 1981 Commentator: Pauline Keng
5. Japanese 'consensus' decision-making	Radio commentary on Daily Digest, SBC, 7 May 1981 Commentator: Pauline Keng
6. An interview with Prof Ezra Vogel (professor of sociology and director of the East Asian Research Centre at Harvard University) on Japan	Telecast on 4 August 1981 Panel: Dr Eddie Kuo, Senior Lecturer, Department of Sociology, NUS; Gopinath Pillai, General Manager, Intraco; Dr Chan Heng Chee, Associate Professor, Political Science, NUS; Toh Thian Ser, Executive Editor, the Singapore Monitor

Figure 5.2: Programmes Run by Singapore Broadcasting Corporation in 1981 on Learning from Japan

Source: Singapore Broadcasting Corporation (1982).

Title	Details
7. Learning from the Japanese experience — a discussion with Prof Ezra Vogel	Telecast on 7 August 1981 Chairman: Wee Mon-Cheng, former Singapore ambassador to Japan and Chairman of SBC Panel: Dr Eddie Kuo, Senior Lecturer, Department of Sociology, NUS; Dr Whang Sun Tze, Executive Member, Singapore Manfacturers' Association; Madam Foo Yee Shoon, Chairman of National Trades Union Congress (NTUC)
8. An interview with Prof Vogel and Dr Namiki (Director and Chief Economist with the Japan Center for Economic Research)	Telecast on 7 August 1981 on 'Friday Background' Interviewer — Yvonne Tan

Figure 5.2: (*Continued*)

followed quickly in 1981. The main events leading to the formation of the Committee on Productivity (COP) and the National Productivity Council (NPC) are summarised in Figure 5.3.

Formation of Committee on Productivity

On 23 April 1981, Dr Wong Kwei Cheong,[1] who succeeded Dr Lee Chiaw Meng as Chairman of NPB from 13 January 1981, formed COP. This took place after his meetings with the major employer groups in Singapore. COP was charged with the responsibility for formulating a set of recommendations to improve work attitudes, productivity and labour-management relations in Singapore. As the *Report of the Committee on Productivity*, published in June 1981, emphasised:

> "*This has become necessary as the subject is crucial to our nation's well-being in the eighties.*"

---

[1] Dr Wong Kwei Cheong was appointed Minister of State (Labour) in June 1981.

Month	Event
1 April	Lee Kuan Yew met officials of the Japanese Chamber of Commerce and Industry, comprising top executives of Japanese firms in Singapore, to discuss the Japanese system of industrial relations and aspects that could be implemented in Singapore.
10 April	Lee Kuan Yew discussed management and productivity issues with Kohei Goshi, founder and Chairman of Japan Productivity Center.
	Employer groups were invited by NPB to submit their views on work attitudes, labour-management relations and productivity.
23 April	Committee on Productivity (COP) was formed by NPB.
June	Lee Kuan Yew met Kohei Goshi in Japan to discuss management and productivity issues further, and expressed interest in emulating the Japanese productivity movement. This later led to the implementation of the Singapore Productivity Development Project (elaborated in Chapter 7).
11 June	*Report of the Committee on Productivity* was published.
17 July	Lee Kuan Yew met representatives of employer groups, together with the unions and government officials, on the COP recommendations. The employers supported the formation of the tripartite productivity council proposed by COP.
8 August	Lee Kuan Yew stressed the importance of productivity in his Eve of National Day message; and said that he had recently met management and union representatives to get them to join the Government in a Productivity Council.
1 September	Government announced appointment of members of National Productivity Council (NPC).
25 September	NPC had its inaugural meeting, and the Productivity Movement was launched.

Figure 5.3: Events in 1981 Leading to Formation of Committee on Productivity and National Productivity Council

Source: Compiled from various reports.

The composition of COP is shown in Figure 5.4. The representatives were drawn from the Government, trade unions and mass media.

S. Chandra Mohan Director of News & Current Affairs Singapore Broadcasting Corporation	Lam Chuan Leong Deputy Secretary (Defence)	Tan Boon Huat Head Establishment Unit Public Service Commission
Douglas Chua Deputy Executive Director National Productivity Board	Ong Yen Her Assistant Director Industrial Relations National Trades Union Congress	Tan Peng Boo Deputy Secretary (Labour)
Foo Meng Tong Deputy Divisional Director Manpower Division Economic Development Board	John Yip Director of Schools Ministry of Education	

Figure 5.4:   Composition of Committee on Productivity

Source: National Productivity Board (1981).

Drawing Lessons from the Japanese

The *Report of the Committee on Productivity* did not state specifically that Japan was used as the model for Singapore. Nonetheless, this was clearly the case, considering the timing of the COP formation, the issues of focus and the recommendations made. In fact, a section in the report titled 'The Japanese System' comes right after 'Introduction.' The section simply says:

> *"The Japanese labour management system, which has considerable success in raising productivity, is characterised by the extent of:*
>
> *a. Job Involvement*
> *b. Small Group Participation*
> *c. Business Welfarism*
> *d. Loyalty and Identification With Company*
> *e. 'Bottom-up' Management*
> *f. House (Enterprise) Unions*
> *g. Multi-functional Job Assignments*
> *h. Seniority Wage System*
> *i. Life-time Employment*

The Committee's opinion is that the above represent roughly the order of feasibility of implementation in Singapore. 'Bottom-up' management, house unions and multi-functional job assignments may take considerable time to evolve. The seniority and life-time employment may never be achieved except in some of the larger organisations and even then limited to a 'core' of skilled workers."

In undertaking its work, COP analysed the various aspects of the Japanese management system in relation to the Singapore environment and proposed what could be adopted or adapted.

Approach Taken and Recommendations

As managing work attitudes, productivity and labour-management relations in a work environment was considered situational, COP was of the view that it could not prescribe specific productivity practices for employers and workers. Instead, its approach was to identify how the desired attitudinal change could be fostered through five areas:

a. Education of the public;
b. Information dissemination and training;
c. Reinforcing company identification;
d. Promotion of labour-management joint consultation; and
e. Government setting an example as an employer.

COP made far-reaching recommendations on the types of practices and policies to adopt in these areas to achieve improvements in work attitudes, productivity and labour-management relations. The recommendations, grouped under the five areas, are summarised in Figure 5.5.

The COP report was released publicly on 14 July 1981 in all the four official languages and became the de facto productivity plan for the 1980s. The media coverage on the report was extensive. Subsequently, the various employer groups and NTUC

Subject Matter	Recommendation
I. Public Education	
a. Productivity Movement	A Productivity Movement should be launched to tackle the productivity issue in its widest context under a Productivity Council. The Council should have the highest level of representation to lend it prestige and weight. It should therefore be chaired by the Minister of State (Labour) and have members drawn from employer groups, NTUC and Government.
b. Productivity Week	The Council should launch a Productivity Week annually for promotional purposes. The Council should also institute a system of national awards to be given to the best Quality Control Circle, Work Excellence Committee, most productive company, etc.
c. Regular publication of productivity indices	The Ministry of Trade and Industry should publish quarterly productivity indices for each economic sector to increase awareness of and give impetus to employers and workers to improve productivity.
d. Media support	The concepts and messages to be included in the general education for the public should cover basic productivity concepts; need for increasing productivity; results of increasing productivity; organisational communication; team work; quality; and development of individual potential.
e. Media Consultative Committee (MCC)	A MCC should be set up for NPB to brief the media and provide a means to receive feedback from the media on the most effective way to promote the Productivity Movement.
f. Singapore Broadcasting Corporation (SBC)	SBC can highlight the benefits of good management practices, team work and labour-management cooperation in companies through news items, forums, radio talks, documentaries, filmlets, etc.
g. Press	The MCC should monitor Press coverage on all matters related to productivity and get the Press to promote the Productivity Movement along similar lines as SBC.

Figure 5.5:   Recommendations of Committee on Productivity

Source: National Productivity Board (1981).

Subject Matter	Recommendation
h. Schools and tertiary institutions	• The Education Ministry should consider including assessment on each pupil's ability to work in groups and his contribution to team effort, to emphasise the value of group effort. • The Education Ministry can consider setting up a unit to administer the project to expose secondary and pre-university pupils to work during their holidays, since this is an effective way of inculcating good work attitudes. • The tertiary institutions should introduce courses or include teachings on human relations since every student will end up working with and managing other people. • The tertiary institutions should increase the proportion of practical work in their courses and incorporate more field project work, industrial attachment, etc. in courses to address employers' view that our graduates are too theoretical in outlook and lack practical experience.
II. Information and Training	
a. Courses	NPB should run more courses with a human management orientation for all levels of workers from senior managers down to supervisors and line workers.
b. Case library	NPB should set up a library of local case studies and reports on management practices to be made available freely to organisations.
c. Course registry	NPB should set up a central registry of management and productivity courses and training programmes to keep tabs on what is happening.
III. Reinforcing Company Identification	
a. Variable bonuses	The ceiling of 3 months' wages of Annual Wage Supplement (AWS) should be lifted; and employers should have the sole discretion to pay AWS based on the company's profitability and the length of service and performance of workers.
b. Company retirement/long service benefits	Special awards/benefits given to workers who have stayed long with the company, should be encouraged since this is an effective way to promote worker loyalty.

Figure 5.5:　(*Continued*)

Subject Matter	Recommendation
c. Reduction of employers' contribution to Central Provident Fund (CPF)	MNCs and Singapore companies with proven track record of good management practices and with more than 300 employees could be given the option to reduce the employers' CPF contribution for new employees from 20% to, say, 11% so that more funds are available to provide more and better benefits for their employees.
d. Exemption from CPF contribution	Companies that have the financial resources should be encouraged to set up their own provident funds to enhance the nexus between workers' welfare and the performance of the company.
e. House unions	• Industry-wide unions, general unions and craft unions should, wherever feasible, be restructured into house unions to help workers identify with the company and its future. • There should be only one union for all levels of staff in one organisation, and the statutory boards should set the example.
f. National Wages Council (NWC)	The Ministry of Labour should review the need for the NWC since wage increases should be a matter for negotiation between the company and the union.
g. Public housing	• The Housing and Development Board (HDB) could consider a scheme of priority allocation of flats to a person who commits to serve his company for a certain period. • HDB could consider the feasibility of a sub-zone scheme which caters flats to applicants who specify preferred sub-zones to stay close to their current work place.
h. Sports and recreation	Government, semi-Government and even union-run sports and recreational facilities should set aside a portion of peak demand periods for company rental only to reinforce company linkage.
i. Business welfarism	The Government should provide only the basic needs like education, health and housing to workers, and leave it to employers to decide the services that will help to attract and retain workers.

Figure 5.5: (*Continued*)

Subject Matter	Recommendation
j. Health	Employers and unions should provide better medical benefits as part of the total reward packages for workers.
k. Public housing subsidy	Employers should play a greater role in helping their employees to purchase public housing, in line with the business welfarism concept.
IV. Promotion of Labour-management Joint Consultation	
a. Work Excellence Committees	Work Excellence Committees as a vehicle to develop joint consultation between management and workers should be widely promoted.
b. Quality Control Circles (QCCs)	• Promotion of QCC activities should be encouraged as they play an important part in promoting workers' involvement and participation at work. • Coordination of the promotion of QCCs should be brought under the Productivity Council as they are a major ingredient of the Productivity Movement.
V. Government as an Employer	
a. Productivity campaign in public sector	A campaign should be mounted within the public sector to increase awareness of the concept and importance of productivity.
b. Staff appraisal	A review should be made of the staff confidential report to give greater emphasis to good human management and ability to motivate staff to strive for higher performance.
c. Work Improvement Teams (WITs)	All Ministries should support the setting up of WITs, which should be the name given for QCCs in the public sector.
d. Staff welfare	There should be a more liberal attitude towards expenditure for supporting social activities for staff members, so as to encourage more social interaction and build up team spirit.
e. House unions in public sector	The Government should move towards house unions in the public sector.

Figure 5.5: (*Continued*)

expressed their support for the report. To encourage greater discussion by Residents' Committee members on the report, NPB and the Residents' Committee Central Secretariat (Prime Minister's Office) organised a seminar with the theme 'Progress through Productivity' on 7 November 1981. The seminar was also intended to familiarise them with the concept of productivity, so that they could convince the citizens of its importance and their role in productivity improvement.

Formation of National Productivity Council

Following the recommendation of COP, NPC was formed on 1 September 1981. The terms of reference of NPC were:

a. To consider the implementation of the recommendations by the Committee on Productivity;
b. To review and analyse the productivity efforts of the country; and
c. To suggest and outline future strategies on an annual basis.

NPC was tripartite in composition, with high levels of representation from the employers, unions, academia and the Government; and with NPB serving as the secretariat and executive arm. As stated in the *NPB Annual Report 1981/82*:

"The National Productivity Board (NPB) is the primary executing agency in Singapore in the field of productivity and the prime implementing agency in support of NPC's Productivity Movement."

Figure 5.6 shows the composition of NPC in its inaugural term of 1 September 1981–31 August 1983.

At the inaugural meeting of NPC on 25 September 1981, Dr Wong Kwei Cheong said:

"One of the main functions of the National Productivity Council will be the launching of a Productivity Movement in Singapore.

Chairman Dr Wong Kwei Cheong Minister of State (Labour) and Chairman, NPB
Deputy Chairman Lee Yock Suan Minister of State (National Development)
Secretary Ng Kiat Chong Deputy Chairman, NPB
Labour Peter Vincent President National Trades Union Congress (NTUC) Dr Wan Soon Bee Deputy Secretary-General, NTUC Eric Cheong Secretary-General Singapore Manual & Mercantile Workers' Union Mustafa Kadir* Deputy Secretary-General, NTUC
Employers M. J. McMahon Member American Business Council G. A. Pourroy Speaker German Business Group K. Mito President Japanese Chamber of Commerce and Industry Tan Eng Joo Representative Singapore Chinese Chamber of Commerce and Industry

Figure 5.6: Composition of National Productivity Council, 1 September 1981–31 August 1983

Note: * Succeeded by Goh Chee Wee, Assistant Secretary-General, NTUC, with effect from 12 January 1983.
Source: National Productivity Council (1983).

Michael Yeo
Honorary Chairman
Singapore Manufacturers' Association

Stephen Lee
Vice-President
Singapore National Employers Federation

Academic Institutions
Prof Lim Pin
Vice-Chancellor
National University of Singapore

Mr Khoo Kay Chai
Principal
Singapore Polytechnic

Government
Ngiam Tong Dow
Permanent Secretary (Trade and Industry)

H. R. Hochstadt
Permanent Secretary (Finance) (Budget)

Dr Han Cheng Fong
Permanent Secretary (Labour)

Goh Kim Leong
Permanent Secretary (Education)

Yeo Seng Teck
Director
Economic Development Board

Figure 5.6: (*Continued*)

*We must have a productive workforce. How can this be achieved?
The National Productivity Council should tackle this problem by seeking to
improve the relationship between workers and employers. ... Productivity as
our Prime Minister explained is 'to get more out of a workforce with the
same working hours'. In order to achieve this, we require a 'better educated,
better trained, better disciplined workforce; with higher skills, higher knowledge and better work attitudes'.*

*... The National Productivity Council will be the forum for a free inter-
change of management concepts. Hopefully, this will represent a major
stride in our search for an elixir to Singapore's personnel management and
industrial relations. "*

The three priorities identified were launch of a nation-wide Productivity Movement, development of a productive workforce, and personnel management and industrial relations. Clearly, the focus was on the human aspects of productivity.

NPC provided a platform for active dialogue among the employers, unions, public sector and educational and professional institutions on the priorities and other issues that had an impact on national and enterprise productivity. In line with the greatest concern then, it focused initially on the human aspects of productivity in its deliberations. These covered in particular the application of good management practices and the moulding of workers' attitudes. As a rallying point, it actively promoted the inculcation of the productivity will, defined as 'the attitude of mind that constantly seeks improvement in work.' NPC also formulated policies to guide the national productivity drive. The details are given in Chapter 6.

Formation of Public Sector Central Productivity Steering Committee

Following the establishment of NPC, the Civil Service set up the Central Productivity Steering Committee (CPSC) on 7 October 1981 to spearhead the Civil Service Productivity Movement. This was in line with COP's recommendation that the Government as an employer should set the example in improving productivity, work attitudes and staff management. As Dr Richard Hu, Minister for Finance, said four years later in a message for the commemorative publication, *Towards Excellence: The Civil Service Productivity Campaign, 1981–1986*:

> *"The seeds of the Productivity Movement in the Civil Service were sown five years ago with the formation of a Committee on Productivity in April 1981. A cardinal recommendation of the Committee was that Government as an employer should set the example in improving productivity, work attitudes and staff management.*
>
> *The fact that the public sector employed approximately 12 per cent of the total workforce was but one reason. Equally important was the need for*

Government to restrain its growth and spending without compromising on the effectiveness and efficiency of the services rendered."

The composition of CPSC, chaired by the Permanent Secretary (Finance) (Budget), is shown in Figure 5.7. The members of the committee comprised the Permanent Secretaries of the larger Ministries and representatives from the larger Civil Service unions.

Chairman
H. R. Hochstadt
Permanent Secretary (Finance) (Budget)/
Permanent Secretary (Law)

Members
Dr Andrew C. K. Chew
Permanent Secretary (Finance)(Public Service)/
Permanent Secretary (Special Duties), Prime Minister's Office/
Head of Civil Service
Lam Chuan Leong
Permanent Secretary (Communications and Information)
Cheong Quee Wah
Permanent Secretary (Environment)
Dr Kwa Soon Bee
Permanent Secretary (Health)/Director of Medical Services
Moh Siew Meng
Permanent Secretary (Labour)/Commissioner for Labour
Koh Cher Siang
Permanent Secretary (National Development)
Dr Chee Yam Cheng
President, Singapore Government Medical, Dental &
Pharmaceutical Officers' Association
Othman Haron Eusofe
Assistant Secretary-General
National Trades Union Congress
G. Kandasamy
General Secretary
Amalgamated Union of Public Employees

Figure 5.7: Composition of Central Productivity Steering Committee
Source: Ogilvy & Mather Public Relations (1986).

The terms of reference of CPSC were:

a. To identify and change or remove procedures and practices which impede teamwork, productivity and quality of work in the Civil Service;

b. To initiate, examine and recommend or introduce measures which would promote teamwork, pride in work, morale and productivity in the Civil Service;

c. To discuss and monitor the implementation of schemes which are aimed at, or have a bearing on, the promotion of productivity, morale and teamwork in the Civil Service;

d. To discuss ways of measuring or assessing productivity, morale and teamwork in the Civil Service;

e. To determine and provide central support services for Ministries and Departments in conducting their own productivity programmes; and

f. To act as a clearing house for Ministries and Departments especially in the dissemination of ideas and feedback on productivity measures and programmes.

The details of the programmes spearheaded by CPSC in the Civil Service Productivity Movement are given in Chapter 6.

Restructuring of National Productivity Board

In conjunction with its role as the executing arm of NPC, NPB was restructured several times during the 1980s. Soon after the launch of the Productivity Movement in September 1981, NPB re-organised itself into Divisions to carry out activities to support the human aspects of productivity. In 1986, two main developments — change in NPB's mandate and the new NPB Building — impacted the course of the national productivity drive spearheaded by NPB.

Re-organisation to Carry Out Activities to Support Human Aspects of Productivity

As a result of the launch of the Productivity Movement and the formation of NPC, NPB, as its secretariat and executing arm, was restructured.

In 1982, a new Board of Directors was appointed to represent the interests of the Government, unions, employers and professional groups from which leading personalities of multinational corporations (MNCs) in Singapore were enlisted. For the first time, three new advisory committees were established, with members drawn from the new Board of Directors and from the industry and trade unions. These three committees, focusing on Training, Consultancy and Occupational Safety and Health respectively, made use of their multinational representation to bring to bear a variety of management and worker concepts from various parts of the world.

In June 1982, Ng Kiat Chong, Secretary of NPC, was appointed to serve concurrently as Deputy Chairman of NPB. With this appointment, the NPC Secretariat was integrated with NPB, enabling the organisation to plan its activities according to NPC's directions and guidelines on the Productivity Movement. From 1 October 1983, Ng Kiat Chong relinquished his Deputy Chairman position to become the Executive Director of NPB. He took over this position from Lim Jit Poh, who had served for just over two years from 1 June 1981–30 September 1983. Prior to that, Dr Goh Keng Leng served for just over a year as Executive Director from 16 April 1980–31 May 1981.

Besides the leadership changes, the organisation structure was revamped. To consolidate its limited resources and develop specialised skills in dealing with the human aspects of productivity, NPB transferred its automation and technology services, including energy management, to the Singapore Institute of Standards and Industrial Research (SISIR), and suspended further work on industrial engineering. Consultancy work was discontinued, except for areas related to the human aspects of productivity (e.g. implementation of quality control circles). From November 1981, it absorbed the training and promotion activities on occupational safety and health from MOL. The final organisation structure comprised six Divisions to carry out the major areas of activities — promotion, training, labour-management relations, planning and policy, occupational safety and health, and administration.

NPB's training function was completely restructured following discussions with other agencies such as the Singapore Institute of

Personnel Management, Singapore Institute of Management, Singapore Training and Development Association, National University of Singapore, the polytechnics and the major employer groups. To support the Productivity Movement, the training programmes were targeted at three levels: top management, i.e. the strategic level where new practices and techniques could be employed to direct operations towards higher output; middle management/supervisory or functional level, where detailed operational practices and techniques could be introduced in areas such as systems management, human resource development and occupational safety and health; and worker or union level, where participation could lead to a more enlightened and better motivated workforce. The various agencies were solicited to make available trainers to help NPB execute its enlarged list of training programmes.

In the field of small group activities and their role in participative management practices to increase productivity, NPB made a concerted drive to establish Quality Control Circles (QCCs) in Singapore. Assistance was sought from the Union of Japanese Scientists and Engineers (JUSE) which had led and coordinated the development of QCCs in Japan.

On the promotional front, NPB sought and secured wide coverage of its activities in the mass media through regular news releases on productivity. Besides publications, TV filmlets were produced in collaboration with SBC and MOL to drive home the productivity message on television.

As a result of all these changes, the character and focus of NPB changed drastically compared with the 1970s. From an organisation that previously emphasised the technological aspects of productivity, NPB had transformed into an organisation that emphasised the human aspects of productivity. This was an abrupt about-turn from the building of its technological capabilities with UNDP's assistance, as described in Chapter 4. The various activities of NPB, as well as NPC, on the human aspects of productivity are elaborated in Chapter 6. Chapter 7 elaborates how the capabilities of NPB on the human aspects of productivity were subsequently built through the Singapore Productivity Development Project (PDP).

Change in NPB's Mandate from August 1986

On 1 August 1986, NPB was transferred from MOL to the Ministry of Trade and Industry (MTI). At the same time, SDF was transferred from EDB to NPB. The rationale for the transfers was given in the press release issued by MTI, which is shown in Figure 5.8.

With the transfer of NPB from MOL to MTI, the organisation had in fact gone a full circle. NPB's predecessor, the National Productivity Centre (NPC*), began in 1967 as an autonomous Division in EDB under MTI. It was then transferred to MOL in 1971 and soon became a statutory board, NPB, in 1972. After 15 years, NPB was back in MTI again.

As a result of the two transfers stated in Figure 5.8, NPB was given a bigger responsibility. Instead of just focusing on the human aspects of productivity, it now had the responsibility for implementing a total approach to productivity, including post-employment training. With this change, the objectives of NPB were revised.

The revised objectives of NPB, as reflected in the National Productivity Board (Amendment) Act 1991, are shown in Figure 5.9. Compared with its objectives in 1972 (Figure 3.2), the only changes now were the additions of sub-objectives ca and cb. These reflected NPB's added responsibilities for post-employment training and the administration of SDF. However, there was no mention of NPB's responsibility for implementing a total approach to productivity.

Nevertheless, to guide its work in implementing a total approach to productivity, NPB developed a framework to capture the key elements of this approach. The framework underlined the need to address all the internal factors affecting both labour productivity and capital productivity at the firm level, and to understand the impact of the various external factors. It also showed how the wealth created through higher productivity would benefit the different stakeholders. The framework was presented by Mah Bow Tan[2], who took over as NPB Chairman from Dr Wong Kwei Cheong on 1 January 1986, at an NPB Certificate Presentation Ceremony on 25 January 1986.

---

[2]Mah Bow Tan was appointed Minister of State (Communications & Information and Trade & Industry) in October 1988.

ON THE TRANSFER OF THE NATIONAL PRODUCTIVITY BOARD (NPB) TO THE MINISTRY OF TRADE AND INDUSTRY

TRANSFER OF NPB TO MTI

In implementing the recommendations of the Economic Committee, the Government has decided to vest responsibility for promoting post-employment training with the National Productivity Board (NPB). This will be in addition to NPB's mission of implementing a total approach to productivity.

So far, NPB has concentrated on improving man-management skills of employers, work attitudes of employees, and labour-management relations. These tasks fitted in well with the responsibilities of the Ministry of Labour (MOL). However, with the new emphasis on a total approach to productivity and the new task of overseeing post-employment training, NPB needs to coordinate more closely with the Ministry of Trade and Industry (MTI) and agencies reporting to MTI, such as SISIR and the Small Enterprise Bureau.

NPB will therefore be transferred from MOL to MTI with effect from 1 August '86. The transfer will give NPB a stronger orientation towards economic development and help it to function more effectively. By comparison in Japan, the Japan Productivity Centre, after which the NPB is modelled, comes under the Ministry of International Trade and Industry (MITI).

With the transfer, the National Productivity Council (NPC) will also come under the purview of MTI.

TRANSFER OF SDF TO NPB

With effect from 1 August '86, the administration of the Skills Development Fund (SDF) will also be transferred from the Economic Development Board (EDB) to NPB, to facilitate NPB's role in skills upgrading and training of workers. Mr Mah Bow Tan will succeed Mr Philip Yeo as Chairman of the SDF Advisory Council. As Chairman NPB, Mr Mah will be in a better position to coordinate the efforts of the SDF and NPB in skills training.

MINISTRY OF TRADE AND INDUSTRY
28 JULY 1986

Figure 5.8:   Press Release on Transfer of NPB to Ministry of Trade and Industry

Source: Ministry of Communications and Information (1986).

a. To promote productivity consciousness in managements, trade union leaders and workers.

b. To provide training facilities for managerial and supervisory personnel in all relevant aspects of modern management including general management, personnel management, management accounting, industrial engineering, achievement motivation and supervisory training.

c. To train workers' representatives in measures for raising labour productivity, and to relate wages and productivity to competitiveness in export markets and industrial relations.

(ca) to promote the development and upgrading of skills and expertise of persons in employment.

(cb) to control and administer the Skills Development Fund in accordance with the Skills Development Levy Act [Cap 306].

d. To foster and promote good industrial relations by training and by promoting the formation of joint consultative councils.

e. To render management consultancy services in the same fields in which training activities are undertaken with a view to assisting industrial enterprises to achieve a general raising of productivity.

f. To assist industrial establishments and trade unions in formulating and rationalising wage policies and wage systems.

g. To assist the Government from time to time in shaping a national wage policy.

h. To undertake manpower and wage studies.

i. To provide a library of books, files and other information material to all interested parties.

Figure 5.9: Objectives of National Productivity Board (NPB) from 1 August 1986
Source: National Productivity Board (Amendment) Act 1991.

To effect its total approach to productivity, NPB added training development, management guidance and productivity measurement to its portfolio; and the activities were rationalised into three categories, viz. promotion, assistance and measurement, supported by review of productivity policies and practices. The rationalisation rested on the premise that in all the activities, four phases were required in a total approach to productivity, viz. awareness, education, action and ownership. Leading the implementation of the total approach to productivity was Koh Juan Kiat, who took over from Ng Kiat Chong as Executive Director of NPB on 1 October 1987.

NPB also began to publicise the definition of productivity which it had formulated earlier to capture the multi-faceted nature of productivity. This definition is shown in Figure 5.10.

The responsibility for a total approach to productivity marked a significant transition in NPB's role. It was also a precursor to further

---

PRODUCTIVITY

Is

AN ATTITUDE OF MIND
that strives for and achieves the habit for improvements,
as well as

THE SYSTEMS AND THE SET OF PRACTICES
that translate that attitude into action:
(A) In and by ourselves
Through
constantly upgrading
our

KNOWLEDGE,
SKILLS,
DISCIPLINE,
INDIVIDUAL EFFORTS
And
TEAMWORK

(B) In our work through
BETTER MANAGEMENT AND WORK METHODS,
COST REDUCTION,
TIMELINESS,
BETTER SYSTEMS
And
BETTER TECHNOLOGY
so as to achieve
HIGH QUALITY PRODUCTS AND SERVICES,
A BIGGER MARKET SHARE
and
A HIGHER STANDARD OF LIVING

Figure 5.10:   Definition of Productivity

Source: National Productivity Board (1990).

developments in the 1990s to strengthen the organisation's role in taking a total approach to productivity. The details are given in Chapter 8.

NPB Building: Symbol of Productivity Drive in Singapore

Besides the change in NPB's mandate, a significant milestone in the 2nd half of the 1980s was the completion of the NPB Building in 1986. For almost 20 years before that, NPB and its predecessor, NPC*, had operated from small rented premises — JTC one-room flats (May 1967–May 1971), 6th floor of Jurong Flatted Factory (June 1971–March 1980) and Cuppage Centre (April 1980–October 1986). The new NPB Building was now one that NPB could call its own.

The NPB Building was built at a cost of $55.5 million and was funded by the Government. Billed as the Training City, the 22-storey building housed all the modern facilities to support the training of the workforce. The details are shown in Figure 5.11.

Facilities	Details
Training rooms	28 lecture rooms, 2 seminar rooms, 1 executive seminar room and 34 syndicate rooms. All the rooms were equipped with a projector, screen, video-cassette recorder, television monitor and white board.
Auditorium	Seating capacity of 480 people. Venue for holding QCC Conventions, seminars, talks and assemblies.
Resource Library	Resource materials, comprising books and audio-visual tapes, on productivity-related subjects. Equipped with a computerised productivity information service; an audio-visual viewing room; and an on-line computerised system that covered cataloguing, acquisitions, circulations, serials and enquiry.
Resource Centre	Equipped with a video production studio and the latest professional grade equipment and facilities to produce quality video programmes to supplement training and in-company productivity efforts.

Figure 5.11:   The Training City at NPB Building

Source: National Productivity Board (1987).

In addition to the training facilities, there were two prominent features at the lobby of the building.

The first feature was a Hall of Fame. This housed the honour rolls of award recipients and other luminaries who had contributed to the Productivity Movement, a map of the key productivity milestones, portraits of productivity experts, and interactive panels for people to learn more about productivity.

The second feature was a mural, together with a sculpture titled 'Excellence,' presented by the Japan Productivity Center (JPC). Symbolising the strong partnership between JPC and NPB in PDP, this was presented in conjunction with the opening of the NPB Building. An identical sculpture was placed in the lobby of the JPC office in Tokyo. The Amp-Box on *Mural from Japan Productivity Center* shows the words on the mural. Besides a short commemoration note, the mural carried a list of the 'Eight Basic Doctrines of Productivity,' signed off by Kohei Goshi, Honorary Chairman of JPC.

Mural from Japan Productivity Center

In commemoration of the opening of the new National Productivity Board (NPB) building, this mural is presented by Japan Productivity Center (JPC) in the hope that the ASEAN Human Resources Development Project proposed by the then Prime Minister of Japan, Mr Zenko Suzuki, in January 1981, will be the cornerstone of the Productivity Movement in Singapore.

October 29, 1986

Eight Basic Doctrines of Productivity

1. Productivity symbolizes one of the highest values that mankind should persistently pursue.
2. Productivity is a concept which signifies a creative culture and brings about the material and spiritual welfare of the human race.
3. Productivity helps to create peace, strengthens democracy, and generates co-operative efforts among a country's government, business, and labour leaders.

(*Continued*)

(*Continued*)

4. Productivity represents a basic code of behavior that should govern the conduct of each and every kind of group and organisation, be it political, governmental, economic, social or familial.
5. Productivity enhances the potential of human beings.
6. Productivity restores the sanctity of labour.
7. Productivity represents a model for individual growth and development.
8. The basic concept of productivity is the vehicle by which the fruits of improved productivity lead to expanded employment opportunities and are fairly distributed among management, labour, and the consumer.

Japan Productivity Center
Honorary Chairman
Kohei Goshi

Source: Mural at NPB Building.

The NPB staff moved into the new NPB Building on 1 November 1986. In conjunction with the official opening of the building on 3 July 1987, Mah Bow Tan, Chairman of NPB, said:

"Today marks the opening of the new NPB Building. It is more than just a landmark in Bukit Merah. It is a permanent symbol of a nation's commitment and desire to achieve excellence and to improve the productivity of its people...
... While we continue with our promotion, assistance and measurement efforts, we have also been tasked with upgrading the skills of our workforce ... we are now able to realise our goals as our building is equipped with training facilities to cater for a thousand managers, supervisors and workers at any one time. Our video production facilities support the training function. So does our Resource Library, with its unique collection and computerised information service ... The resources are all in place at our Training City."

In officiating at the event, Lee Hsien Loong, Minister for Trade and Industry, added:

"NPB's physical expansion is in keeping with its expanded responsibilities. NPB has taken the Productivity Movement through all its phases of development: from promoting productivity awareness, to setting up WITs and

QCCs, to action at the workplace, and then to a total approach to productivity. In every phase, one core value has remained unchanged: a steadfast commitment to training."

Together, the NPB Building, the 'hardware' aspect of the productivity drive, and PDP, the 'software' aspect, contributed much to the building of a strong productivity competency infrastructure in Singapore. In addition, the NPB Building became the symbol of the national productivity drive. It was indeed a far cry from the humble beginnings of NPB's predecessor, NPC.*

Chapter 6

1980s: Decade of Intense
Productivity Drive

---

*"Concentrating on productivity will make today better than yesterday.
And tomorrow better than today. This is the way to prosperity and security."*

*Prime Minister Lee Kuan Yew
Opening of Productivity Month
31 October 1986*

Two Periods of Productivity Drive in the 1980s

The productivity drive in the decade of the 1980s can be divided broadly into two periods. The first period spans the time when the National Productivity Board (NPB) was part of the Ministry of Labour (MOL) until 31 July 1986. The second period covers the time after the transfer of NPB to the Ministry of Trade and Industry (MTI) on 1 August 1986. The transfer marked the transition from a focus on the human aspects of productivity to a total approach to productivity by NPB.

The 1980s also witnessed the implementation of the 7-year Productivity Development Project (PDP) in Singapore from 1983–1990 with funding from the Japanese Government. The project was aimed primarily at building the capability of NPB for the national productivity drive, and is elaborated in Chapter 7.

143

Launch of Productivity Movement

Following the recommendation of the Committee on Productivity (COP), the nation-wide Productivity Movement was launched by the National Productivity Council (NPC) at its inaugural meeting on 25 September 1981. This was the first nation-wide, high-octane and sustained Productivity Movement, even though this was mooted as early as the 1960s, executed in patches in the late 1960s and launched as a one-time productivity campaign in the 1970s.

In his speech at the launch event, Dr Wong Kwei Cheong, Chairman of NPC, said:

> *"Through the Productivity Movement, we aim to inculcate the concept of productivity in the whole of the people of Singapore … Let us bear in mind that it has to be a 'movement' and not a 'campaign'. A movement is a continuous process, whereas a campaign has a finite lifetime."*

Recalling the launch of the Productivity Movement 18 years later in 1999, Lee Kuan Yew, Senior Minister, said:

> *"I discussed the promotion of a productivity movement with groups of Japanese, American and European employers in Singapore. Then I met Mr Kohei Goshi, chairman of the Japan Productivity Centre, and enlisted his advice. Our National Productivity Board formed a Committee on Productivity in 1981. Within five months, the Productivity Movement was launched, with Japanese help. Our objective was simple: to make productivity a way of life for everyone, from the CEO to the supervisor to the worker. We had to convince our workers that higher productivity is as much in their interest as of management. It ensured them job security by making them competitive internationally."*

Lee Kuan Yew's recollection was made in his speech at the Inauguration of the 1999 Productivity Campaign on 9 April 1999, which was his seventh and last appearance at the annual event.

Guiding Principles of the Productivity Movement

NPC set out four guiding principles of the Productivity Movement, which were adapted from Japan Productivity Center (JPC). These are summarised in Figure 6.1.

1. Higher productivity means producing better quality goods and services at competitive prices. This increases sales, attracts investments and expands business.
2. Improvements in productivity will increase the number of jobs available in Singapore. In striving for higher productivity, job changes will take place and the government, employers and labour must work together to prepare and retrain the workforce to become adaptable to these changes.
3. In introducing measures to increase productivity, management and labour must cooperate in discussing, studying and implementing such measures.
4. The gains from higher productivity must be shared among investors, shareholders, employers, workers and consumers in such a way that it will motivate all to put in greater effort to improve the competitiveness of our goods and services and thus increase the gains further.

Figure 6.1:   Four Guiding Principles of the Productivity Movement

Source: National Productivity Board (1987).

These principles were publicised widely to the various stakeholders to provide a common frame of reference to everyone. They explained clearly the meaning of productivity, the strategies required, the benefits to businesses and the workforce, and the sharing of the consequent gains from higher productivity.

Key Areas of Activities in the Productivity Movement

Figure 6.2 shows the key areas of activities in the Productivity Movement in the two periods of the 1980s. Over the years, NPC identified and gave focused attention to certain areas. NPB, as the national productivity organisation, acted as the coordinating and executing arm of NPC to effect its recommendations. Its mission of 'To make Singapore a highly productive nation' reflected its role concisely. This was revised to 'To improve productivity through the

1981–July 1986	August 1986–1989
1. Promotion of productivity	1. Promotion of productivity • including fostering of good labour- management relations
2. Fostering of good labour- management relations	—
3. Training and education	2. Assistance to companies • Training and training development • Management guidance
	3. Measurement of productivity
4. Review of productivity policies and practices	4. Review of productivity policies and practices

Figure 6.2:   Key Areas of Activities in the Two Periods of the 1980s

Source: National Productivity Board, *Annual Report*, various years.

cooperative actions of employers, unions and workers' in 1989 to underline the need for labour and management to work harmoniously for a common purpose.

Hence, the productivity drive in the 1980s was very much associated with the national-level activities carried out by NPB, both by itself and in partnership with others. This was also the case for NPB's successor in the 1990s, as detailed in Chapters 8 and 9.

In the first period of the 1980s, the focus was on promoting the human aspects of productivity. The key areas of activities were documented in NPB's publication titled *Tomorrow Shall be Better than Today — A Productivity Action Plan*, published in 1983.[1] These are detailed below together with the activities in the second period of the 1980s.

Between the two periods of the 1980s, the nature of the activities changed somewhat. This was the result of the two major

---

[1] Although it was called a productivity action plan, the publication was more a listing of activities for six areas, viz. promotion, seminars and study missions, managerial and supervisory training, specific productivity schemes, in-house training, and resource centre.

developments in 1986 — change in NPB's mandate and completion of the new NPB Building.

Promoting Productivity and Inculcating Productivity Will through the Annual Campaign

The most visible aspect of the Productivity Movement in the 1980s was the nation-wide productivity campaign held yearly. As noted in Chapter 5, the campaign was mooted by Prime Minister Lee Kuan Yew in his National Day Rally on 17 August 1980. The first campaign was held in November 1982, following the launch of the Productivity Movement in September 1981.

Every year, the productivity mascot, productivity songs and campaign slogans featured prominently in the campaign.

Productivity Mascot: Teamy the Bee

To give an identity to the Productivity Movement, a productivity mascot was used to front all publicity related to the campaign. The mascot took the form of a bee known as Teamy, which came from the word 'team'. This was chosen after a 2-month discussion by a 4-person team comprising Ng Kiat Chong, Deputy Chairman of NPB; Baskaran Nair, Head (Special Duties), Ministry of Culture; Vince Khoo, President of Association of Accredited Advertising Agents; and Toh Thian Ser, Executive Editor, The Singapore Monitor.

Teamy was chosen as the mascot because of the positive association of bees with high productivity – organised and industrious, working as a team and communicating well among themselves. Teamy thus projected the image of teamwork and industry. Since these same attributes were also found in ants, the team debated whether a bee or an ant should be the mascot. The decision was to go for the bee because it had wings and could fly, which was a positive connotation for the productivity drive.

Teamy was first introduced as the productivity mascot on 1 September 1982, and immediately became a well-known and likeable personality with both adults and children. The only difference between Teamy and an actual bee was the removal of the sting from Teamy to make it look friendly. Teamy was used to spread the productivity message through its appearance on printed materials, television and cinema screens, bus panels, stickers, posters and other promotional materials all over Singapore; and in high-profile events organised by NPB and companies.

A Teamy Club was launched on 15 September 1985 for children between 6 and 12 years old. This was in response to the 600 children who wrote fan letters to Teamy through NPB's newsletter, *Singapore Productivity News (Home Edition)*, which carried a comics feature called 'The Adventures of Teamy, the Bee'. The club organised activities such as 'Tell a Productivity Story', quiz sessions and competitions. Through such events, young fans of Teamy learned the value of teamwork and good work attitude, as well as the importance of being hardworking, punctual and careful in work. On 2 December 1988, the Teamy Club was transferred to the Sharity Club to better synergise the promotion of teamwork, punctuality and good work attitude, as exemplified by Teamy the Bee, and caring and sharing, as exemplified by Sharity the Elephant.

Productivity Songs

In addition to the mascot, two productivity songs were composed in the four official languages: 'Come on Singapore' and 'Good Better Best'. These catchy songs were played over and over again on TV and radio and in the various productivity events. The lyrics of the two songs in English are given in the Amp-Box on *Lyrics of Productivity Songs*.

Judging from recent online posts, the songs, as well as the mascot, have left a lasting impression on the minds of Singaporeans. Examples of the posts are given in the Amp-Box on *Recollection of Teamy the Bee and Productivity Songs*.

Lyrics of Productivity Songs	
Come on Singapore	**Good Better Best**
We all know what hard work means	At work or at play
It's the heart of Singapore	At home or in school
But maybe we have forgotten	If what you have done is good
What it's like to be really poor	If what you have done is only good
So look around the world and see	Then try and make it better
What's happening out there	Better
And let's not lose the things we've gained	Better all the time
Because we don't prepare	
Chorus	Work study or play
We have a plan	Night or day
We have a plan	If what you feel is better
We're going to work together even better	If what you feel is only better
Yes we can	Could with teamwork be the best
Together we can do much more	Teamy
We'll do it even better than we did before	Teamy for the best
Come on Singapore	
We have a plan	*Chorus*
We have a plan	Good better best
We're going to work together even better	Never let it rest
Yes we can	Till your good is better
Together we can do much more	And your better best
We'll do it even better than we did before	To achieve the best
Come on Singapore	Let that be your quest
	Through Productivity
	A better safer
	Happier life
Source: National Productivity Board (undated).	

Campaign Slogans

Each year, the campaign was accompanied by a slogan which reflected the prevailing concern. Figure 6.3 shows the slogans used for the various years.

Broadly, the slogans chosen from 1982 to 1985 were in line with the emphasis on the human aspects of productivity when NPB

Recollection of Teamy the Bee and Productivity Songs
"I remember being in primary 3, when Teamy the bee was born! Also I have never forgotten Teamy's song … 'Good better best! Never let it rest, If it's good, make it better, if it's better, make it best!'. Can't believe how some childhood memories never fade. It was from Teamy that I also learned the meaning of productivity. A huge word, underpinned by abstract concepts for a child of about 10 years old. My childhood understanding of productivity revolved around industrious and hardworking bees, where cooperation helps make things, best! I think that this understanding fuels my working life now. It's amazing how some subtle messages are never lost!"   Joyce Tan   28 May 2012
"Anyone remember Teamy the Productivity bee? There is even a jingle that goes with it. I think it's like this- Good better best/ Never let it rest/ Till your good is better/ and your better, best. I'm amazed I can remember that."   Pinky   6 August 2013
"I've always remembered that song and now I have it stuck in my head! They played it on TV a lot."   Our Busy Life   6 August 2013
Source: Online posts, 2016.

Year	Slogan
1982	Together We Work Better
1983	Come On Singapore — Together We Work Better
1984	Come On Singapore — Let's All Do A Little Bit More
1985	Come On Singapore — Let's All Be The Best We Can Be
1986	Now's The Time…We Must Be The Best We Can Be
1987	Be The Best That We Can Be — Could You Sign Your Work With Pride?
1988	Train Up — Be The Best You Can Be
1989	Make 'Another Satisfied Customer' Today

Figure 6.3: Productivity Campaign Slogans, 1982–1989

Source: National Productivity Board, *Annual Report*, various years.

was under the purview of MOL. The productivity messages revolved around the need for higher productivity, and the importance of teamwork, human relations, worker participation and better labour-management relations. From 1986, a gradual shift began as NPB came under the purview of MTI and was responsible for a total approach to productivity, including post-employment training. Besides the messages in the first half of the 1980s, attention turned to education and training for higher skills, and quality at work, including error-free products, pride in work and customer satisfaction.

The emphasis on quality in the second period of the 1980s was influenced by the quality banner that was flying high worldwide at that time. A major reason for this was the association of high quality with Japanese products that were flooding the market and beating the competition. This was further buttressed by the highly influential writings and teachings of three quality gurus, namely, W. Edwards Deming, Joseph M. Juran and Philip B. Crosby, and by observations of the importance of quality by H. A. M. Cliteur, an expert attached to NPB.

Productivity Month

The start of the productivity campaign each year began in November of the preceding year, so as to give organisations adequate time to prepare their productivity plans for the year ahead. To give prominence to this and to emphasise its importance, November was designated the Productivity Month. This was a variation of COP's recommendation of a Productivity Week, and was the time of the year when the intensity of productivity promotion activities was at its peak.

The launch of the Productivity Month each year was officiated by a ministerial-level Guest-of-Honour to signify the importance attached to the event by the Government. The details are shown in Figure 6.4.

Significantly, Lee Kuan Yew, as the Prime Minister, personally officiated at six of the eight launches. Of the remaining two, one

Year	Launch date	Guest-of-Honour (GOH)	Theme of GOH's speech
1982	1 November	Prime Minister Lee Kuan Yew	Productivity: who benefits?
1983	1 November	Prime Minister Lee Kuan Yew	Productivity: time for action
1984	1 November	Prime Minister Lee Kuan Yew	Productivity: the key to continuing growth
1985	8 November	Prime Minister Lee Kuan Yew	Factors that hindered productivity most
1986	31 October	Prime Minister Lee Kuan Yew	Optimism with progress made (citing Kohei Goshi, Chairman, and Jinnosuke Miyai, President, of JPC)
1987	2 November	Minister for Trade and Industry Lee Hsien Loong	Excellence through quality (citing Kohei Goshi, Chairman of JPC)
1988	1 November	Prime Minister Lee Kuan Yew	Need for continuous improvement in productivity (citing Kohei Goshi, Chairman of JPC)
1989	1 November	Deputy Prime Minister Goh Chok Tong	A decade of keener competition ahead

Figure 6.4:   Launch of Productivity Month, 1982–1989

Source: National Productivity Board, *Annual Report*, various years.

was officiated by Deputy Prime Minister Goh Chok Tong and the other by Trade and Industry Minister Lee Hsien Loong. Besides emphasising the significance of the event, the high level of the Guest-of-Honour was intended to generate widespread publicity in the media following the event. The significance of this point came across poignantly when publicity for the event declined in 1987 because Prime Minister Lee Kuan Yew did not officiate at the event. This prompted him to say in the following year:

> "I launched the first Productivity Month six years ago and have done so every year, except for last year. Then it was launched by BG Lee Hsien Loong, Minister for Trade & Industry. I gave him a letter I received from a former Chairman and President of the Japan Productivity Center (JPC) to

include in his speech. He did so. But his speech did not receive much press or TV coverage. I was disappointed. I could not understand how the media could believe that because I had not launched it, therefore productivity had become less important."

Broadly, like the campaign slogans, the themes of the speeches from 1982 to 1985 were in line with the emphasis on the human aspects of productivity. In fact, in each of the years, Lee Kuan Yew cited findings from the year's Survey on Productivity Attitudes conducted by Times Publishing. In 1986, he spoke of the expanded responsibilities of NPB, among other things. Subsequently, there was greater focus on quality which was considered an important complement of efficiency, the narrow definition of productivity.

Productivity Awards

As part of the programme for the Productivity Month launch, awards were given out to recognise sustained efforts to increase productivity and the results achieved. Coming under the umbrella of the National Productivity Award (NPA), the awards were given to companies for the first time in 1983. In 1986, NPA was extended to individuals. These awards represented the highest form of recognition for outstanding productivity performance. They were also intended to give 'a face' to the winners, who could then serve as role models for others. Between 1983 and 1989, 41 awards were given to companies and 47 to individuals.

Events and Activities Organised in Conjunction with Productivity Campaign

Nation-wide, many promotion activities were organised, especially during the Productivity Month. The activities organised by NPB included National Productivity Congress, Singapore Productivity Lecture, Breakfast Talks for CEOs, CEO Forum, productivity talks at community centres and schools, mobile productivity exhibitions at community centres, seminars and competitions. NPB also distributed promotional materials (posters, pamphlets, stickers, badges, memo pads, etc.) widely to organisations, both in the private sector and the public sector. To ensure a good reach of the productivity message to a wide cross-section of the population, various channels were used for the promotion. These included the screening of filmlets and documentaries during prime time on television, and productivity sketches over radio and Rediffusion. NPB also participated in career exhibitions and organised exhibitions in schools.

The Civil Service, Ministry of Defence (MINDEF), National Trades Union Congress (NTUC), grassroots organisations and educational institutions participated actively with their own activities. Similarly, many employer groups organised seminars and workshops for their member companies. Companies themselves organised their own in-house productivity campaigns, programmes and activities (e.g. poster and slogan competitions, suggestion schemes, talks, seminars and exhibitions) to increase productivity consciousness.

Promoting Productivity and Inculcating Productivity Will through Activities Beyond the Productivity Campaign

The campaign, with its high profile, visibility and pervasiveness, played an important role in promoting productivity and inculcating the productivity will. Nevertheless, there were other activities beyond the campaign that were equally important.

Productivity Promotion through Participation

To encourage more action at the workplace, NPB launched the Productivity Promotion through Participation (3Ps) programme in June 1984. The aim was to encourage companies to start their own in-house productivity promotion programmes to make workers understand the meaning of productivity and take actions to improve it. To promote and encourage the adoption of 3Ps, workshops and clinics were held regularly. NPB also produced a publication titled *3Ps: Productivity Promotion Programme at the Work*

Place, which provided guidelines on the implementation of 3Ps in companies.

Publications

Three serial productivity publications were launched by NPB. The first publication, *Singapore Productivity News* (SPN), started in June 1981, just before the launch of the Productivity Movement in September. A 4-page monthly newsletter, it was distributed free to companies, unions, employer groups, community centres, government agencies, the press and other organisations. The aim was for SPN to serve as a vehicle to disseminate productivity messages to management staff, supervisors, workers, students and the general public. In June 1984, the *Singapore Productivity News (Home Edition)* was published alongside the company edition to reach out directly to primary school children and their families.

In March 1982, NPB began publishing a second serial productivity publication titled *Productivity Digest.*[2] This publication was a successor of NPB's earlier publication *Minimax,* which ran from April 1972 to February 1982. Initially produced on a bi-monthly basis, *Productivity Digest* became a monthly publication from March 1983. Priced at a nominal fee, it became NPB's flagship publication on productivity subjects and matters related to the Productivity Movement. From May 1988–June 1990, the centrefold of the publication carried *SME Newsletter* to cater to the needs of small and medium enterprises (SMEs). The newsletter was published jointly by NPB, Economic Development Board (EDB), National Computer Board (NCB), Singapore Institute of Standards and Industrial Research (SISIR), Singapore Tourist Promotion Board (STPB) and Trade Development Board (TDB). From July 1990, *SME Newsletter* was renamed *Singapore Enterprise* and published as a separate newsletter. *Productivity Digest* itself ran for 23 years until June 2005. SPN was merged with *Productivity Digest* from 1 November 1987, while the

---

[2]From March 1982 to December 1985, *Productivity Digest* was published jointly by NPB and the National Productivity Association.

Home Edition ran until December 1988 when the Teamy Club was transferred to the Sharity Club.

The third serial publication, *PINS and Needles*, was published from 1989. Each issue featured a specific productivity-related topic, with articles sourced from well-known journals and presented in an easy-to-read and concise format. Produced quarterly initially, it went bi-monthly from July 1991. The publication ran until July–August 1996.

Besides these three serial productivity publications, NPB produced a long list of subject-specific publications. The subjects included productivity concepts and applications, quality control circles, suggestion scheme, productivity management, training and labour-management relations.

Productivity Information Service

A Productivity Information Service (PINS) was launched in May 1984 to offer companies access to abstracts of productivity articles obtained from different sources. In November 1988, an online PINS was introduced for subscribers to access a database of some 7000 article abstracts via a modem, a communication software and a personal computer.

National Centre for In-House Publications

In-house publications were considered an important vehicle to promote the productivity message. Hence, the National Centre for In-house Publications (NCIP) was set up by NPB in 1983 to register in-house newsletters. NPB also organised the Best In-house Newsletter Awards Competition, and ran a training programme on 'Better Employer-Employee Communication through the In-house Publication'. The awards were presented until 1990.

Productivity Activist Scheme

On 29 August 1989, NPB launched the Productivity Activist Scheme. The aim was to induct committed individuals to play the role of catalysts in enthusing, energising and leading their colleagues in productivity improvement programmes. Key Activists comprised individuals who were distinguished by their high level of involvement in productivity improvement. They included past Productivity Award winners, Quality Control Circle (QCC) facilitators, trainers, productivity managers, and members of professional associations and productivity steering committees. Activists comprised members of the workforce who had participated in productivity activities either at the company or national level. They included members of QCCs, Work Excellence Committees and productivity associations. All the activists received benefits such as complimentary subscription to *Productivity Digest*, free membership of the NPB Resource Library and invitations to selected events.

Productivity Managers

In 1986, NPB began to promote the need for productivity managers to coordinate and sustain productivity improvement activities in companies. To emphasise the importance of productivity management, 'Managing Productivity — the Key to Business Efficiency' was chosen as the theme of the 1986 Productivity Congress. A study mission to the United States was organised in November 1986 to tap the American experience on productivity management. In 1988, NPB released a publication titled *Handbook on Productivity Management* to guide companies on how they could manage productivity holistically under the charge of a Productivity Manager.

Fostering Good Labour-Management Relations

NPB undertook several activities to actively promote harmonious labour-management relations in companies.

Labour-Management Relations Action Plan

Under the aegis of the NPC Steering Committee on Labour-Management Cooperation, a report titled *Towards Better*

Labour-Management Relations — An Action Plan was completed and released in May 1985. The objectives of the report were to enhance awareness of the importance of labour-management relations for higher productivity; provide a basis for common understanding between employers, unions and employees on the key issues; serve as resource material for an appreciation of the wide range of cooperation opportunities; and generate discussions and interests on labour-management relations in Singapore. Following the publication of the report, NPB organised discussion sessions and workshops to disseminate its findings and recommendations to senior managers, union leaders and industrial relations officers.

Conferences and Workshops

Conferences and workshops were organised to impart knowledge on effective labour-management practices. In 1984, the 1st National LMR[3] Conference was organised under the auspices of the NPC Steering Committee on Labour-Management Cooperation. The 1st Human Resource Development Conference was held in April 1985.

Work Excellence Committees

Although much effort was made to promote productivity committees in the 1970s, there was little success. This was due to lack of support and participation from the top management of companies and poor understanding of the role of joint consultation in the pursuit of higher productivity. To redress the situation, NTUC started a campaign in 1981 to promote the productivity committees, which became known as Work Excellence Committees (WECs). These committees aimed to foster good labour-management relations within an organisation, provide a platform to facilitate communication and consultation, study productivity challenges and discuss solutions, conduct annual surveys to assess the morale and work attitudes of employees, drive the formation of QCCs to improve productivity, and

---

[3]LMR was used as the short form for Labour-Management Relations.

organise social, cultural and recreational activities to promote interactions between workers and management. Compared with the earlier productivity committees and work councils, WECs were formed only where there was support from the top management.

Together with NTUC, NPB promoted WECs actively. In February 1982, it established a special unit to help companies set up WECs. The assistance rendered included conducting residential teambuilding workshops to foster trust and cooperation between management and labour, training the WEC members, providing advisory-consultancy services to develop organisation-wide communication systems and programmes to enhance employee morale, and administering employee attitude surveys to determine the level of morale in the organisation. Industrial committees comprising NPB and union representatives were established to coordinate work excellence activities in the various industries.

High-profile activities to promote WECs included the first tripartite convention on 'Work Excellence through Joint Consultation,' organised by NTUC in collaboration with NPB and the employer groups on 29–30 April 1983, and a National Work Excellence Conference initiated under the auspices of the NPC Steering Committee on Labour-Management Cooperation in 1984. Other significant activities were organisation of a study mission to Japan in November 1982 to expose participants to the practice of joint consultation and to share the findings with the industry, and production of a publication on *Work Excellence Programme* in 1984 to serve as a guide for companies.

Company Welfarism through Employers' Contributions Scheme

In line with COP's recommendation of a company welfare scheme aimed at enhancing the employer-employee nexus, NPC promoted the Company Welfarism through Employers' Contributions (CoWEC) scheme. The scheme was launched in 1984 following the Government's approval and the amendment of the Central Provident Fund (CPF) Act on 20 December 1983. Under the scheme, the employers' 25 per cent contributions were split into 15 per cent for CPF and 10 per cent for CoWEC, which was placed in a trust fund

---

1st Batch

a. Chartered Industries of Singapore (Group)
b. Hitachi Zosen Robin Dockyard (Pte) Ltd
c. Isetan Pte Ltd
d. Jurong Engineering Pte Ltd
e. Matsushita Electronics (S) Pte Ltd
f. NTUC Transport Group
g. Shangri-La Hotel
h. Singapore Automotive Engineering (Group)
i. Tomy (S) Pte Ltd
j. United Overseas Bank (Group)

2nd Batch

a. DBS Bank
b. Emporium Holdings (S) Pte Ltd
c. Hewlett Packard (S) Pte Ltd
d. Hong Kong Bank
e. Hyatt Regency Hotel
f. NEC (S) Pte Ltd
g. Ordnance Development & Engineering Co. of Singapore
h. Overseas Union Bank
i. Singapore Aircraft Industries (Group)
j. Singapore Time Pte Ltd

Figure 6.5: List of Participating Companies in the CoWEC Scheme
Source: National Productivity Council (1985).

for investments. The incomes from the investments were then used for the provision of welfare benefits.

The CoWEC scheme was implemented on a pilot basis by 20 companies for a period of 3–5 years. Figure 6.5 shows the list of companies that participated in the CoWEC scheme.

House Unions

As recommended by COP, MOL encouraged the formation of house unions in companies. The focus was on companies with 500 or more employees, a size that was considered the threshold for house unions to be meaningful.

Industrial Dialogue Committees

At the industry level, NPB promoted the formation of industrial dialogue committees (IDCs) to spearhead labour-management cooperation. Each IDC served as the link between the industry and the NPC Sub-Committee on Labour-Management Cooperation by translating the recommendations of the committee into workable actions for the companies to implement. In addition, it discussed issues and resolved common problems confronting the industry.

Quality Control Circles

NPB first introduced QCCs in 1980 to promote higher productivity through greater participation and teamwork among workers. To learn from the Japanese experience, Ichiro Miyauchi from the Union of Japanese Scientists and Engineers (JUSE), the main coordinating body for QCC activities in Japan, was invited to Singapore. During his 3-week visit, he conducted a QCC training course for managers and engineers, provided consultancy services to companies, and delivered a dinner talk to members of the National Productivity Association (NPA*). Following that, NPB conducted courses to train QCC facilitators and employees. Roadshows and talks were also held in vocational institutes to introduce the concept and benefits of QCCs to new entrants to the workforce.

From 1982, NPB began to promote QCCs more widely. A logo depicting QCC members in discussion was designed to give a distinct identity to the QCC movement. To equip the workforce with the necessary skills, NPB organised courses for QCC leaders, members and facilitators. Seminars, workshops and forums were also organised. In addition, a resource centre was set up to offer advice and assistance to companies in their QCC implementation. In September 1983, NPB set up the National Registration Centre for QC Circles to encourage more companies to set up QCCs and monitor their growth In the public sector, QCCs were also widely promoted under the name of Work Improvement Teams (WITs).

In 1985, NPB set up the Singapore Association of QC Circles (SAQCC) to involve enthusiasts in the development of QCC activities.

SAQCC organised workshops, company visits and other educational activities to enable sharing of knowledge and networking among the QCC activists. It also formed QCC Clubs for companies located near each other, so as to develop common programmes to sustain interest in their QCCs and to provide judges for the company QCC Conventions.

Another instrument used by NPB to sustain QCCs was national recognition. For this purpose, NPB organised a National QCC Convention every year, beginning in November 1982, to provide a platform for QCCs to present their projects. From 1983, National QCC Awards were given to outstanding QCC organisations, circles, managers and facilitators.

Yet another initiative to sustain interest in QCCs was the International Exposition of QC Circles (IEQCC), which was first organised by NPB in November 1984. The annual IEQCC enabled interaction and learning among the QCCs from various countries.

To provide a channel of communication with the QCC members in Singapore, NPB began to publish a bi-monthly newsletter titled *Teamworker* from September/October 1983. Every issue of the newsletter featured a 'Circle in Action' to highlight its achievements and to encourage more workers to participate in QCCs. From March 1990, it was converted into a generic workers' newsletter, covering issues such as teamwork, customer satisfaction and quality that were of direct interest to workers. The newsletter ran until January/February 1992.

Training and Education

Education

In February 1982, NPC appointed a Sub-Committee on Education to implement COP's recommendations on education, and to examine educational programmes to improve productivity and work attitudes of students before their entry into the job market. The Sub-Committee recommended the introduction of human relations courses, human resource management programmes and industrial attachment in the curricula of the various educational institutes and schools.

The Sub-Committee also established three task forces to undertake in-depth studies of specific issues. These were:

a. Task Force on Learning of Productivity in Schools
    Its main recommendation centred on creating opportunities and an environment for students to learn and experience the the benefits of good work attitudes and habits. An activity manual was compiled for teachers to help them create such opportunities.
b. Task Force on Career Guidance to Students
    It made recommendations on how to effectively match students with jobs, based on an extensive survey of practices among all secondary schools and a sample of industries.
c. Task Force on Practical Training
    It introduced a new industrial attachment programme for engineering students in the polytechnics and universities to expose them to the total operations of a company.

Training in Tertiary Institutions and Schools

Human resource management (HRM) contents were introduced in the tertiary institutions in various forms. At National University of Singapore (NUS), a HRM course, first offered in 1982, was extended to all faculties by 1985. At Nanyang Technological University (NTU), second and fourth year students were assigned group projects to enable them to appreciate teamwork and good human relations. At Singapore Polytechnic, HRM-related topics were incorporated into the existing syllabi; whereas, at Ngee Ann Polytechnic, subjects related to human relations were offered in all its full-time diploma courses. At the Institute of Education, courses emphasising human relations were included in its various programmes.

In schools, formal curricula teaching teamwork, human relations and productivity were introduced. They took various forms, such as group work, moral education and peer-tutoring. In addition, topics on productivity were included in school essays to give students a chance to express their views on productivity. The Vocational and

Industrial Training Board (VITB) adopted two approaches to inculcate good work attitudes in students: inclusion of a human relations module in the curriculum, and introduction of activities such as skills competitions promoting good work attitudes as part of the vocational training.

Training of Workforce

To support the Productivity Movement, NPB organised various training programmes for managers, supervisors and workers in the first period of the 1980s. It continued to run the established training programmes from the 1970s, including courses such as industrial engineering and production management to boost business, courses on computing such as data processing and computer applications, and occupational safety and health courses.

In line with the emphasis on the human aspects of productivity, new training programmes on labour-management relations, managerial and supervisory skills, and QCCs were launched. Special emphasis was given to people-management skills. To promote in-house training, NPB offered train-the-trainer programmes to help companies set up their own training departments or to get their line managers to be more effective instructors. It also incorporated the human aspects of management and the 'productivity will' in its training programmes.

A Productivity Training Unit was formed to take charge of training in productivity management. It covered areas such as productivity induction, facilitation and management; productivity practices and techniques; and productivity measurement.

Besides training programmes, NPB organised various seminars, workshops and study missions. Two significant activities were the first Productivity Congress in 1982, attended by about 500 senior executives from the industry, government organisations and unions; and the first Singapore Productivity Lecture in 1983, attended by 1000 senior executives.

NPB also actively assisted and collaborated with various trade and industry associations to organise seminars and courses to spread the productivity message and upgrade the people management skills of their members. These included Singapore Hotel Association, Singapore Retail Merchants Association, Singapore National Employers Federation, Singapore Association of Shipbuilders and Repairers, Singapore Manufacturers' Association and Singapore Chinese Chamber of Commerce & Industry.

In September 1980, NPB, together with NPA*, partnered the University of Chicago to conduct programmes for top executives in Singapore. Following the success of the programme, it collaborated with the university to launch an annual Top Management Development Programme on 24 March 1981. It was the first of its kind offered to local entrepreneurs and senior executives. In 1982, NPB started a similar programme with the National Taiwan University for Mandarin-speaking executives, and another diploma course in financial management with the New York University. In the following year, it launched training programmes on training skills and human resource development in collaboration with the George Washington University School of Education and Human Resource Development.

To build up a core of local trainers, NPB launched a series of train-the-trainer programmes for its staff and the industry. Foreign trainers were also engaged to complement the pool of local trainers. These included trainers from established institutions such as JPC and JUSE, and headquarters of multinational corporations (MNCs) in Singapore such as General Electric, General Motors and Philips.

In May 1985, NPB began to publish a bi-monthly newsletter titled *Singapore Training News*. The aim was to spur training by companies by featuring articles on training efforts on the local scene and other useful information on training. The newsletter ran till January–February 1988, after which it was merged with *Productivity Digest*, NPB's flagship publication.

From August 1986, NPB stepped up the pace of training and intensified training development as it took on the responsibility for post-employment training. In addition to running the various training courses, it launched several major training initiatives. These are summarised in Figure 6.6.

Initiative	Details
National Plan for Workforce Training and Development	With its responsibility for post-employment training, NPB undertook a review of the training situation in Singapore and proposed strategies for the future. These were then tabled for discussion by NPC and subsequently incorporated in a plan. Titled *Initiatives for Reskilling the Workforce*, the plan was published in May 1987.
Worker Training Plan	The Worker Training Plan scheme was introduced in May 1987 to encourage companies to systematically plan and implement training activities for their junior-level employees.
Report on Upgrading the Skills of Workers Aged 40–50	The report by NPB, released in May 1989, highlighted the need for training of mature workers.
Institute for Productivity Training	NPB set up its Institute for Productivity Training in March 1988 to offer a comprehensive suite of productivity-related programmes for companies and the workforce.
SME Training	With its responsibility for implementing a total approach to productivity, NPB began to introduce a series of short training courses tailored to the needs of SMEs. The aim was to equip them with the knowledge and skills to improve productivity.
National Training Packages	National training packages such as QCC 2000, Supervisor Plus, National Quality Awareness and On-the-Job Training were developed. The aim was to raise the standard of training by training providers.
COSEC Programme	The Core Skills for Effectiveness and Change (COSEC) programme was launched in 1986. It covered the core skills of communication, personal effectiveness, problem solving, work economics, computer literacy and quality. The aim was to equip workers with transferable skills to function more effectively on the job and to cope with the rapidly changing environment at the workplace.
Cross-Field Programme	NPB partnered Brain Dynamics Company Ltd, a Japanese consultancy firm, in July 1988 to launch the programme. A 'learning through action' programme, it was aimed at promoting teamwork, leadership and communication skills among middle management, supervisors and workers. It was the first time that the programme had been conducted outside Japan.

Figure 6.6:   Major Training Initiatives in Second Period of 1980s

Source: National Productivity Board, *Annual Report*, various years.

Initiative	Details
Retail Sales Assistants Training Programme	NPB partnered Singapore Retail Merchants Association and VITB to develop the programme to raise service quality levels in small retail outlets, as well as large department stores and supermarkets. The programme was launched in July 1989.
Training Partnerships	NPB partnered various reputable organisations to set up training centres and develop training programmes for the industry. The first NPB-private sector training partnership, NPB-IBM Information Technology Programme for Office Workers, was launched in 1988. This was followed by the NPB-Festo Industrial Automation Programme in July 1989.
INTRO Scheme	The Increasing Training Opportunities (INTRO) scheme was launched in November 1987. It was designed to encourage companies with good in-house training programmes and facilities to share their resources with participants from other companies.
National Training Directory	The National Training Directory, covering the major training programmes and training competencies in Singapore, was initiated in 1987. The aim was to provide comprehensive information to companies and the workforce.
Framework for Certification of Service Skills	The framework was launched on 29 June 1989 to raise the standard of service skills through training and certification. It was developed under the aegis of the Committee on Certification of Service Skills set up by NPB and VITB in October 1987.
National Training Award	The award was introduced in 1988 to recognise organisations for their outstanding efforts in employee training and development. The aim was to encourage companies and the workforce to invest in training.

Figure 6.6: (*Continued*)

Management Guidance and Productivity Measurement

With its new responsibility for implementing a total approach to productivity, NPB set up a Management Guidance Centre (MGC) in February 1986. The primary aims were to assist companies, particularly SMEs, to improve their business efficiency and productivity management, and to highlight successful cases to serve as models for others to emulate. MGC also promoted the growth of management consultancy services for SMEs.

In the area of productivity measurement, NPB developed appropriate systems of measurement at the sector and enterprise levels to complement those at the national level. In addition to tracking performance, the measures provided yardsticks for wage-setting. Besides producing publications on productivity measurement, NPB assisted companies to set up measurement systems through its MGC.

Figure 6.7 summarises the major management guidance and productivity measurement initiatives undertaken in the second period of the 1980s.

Initiative	Details
Management Guidance Services	NPB focused on certain areas of assistance to SMEs, viz. industrial engineering, management information system, labour-management relations, productivity measurement, wage reform and diagnostic service. For other areas of assistance required, the projects were referred to NPB's Associate Consultants.
Associate Consultants Scheme	The scheme, launched on 31 August 1988, aimed to promote the growth of management consultancy services, particularly those specialising in SMEs. The Associate Consultants were selected by a Review Panel and were involved in NPB's projects.
Diploma in Management Consultancy	In January 1987, NPB, together with JPC, offered the pro-gramme to train individuals to be qualified consultants to assist SMEs. The curriculum was based on materials developed under the Productivity Development Project (PDP).
PROMIS Scheme	The Productivity Managers in Small and Medium Enterprises (PROMIS) scheme was launched on 6 October 1987 to help SMEs with the need for further hand-holding after the completion of a consultancy project. This was done through the attachment of a NPB consultant as a Productivity Manager in the company for 6 + 6 months.

Figure 6.7: Major Management Guidance and Productivity Measurement Initiatives in Second Period of 1980s

Source: National Productivity Board, *Annual Report,* various years.

Initiative	Details
PROMPT	The Productivity Management and Project Team (PROMPT) project was launched on 27 April 1989 to help selected industries upgrade their productivity. For each industry, a PROMPT team was responsible for analysing the productivity trends in the industry, identifying major problem areas and making recommendations for improvement. The six industries selected to pilot PROMPT were garment, food manufacturing, restaurant, hotel, retail and finance.
NPB-ENDEC Centre for Inter-firm Comparison	NPB partnered the NTI-Peat Marwick Entrepreneurship Development Centre (ENDEC) in 1989 to develop the centre. The aim was to help industries compute productivity and financial indicators, so as to establish the link between company performance and rewards.
5S Good Housekeeping	On 23 May 1989, NPB set up a Good Housekeeping Advisory Committee to spearhead the nation-wide promotion of good housekeeping practices. This was based on the Japanese housekeeping concept of 5S – encompassing seiri (throw unnecessary things away), seiton (arrange necessary things in order), seisi (clean workplace thoroughly), seiketsu (maintain high standard of housekeeping at all times) and shitsuke (train people to adhere to good housekeeping discipline independently).
Productivity Measurement, Productivity Gainsharing and Flexible Wage Systems	Based on materials developed under PDP, NPB provided consultancy to companies on productivity measurement, productivity gainsharing and flexible wage systems. This was supported by its publications such as *Principles and Applications of Value Added Analysis, Daily Value Added Analysis: A Company Manual, Getting Your Flexible Wage System Right*, and *Report on Productivity Gainsharing*. Seminars and workshops were also conducted. In addition, quarterly and annual productivity statistics were published by NPB through its *Quarterly Bulletin of Productivity Statistics* and *Annual Bulletin of Productivity Statistics*.
Integrated Productivity Improvement (IPI) Approach	The objective of the IPI approach was to disseminate concepts such as Just-in-Time, Total Quality Control, Total Productive Maintenance and Basic Industrial Engineering from Japan (through the PDP) to the industry. To meet the specific requirements of the industries, several IPI task forces were formed in 1987.

Figure 6.7: (*Continued*)

Review of Productivity Policies and Practices

In the 1980s, NPC set up six committees to review the policies and practices, promote concepts and practices, and address the factors affecting productivity in the various sectors. A summary of the committees and their activities is given in Figure 6.8.

Besides the six committees, NPC formed the Committee on Promoting a Training Tradition in June 1986. This was in line with the growing emphasis on training in the second period of the 1980s. In the same month, NPB and MOL formed the tripartite Committee on Third Shift to study how third-shift work could be promoted widely. NPC also set up a tripartite Task Force on Job Hopping in March 1988 to address employers' continued concern with the problem of job-hopping among workers.

In addition to tapping the committees for inputs, NPB carried out an Annual Productivity Survey to gauge the progress of the Productivity Movement. The focus was on the attitudes and actions taken by the workforce to improve productivity. As the executive arm of NPC, NPB also met with representatives of employer groups and unions regularly to seek their feedback on productivity-related issues. The views given served as inputs for the productivity plans and policies formulated by NPC; and some of them were forwarded to the relevant ministries and statutory boards for their follow-up. The major issues raised spanned a wide coverage — job hopping; promotion of productivity; education and training; labour market; productivity measurement, gainsharing and flexible wage systems; rising costs; and local industries. The employers and unions were unanimous in stressing that the productivity promotion effort should continue without let or hindrance. The reason was that the national-level promotion had provided the umbrella for companies to initiate productivity-related activities, and made workers more aware of the need for high productivity.

In line with its eclectic approach of learning from the best on productivity promotion, NPC sought the advice of an expert, H. A. M. Cliteur, Senior Director, Technical Efficiency & Organisation Department of Philips in the Netherlands, between 1982 and 1986.

Committee	Highlights of Activities
Committee on Promotion of the Productivity Movement (initially known as Media Consultative Committee)	• Acted as vehicle for NPC to receive feedback from the media on the most effective ways to promote the Productivity Movement. • Ensured effective dissemination of information on the deliberations of NPC. • Provided guidance on NPB's advertising and promotion efforts.
Sub-Committee on Productivity in the Commerce Sector	• Set up to improve practices in the hotel and retail sectors. • Recommended measures to: — improve practices such as streamlining of licensing procedures, automation and mechanisation, and hiring of part-time workers. — promote job enlargement and enrichment to better utilise the existing manpower. • Introduced standards for HRM practices and quality of service. • Commissioned NUS to conduct a survey of the retail trade in 1987, the findings of which were used to formulate measures for productivity improvement.
Sub-Committee on Productivity in the Manufacturing Sector	• 1st report submitted to NPC in October 1985. — Focused on work attitudes and skills as having the greatest bearing on productivity, based on a survey of factors affecting productivity in the manufacturing sector. — Recommended measures to: ▪ promote productivity at the industry and company levels, training and quality, mechanisation, automation, computerisation and rational utilisation of human resources. ▪ attract more women into the labour force. • 2nd report submitted to NPC in 1988. — Recommended: ▪ Implementation of a grading system for skills of workers. ▪ Upgrading of production management. ▪ Promotion of quality management.

Figure 6.8: Summary of NPC Committees and their Activities
Source: National Productivity Council (1985).

Committee	Highlights of Activities
Sub-Committee on Productivity through Quality and Reliability	• Set up to improve the competitiveness of Singapore-made products and services. • Promoted concepts of quality and reliability among private sector companies. • Developed national programme on Total Quality Control (TQC) for manufacturing, service and supporting industries. • Organised TQC study mission to Japan to learn Japanese practices and adapt them to local industries. • Implemented a project to upgrade the operations of local supporting industries and to develop a mutually beneficial supplier-client relationship between local industries and MNCs.
Steering Committee on Labour-Management Cooperation	• Provided guidelines on effective promotion and implementation mechanisms for employee-employer cooperation. • Developed action plan towards better labour-management relations. • Organised study mission to Japan to learn how Japanese companies deal with the impact of new technology on their workers. • Simplified labour-management relations concepts for workers.
Sub-Committee on Education	• Introduced human relations courses and productivity-related activities into the formal curriculum of educational institutions. • Conducted a study on how productivity concepts could be effectively learnt in an informal school environment. • Enhanced cooperation between industry and educational institutions. • Reviewed existing career guidance system to ensure a better match between the person and his job.

Figure 6.8: (*Continued*)

His views were summarised in two reports, namely, *Observations and Recommendations on the Productivity Movement in Singapore,* published in 1982, and *Coming on Stream: A Report on the Productivity Movement as at the End of 1986,* published in 1986. One of the major recommendations was that quality should be an integral part of the total approach to productivity, and that there should be a Quality Movement fused with the Productivity Movement. This recommendation had a major influence on the directions taken in the productivity campaign and in other activities. An immediate follow-up action was the formation of the Committee on Promotion of Quality jointly by NPB and SISIR in April 1987. The aim of the committee was to recommend ways to promote quality effectively within the Productivity Movement.

From 1986 to 1993, NPC published a yearly *Productivity Statement* to review the progress of actions taken on the various issues, highlight the current issues of concern, and outline the directions for the future.[4] In 1994, this was renamed *Productivity & Quality Statement.* The rationale for this is explained in Chapter 8.

A major highlight was NPC's meeting with the Minister for Trade and Industry, Lee Hsien Loong, in December 1987. The aim was to provide an update on NPC's work and to discuss various productivity-related issues.

Productivity Promotion in the Public Sector

Following the establishment of the Central Productivity Steering Committee (CPSC) on 7 October 1981 to spearhead the Civil Service Productivity Movement, many activities were undertaken simultaneously. These can be grouped under six areas of focus, which are summarised in Figure 6.9.

The many activities undertaken in the Civil Service Productivity Movement underlined the good progress made within a short period. As in many other aspects of the economy, the public sector played an important lead role in the national productivity drive.

---

[4]From 1984 to 1987, NPB published a yearly *Productivity Survey of Singapore.* This was discontinued when *Productivity Statement* began to be published.

Area	Details
Promoting productivity	• Annual campaign organised since 1982 to address specific needs related to promotion of productivity awareness and introduction of productivity measures. • Campaign restructured and spread throughout the year from 1984 to coincide with the Government's financial year (rather than running concurrently with the national Productivity Month) to emphasise the need for continuous improvement in productivity. • Seminars, WITS events, exhibitions and Open Houses on productivity improvements in the Government, included in campaign programmes. • All Ministries, Departments and Statutory Boards encouraged to organise their own productivity campaigns and programmes in addition to the Civil Service Productivity Campaign. • Extensive productivity measurement programme embarked upon to measure achievements in public sector operations.
Training and skills development	• Training of full range of common skills required in the Civil Service, undertaken by the Civil Service Institute (CSI). • WITS movement supported by CSI training courses. • Component on attitudinal and behavioural change for greater productivity incorporated in all CSI courses. • Trainers carefully selected to ensure provision of the best standard of training.
Teamwork	• Teamwork promoted through WITS movement. • WITS Development Unit set up in CSI. • Employees given the opportunity to participate in decision-making and achieve the organisation's goals by participating in WITS. • Employees motivated through WITS participation, as a result of greater sense of belonging, pride in work and direct contribution to productivity improvement. • Applicability of QCC concept in the Civil Service accepted, as a result of WITS Movement.

Figure 6.9:　Areas of Focus of Civil Service Productivity Movement
Source: Ogilvy & Mather Public Relations (1986).

Area	Details
People-centred management	• People-centred management emphasised in recognition of manpower as the critical factor in every organisation. • Terms and conditions of service for civil servants extensively reviewed and upgraded. • Part-time Employment Scheme introduced in 1981 to encourage married female officers who had left the service to rejoin the workforce; flexible working hours introduced in 1983. • No-Pay Leave Scheme for Child Care introduced in 1982 for married female officers. • Half-Day Leave Scheme introduced in December 1984. • Performance appraisal and career development system improved based on the system used by Shell Company.
Technology	• Civil Service Computerisation Programme (CSCP) launched by National Computer Board (NCB) in October 1981 to computerise operations in the Civil Service, and to decentralise computing facilities to Government Ministries and Departments. • Team of trained personnel assembled in NCB to help the Civil Service computerise rapidly. • New areas of IT introduced — email and scheduling systems, electronic document systems, dial-up access to government databases, and application systems that cut across the Civil Service (e.g. financial management and control system).
Working Environment	• Office layout planning and space utilisation practices in the Civil Service reviewed as a result of the rapid growth in use of electronics and automated office equipment. • Ergonomics in office design given attention. • Work procedures and systems revised to complement new office design and layout.

Figure 6.9: (*Continued*)

Productivity Drive in the 1980s in Retrospect

The decade of the 1980s was in many ways the golden era of the national productivity drive. The Government's strategy was directed at restructuring the economy for high productivity growth to underpin economic growth. The policy intent, even during the 1985 recession, was to restructure the economy to achieve high productivity growth. The *Report of the Committee on Productivity* provided the de facto productivity plan to guide activities in the 1980s. The subsequent launch of the Productivity Movement resulted in a slew of activities directed at the human aspects of productivity in the first period of the 1980s, and extended to a total approach to productivity in the second period of the decade. The Movement received the highest level of support from the Government, no less than Prime Minister Lee Kuan Yew himself. At the same time, the 7-year PDP and the new NPB Building built up the productivity infrastructure and competencies significantly.

However, even when the productivity buzz was very much in the air, the labour force continued to grow, mainly through the import of foreign labour. Although the Government recognised the need to reduce the reliance on foreign workers in the longer term, it took the pragmatic approach of responding to the short-term labour needs of companies. From 1.07 million, with a foreign labour share of 7.3 per cent in 1980, the labour force increased to 1.54 million in 1990, with a foreign labour share of 16.1 per cent. For the 1980s as a whole, the average annual productivity growth was a fairly high 4.4 per cent, contributing 59 per cent to the average annual GDP growth of 7.5 per cent. This growth rate was slightly higher than the 3–4 per cent projected by the *Report of the Economic Committee*, albeit lower than the 6–8 per cent target in the *Economic Development Plan for the Eighties.*

Chapter 7

Singapore Productivity Development Project: 1983–1990

"The PDP has contributed in helping NPB to spearhead the Productivity Movement in Singapore. It is through the PDP that we learned more about QCCs, JIT, TQC, 5S(housekeeping) and other productivity improvement techniques which have been introduced to companies in Singapore."

Mah Bow Tan
Minister of State (Trade & Industry and Communications & Information)
and Chairman, NPB
Further Fields to Conquer — A PDP Commemorative Publication
1990

Critical Role of Productivity Development Project in Singapore's Productivity Movement

During the fledgling stage of the Productivity Movement in Singapore, an important programme was implemented to build the productivity infrastructure and the capabilities of the National Productivity Board (NPB). This programme was termed the Singapore Productivity Development Project (PDP) by NPB and the Ministry of Labour (MOL), its parent ministry. PDP was a US$20 million programme funded by the Japanese Government and implemented over a 7-year period from 1983 to 1990. Through PDP, the Singapore Productivity Movement received a boost from Japan, the forerunner of productivity and a widely-acclaimed economic powerhouse.

Background to the Productivity Development Project

In January 1981, Zenko Suzuki, Prime Minister of Japan, pledged a total of US$100 million for the implementation of the Human Resources Development (HRD) Project in the five Association of Southeast Asian Nations (ASEAN) countries, when he visited them. This was part of Japan's diplomatic efforts to promote peace and stability in Asia, as well as to build close relationship with the Asian countries.

Date	Milestone
1981	
January	Zenko Suzuki, Prime Minister of Japan, visited the ASEAN countries and pledged a total of US$100 million for the implementation of the HRD Project in these countries.
April	The Singapore delegation to the 1st Japan-ASEAN Meeting on Human Resources Development, held in Tokyo, proposed setting up an Institute for Continuing Occupation Development (ICOD).
August	A fact-finding mission from the Japan Ministry of Foreign Affairs visited Singapore on 17 August 1981 to study the feasibility of the proposed ICOD project.
October	The 2nd Japan-ASEAN Meeting on Human Resources Development, held in Jakarta on 7 October 1981, agreed that the US$100 million fund be allocated equally among the five countries to assist them in their development of human resources.
1982	
February	A delegation from Japan visited NPB to discuss matters related to the request for experts under the ICOD project.
March	A Singapore team visited Japan to look into staff development activities available in Japan under the ICOD fellowship grants.
March–June	MOL and NPB re-evaluated the ICOD project and decided to propose a project on productivity instead.

Figure 7.1:   Events Culminating in Productivity Development Project

Source: National Productivity Board and Japan International Cooperation Agency (1990).

June	Ng Kiat Chong, NPB's Deputy Chairman, led a Singapore mission to Japan on 18 June 1982 to present PDP, a project proposal on productivity, to the Japanese authorities.
November	The Japanese Preliminary Survey Team, led by S. Horiuchi, Director (Second Technical Cooperation Division), Ministry of Foreign Affairs, visited Singapore from 21 November–2 December 1982 to firm up PDP with the Singapore authorities.
1983	
February	A Japanese Survey Team on Technical Cooperation and Basic Design for PDP visited Singapore on 28 February 1983 to discuss, inter alia, the setting up of a training centre to disseminate productivity-related concepts.
March	The PDP Basic Design Preliminary Survey Team visited NPB from 2–12 March 1983 to collect information for preparation of the preliminary study for the basic design of the new NPB Building.
June	The agreement on PDP, termed 'Record of Discussions for the Singapore Productivity Development Project,' was signed on 11 June 1983. The signatories were H. Suzuki, Director (Technical Cooperation Division), Ministry of International Trade and Industry, representing Japan; and Ng Kiat Chong, NPB's Deputy Chairman, representing Singapore. This date marked the official commencement of PDP.

Figure 7.1: (*Continued*)

The visit by Zenko Suzuki and the subsequent events culminated in the implementation of PDP in Singapore. The details are shown in Figure 7.1. From the series of events, it is evident that the final form of the project implemented under the Japan-funded HRD Project, viz. PDP, turned out to be quite different from Singapore's original intent, which was the ICOD project.

The Government decided on PDP instead of the ICOD project as the priority was to transfer Japanese productivity improvement know-how to the nation. This decision was prompted by the launch of the Productivity Movement in Singapore in September 1981 and Singapore's desire to learn from Japan, the details of which are given in Chapter 5.

Country	Project
Singapore	Singapore Productivity Development Project
Indonesia	Vocational Training Instructors and Small Business Educators Training Center
Malaysia	Center for Instructors and Advanced Skills Training
Philippines	Human Resources Center
Thailand	Primary Health Care Training Center

Figure 7.2:   Final Form of Japan's HRD Project in the ASEAN Countries

Source: Japan International Cooperation Agency (2000).

As the Acting Minister for Labour, Prof S. Jayakumar, said later at the First Exchange of Notes for PDP on 7 December 1983:

> *"It is the intention of Government, through the NPB, to foster a highly productive work force where every worker will want to achieve higher productivity ... The Project is very timely because Singapore will receive the technical assistance at a time when the Productivity Movement is being nurtured."*

Figure 7.2 summarises the final form of the HRD Project undertaken. While the other four ASEAN countries selected projects that fell squarely within the usual scope of HRD, Singapore chose something broader in scope in line with the needs of the economy. As reported by Japan International Cooperation Agency (2016):

> *"Most ASEAN countries requested the establishment of a training centre for developing industrial human resources. However, Lee [Kuan Yew] considered it as a golden opportunity and suggested that Japan assist Singapore to develop human resources with Japan's 'Productivity Movement' as a model. He had planned and thought for some time*

that the key to Japan's economic development was its successful 'Productivity Movement.'

Framework for the Productivity Development Project

The Japan International Cooperation Agency (JICA) was identified as the body from Japan to oversee the implementation of PDP, while the Japan Productivity Center (JPC) was responsible for carrying out the programmes. Both of them constituted the Japan team for PDP. From Singapore, NPB was the Singapore team charged with the responsibility for working with JICA and JPC to implement PDP successfully.

PDP consisted of two components, viz. Technical Cooperation and Grant Aid, which were implemented concurrently. The original intention was for these two components to be executed over five years, from 1983 to 1988. Subsequently, in February 1988, it was agreed that the implementation would be extended by another two years, from 1988 to 1990.

Technical Cooperation

The Technical Cooperation component aimed to build the capabilities of individuals to drive productivity in Singapore. The initial focus was on the NPB staff but this was later extended to personnel in the industry as well. The following two activities were covered under this component:

a. Despatch of Japanese experts to Singapore, on long-term and short-term durations, to help NPB develop new programmes on productivity and to improve existing programmes; and

b. Fellowship training for NPB staff initially, and local companies subsequently, to learn productivity techniques and practices in Japan and to be immersed in the Japanese working environment.

The subject matters included in these two activities were wide-ranging. They comprised:

a. Audio-visual technology;
b. Consultancy for small and medium enterprises;
c. Industrial engineering;
d. Management and supervisory development;
e. Labour-management relations;
f. Occupational safety and health;
g. Productivity measurement;
h. Quality control circles; and
i. Total quality control.

Grant Aid

The Grant Aid component focused on developing NPB into a centre of excellence for the training of managers and supervisors and for the promotion of productivity. This was achieved by setting up a Resource Centre in NPB, equipped with appropriate equipment for training and for the production of training and promotional materials. The following were covered under this component:

a. Training and computer equipment;
b. Training materials and publications; and
c. Audio and video equipment and production and post-production facilities.

In addition, the Grant Aid covered the setting up of a Safety and Exhibition Centre and Industrial Hygiene Laboratory. This project was undertaken by MOL's Occupational Safety and Health Department.

Four Phases of Productivity Technology Transfer from Japan to Singapore

The transfer of both the hard and soft aspects of productivity technology from Japan to Singapore was effected through four phases of

Phase	Period	Chief Advisor
Preparatory	June 1983–March 1985	Kazuo Ishihara
Restructuring	April 1985–October 1986	Kiyohiko Sakurai
Implementing	November 1986–June 1988	Yasushi Fukuda
Follow-up	June 1988–June 1990	

Figure 7.3: Four Phases of the Productivity Development Project

Source: National Productivity Board and Japan International Cooperation Agency (1990).

PDP. These were named Preparatory Phase, Restructuring Phase, Implementing Phase and Follow-up Phase. The implementation of each phase was overseen by a Chief Advisor from Japan. The details are summarised in Figure 7.3.

Preparatory Phase: June 1983–March 1985

The term 'Preparatory Phase' was used for the first phase as it was a period for the teams from Japan and Singapore to establish clear understanding of each other's expectations and to clarify the roles of the Japanese experts and NPB staff.

Beyond working out the details for the implementation of specific programmes, the first phase of PDP saw the despatch of long-term (one year or more) Japanese experts to Singapore and fellowship training for NPB staff in Japan. This enabled the NPB staff to gain basic understanding of Japanese productivity concepts and practices. In addition, a video resource centre was set up, and some equipment and training materials were transferred to NPB.

The milestones of the Preparatory Phase are shown in Figure 7.4.

Restructuring Phase: April 1985–October 1986

This phase was termed 'Restructuring Phase' as the focus was on restructuring the capabilities of NPB to provide direct assistance to

Date	Milestone
1983	
July	NPB study mission visited Japan to look at the latest video equipment and hardware.
October	Kazuo Ishihara, Chief Advisor, and 1st batch of 6 long-term experts (LTEs) arrived in Singapore.
November	1st batch of short-term experts (STEs) came to Singapore to carry out specific studies and areas of work to complement the LTEs.
December	Phase I transfer of equipment, teaching materials, audio-visual aids and booklets to NPB was initiated in conjunction with the signing of the First Exchange of Notes for the Productivity Development Project between Japan and Singapore on 7 December 1983.
1984	
February	1st batch of 33 PDP Fellows went to Japan for training — covering areas such as general concepts of productivity, human resource management, training of trainers, and corporate planning.
May	FY84/85 Annual Workplan for PDP was signed on 22 May 1984 between the Japanese Technical Guidance Team and NPB, providing for despatch of experts to give advice on productivity measurement methodologies, labour-management relations, QCCs, etc.
June	Phase II transfer of teaching materials, audio-visual aids and booklets to NPB was initiated in conjunction with the Second Exchange of Notes signed on 27 June 1984.
October	2nd batch of 35 PDP Fellows went to Japan for training.
November	A video resource centre, equipped with 2 high-grade camera systems including video and audio switching/mixing facilities, was set up in NPB's premises at Cuppage Centre.
1985	
March	Kiyohiko Sakurai arrived as the new Chief Advisor on 29 March 1985.

Figure 7.4: Milestones of Preparatory Phase of PDP

Source: National Productivity Board and Japan International Cooperation Agency (1990).

companies in improving productivity. For this purpose, a Model Company Project was conceived in April 1985. The aims were to assist selected companies to become models of highly productive enterprises for others to emulate, and to underline the usefulness of seeking consultancy services, particularly for companies that did not have their own resources for productivity improvement.

In June 1985, NPB formed a Steering Committee on Model Companies comprising its senior management and the Japanese long-term experts. In total, nine model companies were selected based on the criteria that some contact had already been established with the companies and that they were willing to participate in productivity programmes.[1] The Japanese experts acted as the leaders for the projects, while on-the-job-training (OJT) was provided to the NPB staff to learn the ropes of management consultancy.

The milestones of the Restructuring Phase are shown in Figure 7.5.

Implementing Phase: November 1986–June 1988

Building on the second phase, the third phase was called 'Implementing Phase' as the focus was on implementing management consultancy widely in the industry to improve productivity. To realise this, efforts were stepped up to develop management consultancy expertise in productivity improvement, not just within NPB but also in the industry. For the first time, fellowship training in Japan was extended to private sector managers and consultants. Upon their return, many of them were appointed associate consultants and referral consultants by NPB to supplement its own expertise in providing consultancy services to the industry. Long-term Japanese experts specialising in management consultancy for small and medium enterprises (SMEs) were also attached to NPB. Unlike in the second phase, the role of the experts shifted from leader to adviser for the NPB project teams.

This phase also marked the signing of the Follow-up Action Plan (1988–1990), which extended PDP for another two years. This was recommended by a JICA Evaluation Team in view of the need to

---

[1] The nine model companies were Asian Machine Pte Ltd, Century Park Sheraton, Fowseng Plastics Industries Pte Ltd, Okamoto (S) Pte Ltd, Watson E. P. Industries Pte Ltd and Yokogawa Electric Singapore in Phase I; and Electro Magnetic (S) Pte Ltd, Enamelled Wire & Cable (S) Pte Ltd and the ESCO Group of Companies in Phase II.

Date	Milestone
1985	
April	FY85/86 Annual Workplan for PDP was signed on 8 April 1985 between the Japanese Technical Guidance Team and NPB, providing for despatch of 11 experts to NPB to give advice on planning & research, labour-management relations, industrial & operations engineering, QCCs, and Occupational Safety & Health.
September	3rd batch of PDP Fellows went to Japan for training, which included an extended period of attachment to Japanese companies to learn how to implement productivity programmes through OJT.
October	The Third Exchange of Notes for PDP was signed on 28 October 1985.
1986	
April	FY86/87 Annual Workplan for PDP was signed on 8 April 1986 between the Japanese Technical Guidance Team and NPB.
July	Yasushi Fukuda arrived as the new Chief Advisor on 12 July 1986. Core Programme for 4th batch of PDP Fellows was conducted in Singapore for the first time.
August	4th PDP Fellowship (Elective Programme) was conducted in Japan, focusing on Management Consultancy.

Figure 7.5:   Milestones of Restructuring Phase of PDP

Source: National Productivity Board and Japan International Cooperation Agency (1990).

further strengthen the efforts expended in the past few years. The extension was also necessary as NPB and JICA had jointly launched the Japan-ASEAN Regional Training Programme to share knowledge on productivity with the ASEAN countries.

The milestones of the Implementing Phase are shown in Figure 7.6.

Follow-up Phase: June 1988–June 1990

The last phase was aptly named 'Follow-up Phase' as the intention was to follow up on, as well as consolidate, all the activities that had been undertaken earlier. The activities in this phase included

Date	Milestone
1986	
December	Training equipment, computers and equipment for the auditorium and the Resource Centre in the new NPB Building at Bukit Merah Central were delivered.
1987	
January	JPC-NPB Diploma in Management Consultancy course was launched.
March	FY87/88 Annual Workplan for PDP was signed on 9 March 1987 between the Japanese Technical Guidance Team and NPB, providing for despatch of experts to give advice on labour-management relations, industrial engineering, production management, quality control and in-company productivity schemes.
August	5th batch of PDP Fellows, comprising 28 participants, went to Japan for Production Management and Labour Management training courses.
1988	
February	Final Evaluation Mission from Japan visited NPB and signed the Follow-up Action Plan (1988–1990) with NPB, providing for 27 STEs to be attached to NPB.
March	Japan-ASEAN Regional Training Programme was jointly launched on 27 March 1988 by NPB and JICA to share knowledge and experience in productivity with 12 participants from the ASEAN countries.

Figure 7.6   Milestones of Implementing Phase of PDP

Source: National Productivity Board and Japan International Cooperation Agency (1990).

further upgrading of the management consultancy skills of the NPB staff through practical OJT, deepening of fundamental productivity practices such as 5S in industry, extension of consultancy services to the service industries, and launch of the Japan-ASEAN Regional Training Programme on Management Consultancy. In May 1990, PDP came to an end, with separate closing ceremonies held in both Japan and Singapore.

The milestones of the Follow-up Phase are shown in Figure 7.7.

Date	Milestone
1988	
August	6th batch of PDP Fellows, comprising 12 participants, went to Japan for training in Management Consultancy.
November	Yasushi Fukuda, Chief Advisor, received award from Prime Minister Lee Kuan Yew at the launch of the 7th Productivity Month for his contribution to the Singapore Productivity Movement.
1989	
March	2nd run of Japan-ASEAN Regional Training Programme was conducted for 17 participants from the ASEAN countries.
April	FY89/90 Annual Workplan for PDP was signed on 3 April 1989 between the Japanese Technical Guidance Team and NPB.
September	7th batch of PDP Fellows, comprising 8 NPB staff, went to Japan for training in Management Consultancy.
1990	
January	16 project leaders from JICA came to Singapore for a 5-day Annual Conference, where PDP was chosen as a successful model for discussion.
March	3rd run of Japan-ASEAN Regional Training Programme, focusing on Management Consultancy, was conducted.
May	PDP Closing Ceremony, hosted by the Singapore Ambassador to Japan, Cheng Tong Fatt, was held in Japan on 18 May 1990. Mah Bow Tan, Minister of State (Trade & Industry and Communications & Information) and Chairman, NPB, and Freddy Soon, Divisional Director (Resources), NPB, were present at the ceremony.
May	PDP Closing Ceremony, hosted by Mah Bow Tan, was held in Singapore on 25 May 1990. T. Yamaguchi, the Japanese Ambassador to Singapore, and K. Yanagiya, President of JICA, graced the occasion. A publication by NPB and JICA titled *Further Fields to Conquer — A PDP Commemorative Publication* was released. On 27 May, a Golf Tournament was also held to commemorate the Closing of PDP. Ong Teng Cheong, 2nd Deputy Prime Minister and NTUC Secretary-General, was the Guest-of-Honour.

Figure 7.7:   Milestones of Follow-Up Phase of PDP

Source: National Productivity Board and Japan International Cooperation Agency (1990).

Challenges in Implementation

The implementation of PDP was anything but smooth-sailing. First, the Japanese had no prior experience with the transfer of the soft aspects of technology, which they called 'humanware', to other countries. Second, cultural differences and the language barrier between the Japanese and Singapore counterparts hindered discussions and agreements on various issues.

In 2000, JICA reported the findings of a third-party evaluation (done by non-JICA experts to ensure neutrality) that it had commissioned on PDP as well as other projects to assess the overall results of cooperation projects. The report concluded (Japan International Cooperation Agency, 2000):

> *"The Productivity Development Project (PDP) did not go well from the beginning, and both the Japanese and Singaporean sides have painful memories ... This improvement of the skills of NPB staff was the first task of the experts. However, it gradually turned out that companies also had only a vague conception of productivity as something that seemed to be a good thing ... In Japan, productivity development was promoted based on the assumption that everybody understood concepts such as the 5S-Method: [Seiri (Organization), Seiton (Tidiness), Seiso (Cleaning), Seiketsu (Hygiene) and Shitsuke (Discipline)], 'quality first' and 'safety first.' However, there were no such foundations in Singapore, and the Japanese side was taken aback ... Factory managers expected Japanese productivity development to work like an instant cure in dirty factories that were not even cleaned properly, where there were things to be done before productivity and quality improvement can be attempted ... Likewise, the Singaporean government officials also grilled the Japanese experts about the lack of visible results merely a year after the project began."*

Subsequently, in 2014, JICA recounted (Japan International Cooperation Agency, 2014):

> *"Transferring productivity development knowhow was a bumpy road at first. The first Japanese approach of 'Just give it a try, and then you'll see' did not go down well in Singapore, where value was placed on practicality and theory."*

To make progress from the bumpy start, a PDP Joint Committee, co-chaired by the Executive Director of NPB and the PDP Chief Advisor, was formed in 1985. The committee met monthly and often had protracted discussions to thrash out issues. As far as possible, they tried to accommodate each other's points of view. As Yasushi Fukuda, PDP Chief Advisor in the third and fourth phases, said (Japan International Cooperation Agency, 2014):

> *"Once a month, we provided the opportunity for members of top management from Japan and Singapore to meet and share their comments and complaints with one another. That worked out very well."*

The give-and-take stance adopted made it possible for PDP to be carried out over the 7-year period without major hitches despite the challenges. As Mah Bow Tan, Minister of State (Trade & Industry and Communications & Information) and Chairman, NPB, said at the closing ceremony of PDP in Singapore on 25 May 1990:

> *"After seven years of working together, Singaporean and Japanese professionals on the project have acquired a mutual understanding and respect for one another's managerial and work styles. The result is an enriched experience for both sides as well as a successful PDP ... the success of the PDP is a result of painstaking effort, perseverance and patience on the part of many individuals."*

This statement underlined the good progress made by the Singapore and Japanese teams in implementing PDP as a result of jointly tackling the challenges faced throughout.

Results of the Productivity Development Project

Implemented at a time when Singapore had to build its productivity capabilities and infrastructure, PDP was most timely and met the nation's needs. No doubt, it provided a strong impetus to the Singapore Productivity Movement in the 1980s.

Result	Details

Capability upgrading of NPB	• NPB as an organisation acquired management consulting capabilities through both training and project work involving more than 200 Japanese experts:
	  a. Core skills — management accounting, industrial engineering, production management, diagnostic skills, morale survey and training needs analysis.
	  b. Specialised consulting skills — just-in-time production, total quality control, total productive maintenance, value engineering, flexible wage system, performance appraisal system, labour-management relations, on-the-job-training, customer service, business simulation.
	• 70 staff completed the basic course on Japanese language, enabling them to understand Japanese language and culture and better appreciate the thinking behind Japanese management philosophy.

Infrastructure upgrading of NPB	• NPB Resource Centre was equipped with professional-grade equipment and staffed with trained producers, technicians and engineers to produce audio-visual aids and programmes for promotion and training. • 100 training manuals and audio-visual aids were developed.
Skills upgrading of NPB staff and industry personnel	• 196 Singaporeans, comprising NPB staff and private sector managers and consultants, were trained in Japan. • Over 15,000 individuals participated in training seminars and workshops conducted by Japanese experts.
Development of pool of consultants	• Management Guidance Centre was established in NPB to administer the various management consultancy programmes for companies. • 220 associate and referral consultants were developed to supplement NPB's efforts in reaching out to the industry.
Assistance received by companies through consultancy	• More than 200 local companies received assistance from NPB consultants and associate consultants and Japanese experts. • Over 100 companies in various industries started 5S good housekeeping practices with the assistance of NPB consultants and Japanese experts. • Over 200 companies in various industries started quality control circle (QCC) activities.

Figure 7.8: Direct Results of Productivity Development Project

Source: National Productivity Board and Japan International Cooperation Agency (1990).

Result	Details
Assistance received by companies on industry-wide basis	• 6 industries — food manufacturing, restaurant, hotel, retail, textile and garments, and finance — were assisted to tackle industry-wide issues through NPB's Productivity Management and Project Team (PROMPT) scheme using NPB consultants and Japanese experts as advisers.
Enhancement of occupational safety and health (OSH)	• Training on OSH was given to managers, supervisors and workers in various industries, thus promoting greater safety and health consciousness at the workplace.
Establishment of centre for regional training	• The Japan-ASEAN Regional Training Programme established NPB as a centre for regional training, and enhanced regional cooperation between Singapore and the other ASEAN countries.

Figure 7.8:   (*Continued*)

The immediate and direct results of PDP are summarised in Figure 7.8.

Recalling JPC's role in his memoirs, Lee Kuan Yew said (Lee, 2000):

> "I approached the Japan Productivity Centre to help us set up a centre and saw the chairman, Kohei Goshi ... He described productivity as a marathon with no finishing line. With his help over the next 10 years, we built up an effective productivity organisation that gradually got the unions and management working together on improving productivity."

Specifically on PDP, Mah Bow Tan said at its closing ceremony:

> "The PDP is a unique project in many ways ... Altogether, some 200 Japanese experts were involved. In the course of their work — training, consultancy, lectures, seminars — they reached out to many Singaporeans — CEOs, managers and workers. With their help, the NPB has developed a pool of 220 referral and associate consultants, who specialise in helping local companies. As a result of the PDP, Japanese productivity management

tools and techniques have gained widespread acceptance in Singapore companies."

Figure 7.9 summarises some representative comments from the PDP Fellows and companies that had received assistance from NPB through PDP.

From the viewpoint of Japan, the PDP implementation was also considered successful. In drawing a conclusion on PDP as well as the

PDP Fellows	Companies
"The PDP Fellowship Programme has given me a broader perspective of management consultancy, in particular on the techniques and know-how which can make management consultancy relevant to enterprises."	*"Services provided by NPB have improved the productivity of our company by 30% and enhanced our competitive edge in the market."*
Adrian Chew, Consulting Principal, ACKA Financial & Management Consultants	Steven Chan, Managing Director, Electro Magnetic (S) Ltd.
"The PDP Fellowship Programme in Management Consultancy has given me insight into the importance of good management consulting skills. The skills and experience gained are tremendously useful in my current work as a consultant."	*"The flexible wage system which NPB consultants and PDP Experts helped to establish in our company proved extremely useful in our staff recruitment and promotion exercises as it links the salary adjustment to productivity and profitability."*
Angela Ho, Manager, SHIMPO Consultancy	Lim Lay Yew, Managing Director, ESCO Group of Companies
"The PDP Training Fellowship was a challenging programme which has enabled me to benefit from the guidance and skills of the Japanese experts. This has helped me to assist companies in various productivity improvement programmes."	*"NPB staff with the assistance of Japanese PDP experts have helped our company to initiate a production monitoring system that cuts down on 'set up' time and improves the 'operation time' of our production system."*
Ramasamy Jeyapal, Senior Consultant, Pannell Kerr Forster	S. M. Loh, Deputy Managing Director, Tat Seng Paper Containers Pte Ltd.

Figure 7.9:   Comments on the Productivity Development Project

Source: National Productivity Board and Japan International Cooperation Agency (1990).

PDP Fellows	Companies
"The management consultancy programme has benefited me enormously in providing solutions to my clients' problems, not only from the financial point of view but also from the perspective of productivity, human resource, marketing and production. It has helped me to consolidate my position in the management consultancy profession."	*"The assistance rendered by NPB consultants has helped my company to achieve a reduction in overall defect rate by 6.5% and an estimated savings of $38,000 during the consultancy programme. Our company looks forward to continued support from NPB."*
Suhaimi Salleh, Managing Director, SS&A Management Consultants Pte Ltd.	Seow Poh Eng, Managing Director, Watson E. P. Industries Pte Ltd.

Figure 7.9:   (*Continued*)

Japan-Singapore Institute of Software Technology, the third-party evaluation commissioned by JICA stated (Japan International Cooperation Agency, 2000):

> *"Both of the projects, which were carried out more or less in parallel during the 1980s, were major factors in changing the industrial structure of Singapore."*

JICA's own evaluation of PDP was equally positive (Japan International Cooperation Agency, 2014):

> *"In previous decades, technical assistance by Japan had often focused on providing hardware, with skills and know-how transferred secondarily. The Singapore Productivity Development Project was noteworthy as a more holistic approach, integrating the transfer of productivity technology with business management techniques and corporate culture in a truly comprehensive management system. This holistic approach today informs JICA's activities around the world, thanks in part to the clear success of its application in Singapore."*

Besides affirming that PDP had been successfully implemented in Singapore, JICA felt that the PDP experience had strengthened its approach to international cooperation projects.

Overall, the implementation of PDP was viewed as a success by the Singapore and Japanese Governments. The same view was shared by the individuals and companies that had benefited from the programme.

Factors Underpinning the Success of the Productivity Development Project

Both JICA and NPB identified four critical factors that had contributed to the success of PDP.

First and foremost, there was high-level government support. Both the Japanese and Singapore Governments gave their full backing to PDP. In particular, Lee Kuan Yew took a personal interest in the Productivity Movement and its progress over the years.

Second, meticulous planning preceded the implementation of the various programmes under PDP. The Annual Workplan outlined the forms of know-how to be transferred to Singapore, the types of Japanese experts needed to upgrade NPB's capabilities in spearheading the Productivity Movement, and the specific roles of the experts in transferring their know-how to Singapore.

Third, a Technology Transfer Plan was formulated to outline the types of management consultancy skills that NPB needed to learn from Japan. Two categories of skills were identified, viz. core skills and specialised skills. Core skills comprised the essential generic skills and knowledge required by NPB consultants. Specialised skills covered in-depth knowledge of specific skills.

Fourth, regular monitoring and feedback sessions were conducted through the PDP Joint Committee. Regular meetings were also held between the NPB Chairman and the long-term Japanese experts to share information and agree on implementation strategies. The primary aim was to ensure that tangible results were obtained from the programmes implemented.

Lasting Legacy of the Productivity Development Project

Beyond the 7-year period in the 1980s, PDP has left a lasting legacy on the relationship between Japan and Singapore in the sphere of productivity. Following the conclusion of PDP, bilateral cooperation with JPC was formally established in December 1990 with the signing of a Memorandum of Understanding (MOU).

The tremendous respect for Kohei Goshi has continued over the years. In fact, two extracts from his letters to Lee Kuan Yew were quoted three times in all by Lee Kuan Yew and Lee Hsien Loong.[2] The first is the comparison of the Productivity Movement with a marathon with no finish line:

> *"All world class marathons are designed to test the athlete's endurance and will to win. Flat courses are inevitably followed by 'heart break hills' and any good athlete knows that you cannot maintain the same pace throughout the marathon if you expect to win."*

The second is an adage from *Guanzi*, emphasising the importance of investing in the upgrading of people:

> *"When planning for one year, there is nothing better than planting grains. When planning for ten years, there is nothing better than planting trees. When planning for a lifetime, there is nothing better than planting men."* [一年之计, 莫如树谷; 十年之计, 莫如树木; 终身之计, 莫如树人].

In his Budget Debate Round-Up Speech on 4 March 2010, Finance Minister Tharman Shanmugaratnam also referred to Kohei Goshi's statement that 'productivity is a marathon with no finish line.'

---

[2]The extracts were quoted in the speech by Prime Minister Lee Kuan Yew at Opening of Productivity Month on 1 November 1988; and in the speeches by Lee Hsien Loong as Minister for Trade and Industry at Opening of Productivity Month on 2 November 1987, and as Prime Minister at Opening of National Productivity Month on 7 October 2014.

When JPC commemorated its 50th anniversary on 1 March 2005, it requested for a special videotaped message from Lee Kuan Yew. This was an unusual request, considering that all the other messages and speeches, including one from Prime Minister Junichiro Koizumi, were in Japanese. In making the request on 9 June 2004, Yasuo Sawama, President of JPC, said:

> *"I believe that the event will be made very meaningful if your Senior Minister Mr Lee Kuan Yew, who has spearheaded productivity movement in Singapore, would kindly honor the event by sending us a video-taped message, and grace the occasion."*

Lee Kuan Yew agreed to the request for a video-message. The message is reproduced in the Amp-Box on *Message from Lee Kuan Yew on the 50th Anniversary of Japan Productivity Center*. It reflects his admiration for the Japanese worker, and gratitude to JPC and the Japanese Government for the help that they had given to Singapore over the years.

Message from Lee Kuan Yew on the 50th Anniversary of Japan Productivity Center

Ladies and Gentlemen

Good Afternoon

I have long admired the quality of the Japanese worker, his total commitment to his job. He was a major factor in Japan's miraculous recovery from the devastation of World War 2 and helped to build the world's second largest industrial economy next to America. The label "Made in Japan" now means top quality.

The Chairman of the Japan Productivity Centre, Mr Kohei Goshi, visited Singapore in 1981. I had approached him for advice on how to build a productivity movement in Singapore. He was impressive. In his mid-70s, he looked ascetic, exuded sincerity and earnestness, and was dedicated to making the Japanese workforce the best in the world. I still remember his

---

(*Continued*)

(*Continued*)

description of productivity as "a marathon with no finishing line. The key to winning this 'marathon' is a combination of inexhaustible energy and the balanced allocation of resources."

The Japanese government made a US$20 million grant to transfer Japanese productivity concepts and know-how to Singapore. Some 200 Singaporeans were trained in Japan, and a further 4,000 trained in Singapore. We have made considerable progress in the last 25 years. Our workers now participate in quality control circles and other worker contributions to improving work methods and increasing efficiency and productivity. But they have some way to go to reach Japanese standards.

We learned from the Japanese the importance of harmonious labour relations. We set out to reverse the adversarial relationship between unions and managements that we inherited from the British. We instituted a tripartite partnership in a National Wages Council of government, management and union, to harmonise relations, generate growth and share the benefits of growth through annually agreed guidelines on wage increases and other perks. These guidelines are reached by consensus between the three parties.

What we learned from the Japanese Productivity Movement, and the way Japanese industrial relations are managed in Japan have helped Singapore to create more harmonious industrial relations. This gave investors, both foreign and local, confidence to invest in Singapore for the long term.

As we travelled along the path Japan travelled, we realised that the foundation of Japanese productivity rested on its culture, one that seeks solidarity between its people and perfection in whatever the Japanese set out to do.

On behalf of Singaporeans, I want to express our gratitude for the friendship and help that the Japan Productivity Centre and the Japanese government have given us over the years. Singapore looks forward to developing further our close friendship and co-operation with Japan in the years to come.

Finally, I congratulate the Japan Productivity Movement on its 50th anniversary and wish it success.

When Lee Kuan Yew passed away on 23 March 2015, Yuzaburo Mogi, the Chairman of JPC, wrote a condolence letter to Prime Minister Lee Hsien Loong. An extract of the letter pertaining to the close relationship between Japan and Singapore is reproduced in the Amp-Box on *Extract of Condolence Letter from Japan Productivity Center on the Demise of Lee Kuan Yew.*

Extract of Condolence Letter from Japan Productivity Center on the Demise of Lee Kuan Yew

The long lasting relationship between Singapore and Japan in the productivity journey commenced the moment when H.E. Mr Lee Kuan Yew and Mr Kohei Goshi, the founder of JPC, first met in 1981. This encounter triggered the subsequent JICA supported Singapore Productivity Development Project (1983–1990) that produced remarkable outputs. H.E. Mr Lee continued to cite Mr Goshi's words in his Productivity Month speeches in every November underlining the strong bond between them. Their tight relationship is also symbolized by two identical sculptures; one sits in the SPRING Singapore office and the other in JPC."

Till this day, the Standards, Productivity and Innovation Board (SPRING), the successor of NPB, and several other agencies in Singapore continue to work closely with JPC on productivity-related matters. This speaks loudly of the strong imprint left by PDP.

IV
1990s

Chapter 8

Establishing Framework to Address Total Factor Productivity in the 1990s

"Judging from the experiences of the developed countries, the main source of Singapore's future productivity growth will have to come from improvements in Total Factor Productivity (TFP), or the efficiency with which labour and capital are used."

Lim Boon Heng
Senior Minister of State (Trade & Industry) and
Chairman, National Productivity Board
Chairman's Statement in NPB Annual Report 1992/1993

Economic Priorities in the 1990s

As a continuation of the work of the Economic Committee, the Ministry of Trade and Industry (MTI) set up the Economic Planning Committee (EPC) in December 1989. Chaired by Mah Bow Tan, Minister of State (Communications & Information and Trade & Industry) and Chairman of National Productivity Board (NPB), EPC was given the responsibility for charting a plan to take Singapore into the 21st century. Its report, *The Strategic Economic Plan*, was published in December 1991. The report identified eight strategic thrusts to propel Singapore's economic and social progress to that of a first league developed country within the next 30 to 40 years.

The eight thrusts were enhancing human resources, promoting national teamwork, becoming internationally oriented, creating a conducive climate for innovation, developing manufacturing and service clusters, spearheading economic redevelopment, maintaining international competitiveness, and reducing vulnerability.

As its focus was long-term in nature, EPC did not lay out a detailed blueprint or specifically address the directions for the 1990s. Essentially, the policies implemented in the 1990s were guided by the Government's emphasis on growing the economy, and by the broad directions from the Economic Committee. From 1990 to 1997, the economy continued to grow at a high 8.4 per cent a year. However, the growth plunged to –2.2 per cent in 1998 when the Asian Financial Crisis struck. This was due to the adverse impact of the crisis on Singapore's economy and cost competitiveness. Export of goods and services to the region was reduced because of the shrinkage of domestic demand in the regional economies. Cost competitiveness was eroded because of the sharp weakening of the regional currencies against the Singapore dollar. This caused Singapore to enter into a recession in 1998 — its second since its independence.

Similar to the situation in 1985, before the full impact of the financial crisis was felt in Singapore, a committee called the Committee on Singapore's Competitiveness (CSC) was set up in May 1997. Led by Minister for Trade and Industry Lee Yock Suan, CSC was formed to assess Singapore's economic competitiveness over the next decade and to propose strategies to strengthen it. With the impending recession brought about by the financial crisis, CSC paid attention to the immediate causes of the recession as well.

As in the 1985 recession, CSC proposed cost-cutting measures to arrest the recession. The measures comprised a reduction in the total wage costs by 15 per cent from the 1997 level, including a cut in the employers' CPF contribution from 20 per cent (partially restored from the 10 per cent after the 1985 recession) to 10 per cent again, and cuts to Government fees and charges. Following the implementation of these measures, the economy recovered strongly and faster than the other regional economies, with a high 8.9 per cent growth in 2000.

Policy Intent on Productivity in the 1990s

In the 1990s, explicit statements by the Government on the need to achieve high productivity were considerably less than those in the 1980s. Nevertheless, the need to press on with economic restructuring and continuous development of the workforce was reiterated by CSC in its report, *Committee on Singapore's Competitiveness*, published in November 1998. As stated in the report:

> " ... *we should step up capability-building and economic restructuring to make our economy more productive ... Currently, we can distinguish the more productive internationally-oriented sectors from the less productive domestically-oriented sectors. It is critical to manage this dualistic nature of the Singapore economy. We must continue to encourage restructuring and upgrading.*
>
> *As knowledge becomes obsolete faster, we also need to equip our workforce with critical enabling skills through continuous education and re-training so that we can continually re-invent ourselves.*"

Similar points were put across in *The Strategic Economic Plan*. For the strategic thrust on 'Enhancing human resources', EPC stressed:

> *"The quality of a nation's manpower is widely regarded as the most important factor in a long-term economic development. Resourcefulness, not resources, will determine success. The key ingredients of the education and training system, which are important for business competitiveness, are:*

> - *A high proportion of the population with nine to ten years of education.*
> - *A high standard of competence.*
> - *Nurturing of the right attitudes and values.*
> - *A high degree of industry relevance.*
> - *Some emphasis on technical education for innovation and foreign languages for international orientation.*
> - *Maximum opportunity and encouragement for every one in the workforce to upgrade their skills and knowledge during their entire career."*

For the strategic thrust on 'Spearheading economic redevelopment', EPC stressed:

> *"In order to continue to grow at relatively high rates, it is necessary to reorganise the way human and physical resources are managed ... These [domestic] services took up about 39 per cent of the workforce in 1989, but accounted for only 9 per cent of GDP. This domestic sector has unfortunately not benefitted significantly from the influx of foreign investments, which bring with it the latest technology and management methods. Upgrading of this sector has been substantially below that of the internationally-oriented sector where the pressure of a much more competitive environment forces companies to upgrade or suffer the consequences."*

Beyond these policy statements, the implementation of a total approach to productivity by NPB, following the Economic Committee's recommendation, gained momentum. First, a 10-year productivity plan for the 1990s was prepared. Second, the emphasis on quality was stepped up. Third, analyses of Singapore's productivity drew attention to the poor performance and, hence, the need to address it. Fourth, the formation of a new agency to succeed NPB strengthened the capabilities to adopt a total approach to productivity.

Productivity 2000 — Setting the Directions for the 1990s

Just as the *Report of the Committee on Productivity* had guided the Productivity Movement in the 1980s, the *Productivity 2000* plan was intended to set the directions for the 1990s. To develop the plan, the National Productivity Council (NPC) formed four tripartite committees in April 1989 — Committee on Labour-Management Cooperation, Committee on Management Practices, Committee on Quality Workforce and Committee on Use of Manpower. Chaired by chief executive officers (CEOs) from the private sector, the committees were given the task of examining the key issues and recommending measures for improvement. The overall goal was to achieve an average annual productivity growth of 4 per cent for the

1990s, which was the top end of the long-term target of 3–4 per cent set by the Economic Committee. It was recognised that this would have to come mainly from the qualitative aspects of productivity, i.e. total factor productivity (TFP) rather than higher capital intensity, and that the quality of the workforce was critical.

The *Productivity 2000* report was published in March 1990. It covered five factors that were considered important for raising TFP, viz. work attitudes, skills upgrading, labour-management cooperation, management practices and manpower utilisation. Figure 8.1 summarises the recommendations in the report.

Key Issue	Recommendation
Positive Work Attitudes	
i. Broadening perception of productivity	• Productivity is a total approach which begins with the right mental attitude. Broadly, it means individuals adding value to the work process in which they are involved. There should be a fundamental shift from the narrow perception of productivity as efficiency. NPB's comprehensive definition of productivity, emphasising the interaction of man, machine and systems, should be promoted. • Teamwork is a critical element of productivity. It should continue to be promoted as it will become even more important in the 1990s.
Skills Upgrading	
ii. Improving the training infrastructure	• The infrastructure of trainers, training content and instructional technology should be improved. • Training programmes should be more effective. There should be better learning opportunities, trainers, training programmes and training facilities. • Trainers should be regarded as performance managers as they are responsible for training human resources. Hence, they should have certain specific skills and competency standards.

Figure 8.1: Recommendations of Productivity 2000

Source: National Productivity Board (1990).

Key Issue	Recommendation
iii. Priming companies to train	• Employers spend about 2 per cent of payroll training 30 per cent of the workforce every year. The target for the 1990s should be 4 per cent of payroll and at least 50 per cent of the workforce trained every year. • Companies should adopt a systematic and structured approach to training. Post-employment training, both on-the-job training (OJT) and off-the-job training (off-JT), should be needs-driven. • OJT should be managed with proper direction from a trained supervisor and the aid of a structured programme. • To encourage smaller companies to train, a training voucher scheme, requiring them to pay only a percentage of the fee for approved courses, could be considered. • Incentives should be considered to step up the training of mature workers. A training leave scheme should be considered to encourage workers to train after working hours.
iv. Developing workforce flexibility	• Multi-skilling should be promoted to help workers adapt to changing job requirements amidst rapid technological advances. • Successful cases of multi-skilling should be publicised as models for others.
Labour-Management Cooperation	
v. Strengthening tripartite partnership	• Tripartite cooperation should continue to be the cornerstone of Singapore's harmonious industrial relations. The principle of tripartism should be enshrined in a Code of Industrial Relations Practices. • A body of industrial relations practitioners should be formed to enable practitioners from unions, Government and the private sector to enhance the sharing of information.
vi. Upgrading professionalism of personnel practitioners and union leaders	• Personnel practitioners form a vital link between labour and management. Hence, they should be adequately trained, knowledgeable in personnel matters, and able to provide sound advice on implementing human resource practices. A new

Figure 8.1:   (*Continued*)

Key Issue	Recommendation
	curriculum should be developed to equip personnel practitioners with the relevant skills for the 1990s. • It is the role of union leaders to educate their members on partnership skills with management, so that both can jointly implement the various company practices and programmes. An effective way of building up partnership skills is to have personnel practitioners and union leaders attend training programmes together.
vii. Managing information as a strategic resource	• Companies should build up a good information exchange and sharing system, not only between management and labour but also among the workers. • Companies should make it part of their corporate philosophy to communicate with all levels of employees, and build the necessary infrastructure to support it.
viii. Balancing the changing aspirations of employees and company objectives	• Companies should attempt to meet their employees' needs by introducing effective quality of worklife programmes that will also improve productivity. • Besides Quality Control Circles and suggestion schemes, companies should think of more innovative ways to create opportunities for their employees' personal growth. Employers should also plan career development paths for their employees. • Employers should consider various forms of flexible work schedules to meet the greater demand for more leisure and a shorter working week, bearing in mind their impact on the company's productivity and competitiveness. • Employee welfare programmes, including flexible reward systems, should address the different needs of a more educated workforce, mature workers and female workers.
Progressive Management Practices	
ix. Managing for higher productivity and competitiveness	• Companies will have to adopt progressive management practices to cope with the increasingly rapid rate of change. What is appropriate will depend on a company's stage of growth, i.e. start-up companies, established companies, and companies that are ready to go global. Each has to adopt an integrated set of

Figure 8.1: (*Continued*)

Key Issue	Recommendation
	management practices based on several fundamental principles, viz. emphasis on quality and customer satisfaction, focus on cost effectiveness, information technology management, human resource management, and flatter organisational hierarchy. Training programmes should be developed for each of the three groups of companies. Selected companies should be assisted to progress to the next stage of development, so that they can serve as models for others.
x. Cooperating to compete	• Linkages among companies will enable them to complement each other's strengths and compete with businesses from other countries. Multi-company collaboration, chain-store alliance and multi-industry collaboration should be promoted.
Effective Use of Manpower	
xi. Re-orienting perception of productive workforce	• The message that a productive workforce includes the effective use of mature workers should be promoted. A national programme teaching managers to manage and motivate their mature employees should be explored.
xii. Putting pride into service	• People should be educated on the right meaning of service, so as to improve service levels. • Self-service in certain areas should be viewed as a solution to optimise use of scarce manpower resources.

Figure 8.1: (*Continued*)

The key issues identified were very much in line with the focus on the qualitative aspects of productivity. However, the report was silent on technological advances (or technical progress), the main determinant of TFP growth.

Increasing Emphasis on Quality

The emphasis on quality, which began in the second half of the 1980s as part of the total approach to productivity, was stepped up in the 1990s. Besides the prominence given to quality in the *Productivity 2000* plan, several important quality-related developments took place in the 1990s.

Quality as Rallying Call for the 1990s

NPB made 'Reaching for Quality: Another 10 Years of Productivity, 1991–2001' its rallying call for the 1990s. As it explained in an article 'Quality Work, Quality Life. 1991 Productivity Month Campaign', published in the November 1991 issue of *Productivity Digest*:

> "*Productivity is traditionally perceived as being synonymous with efficiency, i.e. maximising output from given resources. This definition is useful as a yardstick to measure improvements at the company, industry and national levels. However, at the operational level, it must be translated into individual actions and promotion of the whole range of productivity attitudes, including pride in work, training, participation in productivity programmes and punctuality. To the workforce, these can be promoted as the different aspects of quality — a term which is readily understood and which has little negative connotations. To the management of companies, these aspects of quality will lead to higher productivity and competitiveness.*
>
> *Promoting quality will therefore lead to the goal of higher productivity. For this reason, quality will be the overarching theme for the productivity campaigns in the next ten years.*"

BERI's Quality of Workforce Index

Since 1980, the US-based Business Environment Risk Intelligence (BERI), a risk assessment agency, had been rating the labour forces of 47 countries including Singapore using its Labour Force Evaluation Measure (LFEM). The measure was based on four factors: legal framework (30%), relative productivity (30%), work attitude (25%) and availability of technical skills (15%). While these factors gave a general indication of the quality of a country's workforce, they were not sufficiently detailed for an accurate assessment. To address this shortcoming, BERI developed a new tool called Quality of Workforce Index (QWI) in 1991. This was based on 18 criteria grouped under three categories, viz. workforce performance (40%), workforce characteristics (35%) and workforce organisation and practices (25%). In conjunction with QWI, F. T. Haner, President and Founder of BERI, was invited by NPB to deliver the Singapore Productivity Lecture on 'Challenge of the 21st Century: A Quality Workforce' on 2 May 1991.

QWI resonated with the call by CSC, EPC and others to build the quality of the workforce. It also strengthened the case for focusing on quality in the Productivity Movement — including quality of the workforce, quality of work and quality of products and services. For NPB, QWI came into focus at the time when Lim Boon Heng[1] became its Chairman, taking over from Mah Bow Tan on 1 October 1991. Just before that, he was Deputy Secretary-General of NTUC and he had met F. T. Haner to discuss LFEM and issues regarding the Singapore workforce.

Because of the strong emphasis on developing the workforce, NPB changed its mission statement in 1992. Just a year before, in 1991, NPB had changed its 1989–1990 mission statement from 'To improve productivity through the cooperative actions of employers, unions and workers' to 'To have highly productive organisations through the cooperation and actions of employers, unions and the workforce,' to focus on organisations. In 1992, this swung to a focus on the workforce to become 'To develop a world-class quality workforce with a rewarding worklife.'

Renaming of National Productivity Council

In 1994, NPC was renamed the National Productivity and Quality Council (NPQC) to reflect the greater emphasis on quality. The rationale for this was explained by Deputy Prime Minister Lee

---

[1] Lim Boon Heng was appointed Senior Minister of State (Trade and Industry) in September 1991.

Hsien Loong at the Inauguration of Productivity Month 1993. He said:

> *"The National Productivity Board and Singapore Institute of Standards and Industrial Research (SISIR) are working on a National Quality Strategy. This will include initiatives to inculcate quality consciousness in the population, and initiatives to promote quality systems.*
>
> *The National Productivity Council (NPC), which comprises representatives from the government, employers, and unions, will supervise the effort. Over the last 12 years the NPC has examined productivity issues, including quality promotion as it relates to productivity. For example, its campaign slogan for this decade is 'Quality Work, Quality Life.' To reflect its greater emphasis and focus on quality, the council will be restructured and renamed the National Productivity and Quality Council (NPQC)."*

In line with the change in name, the annual *Productivity Statement*, published by NPC from 1986 to 1993, was renamed *Productivity & Quality Statement* in 1994.

Announcement of Singapore Quality Award

At the same Inauguration of Productivity Month 1993 event, Lee Hsien Loong announced the plan to launch the Singapore Quality Award (SQA).[2] Explaining the rationale, he said:

> *"The Japanese have awarded the Deming Prize since 1951. The Americans have the Malcolm Baldrige National Quality Award. The European Quality Award was instituted last year to spearhead their quality drive. The Newly Industrialising Economies (NIEs) have also been trying to build up their quality image. Taiwan, for instance, has embarked on a programme to make the label 'Made in Taiwan' synonymous with quality.*
>
> *We will institute a national quality award for companies which excel in quality. It will be called the Singapore Quality Award. The Prime*

---

[2] Initially, SQA was given to organisations for their attainment of quality excellence. In 1997, it was repositioned as the pinnacle award for business excellence.

Minister will be its patron. NPB and SISIR will launch the award with the support of several sponsoring companies in early 1995. It will confer recognition on those who have excelled in quality, and encourage others to strive to achieve it. It will symbolise the pinnacle of quality achievement for companies in Singapore. "

Findings on Singapore's Poor Performance on Total Factor Productivity

An unexpected impetus to the adoption of a total approach to productivity came from the analyses of Singapore's TFP performance by two foreign academics in the 1990s.

In comparing the productivity growth performances of Hong Kong and Singapore, Alwyn Young (1992) wrote:

"Fully 56% of the increase in output per worker in Hong Kong between 1971 and 1990 is attributable to TFP growth ... Overall, between 1970 and 1990, total factor productivity growth contributed −8% of output growth in Singapore. Capital accumulation explains 117% of the increase in output per worker in the Singaporean economy during this period ...

... Clearly, in the postwar era, both Hong Kong and Singapore experienced rapid structural transformation ... One is left with the indelible impression, however, that Singapore, which started much later, traversed many of the same industries as Hong Kong, but in a much more compressed time frame ... Economic history and empirical studies of technical change strongly suggest that new technologies do not achieve their full productive potential at their moment of invention. Experience gained in the use of new techniques seems to allow large gains in productivity by introducing a series of small improvements on otherwise unchanged technologies ... A premature movement up the technological ladder results in a fall in measured productivity. Thus, fundamentally, I am arguing that Singapore is a victim of its own targeting policies. In individual sectors, Singapore probably has experienced total factor productivity growth. This improvement in productivity, however, is masked by the further and further movement beyond the society's level of industrial maturity. "

Similarly, in debunking the belief that Asia's growth was a miracle, Paul Krugman (1994) wrote:

"Between 1966 and 1990, the Singaporean economy grew by a remarkable 8.5 percent per annum, three times as fast as the United States; per capita income grew at a 6.6 percent rate, roughly doubling every decade. This achievement seems to be a kind of economic miracle. But the miracle turns out to have been based on perspiration rather than inspiration: Singapore grew through a mobilization of resources that would have done Stalin proud ... all of Singapore's growth can be explained by increases in measured inputs. There is no sign at all of increased efficiency. In this sense, the growth of Lee Kuan Yew's Singapore is an economic twin of the growth of Stalin's Soviet Union — growth achieved purely through mobilization of resources.

... Economic growth that is based on expansion of inputs, rather than on growth in output per unit of input, is inevitably subject to diminishing returns ... So one can immediately conclude that Singapore is unlikely to achieve future growth rates comparable to those of the past."

The findings from these two analyses drew strong reactions and rebuttals from the highest level of the Singapore Government.

In the 9 October 1995 issue of *The Asian Wall Street Journal,* Urban C. Lehner wrote:

"When Stanford University economist Paul Krugman encountered Singapore's Senior Minister Lee Kuan Yew a few months ago at a meeting of J P Morgan & Co's advisers, they wasted little time on pleasantries. As both men recall it, Mr Lee launched straight into a decidedly mixed assessment of Mr Krugman's pessimistic views on growth prospects for Asia, and especially Singapore."

In his speech at the 1995/96 Productivity Campaign launch on 15 November 1995, Deputy Prime Minister Lee Hsien Loong said:

"For the last 35 years, Singapore has depended heavily on increases in labour and capital investments to fuel economic growth. Labour and

capital will continue to be important in the future. But economists question whether input-driven growth of this nature can be sustained indefinitely. Paul Krugman of Stanford University recently published an article called 'The Myth of Asia's Miracle.' He concluded that East Asia's high growth is neither a miracle nor a mystery. It can be simply explained by increases in measured inputs — i.e. labour and capital. It is therefore unsustainable, just like the high growth of the Soviet Union in the 1950s and 1960s, which also depended on massive inputs of labour and capital.

Paul Krugman's argument over-simplifies what has happened in East Asia. If the East Asian miracle is so straightforward, why have similar miracles not happened in other parts of the world? ... But Krugman has a point. As economies reach maturity, it becomes harder to increase output by raising inputs of labour and capital. With full employment, it is no longer easy to increase the labour force, by employing idle workers or redeploying underemployed ones. Heavy capital investments eventually reach the point of diminishing returns, because successive increments of more of the same yield less and less incremental results. To sustain economic growth and competitiveness, we then need to make smarter use of our labour and capital resources, and encourage innovations to achieve greater output per unit input. Economists call this Total Factor Productivity, or TFP."

Soon after, Prime Minister Goh Chok Tong addressed the same issue albeit without naming the two economists. In his keynote address at the 20th Federation of ASEAN Economic Associations (FAEA) Conference on 7 December 1995, he said:

"Recently, some Western economists have downplayed the significance of East Asian growth. They derided that most East Asian countries derived their economic growth primarily from employing more capital and labour, with little contribution from productivity ... Identifying economic growth as either input-driven or efficiency-driven, however, misses the larger point that the first priority is to get development going ... But as East Asian countries move closer to the production frontier, they would have to increasingly rely on generating ideas or technology of their own to sustain growth ... Our strategy in the past of relying on foreign capital and ideas will not be enough to see us through the new competitive economic environment of the 21st century. We will have to be more efficient and innovative. We have reached a stage where Total Factor Productivity becomes more than just a

theoretical concept. Will the Singapore economy collapse because it was puffed up by steriods as some economists believed it might? We do not think so. We will invest heavily in education and retraining, in organisation and motivation, to combine inputs with increased efficiency, new ideas and technology. Above all, we will continue to emphasise good government and right macro-economic and social policies, to entrench the virtuous circle of good government, growth and benefits."

The official Government stance seemed to suggest that the statistical analyses were too simplistic or even misguided. There was optimism that as Singapore became a more developed economy, TFP growth could be increased through appropriate policy.

Ironically, Singapore's poor TFP performance and the need to improve it had been uncovered much earlier by Singapore economists and others. As early as 1982, Tsao Yuan (1982) found that TFP in Singapore manufacturing had stagnated in the 1970s. In 1988, NPC's *Productivity Statement 1988* stated the following:

"In developed countries, TFP accounts for more than half, or 50–55%, of their GDP growth over a sustained period......Most of the economic growth [in Singapore from 1981 to 1987] was achieved by large investments in capital. Capital's contribution increased from 91.4% during 1981–84 to 118.1% for the period 1984–87. The declining growth in the workforce pulled GDP growth down by 28.8%.

Between 1981 and 1984, the contribution of TFP to economic growth was nominal (–9.5%). However, during the 1984–87 period, the TFP contribution improved significantly (10.7%) ... Our future growth will depend not only on higher value-added capital investments but also on increases in TFP."

Similarly, the need to focus on TFP was the start-point for NPC's *Productivity 2000* plan for the 1990s. The plan stated the following:

"Between 1966, a year after its independence, and 1980, Singapore attained a high annual economic growth of 10.4 per cent. This growth was achieved mainly through the promotion of new businesses, either by attracting new ones from overseas or encouraging existing ones to expand.

Increases in the use of capital and labour were the major sources of growth during this period. Contribution of total factor productivity (TFP), or the efficiency with which labour and capital are used, was minimal (4% for 1966–72, –11% for 1972–80, –2% for 1980–84, and 17% for 1984–88%). This trend was reversed in the latter part of the 1980s when the contribution of TFP to economic growth improved significantly. In the 1990s, TFP or the qualitative aspects of productivity will become more important."

Apparently, these earlier findings and statements did not strike a chord until the analyses by Alwyn Young and Paul Krugman were publicised.

Task Force on Institutional Reform for Productivity and Quality Improvements

Taking the TFP challenge seriously, MTI formed a multi-agency Task Force on Institutional Reform for Productivity and Quality Improvements in March 1995. The terms of reference of the task force were to propose the appropriate institutional reform to take Singapore's productivity growth to a new height, and to enhance Singapore's economic capability and competitiveness. The composition of the task force is shown in Figure 8.2.

The task force released its report on 1 November 1995. The report made the following observation, which was similar to the earlier analyses of Singapore's TFP performance:

> *"As Singapore progresses as an innovation-driven economy, its focus must be on the qualitative aspects of improvement to enhance total economic capabilities and competitiveness — making the best use of labour and capital resources, and putting in place systems that will encourage innovations and achieve greater output per unit input. In short, we have to focus on TFP.*
>
> *... Manpower development, economic restructuring and technical progress are the three major sources of future TFP growth. ... While SISIR's activities cover largely the technological aspect of TFP, NPB's focus is on the 'software' aspects — including workforce skills and work*

Name	Designation
Chairman	
Goh Chee Wee	Minister of State (Trade & Industry)
Coordinator	
Lee Suan Hiang	Chief Executive, NPB
Members	
Low Sin Leng	Deputy Secretary, MTI
Khoo Lee Meng	Chief Executive, SISIR
Dr Steve Lai Mun Fook	Assistant Chief Executive, SISIR
Nicky Tay	Director, Standards, SISIR
Freddy Soon	Divisional Director, NPB
Henry Heng	Divisional Director, NPB
Khoo Seok Lin	Director, Human Resources, EDB
Dr Low Teck Seng	Director, Magnetics Technology Centre
Lim Geok Hwee	Deputy Director, Planning & Research, NTUC
Secretariat	
Woon Kin Chung	Director, Planning & Research, NPB
Ellen Yeo	Head, Planning, NPB

Figure 8.2: Task Force on Institutional Reform for Productivity and Quality Improvements
Source: National Productivity Board (1995a).

attitudes; labour-management relations; and public education on pro-ductivity concepts. EDB is involved in enterprise and industry cluster development and provides various incentives for companies to upgrade themselves.

Because of the interdependence of the TFP factors, a holistic approach to managing manpower development (specifically in-employment training), economic restructuring and technical progress is required to derive maximum results.

.... In view of the above considerations, the Task Force proposes that an executive body be established under MTI with the mission of increasing Singapore's overall TFP growth, and through it, helping to enhance economic competitiveness. It will focus on in-employment training, economic restructuring and technical progress to achieve its

mission. This new agency, referred to as Singapore Productivity and Standards Board (SPSB) in this report, will integrate the functions of the present NPB and SISIR and take over the SME development function from EDB."

These points were conveyed by Lee Hsien Loong in his speech at the 1995/96 Productivity Campaign launch. In drawing the conclusion on the need to focus on TFP, he said:

"At present, both NPB and SISIR are in charge of areas related to manpower development, industry development and technology application and diffusion. EDB is also involved in enterprise and industry development, and providing various incentives for companies to upgrade. While the efforts of all these individual agencies contribute to TFP growth, they need to be coordinated and integrated properly, to prevent overlaps or gaps in our efforts.

That is why the Government has decided to merge NPB and SISIR to form the Singapore Productivity and Standards Board (SPSB). SPSB can then take a total approach to managing the key determinants of TFP. Mr Goh Chee Wee explained this two weeks ago when he released the Task Force Report on Institutional Reform for Productivity & Quality Improvements."

Formation of Singapore Productivity and Standards Board

Thereafter, the Singapore Productivity and Standards Board (PSB) was formed on 1 April 1996 through the merger of NPB and the Singapore Institute of Standards and Industrial Research (SISIR), as well as the transfer of the small and medium enterprise (SME) development function from the Economic Development Board (EDB) to the new organisation. With this merger, several of the functions that had been transferred from NPB to SISIR in 1982, when the Productivity Movement was launched, were now together again with NPB's other functions. Figure 8.3 shows the functions of PSB, as reflected in the Singapore Productivity and Standards Board Act 1995.

Compared with the functions of NPB (Figure 5.9), all of PSB's functions, except for c, were practically new or reworded. This reflected the combined responsibilities of NPB and SISIR coming together in PSB to enable it to manage TFP. Significantly, instead of

a. To raise productivity and improve competitiveness through manpower development, economic restructuring, technical progress, standardisation and any other activity considered necessary or desirable.

b. To promote, facilitate and assist in the development and upgrading of skills and expertise of persons preparing to join the workforce, persons in the workforce and persons rejoining the workforce.

c. To administer the Skills Development Fund in accordance with the Skills Development Levy Act [Cap. 306].

d. To promote, facilitate and assist in the development and upgrading of industry and enterprises and support the growth of small and medium enterprises.

e. To serve as the national standards body and to promote and facilitate the national standardisation programme and the participation of Singapore in international standardisation activities.

f. To promote and facilitate the adoption of practices that enhance the safety, efficiency and quality of products, processes and technology in industry.

g. To promote, facilitate and assist in the development, application and diffusion of technology in industry.

h. To advise the Government and industrial, commercial, trading and other organisations in respect of matters relating to productivity and standards.

i. To represent the Government internationally in respect of matters relating to productivity, standards and conformity assessment.

j. To perform such other functions as are conferred on the Board by any other written law.

Figure 8.3: Functions of Singapore Productivity and Standards Board (PSB) from 1 April 1996
Source: Singapore Productivity and Standards Board Act 1995.

NPB's function of 'to promote productivity consciousness,' PSB now had the more measurable function of 'to raise productivity and improve competitiveness.' This was made possible through the combination and integration of the competencies of NPB, SISIR and EDB's SME Development Division in the new PSB.

Lee Suan Hiang, who came on board NPB as its Chief Executive on 1 February 1995, became Chief Executive of PSB upon its formation. Over the period 16 April–6 May 1996, he announced PSB's mission and six thrusts to the media. These are summarised in Figure 8.4.

Mission (1996): To raise productivity so as to enhance Singapore's competitiveness and economic growth	
Mission (from 1997): To raise productivity so as to enhance Singapore's competitiveness and economic growth for a better quality of life for our people	
Thrust	**Strategy**
Productivity promotion	• Instilling a mindset for productivity • Fostering an environment for productivity improvement
Manpower development	• Upgrading skills to meet industry requirements • Improving utilisation of human resources
Technology application	• Promoting ownership and investment in technology • Increasing level of innovation in industry
Industry development	• Facilitating restructuring of the economy • Accelerating growth of SMEs
Standards & quality development	• Improving overseas market access • Improving quality of Singapore-made products and services
Incentives management	• Developing enterprises • Developing individuals

Figure 8.4:   PSB's Mission, Thrusts and Strategies

Source: Singapore Productivity and Standards Board, *Annual Report*, various issues.

The formation of PSB culminated the development of organisational capabilities to address Singapore's productivity growth. The organisation was now at its strongest point as a productivity competency centre. Prior to the formation of PSB, NPB had built up its capabilities with considerable assistance from the United Nations Development Programme (UNDP) in the 1970s and the Productivity Development Project (PDP) in the 1980s. With the merger of NPB and SISIR[3], the new PSB was better equipped than NPB alone in addressing Singapore's TFP growth. The contrast is clear when PSB's mission ('To raise productivity so as to enhance Singapore's competitiveness and economic growth') is compared with NPB's mission ('To develop a world-class quality workforce with a rewarding worklife'). A year later, in 1997, PSB added the words 'for a better quality of life for our people' to its mission statement to underline the ultimate outcome of raising productivity.

Publishing Statistics on TFP Performance

In view of the attention given to TFP, the Department of Statistics began to monitor and publish statistics on Singapore's TFP performance, albeit using the term multifactor productivity (MFP).[4] It started with the publication of an Occasional Paper titled *Multifactor Productivity Growth in Singapore: Concepts, Methodology and Trends* in October 1997. Subsequently, from 2000, it began publishing estimates of annual MFP growth in its *Yearbook of Statistics*.

Paying Attention to Innovation

In conjunction with the focus on TFP and the impending formation of PSB, greater attention was paid to innovation from 1995. The rationale was explained by Lee Hsien Loong in his speech at the 1995/96 Productivity Campaign launch. He said:

> *"For the last five years, the Productivity Movement has focused on the theme of promoting quality. We have emphasised work excellence, and meeting*

---

[3]Like NPB in the 1970s, SISIR received significant assistance from UNDP in the 1980s. In particular, assistance was rendered in four areas: Applied Metrology Project, Development of Institutional Capability to Provide Supporting Technical Services to Industry, Development of Materials Technology and Application Centre, and Development of Modern Chemical Centre for Materials Evaluation.

[4]As explained in the Amp-Box on *Productivity Primer* in Chapter 1, multifactor productivity (MFP) is an alternative term that is used by some analysts and institutions in place of total factor productivity (TFP).

world-class standards in products, services and work. We have made progress inculcating a quality mindset among our companies and workers ...

But trying to match the best standards in the world today will still not be good enough. By the time we achieve these standards, they will no longer be the best, because others will have made fresh breakthroughs and moved ahead. To keep abreast of others, we need to couple quality with innovation. Then, we can make qualitatively better use of labour and capital, develop breakthrough ideas that open up new frontiers, and raise TFP."

The need to focus on innovation was also elaborated by NPB in its publication *Singapore's Productivity Movement: 1995–2000. Innovation & Quality*, published in November 1995. The following points were emphasised:

"As the Singapore economy advances into the innovation phase of its development, which will be driven by new sources of growth, the Productivity Movement will once again prepare the nation for the challenges ahead ...

The challenge in the next five years is to transform the Singapore economy so as to get higher output per unit input, or higher TFP ... What is required is a total commitment to Innovation and Quality, as this is what achieving higher TFP is all about ...

While the focus on quality is a logical continuation of past efforts, the emphasis on innovation signals the need for new strategies. Quality connotes excellence and meeting of world-class standards, be it in products, services or work — a theme of the Productivity Movement in the last five years. Innovation connotes a commitment to change and the need to challenge frontiers and seek breakthrough ideas rather than incremental changes."

With the formation of PSB, the emphasis on innovation moved several notches higher.

Chapter 9

1990s: Intensification of Total Approach to Productivity

"Between 1980 and 1994, TFP growth averaged a respectable 1.1 per cent per year. For the next decade, we should aim to raise TFP growth to at least two per cent a year. This will support an overall productivity growth of four per cent, and economic growth of seven per cent."

Deputy Prime Minister Lee Hsien Loong
Launch of 1995/96 Productivity Campaign
15 November 1995

Two Periods of Productivity Drive in the 1990s

Just as in the 1980s, the productivity drive in the 1990s can be divided broadly into two periods. The first period spans the time when the National Productivity Board (NPB) was the agency responsible for productivity in Singapore until 31 March 1996. The second period covers the time from 1 April 1996 when the Singapore Productivity and Standards Board (PSB) was formed through the merger of NPB and the Singapore Institute of Standards and Industrial Research (SISIR). The formation of PSB marked the formal assignment of responsibility to a single agency for increasing Singapore's total factor productivity (TFP) growth.

Setting Specific Goals

In line with the principles of Toyota's lean production system, each of the two periods of the 1990s was guided by a set of doubling or

225

halving goals.[1] These principles were strongly advocated by Lim Boon Heng when he became the Chairman of NPB from 1 October 1991. Besides his chairmanship of NPB, he was concurrently Secretary-General of the National Trades Union Congress (NTUC) from 1 October 1993, which meant that NPB enjoyed a symbiotic relationship with NTUC. Lim Boon Heng was also well known for personally conducting productivity learning sessions for the leaders and members of the trade unions.

Vision 95

To set the directions for the productivity drive in the first period of the 1990s, NPB formulated a 3-year plan called Vision 95 in March 1992. In its *Annual Report 1991–1992*, it stated:

> *"NPB's action plan for 1992–1995, termed Vision 95, supports the Ministry of Trade and Industry (MTI)'s Strategic Economic Plan and the National Productivity Council (NPC)'s Productivity 2000 Report."*

What appeared to be misaligned, however, was its mission of 'To develop a world-class quality workforce with a rewarding work-life.' This was much narrower in scope compared with Vision 95.

The overall goal of Vision 95 was to double the 14 per cent contribution of TFP to productivity growth by the year 2000. This was an unusual goal, considering the methodological and data difficulties associated with the measurement of TFP. Nevertheless, it served as a stretch target to spur action. To attain the overall goal, the plan set out strategies for doubling current achievements in four areas: economic redevelopment of domestic industries, employee involvement, skills upgrading and quality work. The details, together with the subsequent achievements, are shown in Figure 9.1. Judged in terms of the specific vision goals, Vision 95 achieved what it was intended to do.

---

[1]Toyota Motor Corporation is famed for its lean production system, which is commonly known as Toyota Production System. A lean production system or, more broadly, a lean enterprise is one that strives to maximise value for its customers and minimise wastes and non-value added steps in all its processes. To achieve this, stretch goals such as doubling of value and halving of costs are set. See Woon and Loo (2017).

	FY92	FY93	FY94	1995
Overall Vision Goal				
Double TFP contribution to productivity by the year 2000	14%	—	—	—
Specific Vision Goals				
Focus Area 1: Economic redevelopment of domestic industries Vision Goal 1: **Double Productivity of Selected Domestic Industries by 1999**	—			Sales improvement of up to 50% achieved by 83% of franchisees converted from existing businesses
• No. of new members of economic groupings/ franchises	29	116	219	406
• No. of economic groupings (e.g. franchises) formed	9	21	36	40
Focus Area 2: Employee involvement Vision Goal 2: **Double Quality Control Circle (QCC) Participation Rate in the Private Sector to 4% by 1995**				
• QCC participation rate in the private sector	2.04%	2.59%	3.18%	3.6%
• No. of new QCC members in the private sector	5,273	11,394	19,291	32,903
• No. of workers trained in QCCs	3,713	6,464	9,343	13,567

Figure 9.1: NPB's Vision 95

Note: All figures (except those with %) from FY93 onwards are cumulative.

Source: National Productivity Board, *Annual Report 1995–1996*.

	FY92	FY93	FY94	1995
Focus Area 3: Skills upgrading Vision Goal 3: **Double Training Investment to 4% of Payroll by 1995**				
• Training as % of payroll	2.05%	3.1%	3.4%	3.6%
• No. of training places supported by Skills Development Fund (SDF)	381,716	887,726	1,381,064	1,842,715
• SDF grant commitment	$70.4m	$167m	$234.7m	$302.3m
• SDF grant disbursement (net)	$47.1m	$97.8m	$163.6m	$206.5m
Focus Area 4: Quality work Vision Goal 4: **Halve Cost of Quality by 1995**	—			9 Cost of Quality (COQ) industry-wide projects completed, with average reduction in quality costs of about 42%
• No. of new companies assisted in implementing Total Quality Process (TQP)	21	56	102	114
• No. of employees trained in TQP	3,377	6,402	12,262	18,635

Figure 9.1: (*Continued*)

Vision 2002

Similar to NPB's Vision 95, PSB formulated its Vision 2002 in 1997. In its *Annual Report 1997–1998*, it said:

> "PSB is tasked with the responsibility of sustaining Singapore's overall growth in total factor productivity (TFP) and enhancing the country's

*competitiveness. The overall target is an average productivity growth of 4%
and TFP growth of 2%. These targets are linked directly to the government's overall economic goal of a sustainable average annual GDP
(gross domestic product) growth of 7% for Singapore.... Recognising that
productivity improvement is a long-haul effort, PSB formulated five goals
in 1997. The five-year goals are aimed at helping Singapore to build up a
world-class workforce and a world-class industry."*

The details of the five goals in Vision 2002, together with the
subsequent achievements in 2002, are shown in Figure 9.2. The list
of wide-ranging vision goals was aligned with PSB's mission of 'To
raise productivity so as to enhance Singapore's competitiveness and
economic growth.'

Looking at the second column of Figure 9.2, it is difficult to
make an assessment of the overall achievement for Vision 2002. The
reason is that either the achievement figures are not available or the
indicators have been changed in some cases.

Productivity Promotion through Annual Campaign

Promoting productivity via the annual campaign continued to be an
'umbrella' strategy for creating an environment that was conducive to
implementing the various productivity initiatives. It was also an important means of reaching out to companies and the workforce through
the four phases of awareness, education, action and ownership.

More emphasis was now given to the multiple facets of productivity because of NPB's responsibility for implementing a total
approach to productivity since 1986, and especially after the formation of PSB in April 1996.

Productivity Mascot

Throughout the 1990s, Teamy continued to be used prominently as
the productivity mascot. In fact in 1994, NPB produced a publication titled *Productivity: Working It Out with Teamy*, which reproduced
the comics featured earlier in its newsletter *Singapore Productivity
News (Home Edition)*. In conjunction with the publication, NPB solicited the views of workers on their impressions of Teamy. The

	2002 (cumulative)
Overall Vision Goal	
• 2% average annual TFP growth	—
• 4% average annual productivity growth	—
Specific Vision Goals [doubling current achievements in five areas]	
1. **Building a World-class Workforce**	
• 50% of workforce with critical enabling skills	49% (FY01)
• 50% of workforce undergoing training	58% (FY02)
2. **Cultivating Commitment to Productivity**	
• 50% of workforce participating in productivity programmes	36% (FY01)
3. **Building World-class Companies**	
• 400 Singapore Quality Class organisations	336 (FY02)
• 200 promising SMEs achieving sales exceeding $30 million	143 (FY01)
4. **Developing Highly Productive Industries**	
• 10 industries with productivity level doubled	Note 1
5. **Facilitating Market Access for Singapore's Exports**	
• Certification and testing recognised in top 10 export markets	Note 2
• Internationally-aligned standards for top export sector (electronics) doubled	Note 3

Figure 9.2: PSB's Vision 2002

Notes:

1. Achievement for this goal was not reported in the Annual Reports. Proxy indicators used were: (a) businesses becoming franchisees/alliance members and shared service users (cumulative of 4972 as at end FY02); (b) no. of SMEs assisted under the Revitalisation Programme (cumulative of 1007 with estimated cost savings of $19.7 million since launch of programme); and no. of participating SMEs in Business Fusion programme (cumulative of 351).
2. Achievement for this goal was not reported in the Annual Reports.
3. This indicator was changed to '% of alignable Singapore Standards aligned with international standards' in FY2001. The achievement was within the range of 75–78% each year.
4. FY01 figures are shown for the indicators in cases where the FY02 figures are not available.

Source: Singapore Productivity and Standards Board, *Annual Report*, various years.

feedback showed that Teamy had endeared itself to many people, both young and old, over the years. The Amp-Box on *What Workers Remember of Teamy* provides the details of the feedback.

What Workers Remember of Teamy
Healthcare
"Teamy was launched in 1982 by (then) Prime Minister Lee Kuan Yew. It spread the message of hard work, team spirit, and positive attitude towards work."   Audrey Tang   Assistant Nursing Administrator   Singapore General Hospital
"There were Teamy badges and stickers, and even essay writing competitions. I think Teamy's impact on staff attitude in SGH can still be seen today."   Yee Peck Fong   Nursing Officer   Singapore General Hospital
Manufacturing
"Teamy taught the importance of being responsible and dedicated to our work — that helped me to understand what productivity was."   Habibah bte Abdul Aziz, 35   Operator (SMS Operation)   Texas Instruments Singapore
"Teamy used to appear on National floats, and ads on buses. It teaches us to work hard ...   Alice Koh Ah Ee, 46   Material Handler   Advanced Micro Devices
"....and to work smart. Now we are always looking for better ways of doing things and improving: we go through training, QCCs and we make suggestions."   Rohan bte Mohd Rajab, 24   Production Operator   Advanced Micro Devices

(Continued)

(Continued)

What Workers Remember of Teamy
"I knew Teamy from posters and newsletters distributed in school, when teachers taught the value of hard work and the importance of working as a team." Sarah Tan, 23 Planner CarnaudMetalbox Packaging
Retail
"In the retail industry, we have to work well together in order to achieve our target...." Mah Ching Wah, 17 Shop Assistant 7-Eleven   *"... Teamy is a role model for workers. It taught the importance of communication and cooperation between colleagues."* Farzana bte Ghalib Abdat, 17 Shop Assistant 7-Eleven
Transportation
"Teamy appeared on TV very often. It encouraged workers to put in their best in whatever they do. That motivates me to work hard at my job, and to do it well." Lee Fai Nam, 39 Senior Technician TIBS Motors Pte Ltd
"Teamy tells us that hard work and teamwork will be rewarded, just as bees are rewarded with the honey they make. I think Teamy has had a positive influence on the workforce." Sim Kwee Tee, 48 Bus driver Singapore Shuttle Bus Pte Ltd
Defence
"My classmates and I learned to sing the productivity song in school." Chong Kok Yew, Nicky, 24 Management Services Officer Productivity Development Consulting Ministry of Defence

(Continued)

(*Continued*)
What Workers Remember of Teamy
"I used to draw Teamy during art lessons in Primary 4. Teamy conveys the importance of trying to better oneself constantly." LCP Goh Kok Hoe, 21 Project Assistant Accounting Consulting Ministry of Defence
"I was too young to understand what productivity was, but I knew Teamy taught us to work hard and to try to solve problems we encounter." LCP Constantine Liardon, 21 Project Assistant Productivity Development Consulting Ministry of Defence
Sports
"Strive for excellence and be proud of your work — that's the message I got from Teamy." Zarinah bte Abdullah, 23 Professional Badminton Player
Source: National Productivity Board (1994).

Private Sector Steering Productivity Campaign

In 1992, NPB appointed a tripartite Productivity Campaign Steering Committee led by a high-level private sector individual. This was a symbolic move to transfer greater ownership of the Productivity Movement to the private sector, although NPB continued to play a major role in executing the campaign. However, it lasted only four years. Figure 9.3 shows the chairmanship of the Productivity Campaign Steering Committee from 1992 to 1995/96.

Campaign Themes

Unlike in the 1980s where there was a campaign slogan each year, broad themes were used in the 1990s except for the first year. These are shown in Figure 9.4.

Year	Chairman of Campaign Committee
1992	Stephen Lee, President, Singapore National Employers Federation (SNEF)
1993	Robert Chua, President, Singapore Manufacturers' Association (SMA)
1994	Tey Ban Lian, Chairman, Singapore Retailers Association (SRA)
1995/96	Patrick Giam, Chairman and CEO, IPC Corporation Ltd.

Figure 9.3: Chairmanship of Productivity Campaign Steering Committee

Source: National Productivity Board, *Annual Report,* various years.

Year	Theme
1990	100% Right — Another Satisfied Customer
1991–1994	Quality Work. Quality Life
1995–1999	Innovation and Quality
	Sub-themes
1995/96	Mastering the Best Practices
1996/97	Mastering the Best Practices
1997	*
1998	Mastering the Best Practices
1999	You Make the Difference

Figure 9.4: Productivity Campaign Themes, 1990–1999

Notes:
1. * There was no launch event in 1997.
2. Productivity Month was changed to Productivity Campaign for the period 1995/96 to 1999.
Source: National Productivity Board, *Annual Report,* various years; Singapore Productivity and Standards Board, *Annual Report,* various years.

For the period 1991–1994, the theme reflected the strong emphasis on quality. In the article 'Quality Work. Quality Life. Linking Efforts with Rewards,' published in the December 1991 issue of *Productivity Digest*, NPB said:

"The Quality Work. Quality Life. theme addresses two questions commonly asked by the workforce: What is expected of me? What's in it for me? ... The

theme will enable the workforce to view themselves more as an integral part of their company — not only in terms of work contribution but also distribution of rewards."

With the growing attention paid to innovation from 1995, innovation was coupled with quality as the theme from 1995 to 1999. In the article 'Charting New Directions for Singapore's Productivity Movement 1995–2000,' published in the November 1995 issue of *Productivity Digest*, NPB emphasised the need for the coupling:

> *"The Singapore economy has progressed from the factor-driven and investment-driven stages to the innovation-driven stage. This means that we can no longer depend on increases in labour and capital investments as our main sources of economic growth and competitiveness. Instead, we have to focus on making the best use of our labour and capital resources. In short, we require a total commitment to Innovation and Quality."*

From 1995/96 to 1998, the sub-theme 'mastering the best practices' was added to underline what companies had to do to compete effectively in the first league of developed countries. In 1999, the sub-theme 'you make the difference' was chosen to reinforce the point that every individual had a role to play in productivity improvement even as the company focused on mastering the best practices.

To convey the various themes together — productivity, quality, innovation and mastering the best practices — a Productivity Campaign Song 1998 was composed. The Amp-Box on *Productivity Campaign Song 1998* shows the lyrics of this song.

Launch of Productivity Month and Campaign

As in the 1980s, November was designated the Productivity Month from 1990 to 1994, and the launch of the Month was officiated by a ministerial-level Guest-of-Honour. The Productivity Month was changed to Productivity Campaign for the period 1995–1999 to emphasise productivity improvement as a continuous process throughout the year and not an activity that could be accomplished in one month of the year. The details are shown in Figure 9.5.

Productivity Campaign Song 1998

What we've achieved through productivity
Helps us **forge ahead** with quality
Working as one
A quality life for all

Now, we have reached a watershed
With the **right approach,**
we need to be well prepared
Giving our all
Reaching our goals, **stand tall**

We're proud
In our endeavours
We're strong
Working together
Heart & Soul
We have what it takes
Through Productivity,

There is a need to persevere
Master the **Best Practices** and
challenge new frontiers
Innovate —
We will succeed, me & you

Ready to give our best
A better **quality of life** that we can share
Master the best world class practices –
Our quest!

Singapore! Let's Rise to be the Best!

Source: Singapore Productivity and Standards Board, *Annual Report 1997–1998.*

Since April was the start of the financial year for most organisations, the financial years 1995/96 and 1996/97 were stated
explicitly in the productivity campaign. Thereafter, a decision was
made to change the launch of the campaign to April since it was
odd for it to take place after the start of the financial year. To
effect this, the year 1997 was skipped since April 1997 was too close

Year	Launch date	Guest-of-Honour (GOH)	Theme of GOH's speech
1990	1 November	Deputy Prime Minister Goh Chok Tong	Need to be productive to stay ahead
1991	1 November	Prime Minister Goh Chok Tong	10th anniversary of the Productivity Movement: sustaining our workforce as the best in the world
1992	3 November	Deputy Prime Minister and Secretary-General NTUC Ong Teng Cheong	Importance of teamwork, skills and good work attitude to productivity improvement
1993	29 October	Deputy Prime Minister Lee Hsien Loong	Need to sustain pace of upgrading and restructuring; announcement of Singapore Quality Award initiative
1994	1 November	Yeo Cheow Tong, Minister for Trade and Industry	Raising the productivity of services
1995/96	15 November	Deputy Prime Minister Lee Hsien Loong	Preparing for the challenges of a developed country
1996/97	31 October	Deputy Prime Minister Tony Tan	Boosting the Productivity Movement through mastering the best practices
1997	*		
1998	3 April	Deputy Prime Minister Lee Hsien Loong	Preparing the Singapore workforce for the challenges ahead
1999	4 April	Senior Minister Lee Kuan Yew	Productivity: every individual makes the difference

Figure 9.5:   Launch of Productivity Month and Campaign, 1990–1999

Notes:
1. * There was no launch event in 1997.
2. Productivity Month was changed to Productivity Campaign for the period 1995/96 to 1999.

Source: National Productivity Board, *Annual Report*, various years; Singapore Productivity and Standards Board, *Annual Report*, various years.

to the last launch on 31 October 1996. Although not explicit, the subsequent two years of 1998 and 1999 referred to financial years.

As in the 1980s, the Guest-of-Honour for each event launch was at a high level. One of the nine events was officiated by Prime Minister Goh Chok Tong, one by Senior Minister Lee Kuan Yew, six at the Deputy Prime Minister level and one by the Minister for Trade and Industry.

Major Initiatives Under the Six Thrusts

As stated in Chapter 8, PSB adopted six thrusts to achieve its Vision 2002 goals. These were productivity promotion, manpower development, technology application, industry development, standards & quality development, and incentives management. The major initiatives implemented under each of these thrusts are summarised in Figure 9.6. For the first period of the 1990s, the programmes were

Programme	Details
Thrust 1: Productivity Promotion	
10th Anniversary of the Productivity Movement	A series of activities was organised to mark the 10th anniversary of the Productivity Movement in 1991. The activities included the Productivity Games, promoting the key attributes of a world-class quality workforce; a TV commercial titled 'Productivity Race'; and a variety show called 'Quality Special — A Tribute to the Singapore Workforce', culminating the 10th anniversary commemoration. Two publications were also produced — *A Tribute to the Singapore Workforce* by NPB, and *The First 10 Years of the Productivity Movement in Singapore: A Review* by the National Productivity Council (NPC).
15th Anniversary of the Productivity Movement	At the inauguration of the 1996/97 Productivity Campaign, PSB gave recognition to its three tripartite partners for their significant contributions to promoting productivity in the last 15 years. The three partners were National Trades Union

Figure 9.6:   Summary of Major Programmes Under the Six Thrusts in the 1990s

Source: National Productivity Board, *Annual Report*, various years; Singapore Productivity and Standards Board, *Annual Report*, various years.

Programme	Details
	Congress (NTUC), Singapore National Employers Federation (SNEF) and the Civil Service. Recognition was also given to the Japan Productivity Center (JPC) for imparting its knowledge and expertise in the areas of quality circles, just-in-time, total quality control and other productivity improvement techniques. The Asian Productivity Organization (APO) received an award for providing an international network of support to Singapore's Productivity Movement. NPC also produced a publication titled *15th Anniversary of the Productivity Movement, 81–96.*
In-company productivity campaign and programmes	As in the 1980s, NPB/PSB worked with industry associations and employer groups to organise productivity programmes for their members. Support was also given to companies to organise their in-house activities — including quality days, productivity displays and campaign launches — in conjunction with the national productivity campaign.
Productivity zones	Productivity zones were set up for organisations in the same geographic location to jointly organise activities and to exchange information and experiences in productivity improvement. The first zone was set up in Jurong in July 1994; this was followed by another in Ang Mo Kio in July 1996.
National Productivity Award (NPA)	In 1990, NPA (Teams) was introduced. Awards were given to 37 companies, 83 individuals and 18 teams for the period 1990–1999. From 1998, NPA (Teams) was discontinued; outstanding teams were recognised through the National Quality Circle Awards instead. From 1999, instead of inviting companies to apply for NPA (Company), only those that had won the National Training Award, Excellent Service Award or National Quality Circle Award previously were considered.
Singapore Quality Award (SQA)	SQA, with the Prime Minister as its patron, was presented for the first time on 21 June 1995 to recognise quality excellence. Texas Instruments Singapore (Pte) Ltd. was the sole recipient. In 1997, SQA was repositioned as the pinnacle award for business excellence.

Figure 9.6: (*Continued*)

Programme	Details
National Best Practice Programme and Singapore Quality Class (SQC)	The programme was launched on 31 October 1996 to provide a framework for organisations to systematically improve themselves to attain world-class standards of business excellence. Following an assessment based on the Business Excellence Assessment for Continuous Improvement (BEACON) tool, companies were invited to join SQC upon achieving a certain standard. In March 1997, the Productivity On-line Benchmarking (PROBE) service was launched. This service was designed to offer companies a quick way to search for information on best practices, and to identify potential benchmarking partners through the Internet.
Productivity Push Programme (PPP) and Integrated Management of Productivity Activities (IMPACT) programme	PPP was launched by NTUC on 24 April 1988 to galvanise workers to have the right attitudes for enhancing productivity, and to work with management to raise the productivity of the company. IMPACT was the anchor programme of PPP and was aimed at helping organisations to adopt a systematic approach to productivity improvement. The programme was supported by PSB, SNEF and the Economic Development Board (EDB).
Excellent Service Award	The award was launched in March 1995 to encourage and motivate workers to deliver quality service and to raise the prestige of a career in the services trades. In the pilot phase in 1995, the award was presented to service providers in the retail, restaurant and hotel trades. This was later extended to other service industries including travel, attractions, airport and land transport.
International Management Action Award	The award was jointly launched by PSB and the Institute of Management Singapore on 27 August 1999. It aimed to recognise up-and-coming individuals who had demonstrated exceptional ability in taking management action to achieve sustainable, tangible results for an organisation, the society or the nation.
Quality Control Circles (QCCs)	In September 1992, a National QCC Task Force, comprising private sector executives, was formed to help NPB chart new strategies to increase the QCC participation in the private sector. The task force released its report on 5 April 1993.

Figure 9.6:	(*Continued*)

Programme	Details
	In July 1993, the Straits Times and NPB jointly organised the Straits Times/NPB Circle Award to recognise QCC members for their outstanding efforts.
	In 1996, PSB introduced the QCC Coaching Scheme to help non-QCC companies set up QCCs, with coaching from experienced QCC organisations.
	In November 1996, PSB removed the word 'Control' from 'Quality Control Circles' and used the term 'Quality Circles' instead. The aim was to rid the misperception that these circles were for manufacturing companies only.
	In 1997, PSB launched the National QC Database on its website. More than 1,800 records of the top award-winning QC projects at the annual conventions were captured in the database.
	In March 1998, the 1st National Quality Circle Quality Week was jointly organised by PSB and the Singapore Association of Quality Circles.
Conference on Quality Service	The first Asia-Pacific Conference on Quality, with the theme 'Quality Service — The New Competitive Edge,' was held on 7 October 1991. Jointly organised by the Singapore Institute of Management (SIM) and NPB, the conference promoted quality service in companies.
Breakfast Talks for CEOs	These talks continued to be organised for CEOs to learn from others who had successfully implemented productivity programmes in their companies.
Best-in-Management Series	This series of lectures, targeted at top management of companies, was launched in March 1993. Prominent speakers included Michael Porter of Harvard Business School and Nicolas Hayek of Swiss Corporation for Microelectronics and Watchmaking.
Mentoring Scheme	Launched in July 1996, this scheme enabled organisations to tap the know-how of others in one or more areas of productivity improvement. These areas included on-the-job training, suggestion scheme, 5S good housekeeping, total quality process and cost of quality.

Figure 9.6:   (*Continued*)

Programme	Details
Industrial Relations Society (Singapore)	The Society, with secretariat support from NPB, was set up in January 1991 to promote and strengthen tripartite cooperation in Singapore. A governing council, comprising members from the Government, unions and the private sector, was formed to manage the society.
Corporate Membership Scheme	NPB introduced the scheme on 4 May 1991 to garner the commitment of chief executive officers (CEOs) to the productivity drive. The corporate members were kept abreast of the latest productivity issues through the CEO Breakfast Talks and selected conferences and seminars. In June 1991, *Corporate Membership Series*, a monthly publication featuring articles of current interest, was launched as an added service to the members.
Productivity Digest	A Chinese version of *Productivity Digest* was introduced jointly by PSB and Singapore Chinese Chamber of Commerce & Industry (SCCCI) in January 1998. The bi-monthly publication was distributed to 4000 SCCCI members together with *Chinese Enterprise*, SCCCI's flagship publication.
Singapore Productivity Casebook	The first *Singapore Productivity Casebook* was launched on 28 April 1995. Jointly produced by PSB and Nanyang Technological University (NTU), the publication featured the productivity practices of leading companies in the areas of quality management, human resource development, technology and innovation. A second casebook, jointly produced by PSB and National University of Singapore (NUS), was launched in October 1995.
National Innovation Framework for Action	In line with the growing emphasis on innovation, the framework was launched at the National Innovation Forum on 7 January 1998 to nurture innovation in Singapore. It was developed jointly by PSB, EDB and National Science and Technology Board (NSTB), with inputs from the industry and agencies such as Construction Industry Development Board (CIDB), National Computer Board (NCB) and Trade Development Board (TDB).

Figure 9.6: (*Continued*)

Programme	Details
Thrust 2: Manpower Development	
Report on 'A World Class Trainer Infrastructure'	NPB released the report in October 1991, culminating the work of an Advisory Panel on Trainers formed in April 1990. The report made major recommendations to upgrade the trainer infrastructure in five key areas: trainer population, training experts, trainer skills standards, respect and recognition for trainers, and training institution network.
OJT 2000 Plan & OJT 21	An OJT 2000 Plan was announced in October 1993 to make on-the-job training (OJT) another pillar in the training infrastructure to improve the quality of the workforce. This later evolved into OJT 21, which was launched on 21 January 2000.
Continuing Education and Training (CET) Committee	A national CET committee was formed in 1997 to review the adequacy of the CET infrastructure in Singapore. The findings and recommendations were submitted to the Cabinet.
Training partnerships	NPB/PSB continued to partner reputable organisations to set up training centres and programmes for the industry. These included Motorola-NPB Training Design Centre (May 1990), Andersen Consulting-NPB Training Technology Centre (October 1990), NPB-SMA Total Quality Process (TQP) programme (November 1990), NPB-Philips Industrial Engineering Programme (January 1991), Work Induction Programme (June 1991) jointly developed by NPB, SNEF and AT&T Microelectronics, McDonald's-NPB Supervisor Orientation Programme (1991), Seiko Instruments-NPB National On-the-Job-Training (OJT) package (July 1991), Prima-NPB Bakery Industry Training Centre (1992), Johnson & Johnson-NPB Company Wellness Centre (May 1992), and Fuji Xerox-NPB Benchmarking Centre (November 1993).
Service Quality Centre	NPB partnered Singapore Airlines in July 1990 to set up the Service Quality (SQ) Centre to provide a comprehensive suite of programmes to train the workforce on service skills.
START	To help mid-career workers overcome their fear of failure, build learning confidence and learn study skills, NPB launched a video-based Learning to Learn programme called START ('Start Training and Re-training') in June 1994.

Figure 9.6: (*Continued*)

Programme	Details
BacktoWork	The programme was a major initiative by the Ministry of Labour (MOL) and PSB, supported by NTUC and SNEF. It was launched on 13 September 1996. The aim was to encourage economically inactive persons such as housewives, retirees and retrenched workers to re-enter the workforce.
Trainer-Manager programme	Launched on 3 September 1992, this was the first national programme to help managers make training part of their responsibilities.
National Supervisors Conference	NPB organised the conference on 8–9 November 1994. This was the first time that such a conference had been organised for supervisors in the manufacturing and service sectors to keep them abreast of skills required for effective supervision.
8 Pillars of Supervision programme	This national programme for successful supervision was launched in August 1995. The 8 pillars were role of a supervisor, communicating for results, leadership and influencing skills, managing work performance, managing change, internal partnership for service excellence, problem solving skills, and productivity & quality improvement.
Critical Enabling Skills Training (CREST)	Launched on 3 November 1998, the programme aimed to equip the workforce with a set of skills to cope with changing workplace demands. The set comprised seven skills identified as critical enablers: learning-to learn, literacy, listening & oral communication, problem-solving & creativity, personal effectiveness, group effectiveness, and organisational effectiveness and leadership.
FAST FORWARD	Launched on 26 June 1990, FAST FORWARD was unique in its use of teletechnology (television, video, audio, telephone and print) for instruction. The aim was to increase training opportunities for the workforce by making training more accessible and learning schedules more flexible.
People Developer Standard (PDS)	Launched on 11 December 1997, PDS aimed to help companies take a systematic approach to staff training and career development. It became the standard for human resources development.
Job Redesign 21	Launched in 1997, the programme aimed to develop labour utilisation consciousness and help companies redesign jobs to improve labour utilisation and productivity.

Figure 9.6: (*Continued*)

Programme	Details
Industry Capability Upgrading (ICP) Plan	To enhance the capability of the workforce on an industry-wide basis, PSB launched the plan on 24 November 1999. The specific objectives were to identify emerging trends and new skills requirements of the key industries, and facilitate the development of new training programmes for enhancing workforce capability.
Manpower Bulletin	A quarterly *Manpower Bulletin* was launched in November 1997 as a mechanism to alert managers and decision-makers on key manpower trends. In January 2000, Manpower Bulletin Online was launched to complement the printed version.
The Training Shop	NPB opened The Training Shop at Parkway Parade Shopping Centre on 26 October 1990. With information as its main 'merchandise' (e.g. training courses, how to choose the appropriate courses and how to apply for courses), The Training Shop aimed to market training as a mass consumer product. Training and productivity-related products, such as publications, videos, multimedia training packages and training aids, were sold in the shop. Another branch was also opened at the NTUC Pasir Ris Resort.
PSB Institute for Productivity Training (IPT)	IPT continued to offer companies and individuals a broad spectrum of courses aimed at improving productivity and functional skills. These included certificate, diploma and advanced diploma and degree programmes; in-company programmes; and workshops. Supervisory training was enhanced in 1995 in view of the important role played by supervisors as 1st-line management in companies. Each year, about 25,000 individuals were trained by IPT.
Thrust 3: Technology Application	
Industry-wide technology diffusion	The programme aimed to facilitate the application of technology in industry. The first phase of the Marine Technology Programme was completed in 1996, and the second phase was launched in 1997. In July 1997, the Logistics Enhancement and Application Programme 21 (LEAP 21) was launched. Technical assistance-related work was also initiated in other industries such as aerospace and disk drive.

Figure 9.6: *(Continued)*

Programme	Details
Technology application solutions	PSB's laboratories undertook a wide range of projects involving the application of technology to help companies in their business operations and product development. These included a solution for precision optical coating manufacturers, application of resin transfer moulding in the manufacture of aerospace components, food preservation and extension of food shelf life, and development of flavourings catering to Asian tastebuds.
MOU on Green Productivity	PSB signed a memorandum of understanding (MOU) with NTU on 6 September 1999 to jointly work on environmental management, environmental engineering and green productivity projects.
Industrial design and product development	The programme helped companies to design and develop innovative products. These included the design of an electronic ballast which consumed less energy and yet offered better lighting than the conventional wire-wounded chokes in fluorescent lights, and design and development of a machine that partially automated the making of rice dumplings.
Automation for higher productivity	The programme aimed to help companies implement cost-effective, robust and total automation solutions to reduce labour content and produce consistently high quality output.
Precision Engineering Application Centre	The Centre, housed within PSB, was officially opened on 5 April 1999. Its aim was to boost the capabilities of the precision engineering industry.
Technology collaborations	Apart from using the expertise of local research institutes, PSB collaborated with overseas technology organisations. In 1997, an agreement was signed with TNO (Netherlands Organisation for Applied Scientific Research) to work on product design, precision engineering, food technology and product testing. This was the second agreement with an overseas technology organisation, the first being with Fraunhofer Gesellschaft of Germany.
National Patent Information Centre (NPIC)	NPIC was set up in September 1996 to provide information and advice on patents and intellectual property.

Figure 9.6: (*Continued*)

Programme	Details
Thrust 4: Industry Development	
Management guidance and productivity upgrading services	Throughout the 1990s, management guidance (under NPB) and productivity upgrading services (under PSB) were provided to companies, particularly small and medium enterprises (SMEs), to help them upgrade. The areas covered were wide-ranging, including industrial & operations engineering, human resource development, total quality management, cost of quality and productivity measurement.
Strategic alliances with industry associations	Strategic alliances with the key industry associations were established to launch joint initiatives for the respective industries. These included alliances with Singapore Confederation of Industries (SCI) (26 September 1996), SNEF (25 November 1996) and SCCCI (16 March 1999).
Productivity Management and Project Team (PROMPT)	The PROMPT initiative was extended to two other industries in 1991 — precision tooling and furniture manufacturing.
Franchising and economic groupings programme	Through the programme, companies were encouraged to upgrade by joining franchises or economic groupings. The first franchise programme, named TRAVELNET for the travel industry, started on 6 March 1991. Subsequently, economic groupings in trades such as electrical appliance, coffee shop, furniture, and laundry and dry cleaning were launched.
Business Fusion programme	The programme was initiated in September 1999 to bring together SMEs in the same value chain so that they could share knowledge, experience and ideas, and jointly develop new and innovative products and services. The trades included motor workshops, industrial tool calibration and silk screen-printing.
Management of Economic Group Assistance (MEGA) Scheme	On 8 December 1992, NPB and EDB jointly launched the MEGA Scheme to promote the formation of economic groupings among small local companies. The Scheme comprised three components, viz. funding for consultancy work, funding for employment of economic group manager, and funding for training of economic group members.

Figure 9.6:   (*Continued*)

Programme	Details
Industry Productivity Programme	Launched in 1999, the programme aimed to achieve maximum economic growth and long-term competitiveness of the economy through the development of productive industries — e.g. construction, food and beverage, logistics, precision engineering and retail.
Transformation projects for local industries	Several transformation projects were initiated from 1997 for the domestic industries — including hotel, healthcare, furniture, chemical, health spa, shipping suppliers and commercial cleaning.
Relocation Upgrading Programme	PSB launched the programme in September 1998, with Housing & Development Board (HDB) and Jurong Town Corporation (JTC) as its partners. The programme comprised an assistance package to help SMEs optimise factory layout, upgrade operations and enhance business upon their relocation from the older HDB and JTC industrial estates to new premises.
Woodlands Relocation Project	Initiated between JTC and PSB in 1996, the project aimed to assist the productivity upgrading of SMEs through a special package designed for the tenants relocating to new premises.
Total Quality Process (TQP)	In April 1991, NPB launched a training-cum-consultancy package on TQP to train managers, supervisors and workers, and to provide consultancy to companies to adopt an integrated company-wide approach to quality. The package, designed by Philip Crosby Associates, was jointly developed by NPB and SMA.
National Cost of Quality (NCOQ) Programme	In October 1998, PSB launched the NCOQ programme to help local businesses, especially SMEs, improve their resource management capabilities. On 19 January 1999, the first National Cost of Quality Conference, featuring speakers from the United States, Japan, Sweden and Singapore, was organised.
ShopNet	On 2 May 1996, NPB launched ShopNet together with NCB. A computer network linking retailers to suppliers, ShopNet covered sales counter operations, stock control, as well as all electronic transactions between the shops and the suppliers.
1st-stop centre for SMEs (SME First Stop)	A 1st-stop centre for SMEs was set up in 1996 to integrate the Government's efforts in upgrading and developing the local enterprise sector.

Figure 9.6:   (*Continued*)

Programme	Details
Promising SME Development Programme	Initiated in April 1996, the programme aimed to provide focused assistance to accelerate the growth of SMEs with the potential to develop into larger local enterprises and eventually regional companies.
Business. Connect	Introduced in 1996, the programme helped local enterprises to seek out and forge business partnerships with foreign companies with complementary capabilities. Supporting Business. Connect was SingaporeConnect, a business-matching service on the Internet.
ASEAN-EU Partenariat	This large-scale business matchmaking event, jointly initiated by the European Union (EU) and Association of Southeast Asian Nations (ASEAN), was held on 10–11 November 1997. It involved 560 SMEs (200 from Singapore) from 20 countries in the EU and ASEAN. The event was organised by a multi-agency committee led by PSB and comprising Ministry of Trade and Industry (MTI), Ministry of Foreign Affairs (MFA), Singapore Tourism Board (STB) and TDB.
Enterprise Development Growth and Expansion (EDGE) programme	Announced in 1998, the programme aimed to give SME entrepreneurs practical training on management skills to develop, grow and expand their business.
Shared Services for SMEs (Triple S) programme	The programme was launched on 25 November 1999 to help SMEs gain economies of scale and lower business costs by using shared services for business functions like procurement, human resource management, accounting and logistics.
Information for Business (In.Biz)	The multi-agency programme aimed to provide an integrated information service to the business community. It was launched on 13 November 1998.
Enterprise newsletter	A monthly newsletter to promote local enterprise development, *The Singapore Enterprise* was launched in 1997. In June 1998, it became a bilingual publication with articles in English and Chinese. The publication was jointly published by PSB, EDB, Enterprise Promotion Centres, NCB, NSTB, STPB and TDB.

Figure 9.6: (*Continued*)

Programme	Details
Zaobao Consultancy Award for Local Companies	Introduced in June 1990 by NPB and Lianhe Zaobao, the award recognised groups, each comprising an outstanding local company, a consultancy company and consultant(s), for their successful completion of consultancy projects. The aim was to highlight local companies which had sought external help and benefited from consultancy, and to project the credibility of consultants in helping companies to improve their productivity.
Thrust 5: Standards & Quality Development	
Standards Council Award	Awards were presented to standards volunteers to recognise their significant contribution to the national standardisation programme. For the first time, the Standardisation Recognition (StaR) Award was given out in 1997 to recognise organisations for their high level of support for the standardisation programme.
Publications	In 1997, *Measurement Matters*, a quarterly newsletter to raise awareness of measurement and its importance to quality and technology in industry, was published. *Standards News* was renamed *Standards and Testing News* to cover testing news as well. Its frequency was also increased from quarterly to bimonthly.
Standards Implementation for Productivity (SIP)	With the formation of PSB, greater emphasis was given to the role of standards in raising productivity, even though quality, safety and health continued to be key priorities for standardisation. An example of a SIP project facilitated by PSB is the standardisation of pallet sizes in the fast-moving consumer goods industry, particularly supermarkets and grocery retailers.
Quality Management System certification schemes	PSB offered various national quality management system certification schemes to help companies bring their goods and services up to international standards. These included the ISO 14000 certification scheme, launched in May 1996 to certify organisations for their commitment to environmental management; the QS 9000 certification scheme, launched in June 1997 to certify automotive suppliers to the mandatory requirements of the 'Big Three' American car makers (General Motors, Ford and Chrysler); the Hazard Analysis Critical Control Point (HACCP) certification system, launched in September 1998; and the Occupational Health and Safety Management System certification scheme, launched on 26 October 1999.

Figure 9.6:   (*Continued*)

Programme	Details
Product Listing Scheme (PLS)	PLS was launched in December 1999. Under the scheme, products tested and found to comply with the relevant safety and performance standards were listed in *Directory of PSB Certified Products under PLS* and issued with a PSB Certificate of Compliance.
Testing products to world standards	As an established and internationally-recognised testing body, PSB continued to provide testing services in different areas, e.g. MRT tunnel lining, Electronic Road Pricing system and HACCP. Under the PSB (Singapore Quality Mark) Certification Scheme, the Singapore Quality Mark was issued to products that had met either a national or international standard of quality performance.
Agreements with Overseas Certification Bodies	As a member of International Certification Network (IQNet), an international fraternity of 26 major national certification bodies, PSB continued to issue IQNet certificates to companies. PSB continued to sign MOUs with reputable overseas certification bodies to eliminate the need for products to be re-certified in overseas markets. These included the MOU with the Japan Audit and Certification Organisation on ISO 14000 environmental certification in 1997, and the product testing agreement with Laboratoir Central Des Industrial Electriques (LCIE) of France in 1998.
Asia-Pacific Laboratory Accreditation Cooperation (APLAC) multilateral mutual recognition arrangement	November 1997 marked the conclusion of the 1st-ever APLAC arrangement, of which the Singapore Laboratory Accreditation Scheme (SINGLAS) was a founding signatory. Involving seven laboratory accreditation bodies in six Asia-Pacific economies, the arrangement provided for mutual recognition of laboratories accredited by each other, thus facilitating cross-border trade between the economies.

Figure 9.6:   (*Continued*)

Programme	Details
Thrust 6: Incentives Management	
Amendment of Skills Development Levy Act to widen definition of grant beneficiaries	The Act was amended on 1 November 1996 to widen the definition of grant beneficiaries of SDF to include the self-employed, contract workers and those seeking employment. The funding criteria were also tweaked over the years to meet the needs of companies and the workforce. For example, in 1999, SDF implemented a revised funding approach based on three main areas, viz. broad-based skills training, certifiable skills training and training in high-end pioneering areas.
Higher-end Skills Training	To support the cluster development strategy outlined in *The Strategic Economic Plan*, SDF worked closely with employers, training providers, EDB and Institute of Technical Education (ITE) from 1992 to develop critical skills required for the strategic clusters.
Training Leave Scheme	As some workers might not be able to attend training after working hours due to family and work commitments, the Training Leave Scheme was launched by SDF in February 1990 to encourage companies to send their employees for training during office hours.
Training Voucher Scheme	Launched in February 1990, the scheme enabled employers to pay only the balance of the course fees after SDF support. This was done by presenting to the training providers the vouchers indicating the percentage of SDF support.
Retraining Voucher Scheme	The scheme was introduced in 1994 to encourage the training of retrenched workers. The workers were trained in the START programme and job-matched with available job vacancies.
Total Company Training Plan (TCTP)	TCTP was launched on 23 October 1996. Replacing the Worker Training Plan scheme, it aimed to encourage companies to adopt a total and systematic approach to training for all levels of staff.
Skills Redevelopment Programme (SRP)	Launched on 20 December 1996, the programme aimed to enhance the employability of workers, particularly those with low skills and low educational qualifications, through skills certification. It was initiated by NTUC, with the support of PSB, EDB and ITE. Funding support was provided by SDF.

Figure 9.6: (*Continued*)

Programme	Details
Local Enterprise Finance Scheme (LEFS) and Local Enterprise Technical Assistance Scheme (LETAS)	With the transfer of the SME development function from EDB to PSB on 1 April 1996, the administration of LEFS and LETAS was transferred as well. In view of the increasing size of local enterprises, the qualifying criterion for LEFS and LETAS was raised from $12m net fixed assets to $15m. In addition, the eligibility criterion on maximum employment size was raised from 100 to 200. The Government's risk sharing was raised from 50% to 70% for LEFS loans advanced by the participating financial institutions (PFIs).
	To encourage SMEs to upgrade and modernise their operations through professional help, PSB increased the LETAS grant quantum for local enterprises with less than $5m fixed assets from 50% to 70% of the allowable cost of engaging an external consultant. A new programme called Consultancy-led Implementation Programme was also launched to assist the larger enterprises, defined as those with turnover of $10m or more. This programme enabled the larger enterprises to engage professionals and consultants to implement their strategic plans.
	Over the years, the funding criteria were tweaked further to take into account the economic environment and the needs of the companies.
Supporting Initiatives	
Research	As in the 1980s, research was a major part of the work of NPB/PSB. The studies undertaken were wide-ranging, e.g. scope of productivity, productivity-wage linkage, employee benefits and quality of worklife, managing productivity in Singapore's multi-cultural environment, and training-productivity linkage.
NUS-PSB Productivity Research Centre	The centre was set up in the NUS Faculty of Business Administration in November 1993 to undertake productivity research using a multi-disciplinary approach.

Figure 9.6: (*Continued*)

mainly under the thrusts of productivity promotion, manpower development, industry development and incentives management.

From the long list of initiatives, it can be concluded that the scope, scale and intensity of activities were stepped up considerably since the formation of PSB on 1 April 1996. This was in line with PSB's responsibility for TFP in Singapore. Nevertheless, in summarising the progress made after 18 years of the Productivity Movement, the National Productivity and Quality Council (NPQC) zoomed in on seven areas. These are summarised in Figure 9.7.

Area	Achievement
Understanding of productivity	As early as 1990, 90% of the workforce had correctly related productivity to good work attitudes, quality improvement and working more efficiently. In 1986, the figure was only 40%.
Action taken to improve productivity	The proportion of the workforce who took action to improve productivity jumped from 54% in 1986 to 91% in 1990.
Participation in productivity programmes	Participation in QCCs shot up from 0.4% of the workforce in 1983 to 9.9% in 1998.
Labour-management cooperation	The number of disputes referred to the Industrial Arbitration Court fell sharply from 122 in 1980 to less than 20 since 1993.
Skills upgrading	Between 1981 and 1998, the annual number of training places supported by SDF increased by more than 17 times, from 32,600 to 564,400. In 1998, employers invested an average of 3.6% of their payroll in training, double the 1.8% in 1988.
Quality management and business excellence	Nine industry-wide projects to reduce the cost of quality were completed. On average, the industries achieved a 42% reduction in quality costs. Targeted especially at SMEs, the TQP package had trained 28,000 managers and staff as at 1998. As at 1998, 110 organisations had become members of SQC, and 5 had won SQA.
Economic groupings	As at 1998, a total of 60 franchises and 8 economic groupings had been formed in 39 trades, with 712 participating members. Through franchising, 8 out of 10 members achieved better sales and 7 out of 10 saw increases in profits.

Figure 9.7:   Progress Made in the Productivity Movement After 18 Years

Source: National Productivity and Quality Council (1999).

Productivity Drive in the 1990s in Retrospect

If the decade of the 1980s is viewed as the golden era of the national productivity drive, the 1990s may be considered the peak of that era. Compared with the 1980s, there were less explicit statements by the Government on the need to achieve high productivity. Nevertheless, both the Economic Planning Committee and the Committee on Singapore's Competitiveness emphasised the need to press on with economic restructuring and continuous development of the work-force. In terms of specific directions for the 1990s, NPC prepared a 10-year productivity plan. To address TFP holistically, PSB was formed through the merger of NPB and SISIR. This culminated the development of organisational capabilities to address Singapore's productivity growth. As regards Government support, the Productivity Movement continued to receive the highest level of support.

However, just as in the 1980s, the labour force continued to grow, mainly through the import of foreign labour. From 1.54 million in 1990, with a foreign labour share of 16.1 per cent, the labour force grew to 2.09 million in 2000, with a foreign labour share that shot up to 28.1 per cent. For the 1990s as a whole, the average annual productivity growth was 3 per cent, at the lower end of the 3–4 per cent projected by the Economic Committee. This contributed 43 per cent to the average annual gross domestic product (GDP) growth of 6.9 per cent during this period, comparable to the 41 per cent in the 1970s albeit lower than the 60 per cent in the 1980s.

V

2000s

Chapter 10

Shifting Productivity Gears in the 2000s

"Having successfully completed the first lap of the Productivity Movement over the last two decades, we must now, together, run the next lap, to be an innovation-driven economy. This is a major transition that we are undergoing — a major change of gears in our economy."

President S. R. Nathan
National Productivity Rally 2002
3 December 2002

Economic Priorities in the 2000s

Although the Singapore economy recovered fully in 2000 after the 1997 Asian Economic Crisis, it was soon thrust into the first decade of the new millennium that was marked by great volatility and uncertainty. First, there were the global electronics downturn and the dot .com crash in 2001. This was followed by the SARS[1] outbreak in 2003 and the global financial crisis in 2007–2008, both of which had devastating effects on economies throughout the world. To counter the impact of these events on the economy, the Government gave high priority to seizing growth opportunities whenever the global conditions were favourable.

The clearest statement of the Government's focus on seizing opportunities for economic growth in the 2000s was made by

---

[1] This is the short form that is commonly used for 'severe acute respiratory syndrome.'

Prime Minister Lee Hsien Loong. In his 2006 National Day Rally, he said:

> *"I think that when the conditions are good and the sun is shining, we should go for it, as fast as we can, as much as we can. Get the growth, put it under our belt, put it aside a little bit, so when the thunderstorm comes again, we will be ready."*

Similarly, in retrospect, Finance Minister Tharman Shanmugaratnam said in his 2010 Budget Statement:

> *"Much of our growth in the last 10 years took place from 2004 to 2007, when our GDP grew an average of 8% per year. We were able to achieve this because companies could obtain the workers they needed to seize opportunities to expand while the environment was favourable ... Our workforce grew rapidly over those four years, by 5% per year, with foreigners accounting for about half of the growth.*
>
> *By going for growth when the conditions allowed, we offset the downturns we experienced earlier in the decade ... The upshot is that by allowing in foreign workers so that we could go for growth in the good years, we reduced unemployment, and raised wages for Singaporeans after the standstill in the first part of the decade ... This was therefore not a strategy of 'growth at all costs', but of growing our economy to raise Singaporean incomes."*

As in the 1980s and 1990s, the Government also kept an eye on the long-term direction for the economy. This was done through the Economic Review Committee (ERC), formed in December 2001. Chaired by Deputy Prime Minister and Minister for Finance Lee Hsien Loong, ERC was given the task of reviewing the current policies and proposing strategies to promote the further growth and development of the economy. The *Report of the Economic Review Committee* was published in February 2003 and was intended to serve as the economic roadmap for the next 15 years. On the expected growth rates in the future, ERC said:

> *"We believe that going forward, our sustainable growth rate would be 3–5 per cent per annum, barring external shocks. This comprises labour force growth of 1–2 per cent and productivity growth of 2–3 per cent."*

To realise this, ERC painted the vision of Singapore being a globalised, entrepreneurial and diversified economy. While addressing the strategic challenges linked to this vision, ERC also tackled the 2001 recession which had contracted the economy by 1 per cent. Like the previous two decades, containment of business costs received top priority. It recommended that any further restoration of the Central Provident Fund (CPF) contribution rate, beyond its current level of 36 per cent, be deferred for two years, and that land and other business costs be managed to maintain cost competitiveness. Following the various measures taken by the Government, the economy recovered quickly with a growth of 4.2 per cent in 2002.

Similarly, with the various measures taken by the Government, including business cost containment and assistance packages, the economy recovered swiftly from the global financial crisis in 2007–2008. Following the collapse of Lehman Brothers in September 2008, Singapore was one of the first Asian countries that had slipped into recession, with a 0.6 per cent contraction of its gross domestic product (GDP) in 2009. However, to the surprise of many analysts and the Government itself, the economy rebounded strongly in 2010 with a growth of 15.2 per cent.

Policy Intent on Productivity in the 2000s

In view of the emphasis on growth in the 2000s, the policy intent on productivity was subdued in comparison with the 1980s and 1990s. Like the *Committee on Singapore's Competitiveness, The Report of the Economic Review Committee* emphasised the need to press on with economic restructuring and continuous development of the workforce. The report stressed:

> *"Restructuring will speed up. There will be more changes to our economy, more companies turning over ... Economic restructuring will inevitably have a major impact on Singaporeans. Job displacements will be more frequent, and employment structure and work arrangements will need to respond flexibly to change. Structural unemployment will be a growing problem, as people whose skills have become redundant fail to find new jobs. We must manage the dislocation and difficulties that economic*

restructuring will bring, and help Singaporeans make the urgent and essential changes.

Training and retraining remain critical to helping Singaporeans upgrade and update their skills, and ensure that they remain employable. The ERC recommends that the Government set up a national Continuing Education and Training (CET) body to oversee the promotion and development of CET in Singapore."

However, the Government's attention turned much more to innovation in the early 2000s. The emphasis on innovation was a culmination of the focus on total factor productivity (TFP), i.e. the qualitative aspects of productivity, and innovation in the 1990s. It was a time when the notion of a new economy, also known as knowledge-based economy (KBE) and innovation-driven economy, was bandied about as the norm in the new millennium. This contrasted with the old economy of the previous millennium that was driven more, as well as constrained, by physical resources. In this context, the concept of national innovative capacity, advanced by Michael Porter of Harvard University and Scott Stern of Northwestern University and the Brookings Institution, came into prominence. This concept was included in *The Global Competitiveness Report 2001–2002*, published by World Economic Forum, and put forward as a major determinant of a country's competitiveness.

ProAct 21: Plan for Innovation-Driven Economy

To prepare Singapore for the innovation-driven phase of development, the National Productivity and Quality Council (NPQC) developed a 10-year plan called ProAct 21 (short for Productivity Action 21).[2] The *ProAct 21* report, released on 6 December 1999, stated its intent as follows:

"The ability to sustain high productivity growth in the innovation-driven phase of development will depend on how well Singapore is able

---

[2]The ProAct 21 name was chosen at a time when many other '21' plans, connoting plans for the 21st century, were being formulated. These included Industry 21, Manpower 21, Retail 21, SME 21, Technopreneurship 21, Tourism 21 and Trade 21.

to manage TFP in the new environment of the next millennium ... Productivity Action 21 (ProAct 21) is a 10-year plan that will build up the capabilities of the workforce and organisations to steer Singapore into the next millennium through strong and sustained productivity growth ... The vision of ProAct 21 is for Singapore to become a knowledge-based economy deriving its competitive edge from productivity. The strategies to achieve this are geared towards building a world-class workforce and world-class industry by providing the right environment and infrastructure."

This intent was elaborated by Lee Suan Hiang, Chief Executive of Singapore Productivity and Standards Board (PSB), in conjunction with the release of *ProAct 21*. He said:

"As Singapore progresses from an industrial economy to a knowledge-based economy, our workforce and organisations must possess world-class capabilities to help maintain Singapore's competitiveness. Since 1980, Singapore's workforce has been rated top by the Business Environment Risk Intelligence (BERI). But there are certain weak areas such as technical skills and work attitudes. The goal is to maintain the top ranking by international agencies such as BERI and make improvements in all aspects of workforce development. In terms of industry and service productivity, Singapore was ranked 20th and 19th respectively in the 1999 World Competitiveness Yearbook. ProAct 21 aims to propel Singapore into the top ranks by 2010."

A summary of the strategic thrusts and initiatives (some of which were ongoing and others new) of *ProAct 21* is given in Figure 10.1.

The release of *ProAct 21* received wide media publicity, and the report was even hailed as a 'slick blueprint' not expected of a national blueprint. Although innovation was emphasised, the plan was wide-ranging, reflecting the total approach to productivity and PSB's role in raising TFP growth. Nevertheless, the course that was taken subsequently deviated somewhat from the plan because of the shift in focus from productivity to innovation, divestment of certain PSB functions, and change in direction of PSB's successor.

Overall Goal: Sustained TFP Growth **Specific Outcomes:** • The best workforce in the world • Among the world's 10 most productive countries in manufacturing and services	
Strategic Thrust	**Initiative**
World-class Workforce *Purpose* 1. A mental revolution, a paradigm shift	• Inculcate a new productivity mindset that goes beyond teamwork, positive attitudes and efficiency to include ingenuity and innovation. The new productivity icon is symbolic of the mental revolution required. • Launch a National Productivity Education Programme to equip the workforce with understanding of productivity concepts and tools in the new economy. • Reposition Quality Circles as innovation and learning groups using new methodologies to focus their attention on breakthrough ideas, collective and continuous learning, and business outcomes.
People 2. Learning, unlearning and relearning	• Increase reach of CREST (Critical Enabling Skills Training) programme to lay the foundation for lifelong learning. • Develop Industry Capability Upgrading Plans to upgrade technical and managerial skills and meet the manpower capability needs of industries. • Establish a National Skills Recognition System to provide a national framework for establishing job skills competencies and alternative skills acquisition routes and certifying workforce skills. • Implement a Work Redesign programme to assist organisations to examine their work processes, review their utilisation of labour and technology, and redesign jobs for higher productivity and better knowledge utilisation.

Figure 10.1:   Summary of Strategic Thrusts and Initiatives of ProAct 21

Source: National Productivity and Quality Council (1999).

World-class Industry *Products and Processes*	
3. Revitalising business, exploiting new technology	• Implement a Product and Process Innovation Programme to help Promising Local Enterprises (PLEs) and Promising Small and Medium Enterprises (PSMEs) develop new and innovative products and processes. • Facilitate joint product and process development projects between buyers and suppliers to raise the capabilities of local supporting industries to that of ODM (original design manufacture) or even OBM (original brand manufacture). • Initiate a TechConnect Programme to facilitate connections between technopreneurs and expert resources, and provide a platform to evaluate innovative ideas and bring them to market. • Establish a centre for innovating products for the tropics to exploit technology to develop niche areas, capitalising on Singapore's strategic location and knowledge of the Asia-Pacific region. • Develop a framework for product excellence to ensure that Singapore-made products meet high international standards of quality.
Practices 4. Managing for business excellence	• Promote the organisational excellence model underpinning the Singapore Quality Award (SQA) widely as the national framework for business excellence. • Develop a roadmap to help organisations build up their management capabilities and systems. • Promote resource management programmes to enable organisations to go beyond cost-cutting to cost management. • Promote assessment of progress made by organisations in the business excellence journey.

Figure 10.1: (*Continued*)

Partnerships	
5. Teaming and twinning	• Step up collaboration of firms for collective competitiveness through avenues such as franchising, economic groupings, business fusion, co-location and Business. Connect. • Support cluster development through industry-wide upgrading.
World-class Infrastructure *Platform* 6. Catalysing higher peformance	• Incentivise the workforce's acquisition of higher skills by continuing to refine the Skills Development Fund (SDF) mechanism. • Establish Industry Productivity Fund to facilitate industry-wide transformation. • Review asset-based definition of SMEs to take into consideration intangible assets. • Introduce an Enterprise Market to help SMEs find sources of financing beyond bank lending. • Reposition the Local Enterprise Technical Assistance Scheme (LETAS) to encourage result-oriented projects.
7. Standards for competitiveness	• Develop performance-based standards that focus on outcomes rather than prescriptive specifications which may stifle innovation by constraining design or materials used. • Develop fast-track Technical References in cases where the normal consensual process of developing standards is not quick enough. • Continue harmonising Singapore Standards to international standards as much as possible, and participating in international and regional standards organisations and fora. • Pursue more bilateral and multilateral market access agreements on product testing and certification. • Launch Standards Implementation for Productivity (SIP) programme to promote the adoption of standards in various industries so as to facilitate inter-operability of systems. • Strengthen physical measurements to underpin the technical infrastructure for standards and conformity assessment.

Figure 10.1:   (*Continued*)

| 8. Harnessing knowledge, creating differential advantage | • Develop an Electronic Business Information Hub to integrate the existing information resources on innovation and productivity, and play the role of an information broker to bridge the supply of and demand for specialised information.
• Set up a National Best Practice Centre to facilitate the widespread adoption of best practices by organisations. |

Figure 10.1: (*Continued*)

Shift in Focus from Productivity to Innovation

A Rallying Call for Innovation

The shift in focus from productivity to innovation[3] was clearly the first major development in the 2000s that led to a change in the course for the productivity drive. Beyond ProAct 21, a series of rapid successive developments underlined the Government's intent to entrench innovation in the economy.

On 11 January 2000, the EDB Society,[4] in partnership with 13 economic agencies, organised the EDB Society & Partners Millennium Conference. The economic agencies included the Ministry of Trade and Industry (MTI), Ministry of Manpower (MOM), Economic Development Board (EDB) and PSB. A highlight of the conference, attended by about 1,000 representatives from the public, private and people sectors, was the focus on innovation to transform Singapore into a KBE. To generate ideas for discussion, Peter Skarzynski, CEO of Strategos, an international consulting firm renowned for helping companies to create new wealth through strategic innovations, was invited to make a presentation. His presentation was titled 'Competing for the Future — Innovation as Revolution.' This was prefaced by a

---

[3]Even though innovation is an important driver of productivity, the two terms are sometimes erroneously perceived as being distinct and unrelated. This misperception equates productivity narrowly with efficiency or value addition while innovation is taken to be synonymous with breakthroughs or value creation.

[4]Set up in 1989, the EDB Society is an association that comprises former and current officers of EDB.

video message from Gary Hamel, Distinguished Professor of Harvard Business School and Chairman of Strategos. Gary Hamel was a highly sought-after speaker on strategy and innovation, and he had just written an influential book titled *Leading the Revolution* describing how organisations could thrive by making innovation a way of life.

Three months later, at the Productivity Campaign Rally on 4 April 2000, Prime Minister Goh Chok Tong affirmed that innovation was a topmost priority for the Government. He said:

> *"The Productivity Movement made a good start in the last five years by adopting 'Innovation and Quality' as its theme. Innovation must now be lifted to a higher plane. Hence, from today, the Productivity Movement will be expanded to become the Productivity and Innovation Movement. It will emphasise, promote and spread Innovation and Value Creation to all sectors of the economy. The National Productivity and Quality Council will also be repositioned accordingly. These are not just name changes. We will give topmost priority to promoting innovation to all segments of society."*

Soon after, in January 2001, the Public Service Division and the MOM Academy organised an innovation training programme for a group of public service officers. The aim was to equip them with leading-edge tools to spearhead innovation in the economy. The trainers were from Strategos.

On 21 April 2001, a Ministerial Innovation Seminar was organised for the Cabinet and top civil servants. This was the clearest indication of the high priority given to innovation by the top echelon of the Government. Leading the seminar was Gary Hamel, who spoke on 'Building National Innovation Capability.' The other speakers were Carleton S. Fiorina, Chairman, President and CEO of Hewlett-Packard; and Paul Light, Douglas Dillon Senior Fellow and Founding Director of Center for Public Service and Vice President and Director of Governmental Studies, Brookings Institution. They spoke on the importance of innovation in the private sector and in the public sector respectively. In addition, Lee Suan Hiang, PSB Chief Executive, made a presentation on 'Blazing the Innovation Revolution — an Innovation Ecosystem for Singapore.' The presentation outlined the national innovation plan for Singapore.

On 1 August 2001, MOM, under the ambit of its MOM and Partners International Advisory Programme, invited Michael Porter to speak to representatives from the civil service, National Trades Union Congress (NTUC), Singapore National Employers Federation (SNEF) and academia. His presentation was on 'The Competitive Advantage of Singapore: Transition to the Innovation Stage.' On the following day, he made a similar presentation to an audience of about 1,200 business and public sector leaders at the New Economy@Singapore: *What's New? What's Next?* conference organised by the EDB Society. Considering his world-renowned reputation as the doyen of competitiveness, his appearance in Singapore was the icing on the cake for the Government's push for innovation. Importantly, Michael Porter linked innovation to productivity. At the conference, he said:

> *"Singapore truly is going to have to step up the pace of innovation, broadly defined, if it's going to have the productivity growth in order to continue to increase its sustainability."*

Barely two weeks later, in his National Day Rally 2001 speech on 19 August 2001, Prime Minister Goh Chok Tong stressed the need to foster a culture of innovation. He said:

> *"Efficiency is important. But it can be easily matched by others, and does not provide a sustained advantage in competitiveness. In the globalised economy that permits rapid spread of technology at low cost, efficiency is only an entry-level requirement. Innovation and imagination give an economy or a company that extra edge. Today, wealth is generated by new ideas, more than by improving the ideas of others. Ironically, to change mindsets in our society, a top-down approach seems unavoidable. But I am clear in my mind that the Government can only stimulate and encourage you to be innovative. It is not possible to direct and drive the population to become innovative.*
>
> *Earlier this year, I invited Professor Gary Hamel, a management consultant, to conduct a seminar on innovation for Ministers and top civil servants. The seminar has generated some good ideas on how we can encourage a more innovative society.*
>
> *I intend to set up a National Innovation Council to push along this change in the thinking of our people. Lim Hng Kiang, who is making several innovative changes in the Health Ministry, will chair this Council."*

The announcement on the setting up of the National Innovation Council capped the series of events linked to the Government's push for innovation.

Proposed National Innovation Council

Lim Hng Kiang, Minister for Health, explained the rationale for setting up the National Innovation Council at the opening of the International Productivity Conference on 2 October 2001. The conference was organised by PSB in conjunction with the 20th anniversary of Singapore's Productivity Movement and the 40th anniversary of the Asian Productivity Organization (APO). He said:

"In the early years, productivity was largely regarded as a cost-reduction strategy and expressed as 'minimize input, maximize output.' Then, quality gained prominence and became the No. 1 priority of industrialists around the world. After nearly two decades, the attention paid to improving quality of goods was extended to improving and re-engineering systems and processes. In recent years, the focus has shifted to the other side of the productivity equation. Innovation has become the new focus of productivity. Industry and enterprises are concerned not only with adding value to products and services, but creating value in order to build greater wealth.

Here in Singapore, the government is setting up a National Innovation Council to nurture and encourage greater innovativeness in the private and public sectors. Our aim is to transform Singapore from an 'efficiency city' to an 'innovation nation,' in which a culture of innovation permeates all aspects of the economy and society.

To do so, the National Innovation Council will develop and coordinate policies and strategies for the National Innovation Movement. It is quite clear that it is not possible to direct and drive the population to become innovative. What we can do is to facilitate, stimulate and nurture an innovative culture in Singapore and an enterprising spirit in all Singaporeans.

The Council will use the National Innovation Plan developed in April this year as the starting framework to guide its work. The Productivity and Standards Board will serve as the Council's secretariat. This will underline the close linkage between productivity and innovation."

Goh Chok Tong elaborated the rationale for the National Innovation Council at the Singapore Innovation Award 2001 Presentation Ceremony on 16 November 2001. He said:

> *"In the last forty years, the Singapore economy has grown on the basis of an investment-driven strategy. We focussed on improving the quality of capital investments. We built up the infrastructure for business. We increased our productivity and enhanced management efficiency.*
>
> *To succeed in the future, however, we must go beyond all these. We have to be more innovative ... How can we take a quantum leap forward to transform Singapore into a world-class innovative nation?*
>
> *I would like to highlight tonight, five key elements of our strategy to create an innovative nation ... First, we must have talent ... Secondly, we need to develop a pervasive innovation mindset in Singapore ... Thirdly, our society needs to be more tolerant of failure ... Fourthly, we need to develop a deep understanding of global market needs and trends ... The last element is having inspiring role models ... The National Innovation Council, to be chaired by Minister Lim Hng Kiang, will co-ordinate our efforts in these five areas. It will also devise other strategies to catalyse greater innovation nation-wide, and look at ways to nurture and develop an innovative culture in Singapore. The members of the Council will be announced shortly."*

These statements on the setting up of the National Innovation Council underlined the Government's firm position on innovation. Nevertheless, with the formation of ERC in December 2001, the setting up of the Council was shelved as the issue of innovation was folded under the committee's wings. Subsequently, the *Report of the Economic Review Committee* did emphasise the importance of innovation but did not dwell extensively on it. As stated in the report:

> *"We must upgrade ourselves and make Singapore a knowledge economy powered by innovation, creativity and entrepreneurship. Apart from knowledge and technical skills, Singaporeans need the right mindset to thrive in an environment of rapid and unpredictable change. In particular, we need to nurture the spirit of entrepreneurship and creativity. We need to strengthen incentives for Singaporeans to be innovative and venture beyond*

their comfort zones. We need to welcome diversity, accept failure, and embrace broader notions of success."

Instead of innovation per se, the focus now shifted to entrepreneurship:

"For the longer term, our basic strategy is to upgrade ourselves and make Singapore a knowledge economy, banking on creativity and innovation to power the economy and tapping the potential of IT in all areas ... [By 2018], Singapore will have graduated into a knowledge-based, innovation-driven economy. We will be a trend-setting city-state, a creative and entrepreneurial society ... the Government should designate a Minister (or Minister of State) to work with the Entrepreneurship 21 Ministerial Committee, and focus on driving the initiatives for a more entrepreneurial Singapore at the operational level."

Instead of a Minister driving innovation, there was now to be a Minister or Minister of State driving entrepreneurship. In fact, soon after that, Raymond Lim, Minister of State (Trade and Industry) was appointed the Minister of State in charge of Entrepreneurship; and on 26 May 2003, the Action Community for Entrepreneurship (ACE), chaired by him, was launched. In the light of this, the National Innovation Council was not formed.

Progress in the pursuit of innovation was most evident in the upstream activity of research and development (R&D), which could potentially lead to widespread innovation in industry through applications of the scientific and technological discoveries.[5] On 1 January 2006, the National Research Foundation (NRF) was established in the Prime Minister's Office. Besides serving as the secretariat to the Research, Innovation and Enterprise Council (RIEC), chaired by the Prime Minister, NRF was given the responsibility for setting the national direction for R&D. Its specific aims were to create a vibrant R&D hub contributing to a knowledge-intensive, innovative and

---

[5] R&D by itself does not automatically lead to innovation and hence higher productivity. For that to happen, there must be receptacles to diffuse the scientific and technological discoveries widely for applications in different sectors of the economy.

entrepreneurial economy, and to make Singapore a magnet for excellence in science and innovation. Its activities included funding strategic initiatives and building R&D capabilities by nurturing research talent.

A major consequence of the various developments was the cessation of the National Productivity and Quality Council (NPQC) after 20 years as the national policy-making body on the Productivity Movement. Apparently, in anticipation of the formation of the National Innovation Council, NPQC had been discontinued to avoid duplication of work. However, it was not reconstituted when the National Innovation Council was not formed.

Divestment of Certain PSB Functions

Government's Policy on Divestment

The second major development in the 2000s was the corporatisation and subsequent divestment of PSB's revenue-generating functions. This was in line with the Government's rethinking of its role in the economy, and, in particular, the view that the Government would divest all its non-core, non-strategic businesses that had alternative service providers in the private sector.

The roots of the thinking on divestment can be traced to the *Report of the Public Sector Divestment Committee*, published in 1987. Chaired by a prominent corporate figure, Michael Fam, the committee recommended the privatisation of selected government-linked companies (GLCs) and entities owned by statutory boards that were competing with the private sector. Subsequently, this same line of thought was emphasised by ERC. On nurturing an entrepreneurial and creative Singapore, the *Report of the Economic Review Committee* addressed the role of the Government with respect to GLCs and ministries and statutory boards. The following recommendations were made:

- *"Institute a 'Yellow Pages' rule to avoid encroaching on the space of the private sector.*
- *Statutory boards to avoid corporatising regulatory functions which could lead to rent-seeking by the enterprise.*

- *Proactively divest enterprises owned by statutory boards where appropriate, through mandatory periodic housekeeping.*
- *Statutory boards to avoid conflicts of interest. Their enterprises should not utilise the name of the statutory board in the domestic market, and the board of directors should be independent of the management of the statutory board. We also need to ensure that these enterprises do not enjoy a moratorium while competing in the market.*"

From PSB to SPRING

On 1 April 2001, PSB corporatised its revenue-generating functions to have a clear demarcation between the profit centres and the cost centres. In conjunction with this, it established PSB Corporation Pte Ltd (PSB Corp) to undertake the functions of training, consultancy services, technology services and testing services; and PSB Certification Pte Ltd (PSB Cert) to undertake management system certification services, which had to be separated from the rest because of conflict of interest. No doubt a major consideration in using the name 'PSB' for the two corporatised entities, instead of keeping it within the statutory board, was its commercial value as the name had already been well-established locally and overseas. This meant that a different name had to be used for the statutory board to distinguish it from the corporatised entities.

Among the many possibilities, Standards, Productivity and Innovation Board (SPRING Singapore, or SPRING in short) was chosen as the name to reflect the organisation's responsibility for innovation in addition to standards and productivity. As George Yeo, Minister for Trade and Industry, said at the Opening Ceremony of OSIM HQ on 25 January 2002:

> *"The Productivity and Standards Board (PSB) has been given the responsibility to promote innovation, in addition to its responsibilities for productivity and standards. What we want to improve in the end is our Total Factor Productivity, for which innovation is critical. Total Factor Productivity goes beyond labour productivity and capital productivity.*

Improvement in Total Factor Productivity is the result of doing many innovative things, big and small, including R&D, improvements in management and morale, reorganization of the workplace and better branding.

The new PSB will play a lead role in raising the productivity of the domestic sector, which comprises almost two-thirds of total business establishments in Singapore and employs half of the total workforce but contributes only one-third of total value added in our economy. To express better its new mission, PSB will be renamed the Standards, Productivity and Innovation Board, or SPRING Singapore in short. SPRING stands for Standards, Productivity and Innovation for Growth. SPRING Singapore will take over from PSB the responsibility to spearhead the National Productivity Movement."

At the same event, George Yeo also announced the restructuring of the Trade Development Board (TDB) into International Enterprise Singapore (IE Singapore) to help local companies grow and internationalise; and the restructuring of the National Science and Technology Board (NSTB) into Agency for Science, Technology and Research (A*STAR) to give greater emphasis to upstream science, engineering and biomedical research. He said:

"The reorganisation of these three statutory boards — I.E. Singapore, SPRING Singapore and A*STAR — are therefore opening exciting new chapters for MTI and will help us remake Singapore for the 21ˢᵗ century — growing our external wing, fostering innovation and total productivity growth, and deepening our capabilities in Science, Technology and Research. Working with other economic agencies and the private sector, they will strengthen the foundations for a new Singapore economy."

SPRING was officially established on 1 April 2002. Figure 10.2 shows the functions of SPRING, as stated in the Standards, Productivity and Innovation Board Act 2002.

Compared with PSB's functions (Figure 8.3), the functions of SPRING reflected its scope of responsibilities after the corporatisation of its revenue-generating activities. The first function underlined its responsibility for TFP and innovation. This replaced the earlier PSB function of 'to raise productivity and improve competitiveness

a) To raise total factor productivity and improve Singapore's competitiveness through productivity and innovation promotion, domestic sector development, standards, conformance, metrology and any other activity considered necessary or desirable.

b) To promote, facilitate and assist in the development and upgrading of skills and expertise of persons preparing to join the workforce, persons in the workforce and persons rejoining the workforce, and to support the growth of small and medium enterprises and any other enterprise requiring its assistance.

c) To administer the Skills Development Fund in accordance with the Skills Development Levy Act [Cap. 306].

d) To assess and certify persons for achievements in productivity, innovation, skills or standards.

(*da*) to register management systems personnel.

e) To promote and facilitate the national standardisation programme and the participation of Singapore in international standardisation activities.

f) To be the accreditation body for the assessment and accreditation of bodies and institutions whose activities include sampling, testing, calibration, inspection or certification.

g) To designate, appoint, authorise or recognise for any purpose any person who performs conformity assessment and any person who performs any test relating to conformity assessment, and to perform all functions necessary or incidental thereto, including

   (i) determining the qualifications of such persons;

  (ii) controlling and regulating the practice of such persons;

 (iii) suspending, lifting the suspension of or withdrawing the designation, appointment, authorisation or recognition of such persons; and

 (iv) establishing, maintaining and developing the standards of practice, and professional conduct and ethics, of such persons;

h) To serve as the national productivity, innovation and standards body, and to advise the Government and industrial, commercial, trading and other organisations in respect of matters relating to productivity, innovation and standards.

i) To represent the Government internationally in respect of matters relating to productivity, innovation, standards and conformity assessment.

(*ia*) to administer the Weights and Measures Act (Cap.349).

j) To perform such other functions as are conferred on the Board by any other written law.

Figure 10.2: Functions of SPRING from 1 April 2002
Source: Standards, Productivity and Innovation Board Act 2002.

through manpower development, economic restructuring, technical progress, standardisation and any other activity considered necessary or desirable.' Considering the elusive nature of TFP, the change was a bold step especially since TFP had not been stated in the PSB Act when PSB was specifically set up to manage it. Nonetheless, the execution of the function was still possible since SPRING fully owned PSB Corp and PSB Cert and could tap their services and align them with its responsibility for raising TFP. However, this situation did not last long.

In line with the plan to divest Government-owned companies according to the 'Yellow Pages' rule, PSB Corp and PSB Cert had to be fully divested at some point in time. Forming them as corporatised entities wholly owned by SPRING was but an essential first step towards full divestment, as the businesses were then subject to market discipline. The ensuing divestment process led ultimately to the sale of PSB Corp and PSB Cert to TÜV SÜD, a leading technical services provider headquartered in Munich, Germany.

On 27 March 2006, SPRING and TÜV SÜD formally inked the documents for the sale of PSB Corp and PSB Cert. At the signing ceremony, Loh Khum Yean, Chief Executive of SPRING, said:

"We have found a good partner in TÜV SÜD — with a solid track record, strong capabilities and a good network of resources. We are confident that TÜV SÜD's firm commitment to grow these two businesses in Singapore and regionally will enable them to grow even faster moving forward. This collaboration will synergise the strengths of both parties."

At the same event, Dr Ruprecht Schattner, CEO and President of TÜV SÜD in Asia Pacific, said:

"PSB is a superb and strategic fit for TÜV SÜD because we have complementary product offerings and we share many traits, including a common public sector heritage, technical expertise, a strong client base, unswerving commitment to quality and a driving ambition to move forward. Our synergies place us well to capture the vast opportunities in Asia for testing, certification, consulting and training."

No doubt there was great potential for PSB Corp and PSB Cert to grow strongly under the well-established TÜV SÜD. Unfortunately, the two entities did not remain as they were. In fact, parts of the PSB businesses were subsequently sold off by TÜV SÜD to others. It would appear that TÜV SÜD was interested primarily in those parts of the businesses of PSB Corp and PSB Cert that were fully aligned with its own core competencies when it purchased the two entities put up for sale by SPRING.

An even more pertinent point is that, in hindsight, the divestment of PSB Corp and PSB Cert had considerably weakened SPRING's capability as the organisation championing TFP. The capability that had been built through the United Nations Development Programme (UNDP) in the 1970s, the Productivity Development Project (PDP) in the 1980s and the formation of PSB in the 1990s was now severely diminished. Ironically, this happened soon after SPRING had explicitly stated 'to raise total factor productivity' as one of its key functions. The new SPRING, minus PSB Corp and PSB Cert, had in fact been transformed from a productivity competency centre to a policy-making body, industry and enterprise development facilitator, and grants administrator.

Change in SPRING's Mission

The third major development in the 2000s was the change in SPRING's mission. From 1997–2003, SPRING's mission was 'To raise productivity so as to enhance Singapore's competitiveness and economic growth for a better quality of life for our people.' This was in line with its role as the national productivity champion. In 2004, this mission was changed to 'To enhance the competitiveness of enterprises for a vibrant Singapore economy.' The change took place soon after Cedric Foo[6] succeeded Lim Boon Heng as Chairman of SPRING on 1 April 2003 and Loh Khum Yean took over from Lee Suan Hiang as Chief Executive on 15 October 2003.

---

[6] Cedric Foo was appointed Minister of State (Defence) in April 2002.

In the SPRING *Annual Report 2003–2004*, Cedric Foo explained the change in SPRING's mission. He said:

> *"Recognising the need to strengthen enterprise-level competitiveness and the fact that functions among some government agencies had changed, SPRING embarked on a strategic planning exercise in November 2003. A major outcome of the exercise is that SPRING will take on the new mission of enhancing enterprise competitiveness for a vibrant Singapore economy … SPRING will work closely with the other government agencies and our industry partners to undertake the new tasks before us. Our vision is to have dynamic and innovative Singapore enterprises that grow to be tomorrow's global companies."*

In a speech to the British Chamber of Commerce on 28 September 2004, Cedric Foo elaborated the rationale for SPRING's new mission. He said:

> *"In order to succeed in the new competitive and uncertain global economic landscape, all enterprises — big and small — must build up their core capabilities and seek new markets to enhance their resilience. According to the 2004 Global Competitiveness Report, this is where Singapore has room for improvement. Singapore enjoys high rankings in the Macroeconomic Environment Index — we were top-placed, in fact, amongst the 102 countries surveyed. However, we did less well in the microeconomic parameters, ranking 4th in terms of the business environment which includes factors such as supporting industries, market context and factor inputs. And where enterprise-level capabilities are concerned, we could only manage a 12th placing.*
>
> *In response to the critical need to focus on the microeconomic factors of competitiveness, the Standards, Productivity and Innovation Board, or SPRING Singapore, has re-positioned itself. Its mission now focuses directly on enhancing the competitiveness of Singapore-based enterprises. To do this, SPRING will pay particular attention to four areas that are critical for enhancing enterprise competitiveness — business environment; industry clusters; enterprise capabilities; and market access."*

The change in SPRING's mission reflected a change in SPRING's role from the national productivity champion to an enterprise development agency helping companies to be competitive. This new role strengthened further when Philip Yeo, former Chairman of EDB and A*STAR, took over from Cedric Foo as Chairman of SPRING on 1 April 2007; and Png Cheong Boon, SPRING's Deputy Chief Executive who was previously from EDB, replaced Loh Khum Yean as Chief Executive on 1 May 2008. The role continued in the 2010s after Png Cheong Boon was succeeded by Tan Kai Hoe (1 May 2013–31 July 2015) and Poon Hong Yuen (1 November 2015–present).[7]

Considering that SPRING was no longer well-positioned to champion TFP after the divestment of PSB Corp and PSB Cert, the change in SPRING's role was a reasonable move. However, from the perspective of the national productivity drive, it meant that there was now a shift in focus from productivity per se to enterprise development.[8] This led to two major consequences. First, there was no longer the national productivity organisation that was long associated with NPB and PSB. Second, productivity promotion ceased since this was not in line with SPRING's new role. The Productivity Movement, which was supposed to be the Productivity and Innovation Movement from 2000, went out of the radar screen; and the annual productivity campaign/rally was discontinued after 2002.

Turning Point in Productivity Drive in the 2000s

The three major developments — shift in focus from productivity to innovation, divestment of certain PSB functions and change in SPRING's mission — were associated with a series of changes that

---

[7]Although the 2010s is outside the period covered in this chapter, this point is included here for completeness since the role of SPRING is not elaborated in Chapters 12 and 13 by virtue of the fact that it is no longer the national productivity organisation.

[8]A focus on enterprise development does not, in itself, mean that productivity is not addressed at all. Some programmes that are implemented to boost enterprise development do raise productivity as well. However, such a focus directs action more towards growth than productivity. This is akin to the focus on economic growth rather than productivity growth at the national level.

collectively marked a turning point in the productivity drive in the 2000s. These changes are summarised in Figure 10.3. Individually, the changes were insignificant. Collectively, they painted a picture of a muted productivity drive in the 2000s. Symbolic of the extensive changes that had taken place was the discontinuation of the flagship *Productivity Digest* in June 2005 — after a run of 23 years from March 1982 following the launch of the Productivity Movement.

What is surprising is that despite the vast changes in the 2000s, there was no corresponding amendment to the SPRING Act which continued to state 'to raise total factor productivity' as one of

Element	As at end 1999	Since 2000	Reason for change
Branding of national productivity drive	Productivity Movement.	Repositioned as Productivity and Innovation Movement in 2000, but discontinued in 2003.	Discontinuation in view of cessation of productivity promotion by SPRING.
Productivity Month/Rally	National Productivity Rally.	Discontinued in 2003.	Discontinuation in view of cessation of productivity promotion by SPRING.
Productivity Council	National Productivity and Quality Council.	Ceased in 2001. Composition of Council shown in PSB *Annual Report 1999–2000* for the last time and discontinued thereafter.	Cessation in view of focus on innovation and impending set-up of National Innovation Council (intended but not formed).
National recognition for productivity achievement	National Productivity Awards.	Ceased after 2002.	No awards given out in view of cessation of annual Productivity Rally.

Figure 10.3: Changes Marking Turning Point in Productivity Drive in the 2000s
Source: Compiled from various sources.

Element	As at end 1999	Since 2000	Reason for change
Name of national productivity organisation (NPO)	Singapore Productivity and Standards Board. Publicly known as Productivity and Standards Board, or PSB in short, underlining its status as the national productivity organisation.	Renamed Standards, Productivity and Innovation Board in 2002. Publicly known as SPRING Singapore or SPRING, an enterprise development agency with 'Enabling Enterprise' as its tagline.	Change of name in 2002 to reflect the Board's role of promoting innovation, in addition to productivity and standards; and to distinguish it from 'PSB', which was transferred to the two corporatised entities set up in 2001. Tagline of 'Enabling Enterprise' added in 2004 to underline the organisation's new role as an enterprise development agency.
Role of NPO	National productivity champion.	Enterprise development agency from 2004. Role changed to enterprise development, after devolvement of certain functions[9]: a. Administration of Skills Development Fund (SDF)	Change of role to strengthen enterprise-level competitiveness, and taking into account changes in functions of some other Government agencies. Transfer to achieve greater synergy in efforts by MOM to

Figure 10.3:　(*Continued*)

---

[9] Following the change in SPRING's role in 2004, the National Metrology Centre was transferred from SPRING to A*STAR in 2007 to harness the synergy between metrology and scientific R&D.

Element	As at end 1999	Since 2000	Reason for change
		transferred from SPRING to MOM on 1 Oct 2002 and subsequently to Singapore Workforce Development Agency (WDA) in September 2003.	integrate workforce development with lifelong learning.
		b. Workforce development function transferred from SPRING to WDA in 2003.	Transfer to rationalise the work with WDA, which was formed in 2003 to lead and drive workforce development in Singapore.
		c. Divestment of PSB Corp and PSB Cert to TÜV SÜD in 2006, following corporatisation in 2001.	Divestment in line with Government's 'Yellow Pages' rule.
Mission of NPO	Mission statement: 'To raise productivity so as to enhance Singapore's competitiveness and economic growth for a better quality of life for our people.'	Changed to 'To enhance the competitiveness of enterprises for a vibrant Singapore economy' in 2004.	Change in mission to reflect organisation's new focus on enterprise development.
Capabilities of NPO	Productivity competency centre, with	Enterprise enabler, with capabilities in policy-making, facilitation of	Change in capabilities arising from change in

Figure 10.3: (*Continued*)

Element	As at end 1999	Since 2000	Reason for change
	'soft' capabilities (productivity promotion, training, consultancy, workforce development, local enterprise development, research) and 'hard' capabilities (technology development, product development & automation, testing & certification, quality assurance, standards & metrology).	industry and enterprise development, and grants administration.	organisation's role and devolvement of certain functions.
Flagship publication of NPO	*Productivity Digest.*	Ceased in June 2005. Replaced by *Enterprise Today* on 1 August 2005; which was then succeeded by *SPRING News* on 1 January 2009.	Cessation in flagship productivity publication arising from change in organisation's role.
Building housing NPO	NPB Building in Bukit Merah, owned by NPB — symbol of the productivity drive in Singapore.	Tenanted premises in Solaris building in Fusionopolis from December 2010, following sale of the NPB Building.	Shift in office to allow SPRING, in its new role, to be together with other Government agencies with the mandate to grow the economy,

Figure 10.3: (*Continued*)

Element	As at end 1999	Since 2000	Reason for change
			including catalysing more R&D activities, for a 'whole-of-Singapore' approach.
Role of NPO's affiliate — Singapore Productivity Association (SPA)	Activities closely aligned with PSB's directions; SPA used directly by PSB to promote productivity.	Activities less aligned with SPRING's directions from 2004; SPA not given the specific role of productivity promotion.	Change due to SPRING's shift in focus from national productivity organisation to enterprise development agency.
Representation as Director on Asian Productivity Organization (APO)	Chairman of PSB.	Chief Executive of SPRING from 2007 to 2014; an Assistant Chief Executive of SPRING from 2015.	Change possibly due to SPRING's shift in focus from national productivity organisation to enterprise development agency.

Figure 10.3: (*Continued*)

SPRING's major functions. Even till today, this function is embedded in the Act, which means that, on paper, SPRING is still the agency responsible for increasing TFP in Singapore. SPRING also continues to represent Singapore on the Asian Productivity Organization (APO), albeit with a lower level of representation. Nevertheless, in terms of its strategies and programmes, SPRING is today an enterprise development agency with special focus on small and medium enterprises (SMEs). The details of this new role of SPRING are given in Chapter 11.

Chapter 11

2000s: Turning Point in the Productivity Drive

"The future Singapore economy cannot thrive on productivity alone. It must be driven by both productivity and innovation. We have to become an innovative society. Let us work towards this goal over the next 10 years."

Prime Minister Goh Chok Tong
Productivity 2000 Campaign Rally
4 April 2000

Two Periods of Productivity Drive in the 2000s

The productivity drive in the 2000s can be divided in a couple of ways. First, there could be a distinction between 1 January 2000–31 March 2002, when Singapore Productivity and Standards Board (PSB) was in existence, and 1 April 2002–31 December 2009, when Standards, Productivity and Innovation Board (SPRING) succeeded PSB. Second, a division could be made between 1 January 2000–31 December 2003, when PSB/SPRING was the national productivity champion, and 1 January 2004–31 December 2009, when SPRING took on the role of an enterprise development agency. Between the two, the latter is more pertinent and is used here since it reflects the change in the organisation's directions and activities more clearly.

Productivity Promotion through Annual Campaign

Continuing from the 1980s and 1990s, productivity promotion through the annual campaign reached its climax in 2001 when the Productivity Movement marked its 20th anniversary. Thereafter, it began to fizzle out and was stopped altogether in 2003 when the productivity campaign was discontinued.

Teamy Replaced by Productivity Icon

In a move that seemed to portend a turning point in the productivity drive in the new decade, Teamy exited the scene in 2000 after 18 long years as Singapore's well-loved productivity mascot. In place of the colourful Teamy was a nondescript productivity icon formed from the letters 'I', for innovation, and 'P', for productivity, superimposed on each other and set within a water droplet, signifying the qualities of flexibility and adaptability. The icon, intended for use in the new millennium, was launched by Deputy Prime Minister Lee Hsien Loong at the Singapore Quality Award (SQA) Presentation event on 21 July 1999. In its publication *ProAct 21*, released on 6 December 1999, the National Productivity and Quality Council (NPQC) elaborated the reason for the change:

> *"Productivity begins with the right mental attitude. As Singapore moves beyond the industrial age paradigm, a new mental model is called for ... The new productivity icon is symbolic of the mental revolution required. The icon is a useful graphical representation and reference point of the qualities needed in the quest for competitiveness and growth. 'Teamy the Bee' was a mascot which captured the teamwork, positive attitudes and efficiency (i.e. producing more with the same amount of inputs or doing things right) needed for success in the factory-based, investment-driven phase of development in the early 1980s. Building on and complementing it, the new icon champions ingenuity and innovation — attributes essential for a world of immense opportunity but intense competition."*

Despite this well-articulated logic for the change in icon, the new productivity icon was not as well-publicised as Teamy and was short-lived. It faded from the scene completely after 2002 when the productivity campaign ended.

Campaign Themes

In 2000, the new 5-year foundation theme of 'Innovation and Value Creation' was adopted for the Productivity Movement to succeed the preceding theme of 'Innovation and Quality'. The aim was to underline the importance of innovation and value creation, as opposed to value addition, as Singapore moved into the innovation-driven phase of development. However, this foundation theme was not used strongly; instead, specific themes were used in 2001 and 2002, as shown in Figure 11.1. In any case, the foundation theme did not run its 5-year course since the productivity campaign was discontinued after 2002.

Productivity Rally

From Productivity Campaign, used during 1995/96–1999, the annual campaign launch event became Productivity Campaign Rally in 2000–2001 and National Productivity Rally in 2002. The term 'rally' was used to underline the importance of garnering the involvement of everyone. Figure 11.2 shows the details of the launch events.

Year	Theme
2000	Innovation and Value Creation
2001	Dare to Dream, Dare to Do, Dare to Make the Difference
2002	Co-creating a Better Tomorrow through Productivity and Innovation

Figure 11.1: Productivity Campaign Themes, 2000–2002

Source: Singapore Productivity and Standards Board, *Annual Report*, various issues; Standards, Productivity and Innovation Board, *Annual Report 2002–2003*.

Year	Launch date	Guest-of-Honour (GOH)	Theme of GOH's speech
2000	4 April	Prime Minister Goh Chok Tong	Innovation: Key to Singapore's future
2001	5 September	Deputy Prime Minister Lee Hsien Loong	20th anniversary of the Productivity Movement: challenges ahead for the Productivity Movement
2002	3 December	President S. R. Nathan	Rallying the nation for the next lap of the Productivity Movement

Figure 11.2:   Productivity Rally, 2000–2002

Source: Singapore Productivity and Standards Board, *Annual Report*, various issues; Standards, Productivity and Innovation Board, *Annual Report 2002–2003*.

The Guests-of-Honour were at the highest levels, with the President gracing what was to be the last launch event in a 20-year history.

The rally in 2001 was especially significant since it marked the 20th anniversary of the Productivity Movement. Besides commemorating 20 years of the Movement, the launch event on 5 September 2001 aimed to garner mass support for the next phase focusing on productivity and innovation. A mass brainstorming session named Thinkathon, involving the 8000 guests present, was held to generate ideas for improving a wide range of issues including healthcare, transportation system and education. The session generated more than 400,000 ideas, which were subsequently evaluated and passed on to the relevant Government agencies for consideration. In addition, a $5 commemorative coin and a productivity orchid, *robinara productivity psb*, were produced. At the event, special awards were also presented to key tripartite partners who had made significant contributions to the Productivity Movement — the past and present chairmen of the NPQC, president of the Singapore National Employers Federation (SNEF), past and present presidents of the National Trades Union Congress

---

The Kallang Declaration

We pledge to give of our best
For the future of Singapore.
Steered by Innovation and Value Creation,
We shall strive for excellence
To raise productivity and competitiveness
For a better quality of life for all.
We dare to dream, we dare to do.
We can and must make the difference.

Source: Abraham, M. (2001).

(NTUC), and past and present Chief Executives of NPB, PSB and SPRING.

The high point of the 2001 rally was the recitation of the productivity pledge, termed the Kallang Declaration, by the 8000-strong audience. The words of the pledge are shown in the Amp-Box on *The Kallang Declaration.*

Key Performance Indicators and Major Programmes in First Period of 2000s: January 2000–December 2003

Figure 11.3 summarises the key performance indicators (KPIs) used by PSB and SPRING to track their achievements before the focus changed to enterprise development. The KPIs were for the three focus areas of Productivity and Innovation, with the strategic objectives of building world-class organisations and developing organisation capabilities; Standards and Metrology, with the strategic objectives of facilitating market access for Singapore's exports and improving productivity through standardisation; and SMEs and Domestic Sector, with the strategic objectives of developing small and medium enterprises (SMEs) as another engine of growth and creating a vibrant and resilient domestic sector.

Focus area	Key performance indicator	FY2001	FY2002	FY2003	Cumulative
Productivity and Innovation	Business Excellence • No. of certified Singapore Quality Class (SQC) organisations*	243	336	436	—
	People Developer Standard • No. of certified People Developer Standard organisations*	292	388	481	—
	Innovation Excellence • No. of certified Singapore Innovation Class organisations*	—	3	39	—
	Service Excellence • No. of certified Singapore Service Class organisations*	—	—	30	—
	Innovation and Quality Circles (IQCs) • No. of organisations implementing IQC*	168	272	381	—
Standards and Metrology	Market Access • No. of agreements, international comparisons and harmonisation programmes to facilitate market access*	310	346	391	—

Figure 11.3: Key Performance Indicators of PSB and SPRING, FY2001–FY2003
Notes: 1. * Cumulative figures since launch of the programme.
    2. # No. of SMEs crossing the sales turnover mark of $10m for the first time.
Source: Standards, Productivity and Innovation Board, *Annual Report 2003–2004.*

Focus area	Key performance indicator	FY2001	FY2002	FY2003	Cumulative
	Standards Implementation for Productivity (SIP) • No. of SIP projects	12	14	5	31
	Standards • No. of new Singapore Standards developed	20	24	20	756
	Accreditation • No. of laboratories, inspection bodies and certification bodies accredited*	170	186	195	—
	• No. of auditors registered	90	78	83	—
	Metrology • No. of companies assisted on measure-ment traceability	853	783	716	—
	Weights and Measures • No. of infringe-ments on weights and measures regu-lations	11	4	3	—
	Consumer Product Safety • No. of accidents reported for controlled items	0	0	1	—
SMEs and Domestic Sector	SME Upgrading • No. of SMEs with sales turnover of more than $10m#	540	220	616	4,246

Figure 11.3: (*Continued*)

Focus area	Key performance indicator	FY2001	FY2002	FY2003	Cumulative
	• No. of enterprises benefiting from changes in industry structure (franchises and economic groupings)	929	505	519	—
	First Point of Contact for SMEs • No. of upgrading cases handled by SME First Stop	7,945	8,532	8,625	—
	Local Enterprise Finance Scheme (LEFS) • No. of LEFS loan applications approved	2,007	3,909	5,327	38,474
	• Value of LEFS loan applications approved	$417m	$573m	$758m	$9,079m
	Local Enterprise Technical Assistance Scheme (LETAS) • No. of LETAS applications approved	3,942	4,889	3,532	26,898
	• Value of LETAS applications approved	$72m	$83m	$37m	$500m

Figure 11.3: (*Continued*)

As there were no targets shown for the KPIs and no attempts to link the impact of the achievements on productivity (labour productivity or total factor productivity), it is not possible to make an assessment of the achievements.

The major programmes contributing to the achievement of the KPIs for the period January 2000–December 2003 are shown in Figure 11.4. The programmes are classified according to the major thrusts of PSB and SPRING when the focus was on productivity.

Programme	Details
1. Productivity Promotion	
International Productivity Conference	In conjunction with the 20th anniversary of the Productivity Movement in Singapore and the 40th anniversary of the Asian Productivity Organization (APO), PSB and APO jointly organised the conference on 2–4 October 2001. The conference was attended by about 600 participants.
National Productivity Award (NPA)	For the period 2000–2012, awards were given to 5 companies and 59 individuals. NPA was discontinued after 2012.
Quality Circles	In 2000, PSB expanded the scope of Quality Circles to address innovation. Hence, they were renamed Innovation and Quality Circles (IQCs). In September 2002, the National Quality Circle Conventions were transformed into a mega National Innovation and Quality Circle Carnival.
Business Excellence Action Mapping (BEAM)	The programme, based on the SQA framework, was launched in 2000 to help SMEs adopt a systematic approach to achieve business excellence.
Insight Programme	This programme was launched in April 2000 to enable managers to learn and understand the best practices of organisations through local study missions.
Best Practice Networks	Best practice networks among Singapore Quality Class (SQC) members were formed in 2000 to enable them to share and learn from best practices in various areas such as inventory management and training effectiveness.
SQC for Private Education Organisations (PEO)	Based on the SQA framework for business excellence, the scheme was launched by SPRING together with Economic Development Board (EDB) in February 2003 to help private schools achieve organisational excellence.
Singapore Innovation Class (I-Class)	The programme was launched in July 2002 to provide organisations with a systematic framework to achieve innovation excellence. Accompanying this was an innovation assessment tool called I-SCORE (Innovation Scoreboard for Organisational Excellence).

Figure 11.4: Major Programmes Contributing to Achievement of KPIs, January 2000–December 2003

Note: The list includes only programmes that were launched for the first time. Subsequent developments or runs of the programmes are not included.

Source: Singapore Productivity and Standards Board, *Annual Report,* various years; Standards, Productivity and Innovation Board, *Annual Report,* various years.

Programme	Details
Singapore Innovation Award	The award, recognising companies for their excellence in innovation practices, was presented for the first time in November 2001.
National Framework for Service Excellence	Released in March 2003, the framework served as the national plan for raising service levels in organisations. It was developed by the Service Excellence 21 Committee, co-chaired by Lee Suan Hiang, SPRING's Chief Executive, and Jennie Chua, President and Chief Operating Officer of Raffles International Ltd.
Singapore Service Class (S-Class)	The programme was launched in August 2003 to provide a framework for organisations to achieve service excellence.
2. Manpower Development	
Training Partnerships	The Hewlett Packard-PSB e-commerce training package for SMEs called GEN Education was developed in November 2000.
National Skills Recognition System (NSRS)	NSRS was launched on 5 September 2000 to provide a national framework for job skills competencies, alternative skills acquisition routes and certification of workforce skills.
Work Redesign 21	The programme, integrating the BacktoWork and Job Redesign 21 programmes, was launched on 24 February 2000 to help companies review their work processes and redesign jobs for higher productivity.
People Excellence 2000	This programme was launched in November 2000 to provide organisations an integrated approach to developing their people. It comprised three components — information system, capability development programmes and recognition system.
Assessment of People Excellence (APEX)	The programme was launched in October 2002 to help organisations assess their progress and make improvements in their people development.
People Excellence Award	Representing the highest national accolade bestowed on organisations for people excellence, the award aimed to recognise the best of the best People Developers. It was given out for the first time in November 2001.

Figure 11.4:   (*Continued*)

Programme	Details
Management Excellence Programme	Launched in August 2003, the programme aimed to develop managers to initiate and implement programmes to boost productivity and innovation in their organisations. As part of the programme, a Management Excellence Network (MExNET) was launched in November 2003. The aim was to form strategic alliances with training providers to develop and deliver management excellence training courses.
WorkforceOne	Launched in 2000, the website served as the electronic first-stop gateway to world-wide information on workforce development.
3. Technology Application	
Growing Enterprises with Technology Upgrading (GET-UP)	The programme was launched by Agency for Science, Technology and Research (A*STAR) in February 2003 to upgrade the technological capabilities of SMEs. SPRING worked with A*STAR to implement the three components of the programme, viz. Technology for Enterprise Capability Upgrading (T-Up), Operation and Technology Roadmapping (OTR) and Technical Advisor Scheme (TA).
4. Industry Development	
Pro-Enterprise Panel (PEP)	PEP was set up by the Government in August 2000 to enhance the business environment. In 2001, SPRING was appointed the secretariat to PEP, working closely with other government agencies to remove barriers to doing business so that entrepreneurship and innovation could thrive.
SME March	The first SME March, a month dedicated annually to SMEs to highlight their importance to Singapore, was launched on 5 March 2001. Throughout March, a wide range of events and activities was organised to enable SMEs and key stakeholders to interact, learn, share and network with each other. In 2002, SME March was extended to a year-long event.
SME Partner Award	To recognise individuals and organisations that had contributed significantly to the development of SMEs, PSB launched the SME Partner Award in 2002.

Figure 11.4: (*Continued*)

Programme	Details
SME Network	The network was launched on 11 November 2002 to provide informal opportunities for chief executives of SMEs to meet, exchange information and discuss business.
Business@lert	Launched in November 2003, the service enabled local enterprises to tap an estimated 90,000 business opportunities in government tenders locally and overseas.
International Small Business Congress	SPRING organised the event in 2003 together with industry partners to promote business linkages between local SMEs and foreign companies and to position Singapore as a SME hub.
Corporate Advisor Programme	The programme was launched in September 2001 to help SMEs grow by tapping the expertise and experience of business advisors acting as mentors for the SMEs.
Economic Value Added Kit for SMEs	PSB unveiled a self-help package on 7 September 2000 to help SMEs implement the economic value added financial tool to track their financial health.
Retail 21	A 10-year Retail 21 plan was launched on 7 March 2001. The vision was to develop Singapore into a world-class centre of retail excellence.
Retail Cluster Development Initiative	A collaboration between SPRING, Singapore Tourism Board (STB) and Singapore Retailers Association (SRA), this initiative was launched in September 2001 as part of the Retail 21 plan. It was the first cluster development approach applied to the retail business.
Franchising and economic groupings programme	The Singapore Franchise Mark was unveiled on 8 March 2000. This certification scheme aimed to give recognition to franchisors for their sound and ethical franchise practices.
Singapore Premium Food Gift programme	The programme was jointly launched by SPRING and STB on 22 February 2002 to promote made-in-Singapore food products by enabling visitors to take home something uniquely Singaporean.
COOL Programme	The COOL Programme for Shopping Centres was launched on 29 April 2003 to put in place good practices to prevent SARS. This was extended to childcare centres on 14 May 2003 and to supermarkets on 20 May 2003.

Figure 11.4: (*Continued*)

Programme	Details
Action Community for Entrepreneurship (ACE)	ACE was launched on 26 May 2003 to promote entrepreneurship by developing an entrepreneurial mindset and culture, improving access to capital for start-ups and reducing the burden of business rules and regulations. PSB/SPRING acted as the lead agency supporting the work of ACE. The key activities of ACE included BlueSky Exchange, a roundtable discussion between entrepreneurs and ACE members; BlueSky Evening, an informal networking session for entrepreneurs and aspiring entrepreneurs; BlueSky Finance Fair, featuring various financial products and services available to businesses; and ACE Speakers' Circuit, jointly organised with schools to promote the spirit of enterprise among students.
Start Up	In 2004, ACE and the Spirit of Enterprise produced 'Start Up,' Singapore's first reality television series on entrepreneurship. The aim was to inspire the spirit of entrepreneurship among Singaporeans.
Singapore@Work	As part of e-commerce adoption, a new TV series, 'Singapore@Work,' was spearheaded by Infocomm Development Authority of Singapore (IDA) and supported by PSB. The series, showcasing SMEs that had successfully embraced e-commerce in their business strategy, was screened in English and Chinese from August 2000 to February 2001.
5. Standards & Quality Development	
Singapore Standardisation Strategy 21 (SSS 21)	A comprehensive strategy setting the direction for Singapore's national standardisation programme for the long term was developed and released in 2001.
Singapore Accreditation Council	On 1 April 2002, the Council was transferred from the Singapore Confederation of Industries (SCI) to SPRING, making it the national authority for the accreditation of conformity assessment bodies.
Standards Development	PSB/SPRING continued to develop and publish standards for adoption by the industry. An example is the Singapore Standards on Exhibition Terminology which was completed in 2003, making Singapore the first country in the world to develop a national standard for the exhibition industry.

Figure 11.4: (*Continued*)

Programme	Details
Requirements for Business Continuity Standard	Launched in 2003, the Standard aimed to increase business and industry confidence in Singapore companies in the face of threats such as SARS, terrorism and computer virus attacks.
Asia Pacific Metrology Programme	An MOU was signed with IBM and Optus on time authentication on 3 December 2003.
6. Incentives Management	
Local Enterprise Finance Scheme (LEFS)-Micro Loan	A new micro loan programme was introduced in November 2001 to help very small companies (10 or less employees) gain access to funds of up to $50,000 for their working capital needs.
Loan Insurance Scheme	The scheme was launched in September 2002 to provide another venue of financing for SMEs through the use of loan insurance.
Jumpstart	In December 2000, PSB introduced this incentive programme to help SMEs defray the cost of implementing e-commerce.
Industry Productivity Fund	The fund was set up in January 2000 to encourage SMEs within and across industries to collaborate on projects with the potential of fundamentally changing strategies, operations and practices of the industry.
Bridging Loan Programme	The programme was launched under LEFS on 17 April 2003 to assist companies in tourism-related sectors affected by SARS.
Deal Flow Connection	Launched in July 2003, this matching platform, fronted by an online portal, aimed to link businesses with good ideas to investors and financiers.
Enterprise Investment Incentive	In 2003, the Technopreneur Investment Incentive, which mitigated the risks of private equity investments in technology start-ups through loan insurance, was expanded into the Enterprise Investment Incentive catering to start-ups in non-tech sectors as well.
Over-the-Counter (OTC) Market	This platform was established in 2003 to provide a more cost-effective and faster means of raising equity through initial public offering (IPO) or capital injection from venture capital.

Figure 11.4:   (*Continued*)

Programme	Details
SPRING SEEDS (Startup Enterprise Development Scheme)	SEEDS was first launched by EDB in 2001 to provide equity financing to promising start-ups in high-tech sectors. In July 2007, it was transferred to SPRING and renamed SPRING SEEDS. The scheme was also expanded to include start-ups in non-high-tech sectors with innovative products and/or processes with intellectual content and strong growth potential across international markets.
Improving Access to Land, Labour and Technology	SPRING continued to facilitate cases of land/space and manpower requirements of local enterprises, by providing information on the appropriate policies and expert resources.
7. Supporting Initiatives	
NUS-PSB Centre for Best Practices	The NUS-PSB Centre for Best Practices was set up on 11 October 2000. The aim was to help SMEs attain quantum leaps in their business competitiveness and productivity through adoption of best practices.

Figure 11.4: (*Continued*)

Key Performance Indicators and Major Programmes in Second Period of 2000s: January 2004–December 2009

As elaborated in Chapter 10, SPRING's focus from January 2004 shifted from productivity to enterprise development. This had a bearing on the KPIs and the programmes implemented. Figure 11.5 summarises the KPIs that SPRING used to track its achievements as an enterprise development agency.

Just like the first period, there were no targets shown for the KPIs and no attempts to link the impact of the achievements on productivity. Hence, it is not possible to make an assessment of the achievements.

The major programmes contributing to the achievement of the KPIs in the second period of the 2000s (January 2004–December 2009) are shown in Figure 11.6. They are classified according to the four strategic thrusts of SPRING when it changed its mission to focus on enterprise development.

Key performance indicator	2004	2005	2006
Entrepreneurial Environment • No. of start-ups	42,217	42,992	45,581
First Point of Contact for SMEs (EnterpriseOne Call Centre) • No. of upgrading cases handled	7,634	7,815	10,522
Local Enterprise Finance Scheme (LEFS) • No. of applications approved • Value of applications approved	5,383 $746m	5,766 $637m	3,165 $398m
Local Enterprise Technical Assistance Scheme (LETAS) • No. of applications approved • Value of applications approved	2,510 $21m	1,264 $8m	1,064 $6m
Organisation Excellence • No. of certifications for organisation excellence standards (cumulative)	1,066	1,194	1,317
Standards • No. of new Technical References and Singapore Standards developed	15	14	17
Metrology • No. of companies assisted on measurement traceability	706	703	587
Accreditation • No. of laboratories, inspection bodies and certification bodies accredited (cumulative)	208	227	241
Standards Implementation for Productivity (SIP) • No. of SIP projects (cumulative)	36	40	50
Mutual Recognition Agreements (MRAs) • No. of MRAs under negotiation/signed/ implemented (cumulative)	14	15	15
Weights and Measures • No. of infringements on weights and measures regulations	3	6	4
Consumer Product Safety • No. of accidents reported for controlled items	0	0	0

Figure 11.5: Key Performance Indicators of SPRING, 2004–2006

Note: The list of KPIs and achievements was not shown in the *Annual Report* after 06/07.

Source: Standards, Productivity and Innovation Board, *Annual Report* 06/07.

Programme	Details
1. Nurturing a Pro-business Environment that Encourages Enterprise Formation and Growth	
EnterpriseOne	EnterpriseOne was launched on 22 February 2006 as a comprehensive gateway for local enterprises to access information and advisory services. It comprised an interactive web portal, business advisory services at the Enterprise Development Centres (EDCs), and market and business information services through EBIS@SBF.
EnterpriseOne Business Information Services (EBIS@ SBF)	The initiative was launched by the Singapore Business Federation (SBF) in August 2007 in partnership with National Library Board (NLB), International Enterprise Singapore (IE Singapore) and SPRING to empower businesses with a suite of information services.
Enterprise Development Centres (EDCs)	To widen the reach to enterprises and entrepreneurs, SPRING set up EDCs with the key business chambers and trade associations, beginning with EDC@ASME which was officially opened on 28 March 2005.
BlueSky Exchange and BlueSky Evening	A BlueSky Exchange was conducted in Mandarin for the first time on 7 May 2004 in response to feedback that there were Mandarin-speaking entrepreneurs who wanted to take part in the exchanges.
BlueSky Festival	The first ACE Bluesky Festival was held from 9–11 July 2004 to celebrate and showcase the spirit of entrepreneurship. The event included a BlueSky Carnival, attracting some 6,000 participants. The 5th anniversary of ACE was celebrated at the BlueSky Festival 2008.
ACE's 'Why Not?' Campaign	Launched in May 2008, the nation-wide campaign garnered more than 400 new ideas on nurturing an entrepreneurial Singapore.
Global Entrepreneurship Week 2008	In 2008, ACE and National University of Singapore (NUS) co-organised the first Global Entrepreneurship Week which saw more than 10,000 participants in its activities. The aim was to introduce entrepreneurship to young people.

Figure 11.6: Major Programmes Contributing to Achievement of KPIs, January 2004–December 2009

Note: The list includes only programmes that were launched for the first time. Subsequent developments or runs of the programmes are not included.

Source: Standards, Productivity and Innovation Board, *Annual Report*, various years.

Programme	Details
Entrepreneurial Talent Development Fund	The fund was set up in July 2004 to develop entrepreneurial talent by encouraging 'learning by doing' among students of institutes of higher learning.
Young Entrepreneurs Scheme for Schools (YES! Schools)	The scheme was launched in October 2008 to nurture and promote entrepreneurship in schools.
Young Entrepreneurs Scheme for Start-ups (YES! Start-ups)	The scheme was launched in November 2008 to nurture and encourage youths to be enterprising and innovative through 'hands-on' entrepreneurship learning.
Variable Interest Loan Scheme (V-Loan)	The scheme was launched in January 2005 to make it easier for higher-risk SMEs to obtain loans, by allowing the participating financial institutions (PFIs) to tailor interest rates and customise loan packages to match the risk profiles of companies.
SME Access Loan	This asset securitisation scheme was launched on 8 April 2005 as a new source of financing for SMEs.
GST Assistance Scheme for SMEs	Announced on 16 February 2007, the scheme aimed to help SMEs registering to be a Goods and Services Tax (GST) trader offset the cost of setting up a GST-compliant accounting information technology (IT) system.
SME Credit Bureau	SPRING launched the Bureau on 21 March 2005 together with the Association of Small and Medium Enterprises (ASME), SBF and Infocredit D&B. It served as Singapore's first central database on credit-related information on SMEs.
Special Risk-sharing Initiative (SRI)	In January 2009, this initiative, together with enhancements to the existing financing schemes, was launched in conjunction with Budget 2009 to help enterprises tide over the economic downturn.
Financial Facilitator Programme	The programme was launched in January 2009 with the EDCs and EBIS@SBF to help SMEs with advice and loan facilitation for the enhanced government financing schemes.

Figure 11.6: (*Continued*)

Programme	Details
2. Supporting and Driving the Development of Key Industry Clusters	
Local Enterprise and Association Development (LEAD) programme	The programme, jointly administered by SPRING and IE Singapore, was launched on 4 May 2005 to develop and work with industry associations to improve the capabilities of SMEs in the respective industry sectors.
Capability Development Programme (CDP)	To help SMEs be more competitive, SPRING launched CDP on 26 October 2006. The specific aims were to enable SMEs to develop capabilities, streamline processes, create new and innovative products, and meet international standards. The industries covered were marine and offshore (October 2006), logistics (November 2006), MedTech (March 2007), food & beverage (March 2007), semiconductor (April 2008) and environmental technology (July 2008).
Centre of Innovation (COI)	COIs were set up to provide dedicated assistance to the respective industries in developing new and innovative products, services and processes. These included COIs for Food at Singapore Polytechnic (May 2007), Marine & Offshore Technology at Ngee Ann Polytechnic (October 2007), Precision Engineering at SIMTech (May 2008), Environmental and Water Technology at Ngee Ann Polytechnic (July 2008), and Electronics at Nanyang Polytechnic (January 2009).
Containerised Traffic System	The system was launched in January 2008 to enhance the competitiveness of the land logistics sector.
Retail National Continuing Education & Training Framework	The framework was launched by Workforce Development Agency (WDA) in October 2004, with support from SPRING and the Retail Academy of Singapore.
Warehouse Retail Scheme	The scheme was piloted in 2004 to provide greater flexibility in the use of industrial land by allowing the retail component of a business, not exceeding 40% of total gross floor area (GFA), to be located on the site. The aim was to achieve greater productivity and cost efficiency by encouraging consolidation of business operations such as logistics, headquarter management functions and retailing in a central location.

Figure 11.6: (*Continued*)

Programme	Details
Apparel Singapore	Apparel Singapore, a mark of distinction and business excellence awarded to exemplary apparel manufacturers of Singapore origin, was launched in July 2008 to boost the global competitiveness of Singapore's apparel manufacturers.
Singapore Mozaic	In March 2008, the Singapore Furniture Industries Council (SFIC) launched Singapore Mozaic, a business-to-business brand encapsulating the essence of Singapore furniture and the distinctive attributes of Singapore furniture companies. Supported by SPRING and IE Singapore, it brought together a collection of successful Singapore furniture companies offering a diverse portfolio of consumer, business and specially-crafted products.
GET Singapore	Launched in March 2009, GET Singapore served as a national marketing platform for local enterprises to showcase their well-designed, high-quality Singapore brands locally and abroad.
Restructuring Programme for Shops	Supported by SPRING, the Housing & Development Board (HDB) launched its Restructuring Programme for Shops in 2005 as part of its effort to revitalise neighbourhood precincts.
Chain Master Pilot Project	The project was launched on 19 May 2005. It aimed to help manufacturing companies meet competition from their rivals in locations with lower cost or larger domestic markets, through better supply chain management.
Certification for Aerospace industry	SPRING and the Association of Aerospace Industries (Singapore) signed an MOU with Performance Review Institute USA in October 2008 to promote certification for the aerospace industry.
International Furniture Centre	The centre was officially opened in December 2007 as part of the strategy to make Singapore an international furniture hub.
SCI Print Technology Institute	The institute was launched in February 2008 to meet the advanced training needs of the print industry and to enhance employability in the industry.
Quality Jewellers of Singapore Scheme	With support from STB, SPRING launched the scheme in October 2004. The aim was to encourage jewellers to ensure the quality of their products and provide excellent service to customers.

Figure 11.6:   (*Continued*)

Programme	Details
The Retail Academy of Singapore	The Academy was launched on 26 July 2004 to build critical skills, enable career advancement and attract talent for the retail sector.
National Retail Scholarship	The scholarship was launched in May 2007 to groom future leaders for the retail sector.
Customer Centric Initiative (CCI)	A multi-agency effort by SPRING, NTUC, WDA, STB and SNEF, CCI was launched for the retail sector on 26 August 2005 to create awareness of the importance of good customer service and improve service quality. Subsequently, this was extended to CCI (food & beverage) in June 2007 and CCI (healthcare) in September 2008.
GEMS Up	A multi-agency effort involving SPRING, STB, WDA, NTUC and Institute of Service Excellence at Singapore Management University (SMU), the Go the Extra Mile for Service (GEMS) movement was first launched in 2005 to improve service levels and achieve an excellent service culture. GEMS Up was launched in September 2009 as the second phase of the national movement to bring service excellence up to the next level.
Singapore Merchandise Branding Programme	The programme aimed to build a brand image for the Singapore retail industry based on quality, value and authenticity, so as to make an impact locally and overseas. It was launched on 27 September 2006 jointly by SRA and SPRING.
Mystery Diner Programme	The programme was launched in February 2006 to improve the service standards and performance of food & beverage establishments.
World Gourmet Summit Lifetime Achievement Award	SPRING sponsored the Award to recognise individuals whose innovation and commitment had contributed significantly to the vibrancy of the Singapore dining experience, and to encourage more F&B players to become visionaries in the industry.
Food Safety Programme	The programme was launched on 25 April 2006 to ensure that the local food & beverage industry serve food meeting international food safety standards, thereby helping them to gain a competitive advantage in accessing overseas markets.

Figure 11.6: (*Continued*)

Programme	Details
Food Import Regulations and Standards Database	The database was launched in July 2007 to facilitate food manufacturers' access to global markets.
HACCP Toolkit	The Hazard Analysis Critical Control Point (HACCP) Toolkit, a self-help tool for HACCP implementation, was launched on 3 December 2004.
Sectoral Service Standards for F&B Companies	The standards were launched in July 2008 for food & beverage companies to assess their service quality.
3. Enhancing the Productivity, Innovation and Capabilities of Enterprises	
Executive Management Programme	In 2005, an Executive Management Programme was developed jointly with Singapore Management University (SMU) to train CEOs of SMEs in the areas of finance, marketing and branding, and strategy.
Business Leaders Initiative	The initiative was launched in January 2008 to enhance management capacity both at the top and middle levels and to build a pipeline of future leaders. It comprised three main components — Advanced Management Programme (AMP), training business owners, CEOs and senior executives; Management Development Scholarship (MDS), co-sponsoring MBA programmes for promising young executives; and Executive Development Scholarship (EDS), sponsoring the studies and work attachments of local undergraduates with passion in entrepreneurship or working for SMEs.
Business Advisors Programme	On 27 March 2009, SMU and SPRING launched the programme to facilitate the matching of independent business advisors with SMEs seeking help on various business and corporate areas.
SME Training for Enhanced Performance and Upgrade (Step-UP)	The programme was launched on 19 July 2006 to identify training gaps and run courses for SMEs, focusing on industry and occupational skills of immediate applicability to the workplace.

Figure 11.6: (*Continued*)

Programme	Details
SME Management Action for Results (SMART)	The programme was launched on 12 October 2006 to help SMEs embark on the business excellence journey through consultancy advice and funding support to develop management systems and processes.
HR Capability Package	The package was launched in October 2008 to help SMEs attract, develop and retain talent.
BrandPact	To help local enterprises develop an effective branding strategy, SPRING partnered IE Singapore on this capability development initiative, which was launched on 7 April 2005.
Intellectual Property Management (IPM) for SMEs Programme	The programme was launched on 23 January 2007 by SPRING and Intellectual Property Organisation of Singapore (IPOS) to help SMEs develop a strategy to create, own, protect and exploit their intellectual property such as brand, design and trade secrets.
Design for Enterprises Initiative	DesignSingapore Council, SPRING and IE Singapore launched the initiative in November 2008 to encourage local enterprises to be design-savvy and leverage design as a strategy to boost competitiveness. Design Engage, a part of this initiative, aimed to help enterprises build their strategic design thinking capabilities.
National Business Continuity Management (BCM) Programme	In December 2008, SPRING launched the programme with SBF, designated the National BCM Centre, to promote and entrench BCM in companies.
Technology Enterprise Commercialisation Scheme (TECS)	The scheme was launched in April 2008 to support enterprises and entrepreneurs to bring their innovative ideas to market through early-stage funding for the research, development and commercialisation of proprietary technology innovations.
Proof-of-Concept Grants	In September 2008, National Research Foundation announced Proof-of-Concept Grants, under the National Framework for Innovation and Enterprise, part of which was for the enhancement of TECS.
Technology Fair	The first Technology Fair was held on 24 March 2005 to increase SMEs' awareness of technology as an enabler of innovation and growth.

Figure 11.6: (*Continued*)

Programme	Details
Technology Innovation Programme (TIP)	Part of the National Science & Technology Plan 2010, TIP was launched on 29 August 2006 to encourage technology innovation and to help SMEs grow their businesses with the help of technology.
Incubator Development Programme (IDP)	The programme was launched in February 2009 to nurture innovative start-ups.
Innovation Voucher Scheme (IVS)	The voucher was launched in March 2008 to encourage SMEs to tap the research institutes' extensive engineering and resource base.
Flu Pandemic Business Continuity Guide	The guide was launched in February 2006 to help SMEs understand the possible impact of a flu pandemic and how they could prepare themselves to ensure business continuity.
Technical Reference on Business Continuity Management System	In 2005, SPRING achieved a world's first in its launch of the technical reference, which would enhance the standing of local enterprises in local and overseas markets.
BUILD (Business Upgrading Initiatives for Long-term Development) package	The package was launched in February 2009 to help SMEs overcome the global economic crisis and build their capabilities for the future.
4. Increasing Enterprises' Access to Markets and Business Opportunities	
GeBIZ mall	The GeBIZ Mall was launched on 24 March 2015 to help SMEs market their goods and services directly to government agencies on the Government Electronic Business portal (GeBIZ).
Government Procurement Guide for SMEs	A new guidebook to help SMEs access information on government procurement procedures was launched on 24 June 2005.

Figure 11.6: (*Continued*)

Programme	Details
Global Sourcing Hub	The hub aimed to connect more than 100,000 SME suppliers to major corporate buyers, and give them a critical edge in visibility and e-commerce capability in the global marketplace. It was launched in January 2006.
Free Trade Agreement (FTA) Guidebooks	In 2005, SPRING published two guidebooks to familiarise enterprises with trading in goods and services under the FTA framework. Other awareness programmes included seminars and news alerts.
Food Conference on Exploring Food Export Opportunities	The conference was organised in July 2008 to share the latest developments and insights on food safety standards, regulations and compliance issues for exports to the United States, Europe, Japan and Korea.
Singapore Standards	SPRING continued to develop and launch standards for adoption. These included standards related to productivity, safety, e-payment, office ergonomics, hotel security and property management.
Participation on International Platforms	SPRING continued to participate actively on platforms such as APEC Sub-Committee on Standards and Conformance, ASEAN Consultative Committee on Standards and Quality, and International Organization for Standardization (ISO) to reduce technical barriers to trade.
Metrology Quality System	SPRING's Metrology Quality System was assessed in September 2004 and found to conform to ISO 17025, a quality management system standard for calibration and testing laboratories. This enabled mutual recognition of national measurement standards and calibration certificates issued by signatories of the global Mutual Recognition Agreement on Measurement.
Singapore Accreditation Council 5-year Plan	SPRING announced the plan in October 2008. The strategic outcomes outlined in the plan were Accreditation, Management/Development and Promotion.

Figure 11.6:   (*Continued*)

Programme	Details
Accreditation Scheme for Biomed Industry	Singapore Accreditation Council (SAC) collaborated with the College of American Pathologists on a joint accreditation programme for the biomed industry. Launched on 31 August 2005, the programme aimed to raise the level of confidence in medical testing services in Singapore.
Good Laboratory Practice (GLP)	Launched on 14 June 2006, the GLP programme enabled GLP-compliant Singapore laboratories to have their pre-clinical studies data accepted in 30 OECD countries, thus avoiding duplicate safety testing and shortening the time-to-market for new products.
ISO Singapore 2005	ISO held its 28th General Assembly in Singapore from 19–23 September 2005. It was hosted by SPRING, the national standards body. This was the first time that a Southeast Asian country had played host to this international standards meeting.
PAC Multilateral Recognition Agreement for Product Certification	In July 2007, SPRING and Pacific Accreditation Cooperation (PAC) signed the agreement to help exporters save certification costs through mutual recognition of product certification.
IEC Quality Assessment System for Electronic Components	In August 2007, SPRING joined the International Electro-technical Commission (IEC) Quality Assessment System for Electronic Components to facilitate exports by electrical and electronic product manufacturers.
SPRING-SCI Council MOU	In March 2008, SPRING and Singapore Chemical Industry (SCI) Council signed an MOU to help Singapore companies meet the EU REACH regulation.
Quality and Standards 2006 (QS2006)	The inaugural QS2006, held from 17–20 October 2006, celebrated 40 years of the National Standardisation Programme. The event showcased how industries and companies could benefit from standards and conformance, and allowed regulators and stakeholders to learn about overseas regulations. A fund to support new initiatives and programmes under the Standards & Conformance plan was also unveiled.

Figure 11.6:   (*Continued*)

Programme	Details
Export Technical Assistance Centre (ETAC)	ETAC was launched on 17 October 2006 to help enterprises understand and navigate the maze of standards, technical regulations and compliance requirements of overseas markets.
Instruments affixed with Accuracy Label	SPRING announced on 9 February 2007 that 40,000 weighing and measuring instruments used for trade in Singapore had been verified accurate and affixed with the Accuracy Label, giving consumers peace of mind in their shopping.
5. Supporting Initiatives	
SPRING Enterprise Conference	The inaugural conference was held on 5 April 2007. Themed 'Enabling Enterprise,' it focused on three key enablers of enterprise growth: people, technology innovation and financing.
SPRING's Flagship Magazine	SPRING's new flagship magazine, *Enterprise Today*, was launched on 1 August 2005. The magazine aimed to address the needs of Singapore's growing local enterprises. This magazine was succeeded by *SPRING News* on 1 January 2009.
Quality and Standards e-news letter	The e-newsletter was launched in April 2008 to update companies on the latest standards and conformance matters.

Figure 11.6: (*Continued*)

A comparison of Figures 11.4 and 11.6 shows clearly the shift of the programmes from productivity to enterprise development. Since productivity promotion was no longer a function undertaken by SPRING from 2004, the corresponding programmes were either discontinued or transferred elsewhere. One of these was the Innovation and Quality Circle (IQC) programme, which was transferred to the Singapore Productivity Association (SPA) in 2008. This included the International Exposition of Innovation and Quality Circles (IEIQC), which was subsequently renamed International Exposition of Team Excellence (IETEX) by SPA. Another programme that was transferred was the International Management Action Award (IMAA).

Productivity Drive in the 2000s in Retrospect

After the intense focus on productivity in the 1980s and 1990s, the 2000s marked a turning point in the national productivity drive. Instead of productivity, the Government's attention turned to innovation, entrepreneurship and growth. NPQC did develop a 10-year productivity plan for the 2000s. However, this was somewhat derailed by the subsequent divestment of a large part of SPRING's core functions as well as the repositioning of SPRING's mission to focus on enterprise development. In terms of institutional capability, the national productivity organisation that was synonymous with PSB faded from the scene after the divestment of PSB Corp and PSB Cert and the repositioning of SPRING. In its place was a new SPRING championing enterprise development, with capabilities in policy-making, facilitation of industry and enterprise development, and grants administration.

It is certainly not the case that the national programmes to improve productivity had ceased in the 2000s. Rather, the efforts were diffused and the hitherto laser focus on productivity became dim as a result of changes in priorities and institutional capabilities. At the same time, the Government's emphasis on growing the economy led to a continued expansion of the labour force, mainly through the import of foreign labour. Compared with the previous two decades, the difference now was that the growth was much higher. From 2.09 million in 2000, with a foreign labour share of 28.1 per cent, the labour force increased by an unprecedented one million to 3.10 million in 2010, with a foreign labour share of 34.7 per cent.

For the 2000s as a whole, the average annual productivity growth was a mere 1.0 per cent, much lower than that in the previous four decades and below the projected sustainable growth rate of 2–3 per cent stated in the *Report of the Economic Review Committee*. This contributed only 21 per cent to the average annual gross domestic product (GDP) growth of 4.8 per cent, compared with the huge 79 per cent from labour arising from the surge in the labour force.

VI

2010s

Chapter 12

Renewing the Productivity Drive in the 2010s[1]

"Our focus on productivity is not new. We had productivity movements in fact going back to the 1970s, then in the 80s and 90s, each with a different focus ... So the productivity effort goes back a long way... It is therefore a continuous and unending effort. This is also why many of the advanced countries are themselves revisiting the issue of productivity, as a basis of sustaining their growth."

Tharman Shanmugaratnam
Minister for Finance
Budget Debate Round-Up Speech 2010
4 March 2010

Economic Priorities in the 2010s

As stated in Chapter 10, the Singapore economy entered the decade of the 2010s on a positive note, growing 15.2 per cent in 2010 after a contraction of 0.6 per cent in 2009. This underlined the resilience of the economy upon implementation of appropriate policies and measures, even if the high growth was partly due to the low base in 2009.

To map out the directions for Singapore in the 2010s, the Economic Strategies Committee (ESC) was formed on 27 May 2009.

---

[1] The cut-off date for the write-up in this chapter is 2 March 2017, the date of the round-up of the debate on Budget 2017.

Its specific task was to develop strategies for Singapore to maximise its opportunities in a new world environment with the aim of achieving sustained and inclusive growth for the decade ahead. The committee was chaired by Minister for Finance Tharman Shanmugaratnam, with members drawn from the public and private sectors and the labour movement.

The *Report of the Economic Strategies Committee* was released on 1 February 2010. In his opening remarks at the press conference to share the report, Tharman Shanmugaratnam summarised the economic priorities in the 2010s which set the context for ESC's recommendations. He said:

> *"This will be an exceptional decade — a decade that is unusual both for its opportunities and its challenge. Our assessment is that the next five to ten years will provide greater opportunities for growth in the world around us than any of the past decades that we have seen — greater opportunities for companies to grow. But at the same time, we will also see greater constraints on growth than we have had in the past. In particular, because of a slower growing workforce, and over time too because we will run up against the limits of our land. We will also have to use energy more efficiently, diversify our sources of energy and play our role over time as a responsible member of the international community in reducing carbon emissions."*

The top priority was thus to capitalise on the opportunities and grow the economy. At the same time, it was clear that the growth of the labour force would decrease. Curtailing the rate of increase of foreign workers became a priority, as the share of foreign workers in the labour force had escalated considerably over the years. As shown in Figure 12.1, the share jumped tenfold from 3.2 per cent in 1970 to 34.7 per cent in 2010.

The policy position on foreign worker dependence was clearly stated in the ESC report:

> *"We should avoid becoming overly dependent on foreign workers, and continue to increase their proportion of the total workforce over the long term ... we cannot increase the number of foreign workers as liberally as we did over the last decade, or else we will run up against real physical and social limits.*

	1970	1980	1990	2000	2010	2016
Labour force (million)	0.65	1.07	1.54	2.09	3.10	3.67
Foreign labour share (%)	3.2	7.3	16.1	28.1	34.7	38.5

Figure 12.1:   Share of Foreign Labour, 1970 to 2016

Source: Department of Statistics, *Yearbook of Statistics,* various issues; Ministry of Manpower, *Labour Force Survey,* various issues.

Further, if access to labour is too easy, companies will have little incentive to invest in productivity improvements, which will affect our efforts to upgrade the skills and wages of lower-income Singaporean workers."

ESC spelt out the overall goal of 'high-skilled people, innovative economy, distinctive global city' for the decade of the 2010s. To realise this goal, seven strategies were proposed: growing through skills and innovation, anchoring Singapore as a Global-Asia Hub, building a vibrant and diverse corporate ecosystem, making innovation pervasive and strengthening commercialisation of R&D, becoming a smart energy economy, enhancing land productivity to secure future growth, and building a distinctive global city and an endearing home. A sustainable gross domestic product (GDP) growth averaging 3–5 per cent a year was projected for the decade ahead, supported by productivity growth of 2–3 per cent a year.

Three weeks after the release of the ESC report, the Government's Budget 2010 set out the actions to implement its recommendations. The focus was on building the capabilities required to transform Singapore into an advanced economy with superior skills, quality jobs and higher incomes. To achieve this, investments would be made to raise productivity, grow globally competitive companies, and include all Singaporeans in the benefits of growth.

Six years after the release of the ESC report, the Committee on the Future Economy (CFE) was convened in January 2016. The committee was given the task of building on ESC's work and addressing the new challenges facing Singapore. Co-chaired by Minister for Finance Heng Swee Keat and Minister for Trade and Industry

(Industry) S. Iswaran, the committee comprised 30 members from the public and private sectors across industries.[2]

The *Report of the Committee on the Future Economy* was released on 9 February 2017. CFE's assessment was that good progress had been made in implementing ESC's recommendations — including developing higher skills in the workforce, growing an innovative economy, and building a distinctive global city. Nevertheless, it emphasised that the world was now very different from the start of the decade, due to long-term structural changes and unexpected events. First, global growth had been subdued and was expected to be lower than that in the previous decade. Second, technological change had escalated and global value chains and production patterns were changing rapidly. Third, protectionist tendencies and anti-globalisation trends had risen.

Despite the challenging global environment, CFE emphasised that there were opportunities for Singapore to seize to thrive in the decade ahead. It underlined the point that:

> *"We cannot know which industries will succeed. What we do know is that Singapore must stay open to trade, talent and ideas, and build deep capabilities. By being innovative, bold and willing to change, and by remaining open to the world, and deepening our knowledge of markets everywhere, our businesses and people can grasp the opportunities that this new environment offers, and Singapore can continue to prosper."*

In line with this, the vision of the future economy was stated as:

> *"Our vision is for us to be the pioneers of the next generation. In the future economy, our people should have deep skills and be inspired to learn throughout their lives; our businesses should be innovative and nimble; our city vibrant, connected to the world, and continually renewing itself; our Government coordinated, inclusive and responsive."*

---

[2] S. Iswaran was appointed co-Chairman of CFE on 16 May 2016. Before that, he was Deputy Chairman. Chan Chun Sing, Minister in the Prime Minister's Office, was appointed Deputy Chairman on 16 May 2016.

To realise this vision, seven mutually-reinforcing strategies were identified: deepen and diversify international connections, acquire and utilise deep skills, strengthen enterprise capabilities to innovate and scale up, build strong digital capabilities, develop a vibrant and connected city of opportunity, develop and implement Industry Transformation Maps (ITMs), and partner each other to enable innovation and growth. Collectively, these strategies would support a GDP growth rate of 2–3 per cent a year over the next decade.

At the media conference held in conjunction with the release of the CFE report, Heng Swee Keat made it clear what the report aimed to do. He said:

> "What the CFE aims to do is to set out the direction and broad strategy rather than a detailed roadmap. We have to develop the agility and adaptability to cope with change and to seize new opportunities."

This statement emphasised the point that it did not make sense to have a detailed roadmap in a highly volatile and uncertain future, and that the best way to be future-ready was to be agile and adaptable.

Policy Intent on Productivity in the 2010s

In a reversal of the policy position taken in the 2000s, productivity was strongly emphasised again in the early 2010s. This was a consequence of the intent to decrease the growth of the labour force, which meant that the slack had to be taken up by productivity to drive economic growth.

In fact, just before the turn of the decade, an Inter-Agency Taskforce on Productivity, jointly led by the Ministry of Manpower (MOM) and Ministry of Trade and Industry (MTI), was set up in February 2009. Headed by Lee Yi Shyan, Minister of State (Trade and Industry and Manpower), the Taskforce focused on the services sector which took up 68 per cent of total employment and lagged the manufacturing sector's productivity. It zoomed in on three sectors — hotel, retail and food & beverage — which were deemed to be less productive compared with other countries. The Taskforce identified four key productivity levers for the three sectors: service standards, innovation, manpower management, and research and benchmarking.

Subsequently, the policy intent on productivity came across strongly in the *Report of the Economic Strategies Committee* and in Budget 2010. On the key challenge faced by Singapore in the future, the ESC report emphasised:

> *"We must shift to achieving GDP growth by expanding productivity rather than the labour force. We must boost productivity in order to stay competitive, upgrade the quality of jobs, and raise our people's incomes. A slower growing workforce makes it all the more important for every enterprise to innovate to create value, and to maximise the potential and performance of every worker. This shift to productivity-driven growth will require major new investments in the skills, expertise and innovative capabilities of our people and businesses over the next decade......*
>
> *We can achieve productivity growth of 2 to 3 percent per year over the next 10 years, more than double the 1 percent achieved over the last decade. This is a challenging target, particularly applied across the economy and not just within a single sector. Attaining it will require a comprehensive national effort."*

To effect the comprehensive national effort, ESC recommended the formation of a high-level national council to oversee and drive efforts to boost productivity and expand continuing education and training. It also recommended a national productivity fund to provide grants to support industry-focused and enterprise-level productivity initiatives at the sectoral level, and a productivity and innovation centre to assist enterprises.

In a clear sign of the Government's intention to carry out ESC's recommendations, Tharman Shanmugaratnam said in his Budget Speech 2010 on 22 February 2010:

> *"The Government has accepted the key thrusts of the ESC report ... Budget 2010 therefore looks beyond the immediate rebound in the economy.*

It focuses on building up the capabilities we need for a phase shift in our economy over the next decade, with growth being based on the quality of our efforts rather than the ever-expanding use of manpower and other resources.

Our key goal is to grow our productivity by 2% to 3% per year over the next decade, more than double the 1% we achieved over the last decade. Raising skills and productivity is the only viable way we can achieve higher wages, and is the best way to help citizens with low incomes. If we achieve this goal, we can raise real incomes by one-third in 10 years."

In the same speech, announcements were made on the formation of the National Productivity and Continuing Education Council (NPCEC), creation of the National Productivity Fund (NPF), and introduction of a Productivity and Innovation Credit (PIC). These would be complemented by gradual increases in the foreign worker levies and tightening of the foreign worker inflow, starting from 2010.

In sharp contrast to the ESC report, the *Report of the Committee on the Future Economy* did not set any target for productivity growth, even as the labour force and the foreign labour share (shown in Figure 12.1) continued to increase. The single substantive statement on productivity is the following in relation to the ITMs:

"Where an industry has good growth prospects, the ITM's task would be to map out the opportunities, invest in capabilities, and help Singaporeans take up good jobs in these industries. Such ITMs should also include strategies to strengthen the nexus between R&D investments and industry plans ...

In contrast, some industries are facing challenges in restructuring, for instance if they are domestically-focused and require large numbers of low-skilled workers. ITMs for such industries will have to focus on strategies to increase their productivity and upgrade their jobs. In these industries, ITMs have to identify the key headwinds, and support companies to transform their operations."

This statement seemed to suggest that the focus on productivity should apply primarily to industries facing challenges in restructuring, whereas other strategies would be more pertinent for the industries with good growth prospects. Clearly, productivity was no longer the mantra that had pervaded the ESC report.

Questions Raised About Renewed Productivity Drive in the Early 2010s

The renewed emphasis on productivity in the early 2010s was a déjà vu for many, especially the older Singaporeans who had been exposed to the Productivity Movement in the 1980s. It led some to ask how the current productivity push was different from the Productivity Movement in the past, why productivity was de-emphasised in the previous decade, and whether the poor productivity performance was due to the lack of consistency in sustaining productivity growth.

An article titled 'ESC Recommendations on Productivity — Paradigm shift or pendulum swing?', published in *The Straits Times* on 6 February 2010, summarised some of the sentiments. Choy Keen Meng, a Nanyang Technological University (NTU) economist, felt that the policy-makers and the people had made a mistake in becoming complacent and losing sight of the productivity issue during the long boom years. Member of Parliament (MP) Mdm Halimah Yacob opined that the focus on economic growth in the 2000s had sidelined questions about whether a growth model based on labour was sustainable. She added that the change in the name and focus for the National Productivity Board (NPB), Singapore Productivity and Standards Board (PSB) and Standards, Productivity and Innovation Board (SPRING) might have caused policy-makers to lose sight of productivity and its related issues.

During the debate on Budget 2010, Nominated Member of Parliament (NMP) Viswa Sadasivan questioned whether the proposed thrust of raising productivity through upgrading skills, innovation and economic restructuring would work. He asked:

> *"Why will it work this time if in spite of all the systematic measures in the past 38 years we've only managed to get productivity up to 1% and then appear to have hit a stone wall?"*

In response, Tharman Shanmugaratnam said in his round-up speech on the Budget 2010 debate on 4 March 2010:

"Some like NMP Viswa Sadasivan thought that our renewed attention to productivity growth reflects the failure of these previous efforts. This is patently not the case.

The Singapore economy of today is a completely transformed place, in most sectors of the economy, compared to what we were 20 to 30 years ago. Since 1980, our productivity levels have more than doubled ... So the productivity effort goes back a long way."

Clearly, the message is that the focus on productivity in the past did make a positive difference to the economy. In elaborating the reason for the focus on productivity in Budget 2010, Tharman Shanmugaratnam, like Lee Kuan Yew and Lee Hsien Loong in the past, referred to Kohei Goshi's statement that 'productivity is a marathon with no finish line.' He added:

"It is therefore a continuous and unending effort. This is also why many of the advanced countries are themselves revisiting the issue of productivity, as a basis of sustaining their growth ... The journey of productivity, innovation and service quality therefore never ends ... It will also get more challenging as we catch up with the leaders and strive for higher levels than before."

What was left unsaid is whether the 'continuous and unending effort' was sustained or whether there was a pause or deceleration in the productivity marathon in the 2000s.

Formation of National Productivity and Continuing Education Council

On 1 April 2010, NPCEC was established to drive the national productivity effort and the development of a national continuing education and training (CET) system. The specific aims of NPCEC were to:

a. Prioritise and champion national productivity initiatives at the sectoral and enterprise levels;

b. Develop a comprehensive, first-class national CET system; and

c. Foster a culture of productivity and continuous learning and upgrading in Singapore.

The composition of the first 2-year term of NPCEC, with tripartite representation from the Government, unions and private sector, is shown in Figure 12.2. Unlike the previous national productivity

	Name	Designation
	Chairman	
1	Teo Chee Hean	Deputy Prime Minister
	Members	
	Government Representatives	
2	Lim Hng Kiang	Minister for Trade and Industry
3	Gan Kim Yong	Minister for Manpower
4	Lim Hwee Hua	Minister in the Prime Minister's Office and Second Minister for Finance and Transport
5	S. Iswaran	Senior Minister of State, Trade and Industry and Education
6	Grace Fu	Senior Minister of State, National Development and Education
7	Lee Yi Shyan	Minister of State, Trade and Industry and Manpower
	Union Representatives	
8	John de Payva	President, National Trades Union Congress (NTUC)
9	Lim Swee Say	Secretary-General, NTUC
10	Lim Kuang Beng	General Secretary, Singapore Industrial and Services Employees' Union (SISEU); and NTUC Central Committee Member
11	Abdul Subhan bin Shamsul Hussein	President, Food, Drinks and Allied Workers' Union (FDAWU)

Figure 12.2: Composition of National Productivity and Continuing Education Council, 1 April 2010–31 March 2012
Source: Ministry of Trade and Industry (2010).

	Name	Designation
	Industry Representatives	
12	Stephen Lee	President, Singapore National Employers Federation
13	Dr Ahmad Magad	President, Singapore Productivity Association
14	Aaron Boey	Asia Pacific President, Levi Strauss
15	Choo Chiau Beng	CEO, Keppel Corp
16	Liew Mun Leong	President and CEO, CapitaLand
17	Douglas Foo	Chairman, Apex-Pal
18	Simon Lam	Venture Director, Shell, Eastern Petroleum Complex
19	Pek Lian Guan	Managing Director, Tiong Seng Contractors Pte Ltd

Figure 12.2:   (*Continued*)

councils which were chaired by a Minister or a Minister of State, NPCEC was chaired by a Deputy Prime Minister to lend clout to the council, as well as to signal the Government's strong commitment to the national productivity drive.

On 9 June 2011, changes were made to the Government representation on NPCEC following the formation of a new Cabinet after the General Election on 7 May 2011. Tharman Shanmugaratnam, promoted to Deputy Prime Minister and concurrently made Minister for Manpower, took over the chairmanship of NPCEC from Teo Chee Hean. Minister for Education Heng Swee Keat, Minister of State for Manpower and National Development Tan Chuan-Jin and Minister of State for Finance and Transport Josephine Teo replaced Gan Kim Yong, Lim Hwee Hua, S. Iswaran and Grace Fu.

The high-level NPCEC was supported by a secretariat staffed by MTI and MOM.

Sectoral Approach to Drive Singapore's Productivity

In the press release, *The National Productivity and Continuing Education Council (NPCEC) Holds Its First Meeting*, dated 30 April 2010, Teo Chee Hean said:

> *"The NPCEC will adopt a holistic approach in its work. We will focus on driving productivity improvements at the worker, enterprise and sectoral levels."*

Subsequently, *The Straits Times* quoted him as saying that this approach was "what sets the new council apart from earlier high-level productivity councils which had focused largely on workers". Placed in historical context, this statement referred to the focus on the human aspects of productivity in the 1980s. As described in Chapter 5, a total approach to productivity was in fact taken from 1986.

What did set the NPCEC apart from the earlier productivity councils was the sectoral approach taken. In contrast to the productivity drive in the past which was executed largely at the national level,[3] NPCEC adopted a sectoral approach to achieve the productivity growth target of 2–3 per cent a year over the next 10 years. This approach entailed a focus on the key sector verticals, complemented by certain horizontal productivity enablers that cut across all sectors.

NPCEC identified 12 priority sectors in 2010, based on their GDP contribution, employment size and potential for productivity improvement. Another four sectors were identified in 2012, bringing the total to 16 sectors covering 55 per cent of Singapore's GDP and 60 per cent of employment. The list of priority sectors is shown in Figure 12.3.

For each sector, a lead agency was identified. The lead agency was responsible for developing the productivity roadmap for the sector in consultation with the unions, public and private sectors, and local and international experts. Once the roadmap was approved by

---

[3]The national productivity councils in the past did address sectoral-level issues as well. However, the emphasis was very much on national-level issues that cut across the various sectors.

	Sector	Lead Agency
1	Construction	Building and Construction Authority (BCA)
2	Electronics	Economic Development Board (EDB)
3	Precision engineering	EDB
4	Transport engineering	EDB
5	General manufacturing	SPRING
6	Retail	SPRING
7	Food & beverage	SPRING
8	Hotels	Singapore Tourism Board (STB)
9	Healthcare	Ministry of Health (MOH)
10	Infocomm and media	Info-communications Development Authority of Singapore (IDA)
11	Logistics and storage	EDB
12	Administrative and support services	• Security industry — Ministry of Home Affairs (MHA) • Cleaning industry — National Environment Agency(NEA) • Landscaping industry — National Parks Board (NParks) • Agriculture industry — Agri-Food & Veterinary Authority of Singapore (AVA)
13	Financial services	Monetary Authority of Singapore (MAS)
14	Accountancy	Singapore Accountancy Commission (SAC)
15	Social services	Ministry of Social and Family Development (MSF)
16	Process construction & maintenance	EDB

Figure 12.3: 16 Priority Sectors for Productivity Improvement

Source: Ministry of Trade and Industry (2010 and 2012); Way to Go website (www.waytogo.sg).

NPCEC, the agency was then responsible for implementing it and reporting the progress periodically.

Work groups were also formed to study the horizontal productivity enablers. These horizontals included CET, research and benchmarking, small and medium enterprises (SMEs), and public communication.

The approach taken was thus very much decentralised, with different agencies being responsible for raising productivity in their respective sectors and held accountable to NPCEC for the progress made. This was a major contrast with the past where NPB, as well as its successors, was the main agency executing many of the initiatives and working with others to implement other programmes. This time round, without a focal point like NPB, much of the coordination and monitoring work was carried out by the NPCEC secretariat jointly staffed by MTI and MOM.

Establishment of National Productivity Fund

To support the national productivity drive, NPF and the Productivity Fund Administration Board (PFAB) were established on 1 November 2010 under the National Productivity Fund Act.

According to the Act, NPF would be used for the following:

a. Provision of financing (but not loans) or incentives (including grants and scholarships) to any public authority, enterprise, educational institution or other person (whether in Singapore or elsewhere) undertaking or facilitating any programme or matters relating to productivity enhancement and continuing education;

b. Payment of expenses incurred by the Board in the performance of its functions and the discharge of its duties under this Act, including any remuneration or allowances payable to the members of the Board who are not public officers; and

c. Payment of all expenses incidental to or arising from the administration, investment and management of moneys in the Fund.

The role of PFAB was to manage and administer NPF, and evaluate and review the proposals relating to the use of the Fund as advised by NPCEC. The NPCEC Chairman chaired the Board of Directors of PFAB, with selected Government representatives as members.

A total of $1 billion was set aside for NPF in 2010 to support initiatives for the first five years. The Government topped it up with another $1 billion in Financial Year (FY) 2011 and $1.5 billion in FY2015 to extend the support beyond the first five years, and to support more productivity and SkillsFuture initiatives.

By the end of FY2014 (ended 31 March 2015), or almost five years since the establishment of NPF, close to $1.6 billion[4] had been allocated to the various productivity plans and initiatives. The construction sector received the lion's share. In 2010, $250 million of NPF was allocated to the Construction Productivity and Capability Fund (CPCF), managed by BCA, to raise the productivity of the construction sector. A second tranche of $450 million was allocated to CPCF in March 2015.

Comprehensive Range of Government Assistance Schemes

The renewed productivity drive was supported by a comprehensive range of government assistance schemes to help the broad base of enterprises across all sectors improve their productivity. Some of the existing schemes were expanded and new ones were introduced. Those related to productivity alone numbered more than a hundred. Figure 12.4 provides a selection of the main schemes to illustrate the wide range of help available.

Besides the various government assistance schemes, PIC was introduced in 2010 as a major tax incentive to boost productivity. This was effected by providing significant tax deductions to incentivise businesses to invest in innovative and productivity enhancement activities. The activities covered six areas: research & development; design projects; registration of patents, trademarks, designs and

---

[4]The figure is arrived at by adding the amounts allocated for each financial year, as reported in the PFAB annual reports submitted to Parliament for FY2010 to FY2014.

Scheme	Administering agency	Description
1st-level enterprise capability development Innovation and Capability Voucher (ICV)	SPRING	Encourage SMEs[5] to take the first step to develop their capabilities by providing them a voucher valued at $5,000 to redeem the cost incurred for: i. consultancy services in the areas of innovation, productivity, human resources, and financial management; and ii. integrated solutions (e.g. mobile ordering and payment system, and fleet management system).
In-depth enterprise capability development Capability Development Grant (CDG)	SPRING	Provide financial assistance to SMEs to build capabilities in ten business areas: brand and marketing strategy, business excellence, business strategy innovation, quality and standards, financial management, human capital development, intellectual property and franchising, productivity improvement, service excellence, and technology innovation.
Industry collaboration Collaborative Industry Project (CIP)	SPRING	Provide funding support to enterprises and industry partners (e.g. trade associations) to form consortia to develop and implement solutions that address challenges faced by the industry.

Figure 12.4: Examples of Enterprise-based Government Assistance Schemes Related to Productivity

Source: SME Portal (www.smeportal.sg); Way to Go website (www.waytogo.sg); websites and press releases of the various administering agencies.

---

[5] SMEs are defined as enterprises that are registered or incorporated in Singapore; have at least 30% local shareholding; and have not more than $100 million group sales turnover or not more than 200 employees under the group.

Scheme	Administering agency	Description
Infocomm technology iSPRINT (Increase SME Productivity with Infocomm Adoption & Transformation)	IDA[6]	Encourage SMEs to adopt infocomm technology (ICT) solutions by providing funding support for: i. Deployment of pre-qualified and customised solutions; ii. Piloting emerging ICT solutions; and iii. Deployment of high-speed connectivity solutions.
Low-wage workers Inclusive Growth Programme (IGP)	Employment and Employability Institute (e2i)	Co-fund enterprises for costs incurred for automation and equipment, process re-engineering, and training associated with productivity improvement projects, with the condition that productivity gains are shared with low-wage workers through wage increases.
Manpower-lean enterprise development Lean Enterprise Development (LED)	Coordinated by a cross-agency LED taskforce comprising Singapore Workforce Development Agency (WDA)[7], SPRING, NTUC, EDB, STB, IDA, BCA and e2i	Provide grants and transitional manpower support to assist the transformation and growth of progressive SMEs that are committed to: i. Becoming more manpower-lean; ii. Building a stronger Singapore core; and iii. Developing better-quality workers.

Figure 12.4: (*Continued*)

---

[6] IDA and Media Development Authority (MDA) were restructured to form two new statutory boards — Government Technology Agency of Singapore (GovTech) and Info-Communications Media Development Authority (IMDA) — with effect from 1 October 2016. iSPRINT is now administered by IMDA.

[7] WDA was reconstituted into a new statutory board, Workforce Singapore (WSG), with effect from 4 October 2016, to drive the transformation of the workforce to support economic growth. At the same time, the implementation of the SkillsFuture movement was transferred from WDA to a new statutory board, SkillsFuture Singapore (SSG), formed under the Ministry of Education.

Scheme	Administering agency	Description
Technology Technology Adoption Programme (TAP)	Agency for Science, Technology and Research (A*STAR)	Help SMEs to adopt technology to improve by: i. Sourcing and matching SMEs with technology solutions or developers; ii. Piloting solutions; and iii. Providing advice on areas that technology can help.
Training Enterprise Training Support (ETS)	WDA	Help businesses, societies and non-profit organisations to increase productivity, train, attract and retain employees through the development of good human resource practices, and review and restructuring of compensation and benefits.

Figure 12.4:   (*Continued*)

plant varieties; acquisition and licensing of intellectual property rights; training of employees; and acquisition and leasing of information technology (IT) and automation equipment.

PIC was initially made available for five years, from Year of Assessment (YA) 2011 to YA 2015. Businesses could deduct 250 per cent of their expenditure incurred for activities in the six qualifying areas from their taxable income, capped at $300,000 per year in each area. They also had the option of converting the tax credit into a non-taxable cash grant at 7 per cent of the qualifying expenditure, up to $21,000 (i.e. 7 per cent of the cap of $300,000).

In FY2014, the Government announced that PIC would be extended to YA 2018. Subsequently, enhancements were made to encourage more businesses, especially SMEs, to improve productivity. The enhancements included a higher tax deduction of 400 per cent of qualifying expenditure, an increase in the cap on qualifying expenditure from $300,000 to $400,000, a higher cap of $600,000 for SMEs (under the PIC+ Scheme), and a dollar-for-dollar matching cash bonus (under the PIC Bonus Scheme).

In Budget Speech 2016, Finance Minister Heng Swee Keat announced that PIC would not be extended beyond YA 2018. This was in line with the Government's plan to shift away from broad-based measures to those that were more targeted at supporting industry transformation under a new $4.5 billion Industry Transformation Programme. The details are given in Chapter 13.

Whither the Productivity Drive in the Second Half of the 2010s?

In a nutshell, the ground was well-tilled for a renewed Productivity Movement in the 2010s. The policy statements, infrastructure and schemes put in place in the early 2010s collectively affirmed the Government's strong commitment to the national productivity drive. Fronting all these was a high-profile NPCEC.

Beyond the halfway mark, however, there appeared to be a change in policy regarding the approach taken to promote productivity. The clearest indication of this was the scarce mention of productivity in the CFE report and in the Budget 2017 Statement. The details are given in Chapter 13.

Chapter 13

2010s: The Big Challenge to Raise Productivity[1]

"In our new situation, productivity becomes more important, not less. Not only is it important to grow our economy, but it is also crucial for raising the incomes of workers. In the short term, wages may rise by themselves in a tight labour market. But in the long term, wage rises can only be sustained through higher productivity. Therefore we have embarked on our next phase of the productivity drive — continuing to upgrade individual workers but also emphasising raising productivity at the industry and company level."

Prime Minister Lee Hsien Loong
Opening of National Productivity Month
7 October 2014

Focus of Productivity Drive in the First Half of the 2010s

When news of the renewed Productivity Movement[2] was made public in 2010, there was much buzz in the media reminiscing the productivity campaigns in the past. Teamy the Bee, the well-known productivity mascot, was featured prominently again in the media. In fact, in 2009, Lee Yi Shyan, Minister of State (Trade and Industry

---

[1]The cut-off date for the write-up in this chapter is 2 March 2017, the date of the round-up of the debate on Budget 2017.
[2]The term 'renewed' or any other similar word was not used in any official statement or document. Nevertheless, judging from the hiatus in the 2000s, the Productivity Movement in the 2010s was clearly a renewal of what had been muted in the previous decade.

and Manpower) had suggested that Teamy could be resurrected and given a makeover to become a Transformer Bee (a la Transformers) to front a new productivity campaign.[3] Similarly, in the Debate on the 2010 Budget, Member of Parliament Dr Ahmad Magad[4], proposed that either Teamy or a new mascot be identified to spur fresh vigour and vitality in the renewed Productivity Movement. He even went on to croon what Teamy had preached, "Good, better, best, never let it rest, if your good is better, make your better best".

The eventual approach taken, however, was quite different. In contrast to the 1980s and 1990s, the campaign aspect of the productivity drive in the first half of the 2010s was very much subdued. Instead, the national productivity drive focused on the implementation of the plans for the priority sectors identified. Supporting this was a small-scale outreach campaign.

Sectoral Productivity Plans and Key Initiatives Rolled Out

As stated in Chapter 12, each of the lead agencies for the 16 priority sectors identified was responsible for developing the productivity roadmap for the sector, getting it approved by the National Productivity and Continuing Education Council (NPCEC), implementing the programmes and reporting the progress periodically.

Figure 13.1 summarises the key issues identified and the programmes rolled out for the priority sectors, as well as other areas. Clearly, many programmes were launched in the first half of the 2010s in the 16 priority sectors to improve productivity. These were complemented by certain horizontal programmes that cut across the sectors. However, the impact of all these programmes on the respective sectors' productivity was not evident. As described below, the productivity performance of the economy and the various sectors at the halfway mark of the 2010s was lacklustre.

---

[3]This suggestion was made in his capacity as Chairman of the Inter-Agency Taskforce on Productivity.
[4]Dr Ahmad Magad was also President of the Management Committee of the Singapore Productivity Association.

Roadmap	Key Initiatives
Sectoral Productivity Roadmaps	
Construction	• A $250 million Construction Productivity and Capability Fund (CPCF) was launched in June 2010 to incentivise skills development, adoption of technology and capability-building in complex civil engineering and building projects. CPCF was topped up by $85 million in 2014. • The Building and Construction Authority (BCA) announced the first 5-year (2010–2015) Construction Productivity Roadmap in March 2011 to meet the target of 2–3% productivity growth a year by 2020. This would be achieved by regulating the demand for and supply of low-cost and lower-skilled foreign manpower, lifting the quality of the workforce, driving technology adoption by imposing regulatory requirements, and offering incentives through CPCF. • A second 3-year (2015[5]-2018) roadmap was launched in March 2015, with an additional $450 million added to CPCF. The second roadmap focused on building a better quality workforce, promoting adoption of technology, and facilitating a better integrated construction value chain. • BCA established the Construction Productivity Centre (CPC) to promote productivity, and the Centre of Construction Information Technology (CCIT) to help the industry adopt new information technology (IT) capabilities. • Various outreach and engagement initiatives were rolled out — including the bi-monthly *BuildSmart* magazine on news and best practices related to construction productivity; an annual Singapore Construction Productivity Week comprising conferences, exhibitions, and competitions; and Construction Productivity Awards. • At the launch of the Singapore Construction Productivity Week on 18 October 2016, the Government announced several measures to raise construction site productivity from an average of 1.3% per annum since 2009 to 3% by 2010. The measures included requiring more productive construction methods and best practices to be adopted at

Figure 13.1: Summary of Key Programmes in the Productivity Roadmaps and the Supporting Horizontal Programmes

Source: Websites, press releases, annual reports, and publications of the lead agencies.

---

[5]This commenced on 1 June 2015.

	public sector projects and Government Land Sale (GLS) sites; facilitating greater upstream collaboration between developers, architects, engineers and contractors to achieve more robust designs, less rework and duplication of efforts, and more efficient construction processes; promoting the adoption of technologies such as design for manufacturing and assembly, robotics and 3D printing; and helping the industry to upgrade through R&D (A Construction Productivity R&D Roadmap was developed by BCA for this purpose).

Electronics	Attention was given to growing and transforming Electronics, which had been a bedrock of Singapore's manufacturing sector. The strategies to grow the sector included:
	  i. Attract high-value added manufacturing activities to Singapore, and anchor them here.
	  ii. Support companies to improve manufacturing efficiency through the adoption of robotics, automation, and advanced manufacturing technologies.
	  iii. Equip Singaporeans with the necessary skills and competencies to take on new jobs and capture new opportunities in the sector.

Precision Engineering	• The Economic Development Board (EDB) and Standards, Productivity and Innovation Board (SPRING) launched a 5-year Precision Engineering Productivity Roadmap in September 2011.
	• The roadmap identified three key strategies to raise the productivity of the sector from $67,000 in 2008 to $178,000 by 2020:
	  i. Industry transformation to help companies move up the value chain.
	  ii. Improvement in operational efficiency at the firm level.
	  iii. Upgrading and developing the workforce.
	• As part of the roadmap, $52 million was allocated to a Precision Engineering Vocational Continuing Education and Training (PEVC) initiative to develop a pipeline of master craftsmen to meet the needs of the manufacturing industries.

Figure 13.1:   (*Continued*)

Transport Engineering	Aerospace was given focused attention. The aim was to support Singapore-based aerospace companies to compete and grow in both the existing stronghold of MRO (maintenance, repair and overhaul) services and new market segments. The strategies were:
	  i. Leverage R&D and innovation to push the frontiers of technology and develop complex capabilities to address industry needs.
	  ii. Support industry-led co-innovation and supplier partnerships.
	  iii. Develop a steady pipeline of highly skilled talent for the industry by deepening synergies between pre-employment education and industry needs.

General Manufacturing	*General Manufacturing*
	• In October 2012, the Singapore Innovation and Productivity Institute (SiPi) was established as the national productivity centre for the manufacturing sector. It was set up by the Singapore Manufacturing Federation (SMF), with support from SPRING.
	• SiPi provided direct assistance to enterprises through research and benchmarking studies, conferences, consultancy services and training. An annual Singapore Innovation and Productivity Conference and Manufacturing Solutions Expo was organised to share best practices and solutions with the industry.
	
	Food Manufacturing
	• SPRING launched a 5-year Food Manufacturing Productivity Plan in November 2011. With a budget of $45 million, the plan aimed to increase the sector's productivity by 20% by 2016.
	• The following strategies were identified in the plan:
	  i. Enhance productivity of food production base through the adoption of productivity tools and benchmarking using a common set of sector-specific productivity indicators.
	  ii. Produce high value added and innovative products to drive exports and increase production volume.
	  iii. Build a skilled workforce by training and improving human resource capabilities.
	• A Food Automation Unit was set up in 2012 to assist companies with food automation solutions, technical expertise, training and advisory services. The unit was established as part of the Food Innovation & Resource Centre (FIRC)@ Singapore Polytechnic.

Figure 13.1: (*Continued*)

	Furniture Manufacturing
	• SPRING launched a Furniture Industry Productivity Plan in October 2011. The aim was to increase the sector's productivity by 20% and raise the sector's global market share from less than 1% to 1.5% by 2015.
	• A budget of $17m was set aside for the 5-year plan to improve the sector's productivity by:
	   i. Training and process optimisation.
	   ii. Strengthening design and branding capabilities.
	   iii. Expanding market share in global markets.

Retail	• SPRING launched the first 5-year (2010–2015) Retail Productivity Plan in April 2011.
	• With a budget of $86 million, the plan aimed to raise the sector's productivity by 25% by 2015 through three key areas:
	   i. Process improvement through the adoption of technology, new concepts and enhanced capabilities.
	   ii. People development through training and better human resource management capabilities.
	   iii. Service improvement to increase sales and value added through the Customer Centric Initiative.
	• In August 2013, SPRING announced the establishment of the Singapore Productivity Centre (SPC) to help companies in the retail and food services sectors through consultancy, training, conferences, benchmarking and applied research studies. A budget of about $10 million, carved out from the Retail and Food Services Productivity Plans, was set aside for SPC over three years.
	• SPRING launched a second 5-year (2016–2020) Retail Productivity Plan in September 2015. This plan built on the strategies in the first plan, and focused more on initiatives driving sales growth, i.e. e-commerce, branding and innovative concepts; and operational efficiency through technology adoption.

Food & Beverage	• SPRING launched the first 5-year (2010–2015) Food Services Productivity Plan in April 2011, with a budget of $75 million. • The plan aimed to raise the sector's productivity by 20% by 2015 through five key strategies: i. Redesign processes to improve workflow and service delivery.

Figure 13.1:   (*Continued*)

	ii. Develop workforce through training and better human resource management capabilities. iii. Promote innovation and improve service standards. iv. Boost outreach by working with partners. v. Provide infrastructural support and expertise to assist companies, through SPC. • SPRING launched a second 5-year (2016–2020) Food Services Productivity Plan in October 2015. This plan focused more on initiatives to facilitate the adoption of manpower-lean formats and sales channels such as vending machines and ready-to-eat meals; and operational efficiency through automation and technology adoption.
Hotel	• The Singapore Tourism Board (STB) rolled out the Hotel Industry Productivity Roadmap in March 2011, with the following key strategies: i. Raise local participation and workforce quality. ii. Enhance customer service. iii. Improve operational efficiency. • A Hotel Industry Expert Panel was set up by STB in February 2014 to review the productivity strategies and initiatives. A report of its recommendations was released in October 2015. The proposed initiatives included the formation of a Hotel Innovation Committee to identify and advise on emerging technologies, and adoption of a basket of sector-specific productivity indicators to facilitate benchmarking among hotels. • STB also funded the set-up of the Hotel Productivity Centre (HPC) to assist the industry through applied research, benchmarking, consultancy, training and sharing of best practices. Launched on 31 March 2015, HPC was set up as a dedicated competency unit within SPC, in partnership with Republic Polytechnic.
Healthcare	• The Healthcare Productivity Roadmap was announced by the Ministry of Health (MOH) in March 2012 to improve the productivity of public healthcare institutions and the Intermediate and Long-Term Care (ILTC) sector. • $130 million was set aside to implement the roadmap over five years (financial years 2012 to 2016). Of this, $110 million was allocated to a Healthcare Productivity Fund — Intermediate and Long-Term Care (HPF-ILTC),

Figure 13.1: (*Continued*)

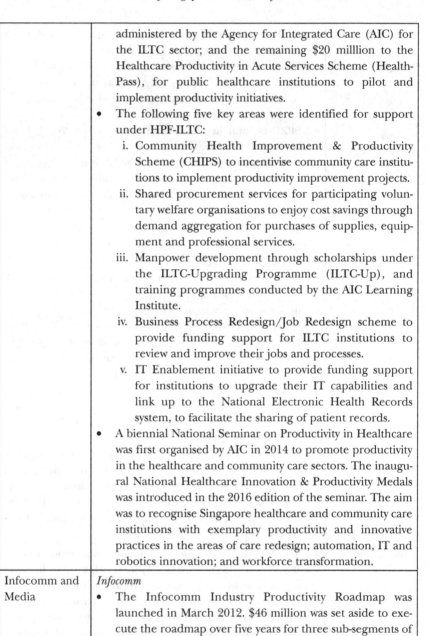

	administered by the Agency for Integrated Care (AIC) for the ILTC sector; and the remaining $20 milllion to the Healthcare Productivity in Acute Services Scheme (Health-Pass), for public healthcare institutions to pilot and implement productivity initiatives.
	
	• The following five key areas were identified for support under HPF-ILTC:
	   i. Community Health Improvement & Productivity Scheme (CHIPS) to incentivise community care institutions to implement productivity improvement projects.
	   ii. Shared procurement services for participating voluntary welfare organisations to enjoy cost savings through demand aggregation for purchases of supplies, equipment and professional services.
	   iii. Manpower development through scholarships under the ILTC-Upgrading Programme (ILTC-Up), and training programmes conducted by the AIC Learning Institute.
	   iv. Business Process Redesign/Job Redesign scheme to provide funding support for ILTC institutions to review and improve their jobs and processes.
	   v. IT Enablement initiative to provide funding support for institutions to upgrade their IT capabilities and link up to the National Electronic Health Records system, to facilitate the sharing of patient records.
	
	• A biennial National Seminar on Productivity in Healthcare was first organised by AIC in 2014 to promote productivity in the healthcare and community care sectors. The inaugural National Healthcare Innovation & Productivity Medals was introduced in the 2016 edition of the seminar. The aim was to recognise Singapore healthcare and community care institutions with exemplary productivity and innovative practices in the areas of care redesign; automation, IT and robotics innovation; and workforce transformation.

Infocomm and Media	*Infocomm* • The Infocomm Industry Productivity Roadmap was launched in March 2012. $46 million was set aside to execute the roadmap over five years for three sub-segments of the infocomm industry: software development, systems integration and IT consultancy.

Figure 13.1:   (*Continued*)

| | • The roadmap aimed to help local infocomm enterprises acquire new capabilities to transform their business models, gain access to tools and resources, and internationalise.
• The following key initiatives were supported by the Infocomm Development Authority of Singapore (IDA) under the roadmap:
 i. Productivity & Productisation Programme Office (PPPO), set up by the Singapore Infocomm Technology Federation, to assist enterprises with resources and advisory services.
 ii. Adoption of specialised productivity software and solutions, with funding support from IDA's iSPRINT (Increase SME Productivity with Infocomm Adoption & Transformation) grant scheme.
 iii. Manpower development through productivity masterclasses and other training programmes identified under the National Infocomm Competency Framework.
 iv. Product development and access to overseas markets, with support from IDA.

Media
The Media Development Authority Singapore (MDA) enhanced its grant schemes to encourage industry professionals to upgrade their skills. Under the Talent Allowance and Enhanced Apprenticeship scheme, freelancers could claim training allowances for attending training programmes, and experienced media practitioners could apply for funding of higher allowances for work attachments. Under MDA's Enterprise Assistance (Productivity) scheme, local media enterprises could enjoy funding support to implement productivity improvement programmes. |
| Logistics and Storage | • EDB and SPRING launched a 5-year productivity roadmap for the logistics and transportation industry in March 2012.
• $42 million was set aside for the roadmap to raise the productivity of the industry by 30% to $130,000 by 2015. Public transport, shipping lines and airlines were excluded from the roadmap.
• The roadmap focused on enhancing supply chain management expertise, and improving operational efficiency and innovation at the enterprise and industry levels. |

Figure 13.1: (*Continued*)

	• To assist the industry, a Centre of Innovation (COI) for Supply Chain Management was jointly set up by SPRING and Republic Polytechnic in January 2012. It aimed to be a one-stop resource centre to help enterprises, especially SMEs, improve their supply chain expertise through innovation, process re-engineering, technology and training. • In October 2015, the Government announced that $15 million had been set aside to pilot and implement the use of Automated Guided Vehicles in warehousing to improve the efficiency of the storage and retrieval processes. Another $20 million was allocated to pilot integrated delivery systems to coordinate and consolidate deliveries from warehouses to shopping malls.
Administrative and Support Services	*Cleaning Industry* • The National Environment Agency (NEA) rolled out the Cleaning Industry Productivity Roadmap in July 2010, in partnership with the Ministry of Manpower (MOM), Singapore Workforce Development Agency (WDA) and the labour movement. • The roadmap had four key thrusts: capability and standards development, training and manpower resources, technology and innovation, and education and outreach. • The following were among the key initiatives rolled out: 　i. Enhanced Clean Mark Accreditation Scheme to help cleaning companies put in place proper systems and processes, especially in the areas of human resource management and process improvement. 　ii. Mandatory licensing of cleaning companies to raise standards. 　iii. Training and certification of cleaners through the Environmental Cleaning Workforce Skills Qualification (WSQ) training programmes. 　iv. Funding support for improving the skills and wages of low-wage workers through job redesign, process improvement and adoption of equipment, under the Inclusive Growth Programme (IGP) administered by Employment and Employability Institute (e2i).

Figure 13.1:   (*Continued*)

Landscape Industry

- The Landscape Industry Productivity Roadmap was launched by the National Parks Board (NParks) in September 2010. The goal was to raise the productivity of the industry by an average of 2.5% per year over the next 10 years.
- A budget of $12 million was set aside for the roadmap to enhance skills and capabilities, and restructure industry operations.
- The following were among the key initiatives rolled out:
  i. Landscape Apprenticeship Programme to train fresh talents for the industry through work assignments, on-the-job training and formal training.
  ii. Nursery Accreditation Scheme to raise the standards of the industry, and encourage adoption of more innovative and productive practices.
  iii. Machinery Training and Hire Facility to allow landscape service providers to lease and try using equipment at low costs.
  iv. Landscape Productivity Grant Scheme to incentivise landscape companies to purchase equipment to improve their productivity.
- NParks also implemented a new tenancy model for land parcels tendered out for bidding by landscape nurseries. Successful tenderers had to commit to meeting the productivity targets set by NParks, and using 90% of the land for nursery operations.
- On 24 September 2016, the Government announced a $5.6 million budget for the landscaping industry over the next four years. Of this sum, $3 million would be set aside for the Landscape Productivity Grant Scheme to top up the $3.6 million allocated to it three years ago. The remaining $2.6 million would be used to fund studies and surveys such as the skills and manpower needed for the industry.

Agriculture Industry

- A $63 million Agriculture Productivity Fund (APF) was launched by the Agri-Food & Veterinary Authority of Singapore (AVA) in August 2014.
- APF aimed to raise the production capabilities of farmers by providing funding support under three schemes;
  i. Basic Farm Capability Upgrading scheme to fund equipment to increase productivity.

Figure 13.1: (*Continued*)

ii. Productivity Enhancement scheme to help farms achieve a significant increase in productivity through automation or advanced/high-tech integrated production systems.

iii. Research & Development (R&D) scheme to fund R&D in innovative technology systems, consultancy services in land intensification, system prototyping and technological system pilot trials.

• To further increase the productivity of the farms and their use of land, AVA put in place new policies and requirements for all land-based farms licensed by them:

i. All farms must use at least 90% of the farm area for agriculture production and uses related to production.

ii. All farms must meet the minimum production levels stipulated by AVA for the various farm types.

Security Industry

• The Security Sector Productivity Working Group was formed in January 2011 to work out a 5-year roadmap to identify impediments to productivity in the security industry, and to develop initiatives and programmes at the sectoral, agency and security officer levels to improve productivity. It comprised representatives from the Ministry of Home Affairs (MHA), MOM, WDA, e2i, Union of Security Employees (USE) and IDA.

• The Roadmap covered measures to:

i. Enhance buyers' awareness of different types of security services/products and their usefulness, and promote relevant incentive schemes to buyers.

ii. Encourage use of technology to improve operations, e.g. central monitoring system to monitor activities on all sites and ensure close command and control of all staff on the sites.

iii. Upgrade skills competencies and promote manpower development of security officers to achieve higher productivity and greater sense of pride in work.

iv. Enhance employment and working conditions of security officers to attract more to join the industry to meet the demand.

• Existing schemes under e2i and IDA were leveraged to encourage the sector to use technology. Buyers who qualified for e2i's best sourcing initiative were eligible for the extended funding to invest in technology.

Figure 13.1: (*Continued*)

Financial Services	The focus was on transforming the sector in the light of technological disruption in the production, delivery and consumption of financial services. The strategies included: i. Leverage technology to create platforms and infrastructures that enable new services, ideas and innovation to thrive across the sector. ii. Encourage adoption of technology in financial institutions to increase efficiency and promote innovation. iii. Raise skills of manpower in the sector, and build a strong local pipeline of specialised talent.
Accountancy	The Institute of Singapore Chartered Accountants (ISCA) rolled out the following productivity-related initiatives: • Pilot Productivity Study for the Accountancy Sector. • Annual productivity benchmarking surveys. • Series of case stories on how some small and medium-sized practices (SMPs) improved their productivity. • One SMP consortium, bringing together a group of SMPs to share resources and develop solutions to increase productivity.
Social Services	In March 2012, the Ministry of Community, Youth and Sports (MCYS) launched two key initiatives to raise the productivity of the social services sector: • A 5-year (2012 to 2016) Social Service Sector Information and Communications Technology (ICT) Masterplan, in collaboration with IDA, to drive the adoption of ICT to improve service delivery and productivity. • An Innovation and Productivity Grant (under the VWOs-Charities Capability Fund) to support voluntary welfare organisations (VWOs) to embark on productivity enhancement, innovation and service improvement projects.
Process Construction & Maintenance (PCM)	• The Government set up a Process Construction & Maintenance Management Committee (PCMMC) in 2013 to coordinate productivity improvement efforts between the Government, plant owners and PCM contractors represented by the Association of Process Industry (ASPRI). • Key initiatives rolled out by PCMMC included the development of a 7,900-bed PCM dormitory near Jurong Island to reduce the time taken for workers to travel to the work sites on the Island, and a data-sharing portal to minimise overlaps in scheduling projects.

Figure 13.1:   (*Continued*)

	• In February 2015, the industry formed a PCM Productivity Council, comprising plant owners, PCM contractors and ASPRI, to improve the productivity of the sector through benchmarking, mechanisation, certification systems and training.
Horizontal Programmes	
Continuing Education and Training (CET)	• MOM and Ministry of Education (MOE) led the effort to increase the number of training places in the polytechnics to provide adult learners with more opportunities to pursue lifelong learning. • Productivity-related courses were introduced in the polytechnics and Institute of Technical Education (ITE). WDA also launched a Productivity Initiatives in Services & Manufacturing (PRISM) initiative in July 2010. This comprised a suite of productivity-related training programmes that managers and supervisors could attend, with support from WDA. • The CET portfolio was transferred to the SkillsFuture Council on 1 November 2014, and subsequently to the Council for Skills, Innovation and Productivity (CSIP) on 20 May 2016.
Low-Wage Workers	• An Inclusive Growth Programme (IGP), administered by e2i, was launched by the labour movement in August 2010. Overseeing the programme was the IGP Committee, formerly known as Cheaper, Better, Faster (CBF) Committee, headed by the Secretary-General of the National Trades Union Congress (NTUC). The members were drawn from the relevant Government agencies and the unions. • The $100 million programme aimed to help companies in all sectors improve their productivity. To be eligible for funding support, the companies must be willing to share the productivity gains with their low-wage workers. • The labour movement introduced a Progressive Wage Model (PWM) in June 2012 to help workers raise their wages through better skills and productivity improvements. The Security, Cleaning and Landscape sectors were the first few to adopt PWM.

Figure 13.1: (*Continued*)

Small- and Medium-sized Enterprises (SMEs)	• SPRING and WDA jointly launched the SME-Productivity Roadmap (SME-PRO) in June 2010 to help SMEs embark on the productivity journey through a 3-step approach: be aware, get trained and take action. • SME-PRO included a Productivity@Work website containing information and resources on productivity methodologies and concepts, government assistance schemes and case stories, with SMEs in mind. • The website was complemented by the Productivity Management Programme that was rolled out through the SME Centres[6] to train, provide advice and assist SMEs to assess and take the first steps to improve their productivity performance.
iSPRINT (SME Productivity with Infocomm Adoption and Transformation)	• In March 2010, IDA, together with SPRING and the Inland Revenue Authority of Singapore (IRAS), launched iSPRINT to help SMEs adopt ICT, which was identified by NPCEC as a key productivity enabler across all sectors. • iSPRINT started off as a $25 million initiative providing funding support for SMEs to adopt various pre-qualified infocomm solutions and subscription to Software as a Service (SaaS) applications. • In Budget 2014, a 3-year $500 million ICT for Productivity and Growth (IPG) programme was introduced to help SMEs increase adoption of ICT solutions. In August 2014, IPG was subsumed under iSPRINT, which was enhanced to include funding support for piloting emerging solutions, and for deployment of high-speed connectivity.

Figure 13.1: (*Continued*)

Public Communication and Engagement

Initial Decentralised Publicity

For the first two years, in 2010 and 2011, the approach taken for productivity promotion was similar to that taken by NPCEC to drive national productivity. By and large, publicity was carried out by the lead agencies and tailored for enterprises in the respective sectors.

---

[6]Prior to 1 April 2013, the SME Centres were known as Enterprise Development Centres (EDCs).

The publicity activities included announcements of plans and targets set for the sector, publications and editorials, television and radio series on success stories and best practices, and annual conferences. Technology was often featured as the solution to address low productivity and reduce reliance on manual labour.

The construction sector provides a good example of the productivity promotion activities undertaken for a specific sector. An annual Singapore Construction Productivity Week was first launched by BCA in April 2011. The Week included a conference to share best practices in innovative construction methods and technologies, an exhibition to showcase related products, a Skilled Builder and Building Information Modelling competition, and Construction Productivity Awards to recognise professionals and builders for their efforts in improving and promoting productivity in the sector.

Besides sector-specific activities, SPRING embarked on a publicity campaign to promote productivity to SMEs at large, under the SME-PRO programme. A key initiative was the Productivity@Work website, which was complemented by the Productivity Management Programme.

'Way to Go' Outreach Campaign

Prior to 3 January 2012, all the sector-vertical and horizontal productivity promotion activities were carried out with no common branding or message linked to the national productivity drive. From then onwards, they were brought together and integrated under the 'Way to Go' outreach campaign launched by NPCEC. Fronting the campaign was a simple logo with the tagline 'Way to Go, Singapore' placed smack in the middle of a circle.

The campaign aimed to promote productivity by featuring real-life cases of companies, employees and employers who had 'found a way' to improve productivity in their organisations. These were featured on print, online, broadcast and outdoor platforms. Collaterals were also produced to help companies take their first step towards improving productivity.

In conjunction with the campaign, a new Way to Go website was set up to serve as a one-stop resource platform and gateway to other resources maintained by the sector lead agencies. Companies and individuals were encouraged to pledge their support to the Productivity Movement, and contribute stories through the website. In 2013, the Way to Go website was integrated into the Productivity@Work website to avoid duplication and dispersion of information.

Compared with the productivity campaign in the 1980s and 1990s, the Way to Go campaign was low-keyed. Initially, the term 'productivity' was not explicitly promoted, as a subtle approach was preferred. Instead, the three I's of 'Initiate', 'Innovate' and 'Impact' were used to illustrate how employees and employers had put in place initiatives to increase productivity. Subsequently, the line 'Here's to Productivity' was added to the Way to Go logo displayed in the various platforms and collaterals, and productivity was more explicitly promoted. It can be deduced from this that the approach taken earlier had been so subdued and subtle that it was not widely known that there was an ongoing productivity campaign. Including the word 'productivity' was thus seen to be necessary. However, the impact of the campaign is unclear as there is no public information on awareness of the campaign or action taken as a result of the campaign.

National Productivity Month

October 2014 saw the revival of the National Productivity Month, which had been canned for more than a decade. Activities for the Month were led by the Singapore Business Federation (SBF) and the Singapore National Employers Federation (SNEF), under the aegis of NPCEC and with support from the sector lead agencies. Unlike in the 1980s and 1990s, there were no jingles, mascot or large-scale publicity blitz that stared in the face. Instead, the National Productivity Month centred on events, which were also a prominent feature in the past campaigns. Figure 13.2 summarises the major events during the Month.

Event	Organiser	Date
• Opening of National Productivity Month	SBF and SNEF, under aegis of NPCEC	7 October
• Singapore Innovation and Productivity Conference & Manufacturing Solutions Expo	SMF	8–10 October
• Manufacturing Productivity Technology Centre Conference and Technology Exhibition 2014	Singapore Institute of Manufacturing Technology (SIMTech), Agency for Science, Technology and Research (A*STAR)	9 October
• National Seminar on Productivity in Healthcare and 4th Intermediate and Long-Term Care (ILTC) Quality Festival 2014	MOH and AIC	9–10 October
• Singapore Construction Productivity Week 2014	BCA	13–16 October
• Hospitality Summit	Singapore Hotel Association (SHA) and STB	14 October
• Singapore Retail Industry Conference 2014	Singapore Retailers Association (SRA) and SPC	16–17 October
• Technology Showcase and SMP Dialogue	Institute of Singapore Chartered Accountants	17 October
• International Singapore Compact CSR Summit	Compact Singapore	16–17 October
• TravelRave	STB	27–31 October
• Food Productivity Conference	SPC and Singapore Productivity Association (SPA)	27–28 October
• 6th Business Excellence Global Conference	SPRING	29–30 October
• 20th Business Excellence Awards and Inaugural Singapore Productivity Awards Ceremony	SPRING, with support from SBF and SNEF	30 October

Figure 13.2:   Major Events During National Productivity Month 2014

Sources: www.waytogo.sg; websites and news releases of organisers.

The National Productivity Month started with an opening ceremony graced by Prime Minister Lee Hsien Loong on 7 October. An exhibition of productivity solutions, including a flying robot waiter, was held in conjunction with the ceremony. This was followed by conferences and other events that had been organised separately by the sector lead agencies prior to 2014.

The 20th Business Excellence Awards and Inaugural Singapore Productivity Awards Ceremony, graced by Deputy Prime Minister Tharman Shanmugaratnam on 30 October, marked the close of the National Productivity Month. The Singapore Productivity Awards was in fact a revival of the National Productivity Awards, which was discontinued in 2003. Six company winners were selected based on their productivity performance and initiatives to drive productivity and innovation. The assessment was undertaken by a committee comprising representatives from trade associations and Government agencies.

Oddly, the National Productivity Month was not sustained after 2014. There was no official word on whether it was a one-time affair or whether there were plans to organise it at regular intervals. What did continue was SBF's Singapore Productivity Awards. The awards were presented to eight companies in 2015 and ten companies in 2016. The sector lead agencies also continued to organise their own productivity conferences and events.

InDIYpendent Campaign

On 8 November 2015, the National Productivity Council (NPC)[7] launched a 'We are InDIYpendent' campaign. The aim was to encourage consumers to embrace self-service facilities, which would in turn incentivise more companies to adopt self-service formats and technologies amidst a tight manpower situation. Directed primarily at the retail and food & beverage sectors, the campaign leveraged celebrities, social and broadcast media, print and out-of-home advertisements, and competitions to engage consumers. Besides the

---

[7]As described below, NPC was the successor of NPCEC.

launch event, the campaign included mystery-spotting activities to encourage consumers to use DIY ('do it yourself') options in their daily lives, videos on the DIY culture, and advertisements featuring different forms of self-service.

Report Card at Halfway Mark of the 2010s

At the halfway mark in 2015, questions on the progress made and the likelihood of achieving the 2–3 per cent productivity growth target for the 2010s were invariably asked. Compared with the past decades, there was greater scrutiny this time round on the achievement of the target in relation to the productivity plans and programmes. The reason is that each of the sectoral plans had their own targets to be achieved through specific programmes, and these sector-level targets were expected to collectively contribute to the overall target of 2–3 per cent productivity growth.

Figure 13.3 shows the achievement for the period 2010–2015 in terms of the average annual productivity growth rates for the economy and the individual sectors.

Sector	Average annual growth (%)
Overall economy	0.4
Manufacturing	1.3
Construction	0.1
Wholesale & retail trade	2.3
Transportation & storage	–0.2
Accommodation & food services	–0.1
Information & communications	0.9
Finance & insurance	4.0
Business services	–0.1
Other services	–0.9

Figure 13.3: Average Annual Productivity (value added per worker) Growth, 2010–2015

Source: Singapore Department of Statistics.

For the economy as a whole, the productivity growth averaged a mere 0.4 per cent a year,[8] well below the target of 2–3 per cent. Other than the blip of 2.3 per cent from 2010 to 2011, the growth was basically flat, falling within the range of –0.5 to 0.5 per cent a year. At the sector level, four of the nine sectors — transportation & storage, accommodation & food services, business services, and other services — experienced negative growth; while construction was stagnant and information & communications grew only marginally. Finance & insurance was the best performer, followed by wholesale & retail trade in a far second position and manufacturing in third position.

Based on the growth numbers alone, the productivity drive did not bring about the desired effect of raising productivity. This is not surprising since it is unrealistic for a 5-year productivity drive to bring about significant results. The task of raising productivity is made more difficult by the fact that the economy is now entrenched with certain structural factors that weigh down productivity. These factors, which are the result of policies taken in the past, are inter-related and fall under three broad categories.[9]

First, the long dependence on low-cost foreign workers to prop up economic growth has had a lingering adverse effect on productivity. In the early years of Singapore's independence, the inflow of foreign workers was needed to support the growing operations of foreign MNCs in the manufacturing sector, but it was later extended to other sectors as well. This has calcified the labour-dependent operating model and weakened the resolve of companies, particularly SMEs, to take the more arduous route of increasing

---

[8]From 2016, the Ministry of Trade and Industry (MTI) started to track and report labour productivity growth figures based on value added per hour worked, in addition to value added per worker, on a regular basis. Using value added per hour worked, the average productivity growth of the economy for 2010–2015 was a higher 1.3 per cent a year.

[9]Besides the structural factors, the year-to-year fluctuations in productivity growth may be attributed to the state of the global economy. The reason is that productivity growth is pro-cyclical in the short-run, especially for a small, open economy like Singapore. See Amp-Box on *Productivity Primer* in Chapter 1.

productivity. SMEs constitute 99 per cent of the total number of establishments in Singapore and employ about 70 per cent of the workforce, but contribute just about half of the gross domestic product (GDP). Their dependence on low-cost foreign labour has slowed the growth of capital intensity, thus depressing productivity growth. Despite the tightening of the foreign worker inflow in recent years and the availability of many productivity programmes, the SMEs have been reluctant or are slow to change their operating model.

Second, the highly dualistic structure of the economy — comprising the more productive export-oriented sectors and the less productive domestically-oriented sectors — retards overall productivity growth. On a long-term basis, the export-oriented sectors — manufacturing, wholesale trade, transportation & storage, accommodation, information & communications, and finance & insurance — are the ones that have lifted the economy's productivity. In contrast, the domestically-oriented sectors — construction, retail trade, food services, business services, and other services — generate low value added but employ a disproportionate number of workers. Comprising mostly SMEs, they are the ones that are most dependent on foreign workers and are the laggards in productivity. As they are not subject to as much competition as the export-oriented sectors, there is less motivation to improve productivity. Consequently, the many initiatives in the sectoral productivity plans have not been able to make a big impact on the respective sectors' productivity.

Third, the less productive domestically-oriented sectors have grown in size over the years. Studies, including those by MTI, have shown that the employment share of these sectors has increased relative to the export-oriented sectors. This means that more labour resources are pumped into the less productive sectors instead of being used to grow the more productive ones, and some unproductive businesses which would otherwise have closed down are sustained by the low-cost labour. The effect of such a structural shift, which has been termed 'growth-reducing structural change,' [10] is a drag on the economy's overall productivity growth.

---

[10]This term was coined by McMillan and Rodrik (2012).

Productivity Drive Beyond the Halfway Mark of the 2010s

What is surprising is that instead of being promoted overtly beyond the halfway mark, the productivity drive began to recede into the background once again. The clearest reflection of this is the brevity of the mention of productivity in the *Report of the Committee on the Future Economy*, as well as the Government's response to this report in the Budget 2017 Statement. In delivering the Statement on 20 February 2017, Finance Minister Heng Swee Keat simply said:

> *"We can aim for quality growth of 2% to 3%, if we press on in our drive for higher productivity and work hard to help everyone who wishes to work find a place in the labour force."*

Similarly, in his speech rounding up the Budget 2017 debate on 2 March 2017, Heng Swee Keat made a brief reference to productivity. He said:

> *"Our demographics are changing. Our labour force growth is slowing down, because of smaller cohorts entering the workforce and a slowdown in foreign worker inflow. To counter this, future growth has to come from sustained productivity growth. We need to help every worker maximise his potential, and support our businesses in innovation. This will put us in good company, among high-income, productive economies."*

Even before the release of the report by the Committee on the Future Economy (CFE) and the Budget 2017 Statement, certain developments portending the direction of the productivity drive had already taken place.

From NPCEC to National Productivity Council

At the National Day Rally on 17 August 2014, Prime Minister Lee Hsien Loong announced the formation of a tripartite committee to develop an integrated system of education, training and career progression, and to promote industry support and recognition for individuals to advance based on skills. The committee, chaired by Deputy Prime Minister Tharman Shanmugaratnam, was subsequently named the SkillsFuture Council. At its first meeting on 5 November 2014, the Council identified four key thrusts to drive the national SkillsFuture effort:

a. Help individuals to make well informed choices in education, training and careers;
b. Develop an integrated, high-quality system of education and training that responds to constantly evolving industry needs;
c. Promote employer recognition and career development based on skills and mastery; and
d. Foster a culture that supports and celebrates lifelong learning.

With this new development, the portfolio of developing a national CET system was handed over from NPCEC to the SkillsFuture Council with effect from 1 November 2014. Following that, NPCEC was renamed National Productivity Council (NPC).

From NPC to Council for Skills, Innovation and Productivity

Between 2015 and 2016, the SkillsFuture movement rolled out several initiatives that were targeted at individuals. These included the SkillsFuture Credit, SkillsFuture Study Awards, SkillsFuture Mid-Career Enhanced Subsidy, and SkillsFuture Earn and Learn Programme. At the industry level, sectoral manpower plans were developed in consultation with the sector lead agencies to identify future skills, and to map out the sector's future skills development and career progression plans. By June 2016, five sectoral manpower plans had been launched — for the hotel, retail, built environment, public bus and food services sectors.

Clearly, synergy could be derived by jointly addressing the sectoral manpower plans, led by the SkillsFuture Council, and the sectoral productivity plans, led by NPC. Furthermore, the various economic agencies had their own economic plans for the sectors under their charge. Hence, it made sense for all these to be integrated so that a holistic approach could be taken to develop and transform the sectors. This was put across by Finance Minister Heng

Swee Keat in his presentation of Budget 2016 on 24 March 2016. He said:

"In Budget 2016, we will launch a new Industry Transformation Programme to take us into the next phase of our development. This builds on our efforts under the Quality Growth Programme, which was introduced in Budget 2013 to achieve inclusive growth driven by innovation and higher productivity. The Industry Transformation Programme will help firms and industries to create new value and drive growth in four ways:

a. *It will involve integrating our different restructuring efforts. Our efforts to raise productivity, develop our people, and drive research and innovation are working, but we can maximise impact by pulling these together.*

b. *We will take a more targeted and sector-focused approach to better meet the needs of firms in each sector.*

c. *We will deepen partnerships between government and the industry, and among industry players to identify challenges, and develop solutions to support transformation.*

d. *And we will place a stronger emphasis on technology adoption and innovation."*

A total of $4.5 billion was set aside for the Industry Transformation Programme to support enterprises and industries. This amount was on top of what had been allocated to research & development (R&D) and the National Productivity Fund (NPF).

Two months later, on 20 May 2016, the Government announced the formation of the Council for Skills, Innovation and Productivity (CSIP) to succeed both NPC and the SkillsFuture Council. The press release on the formation of CSIP provided the rationale:

"A tripartite Council for Skills, Innovation and Productivity (CSIP) will be established with effect from 20 May 2016, to take forward the efforts undertaken to date by the SkillsFuture Council and the National Productivity Council (NPC). The CSIP will also develop and implement the Industry Transformation Maps announced in Budget 2016. ... The CSIP will therefore integrate and achieve maximum synergies between our skills, innovation and productivity efforts. Each of these three dimensions will be reflected in the development of Industry Transformation Maps for key clusters of our economy.

In sum, the CSIP aims to develop skills for the future and support productivity-led economic growth by:

a. *Advancing SkillsFuture: Developing an integrated system of education, training, and career progression for all Singaporeans;*
b. *Driving industry transformation: Overseeing implementation of plans for key clusters through skills development, innovation, productivity and internationalisation strategies; and*
c. *Fostering a culture of innovation and lifelong learning in Singapore."*

Chairing CSIP is Deputy Prime Minister and Coordinating Minister for Economic and Social Policies Tharman Shanmugaratnam. The members are from the public and private sectors, unions, and educational and training institutions. Figure 13.4 shows the composition of CSIP at the time of its formation.

	Name	Designation
	Chairman	
1	Tharman Shanmugaratnam	Deputy Prime Minister and Coordinating Minister for Economic and Social Policies
	Members	
	Government Representatives	
2	Heng Swee Keat	Minister for Finance
3	Lim Hng Kiang	Minister for Trade and Industry (Trade)
4	Lim Swee Say	Minister for Manpower
5	S. Iswaran	Minister for Trade and Industry (Industry)
6	Ong Ye Kung	Acting Minister for Education (Higher Education & Skills)
7	Denise Phua	Mayor, Central Singapore District
	Union Representatives	
8	Mary Liew	President, NTUC
9	Chan Chun Sing	Secretary-General, NTUC

Figure 13.4: Composition of Council for Skills, Innovation and Productivity as at 20 May 2016

Source: Singapore Workforce Development Agency (2016).

	Name	Designation
	Educational Institutions	
10	Professor Tan Thiam Soon	President, Singapore Institute of Technology
11	Professor Arnoud De Meyer	President, Singapore Management University
	Industry Representatives	
12	Dr Robert Yap	Chairman, Singapore National Employers Federation
13	Teo Siong Seng	Chairman, Singapore Business Federation
14	Thomas Chua	President, Singapore Chinese Chamber of Commerce & Industry
15	Andrew Chong	Regional President & Managing Director, Infineon Technologies Asia Pacific Pte Ltd
16	Wayne Hunt	Managing Director, AsiaPac Executive Insights Pte Ltd
17	Jamie Lim	Regional Marketing Director, Scanteak
18	Lim Kuo-Yi	Managing Director and Partner, Monk's Hill Ventures
19	Lim Ming Yan	President and Group CEO, CapitaLand
20	Kenneth Loo	Executive Director and Chief Operating Officer, Straits Construction
21	Peter Meinshausen	Regional President, South East Asia, Australia, & New Zealand, Evonik
22	Vincent Tan	Vice President, Restaurant Association of Singapore
23	Tham Sai Choy	Managing Partner, KPMG in Singapore
24	Oliver Tonby	Managing Partner, McKinsey, Southeast Asia
25	Grace Yeow	Managing Director, Fluidigm
26	Zulkifli Bin Baharudin	Chairman, ITL Corporation

Figure 13.4: (*Continued*)

Productivity Subsumed Under Industry Transformation Maps

On 8 September 2016, Tharman Shanmugaratnam provided more details of the Industry Transformation Maps (ITMs) being developed under the aegis of CSIP. In his speech at the Opening of Select

Group's Corporate Headquarters and Launch of the Food Services Industry Transformation Map (ITM),[11] he said:

> *"The Food Services ITM is one of 23 ITMs being developed under the $4.5 billion Industry Transformation Programme announced in this year's Budget ... The Council for Skills, Innovation and Productivity (CSIP) will take overall responsibility for the implementation of the 23 ITMs. To do so, the CSIP is setting up 6 subcommittees. Each of the subcommittees will oversee a group of ITMs within the same broad cluster of industries.*
>
> *A few government agencies, TACs, and unions will be involved in each ITM. For clarity and accountability within the Government, we will have one government agency assume overall responsibility for each ITM, and will coordinate among agencies and with our tripartite partners. Similarly, at the cluster level, one government agency will take the lead.*
>
> *The Food Services ITM is a good example. Together with the Retail, Food Manufacturing and Hotel ITMs, it falls under the Lifestyle cluster. Senior Minister of State Sim Ann and Managing Director of Select Group Mr. Vincent Tan will co-chair a team of experienced industry practitioners and unionists to oversee the implementation of the ITMs for the Lifestyle cluster.*
>
> *SPRING, which is the lead agency for the Food Services ITM, is also the lead for the Lifestyle Cluster. In this role, SPRING will coordinate across agencies — it is a long list, including IES, HDB, EDB, STB, JTC, WDA, IDA, URA, NEA, AVA, and A*STAR! The long list illustrates the many Government functions and capabilities that can help advance industry transformation — approving use of space, promoting ICT use, marketing the industry to tourists, and so on. Every agency must be involved in supporting industry transformation.*
>
> *But it is also why we need both tight coordination in Government and clear accountability. Hence, at the end of the day, SPRING will take the lead and be responsible for the Lifestyle cluster's progress."*

---

[11] The Food Services ITM was the first of the 23 ITMs launched. Following this, five other ITMs were launched in 2016 — Retail (15 September), Precision Engineering (12 October), Logistics (16 November), Food Manufacturing (18 November) and Hotels (21 November).

Figure 13.5 shows the details of the structure for the development of the ITMs. The 23 industries identified contribute more than 80 per cent of Singapore's GDP. Laying out the growth and transformation strategies for the industries over the next five years, the ITMs are to be developed and implemented in collaboration with the industry partners. Each ITM will integrate the Government's strategies for productivity improvement, skills development, innovation and internationalisation to achieve maximum effectiveness and impact.

The latest endorsement of the importance of ITMs was made by CFE, which identified 'Develop and implement Industry Transformation Maps' as one of the seven economic strategies for the next decade. In fact, the CFE report emphasised that ITMs would be critical for implementing all the strategies coherently and addressing the specific needs of the different industries. Hence, it recommended that ITMs be championed as the platform for integrative planning and implementation. It also recommended that in the next phase of ITMs, a cluster-based approach be taken to maximise synergies across industries and boost the transformation of clusters of industries. Within two weeks of the release of the CFE report, the Government responded by topping up NPF by another $1 billion to support industry transformation. This was announced by Heng Swee Keat in the Budget 2017 Statement.

With the ITMs, productivity is now integrated with three other strategies, which means that the hitherto productivity drive is no longer a separate movement. In effect, the sectoral productivity plans, including the productivity growth targets for the sectors, are now folded under the ITMs. This is the case for the sectors or industries that have developed their productivity plans earlier and which have been identified for the development of ITMs. The majority of them fall into this category. The exceptions are the administrative & support services (landscape and agriculture industries) and social services sectors. For the ITMs, the new industries identified are

Desired outcomes

Employers

- Strategies that provide integrated assistance across domains
- Stronger support for innovation and internationalisation
- Single government agency to integrate transformation efforts

Employees

- New and re-designed jobs with better wages
- More opportunities overseas
- Stronger support for upgrading and skills deepening

23 industries grouped under 6 clusters

Manufacturing	Built Environment	Trade & Connectivity	Essential Domestic Services	Modern Services	Lifestyle
• Precision engineering [Economic Development Board (EDB)] • Energy & chemicals (EDB) • Marine & offshore (EDB) • Electronics (EDB) • Aerospace (EDB)	• Construction [Building and Construction Authority (BCA)] • Real estate [Council for Estates Agency (CEA)] • Cleaning [National Environment Agency (NEA)] • Security [Ministry of Home Affairs (MHA)]	• Wholesale trade [International Enterprise Singapore (IES)] • Land transport [Land Transport Authority (LTA)] • Sea transport [Maritime and Port Authority of Singapore (MPA)] • Air transport [Civil Aviation Authority of Singapore (CAAS)] • Logistics (EDB)	• Healthcare [Ministry of Health (MOH)] • Education [Ministry of Education (MOE)]	• Professional services (EDB) • Financial services [Monetary Authority of Singapore (MAS)] • ICT and media [Ministry of Communications and Information (MCI)]	• Food manufacturing [Standards, Productivity and Innovation Board (SPRING)] • Food services (SPRING) • Hotels [Singapore Tourism Board (STB)] • Retail (SPRING)

4 strategies			
Productivity	**Jobs & skills**	**Innovation**	**Internationalisation**
• Shift towards higher-value added activities • Drive operational excellence • Establish shared industry platforms for mass adoption	• Promote manpower-lean enterprise development • Equip Singaporeans with skills to support the shift to greater value creation • Develop comprehensive ecosystem for skills development and lifelong learning • Strengthen enterprise HR capabilities to maximise workforce potential	• Leverage technology to drive innovation and value-creation • Build enterprise capabilities and sector infrastructure • Develop own products and brands	• Develop core of globally-competitive local enterprises • Access global markets through digital channels • Leverage international networks for market access

2 supporting horizontals	
Promoting ICT adoption across the economy	Promoting skills development across the economy

Figure 13.5: Structure for Development of Industry Transformation Maps

Note. Agencies in brackets are the lead agencies.

Source. Ministry of Trade and Industry (2016b and 2016c).

marine & offshore, real estate, air transport, sea transport, land transport, wholesale trade, education and professional services. [12]

Focus on Boosting Innovation Beyond the Halfway Mark of the 2010s

As in the early 2000s, the focus shifted from productivity to innovation beyond the halfway mark of the 2010s. This was evident from certain developments.

Research, Innovation and Enterprise 2020 Plan

In a separate track from the mainstream of productivity, R&D and innovation received a boost when the Research, Innovation and Enterprise 2020 Plan (RIE 2020) was unveiled by Prime Minister Lee Hsien Loong on 8 January 2016. Backed by a budget of $19 billion, the plan spells out the directions for Singapore's R&D efforts over the next five years (2016–2020). Compared with the budget for RIE 2015, the budget of $19 billion is an 18 per cent increase.[13] Overall, R&D spending will be sustained at about 1 per cent of GDP.

In terms of focus areas, RIE2020 is more selective and targeted in its support of R&D initiatives to maximise impact in areas where Singapore has the competitive advantage or where important national priorities need to be met. Instead of the two broad categories of 'private R&D' and 'public R&D' funding in RIE2015, the funding in RIE2020 focuses on four primary technology domains, or 'verticals.' These are advanced manufacturing and engineering,

---

[12]Marine & offshore is under the transport engineering sector but no productivity roadmap was developed for it. Similarly, air transport, sea transport and land transport are under the logistics and storage sector but they were excluded from the productivity roadmap for that sector.

[13]RIE2020 is Singapore's 6th science & technology plan. The previous plans were National Technology Plan 1995 (budget of $2b), National Science & Technology Plan 2000 ($4b), Science & Technology 2005 Plan ($6b), Science & Technology 2010 Plan ($13.5b) and RIE2015 ($16b).

health and biomedical sciences, services and digital economy, and urban solutions and sustainability. These four domains aim to deepen the technological capabilities and competitiveness of the manufacturing and engineering sectors, advance human health and wellness, leverage digital capabilities to raise productivity, and meet national priorities such as developing a reinforced cybersecurity infrastructure and system.

To support the four technology domains, three cross-cutting programmes, or 'horizontals', are given attention. These are academic research to ensure excellent science, manpower programme to yield a strong pipeline of talent, and innovation and enterprise programme to generate value creation. To spur R&D in the private sector, RIE2020 emphasises public-private collaboration and the participation of MNCs, large local enterprises (LLEs) and SMEs. What is particularly important from the productivity viewpoint is that commercialisation of technology is given emphasis to translate R&D investments into products, services and solutions.

The details of the plan to bring new technological developments to market were announced by Teo Chee Hean, Deputy Prime Minister and Chairman of the National Research Foundation (NRF), at the opening of the Singapore Week of Innovation and Technology [14] on 20 September 2016. Out of the $19 billion RIE2020 budget, $4 billion has been carved out for industry-research collaboration so that enterprises can capture the value of R&D when it is brought to market. To facilitate the collaboration, technology consortia, acting as the bridge between industry partners and researchers, will be set up to help direct applied research to the development of new products and services. These various initiatives complement the integrated multi-agency approach taken for the ITMs, which will help enterprises to innovate and internationalise their products and services.

---

[14]The inaugural Singapore Week of Innovation and Technology, or Switch in short, was held during 19-21 September 2016. It featured exhibitions, conferences and workshops revolving around entrepreneurship and technology innovation. The event was organised by 23 partners from both the public and private sectors.

Committee on the Future Economy and Budget 2017

In place of productivity in the *Report of the Economic Strategies Committee*, innovation came across as a major theme in the *Report of the Committee on the Future Economy*. Of the seven strategies, one emphasised the need to strengthen enterprise capabilities to innovate and scale up, and another stressed the importance of partnering each other to enable innovation and growth.

In conjunction with the strategy on 'Strengthen Enterprise Capabilities to Innovate and Scale Up', the CFE report stressed the importance of RIE2020 to companies and the need for commercialisation of R&D. As stated in the report:

> *"Companies can also tap on the Research Innovation Enterprise 2020 Plan (RIE2020) to develop innovative and viable commercial products. Companies that have strong growth potential can be supported to scale up and internationalise."*

Specific recommendations were made in the CFE report to boost innovation. These included setting up a Global Innovation Alliance to build networks to facilitate innovation; strengthening the innovation ecosystem by establishing commercially-oriented entities to better commercialise research findings and intellectual property (IP) of research institutions, and developing a standardised IP protocol for all public agencies and publicly-funded research performers to simplify the commercialisation process; and creating a regulatory environment to support innovation and risk-taking.

In line with the focus of the *Report of the Committee on the Future Economy*, innovation received prominence in the Budget 2017 Statement. Under the title of 'An Innovative and Connected Economy', the Statement emphasised:

> *"As we mature as an economy, we must compete on the quality and novelty of our ideas, and our ability to create value. We need to build a strong innovation and enterprise engine, to complement our traditional strengths in efficiency and speed. These moves will entail building capabilities of our enterprises, the capabilities of our people, and bringing all parts together in*

partnership to act as one agile, adaptable whole. This, in essence, is the key
thrust of the CFE recommendations.....
......there are three capabilities that many firms will need in
common — being able to use digital technology, embrace innovation, and
scale up."

Specific initiatives to boost innovation were also announced.
These included helping companies to identify technology to spur
innovation (A*STAR Operation and Technology Roadmapping),
improving companies' access to intellectual property (through
Intellectual Property Intermediary), supporting companies in the
use of advanced machine tools for prototyping and testing (Tech
Access Initiative), and facilitating Singaporeans to gain overseas
experience, build networks and collaborate with their counterparts
in other innovative cities (Global Innovation Alliance).

In addition, the Budget 2017 Statement underlined the role of
Government agencies in boosting innovation. The enabling roles of
the agencies included striking a balance between managing risk and
creating the space to test innovations, creating regulatory sandboxes
within which some rules could be suspended to allow greater exper-
imentation, and making risk assessments for new products and
services more swift and effective.

A culture of innovation was also stressed by Heng Swee Keat in
his round-up speech on the Budget 2017 debate. He said:

"The CFE strategies are part of a broader movement, to develop a pervasive
culture of innovation, nimbleness and adaptability. This will not take
place overnight, and Budget 2017 is but a step in that direction and builds
on what the CFE has put forward."

Productivity Drive in the 2010s in Retrospect

The beginning of the 2010s created much buzz and excitement, as
it was reminiscent of the early 1980s when the nation-wide Productivity
Movement was launched. After the hiatus in the productivity drive
in the 2000s, the intense focus on productivity once again was very

glaring. It soon became clear that the approach taken was going to be different. Instead of national-level productivity promotion, a sectoral approach to productivity improvement was taken. Instead of a single national productivity champion, different lead Government agencies were assigned the responsibility for different sectors. And instead of a high-octane productivity campaign, a subdued and subtle approach was adopted to promote productivity.

At the halfway mark of the 2010s, the outcome was limited, both in terms of the publicity generated and the productivity growth achieved. The average productivity growth of 0.4 per cent a year from 2010–2015 was less than half of what was already a low 1 per cent a year in the 2000s, and it was well below the targeted range of 2–3 per cent for the entire decade.

Beyond the halfway mark, the productivity drive, in the form that was implemented in the first half of the 2010s, came to an abrupt halt. Instead of being on a separate high-profile track on its own, productivity was now subsumed under the ITMs as one of four strategies. This was an about-turn on the approach taken to promote productivity in the first half of the 2010s. The ITM approach, first put forward in Budget 2016, was strongly affirmed as the preferred approach to industry transformation in the CFE Report and in Budget 2017. Furthermore, innovation, rather than productivity, began to hog the limelight.

VII
Epilogue

Chapter 14

Back to the Future

"One of the more notable character traits of the Singaporean is his unconcern for the history of his country ... I should like to end as I began, by exhorting Singaporeans to take more interest in the history of their country — its founding, development and progress."

Dr Goh Keng Swee
Minister for Finance
Speech at the Opening of the '150 Years of Development' Exhibition
at Elizabeth Walk
1 August 1969

Reflecting on the Past

A distinguishing characteristic of the Singapore Government is its forward-looking orientation and ability to plan for the future. Public officers are constantly reminded of the need to look ahead, and they are taught how to do so. Scenario planning is done in the same vein as corporate planning. At the same time, the officers are told that they should be grounded in the past. In his speech at the 2010 Administrative Service Dinner and Promotion Ceremony on 30 March 2010, Teo Chee Hean, Deputy Prime Minister and Minister in Charge of the Civil Service, said:

"It is not our nature to remain content with the status quo and rest on our laurels; we should always look ahead. But even as we think about the future, we must not forget the past for we can learn many things from the

past as well ... PSD [Public Service Division] has also been working on a book to capture the 50-year history of the Public Service — from the time Singaporeans took over the Service from the British in 1959 ... The Public Service book is our link to the past, the valuable lessons it can offer."

This book on Singapore's productivity drive in the last 50 years is similar to the Public Service book in providing a link to the past. With a 50-year history, the productivity drive can certainly offer much thought for reflection and lessons for the future.

Fundamentals that Have Served Singapore's Productivity Drive Well

Like many other areas of the economy and society, the Government has done an impressive job in attempting to raise productivity in the past five decades even if the results are not sterling. As stated in Chapter 1, Singapore's experience is benchmarked by many other countries and it has been the subject of study by academics and researchers.

Looking back at the 50-year history, certain fundamentals that have served Singapore's productivity drive well can be distilled.[1] These are:

a. Political stability;
b. Role of Government;
c. Tripartism; and
d. Eclectic learning approach.

Political Stability

Political stability is a sine qua non of economic progress. The reason is that the degree of political stability has a direct impact on the

---

[1] Many of the fundamentals underpinning the productivity drive are the same as those that have been widely cited for Singapore's economic progress. Only the macro-level fundamentals that have been critical to the progress of the productivity drive are listed here. From this list, a longer list of key success factors can be derived.

various sources of economic growth in a country — including physical capital accumulation, foreign trade and investment, and technology advancement. Various studies have substantiated this relationship. An example is the detailed study by Alesina, *et al.* (1992), covering 113 countries including Singapore, for the period 1950–1982. Using a model in which several economic determinants were accounted for, the study reached the robust conclusion of an inverse relationship between political instability and economic growth.

Without the precondition of political stability, it is fruitless to channel energies and resources into productivity improvement. Soon after Singapore had become a self-governing State in 1959, productivity was recognised as being critical to the economy. Yet, as Dr Goh Keng Swee, Minister for Finance, said plainly in 1964, he did not support the idea of setting up a productivity centre then because "the Communists were in full cry, and nothing worthwhile would have been achieved". With the Communists in check thereafter, the political situation stabilised and the pursuit of productivity became meaningful. Since then, the state of political stability has improved by leaps and bounds, with the People's Action Party (PAP) forming the Government from 1959. Today, this is often taken for granted because it appears to be the norm.

The extreme importance of political stability to the productivity drive cannot be overstated. This point comes across clearly when one looks at the member economies of the Asian Productivity Organization (APO). Because of political instability, some of the economies have not been able to progress much over the years even though they had a head start compared with Singapore.

Role of Government

Singapore is well known for the Government's interventionist approach in developing the economy. More than 20 years ago, The World Bank concluded that this approach had benefited Singapore, as well as other high-performing East Asian economies. This was attributed to three prerequisites that were met by the interventions.

First, they addressed problems in the functioning of markets. Second, they took place within the context of good, fundamental policies. Third, they were monitored closely against appropriate economic performance criteria. In short, the institutional context within which the interventionist policies were implemented was as important to their success as the policies themselves (The World Bank, 1993).

The World Bank's findings apply to the Government's role in the national productivity drive. Systematic planning, implementation and monitoring are pervasive — including the policies and plans, infrastructure, institutions, campaigns, programmes and public communication. In the 1980s, the National Productivity Council (NPC) was given the responsibility for overseeing the national productivity drive. Today, the Council for Skills, Innovation and Productivity (CSIP) plays that role. The Government's philosophy is well summed up by the words "Productivity is never an accident. It is always the result of a commitment to excellence, intelligent planning, and focused effort" (attributed to Paul J. Meyer, an American businessman and founder of Success Motivation Institute).

More importantly, the systematic planning and implementation of the productivity policies and plans is led by the top-level leadership in the Government. Prime Minister Lee Kuan Yew's personal commitment and involvement in the Productivity Movement in the 1980s were critical to its significant progress. This top-level leadership has continued over the years. CSIP is chaired by Deputy Prime Minister Tharman Shanmugaratnam, giving the council the clout to implement policies that fall under the charge of different Government ministries.

Tripartism

Tripartism, involving the collaboration between unions, employers and the Government, is critical in many aspects of the Singapore economy. Viewed against the history of industrial strife and confrontation in the 1950s and 1960s, tripartism has promoted harmonious labour-management relations and enhanced Singapore's economic competitiveness significantly. Today, the tripartite partners — National Trades Union Congress (NTUC), Singapore National Employers Federation (SNEF) and Ministry of Manpower (MOM) — are represented on many national-level committees formed to oversee various aspects of the economy. The most prominent of these committees is the National Wages Council (NWC).

Over the years, the national productivity drive has benefited much from tripartism. In the early 1960s, the productivity drive could not get off the ground not just because of the turbulent political situation; the hostile state of labour-management relations made it impossible to focus on productivity. The need for tripartism (although the term was not used then) was clearly put across by Dr Goh Keng Swee, Minister for Finance, in 1961 when he said, "It is necessary to have all three parties working towards an agreed objective and agreeing also on the means whereby inevitable differences must be resolved."

The National Productivity Centre was established in 1967 to kick-start the productivity drive only after *The Charter for Industrial Progress and the Productivity Code of Practice* had been signed by representatives of the unions and employer groups with strong backing from the Government. In the subsequent decades, the tripartite partners worked together to push the productivity agenda to all segments of the economy and society. Beginning from NPC in 1981, the tripartite representation has been sustained over the years — all the way to the National Productivity and Continuing Education Council (NPCEC) in 2010 and CSIP in 2016.

Like political stability, tripartism is often assumed to be the natural order of things in Singapore. The reality is that it is a unique institution that has been painstakingly built over the years; and it is something that is not found in many other countries, which are often plagued by a trust deficit between the various parties. Platforms highlighting the role of tripartism — such as the 'Pioneering The Future Series' organised by the EDB Society and The Straits Times on 26 February 2016 — are useful in reminding everyone that tripartism should not be taken for granted. For the same reason, it is significant that the *Report of the Committee on the Future Economy* emphasised that "tripartism in Singapore has been a key competitive advantage for us. Our good industrial relations remain an enduring strength."

Eclectic Learning Approach

The Singapore Government has prided itself in the fact that it adopts an eclectic approach in tackling any issue. Instead of taking a textbook approach or re-inventing the wheel, it openly learns from others, makes modifications and improvements appropriately, and then applies the lessons to the economy. It has in fact been engaging in what is known as 'benchmarking' in the 'management field, even without using the term.

The eclectic learning approach has contributed much to the advancement of the national productivity drive. In the 1960s and 1970s, assistance from the United Nations Development Programme (UNDP) was sought. As a result, Singapore was able to kick-start its own national productivity organisation, build the requisite competencies, and launch various activities to get the productivity drive underway. In the 1980s, the Productivity Movement received a tremendous boost from the Productivity Development Project (PDP) funded by the Government of Japan. In addition to building the competencies of NPB, individuals and companies, PDP supported the fledgling national Productivity Movement that was launched in September 1981.

Besides the large-scale assistance from UNDP and PDP, Singapore learned much from the other national productivity organisations, overseas institutions and companies, and individual experts. By integrating the lessons from these various sources, the Government has been able to take a uniquely Singapore approach that is appropriate for the local environment.

Issues for Reflection

No doubt, Singapore has come a long way in its 50-year productivity journey. Compared with its nascent years in the 1960s, the national productivity drive has made much progress. Nevertheless, in the spirit of continuous improvement and in the quest for higher benchmarks of performance, there is the possibility of doing better in the future.

The rest of this chapter draws out the main issues from the preceding chapters for reflection. The issues are presented not primarily for their historical curiosity but for the fact that they will still have to be dealt with in the future, even though the environment is different. Based on the information available and with the benefit of hindsight, certain views are presented on each of the issues. The aim is not to criticise any policy decision taken in the past, but to facilitate and stimulate discussion on what needs to be done for the future based on lessons from the past.

Diverse interpretations can be made and conclusions reached when the various issues are examined by different individuals. It is therefore highly unlikely that there will be consensus on the views laid out. In fact, it is more likely that there will be disagreements or even protestations by some individuals or representatives of certain Government agencies or other organisations. This is a positive outcome if it leads to serious reflection, thorough discussion and good planning for the uncharted territory that lies ahead. As Prime Minister Lee Hsien Loong said at Camp Sequoia, hosted by Sequoia Capital, on 24 February 2017:

> *"You need people who have their own views, whose views you respect, whom you can have a productive disagreement with, and work out ideas which you might not have come up with, or who improve on ideas you had."*

The main issues for reflection are grouped under the following ten headings:

a. Understanding historical context in conjunction with planned changes;
b. Factoring in wide spectrum of views and opinions;
c. Promoting productivity consistently;
d. Leading with a single national productivity champion;
e. Balancing national approach and sectoral approach;

f. Understanding the multiple aspects of productivity;
g. Focusing on particular aspects of productivity at any point in time;
h. Building the productivity culture;
i. Balancing form and substance in productivity drive; and
j. Learning from the experience of others.

Understanding Historical Context in Conjunction with Planned Changes

A policy is never an absolute. It is made and implemented according to the prevailing circumstances. The policy may have to be modified or even discarded when the environment changes. On the other hand, it may continue to be relevant even in a new environment. So, it is important for a policy, as well as its raison d'etre, to be reviewed against its historical context when a change is being considered.

Looking at the record in the last five decades, it is arguable whether some of the policies had fully taken into account the historical facts before they were implemented. A prime example is the corporatisation and subsequent divestment of certain core functions of the Singapore Productivity and Standards Board (PSB) from 2002. It seemed that the primary driving force for the decision taken was the policy of the Government to divest all its non-strategic businesses that had alternative service providers in the private sector. Because some of the PSB functions were considered non-strategic and had alternative service providers, albeit not within a single entity, they were eventually divested in 2006. It would appear that there was little consideration of the reason for the establishment of PSB, as well as its predecessors, in the first place. Apparently, three decades of building the national productivity organisation — with assistance from UNDP in the 1970s and PDP in the 1980s, and merger of the National Productivity Board (NPB) and the Singapore Institute of Standards and Industrial Research (SISIR) in the 1990s — did not carry much weight in the divestment decision.

Ironically, in the late 2000s, in preparation for the renewed Productivity Movement, the policy-makers turned their attention to the regional countries to learn about their productivity centres. These were the same countries that had previously learnt earnestly from Singapore, which was then a highly-sought benchmarked country. In the early 2010s, a decision was made to recreate, as it were, the productivity organisation that had existed earlier, albeit in a different form (see 'Leading with a Single National Productivity Champion' below). This inevitably raises the question of whether the PSB divestment was done too hastily without adequate knowledge of the historical facts.

Understanding the historical context of a policy is particularly important when there is a change of policy-makers, which happens all the time. Starting with a clean slate, with no consideration of the past, is not a good practice. Hence, any sign of the non-invented-here (NIH) syndrome creeping in must be nipped in the bud.

Factoring in Wide Spectrum of Views and Opinions

Many studies have been done, both locally and overseas, on various aspects of Singapore's productivity drive and performance. Similarly, there have been numerous studies on Singapore's labour policy and its impact on long-term productivity growth. The resulting numbers and conclusions from the studies, some of which are presented in this book, are telling. Trend numbers such as the sharp drop in productivity growth and the steep rise in foreign labour share over the decades are startling. The studies have also identified policies that contributed to Singapore's lacklustre productivity performance, and proposed possible solutions to turn the tide. Such studies continue to be done every year.

A problem is that many of the studies are done by academics, and they tend to be inaccessible because of their academic orientation and publication in journals that are not usually read by non-academics. Prior to the article on 'The Myth of Asia's Miracle' by Paul Krugman, there were several academic studies that had highlighted Singapore's low TFP performance. However, they did not receive widespread attention until Paul Krugman, himself a highly-acclaimed theorist, wrote the piece for non-academics.

It is certainly not the case that the policy-makers are totally unaware of the studies done by academics and other researchers. It is a question of how much attention is given to these studies, and whether the findings get disseminated to the appropriate decision-makers. What is particularly problematic is the chasm that exists between the academic world and the policy-making world. This chasm is created by the traditional assessment yardstick used in the academia, which rates academics primarily on their esoteric publications in top-tier journals. Consequently, there is little incentive for the academics to contribute to policy-making.

Even when the findings of a study are disseminated, the receptacle may not always be open, especially when the conclusions reached, views expressed and recommendations made are different from the policy-makers' worldview. A clear example is the strong rebuttal of the findings by Alwyn Young and Paul Krugman on Singapore's poor total factor productivity (TFP) performance. It is therefore not surprising to read statements from academics such as:

> *"What is more relevant for policy development in Singapore is not so much which studies are correct but what the Singapore government thought of the points being made in the debate ... Here we have seen what could be thought of as the technocrats' reaction to studies that seemed to show that Singapore was not a very efficient economy. They did their own calculations trying to show that things were not as bad as the earlier studies had shown, provided references to other studies for ministerial speeches and did something about measuring and monitoring the supposed crucial variable and set up institutions and policies to improve things."*

This statement was made by Peebles and Wilson (2002) in conjunction with their review of the studies on Singapore's TFP performance. No doubt, this strikes a chord among policy-makers. In this case, there was at least an attempt to take action to improve things.

Another example of a statement made by academics (Pang and Lim, 2016) in a similar vein is the following:

> *"Singapore's state-driven, foreign-led, export-oriented development model since independence has delivered high GDP growth for over four decades primarily through factor accumulation — chiefly foreign manufacturing investment, high domestic savings, and vast inputs of foreign skilled and unskilled labor. This high-growth achievement, and a very high share for profits in GDP, has occurred at the expense of productivity growth, and more recently, of citizens' social welfare.*
>
> *Singapore economists have long called for a change in this model, recommending a refocus away from subsidized manufacturing for a global market toward market-based services for the Asian and Southeast Asian region, in line with Singapore's unique competitive advantage as a city-state in a fast-growing geography."*

Obviously, the point is not that policy-makers should be swayed by the findings and recommendations of academics, researchers and other analysts. Rather, there is a wide spectrum of studies done by experts outside the policy-making arena, which should be monitored, considered and analysed to draw insights. The chasm between the academic world and the policy-making world needs to be bridged. Greater interaction between the two worlds and openness to alternative views, including dissenting opinions, will enable better policy formulation.

Promoting Productivity Consistently

Throughout Singapore's 50-year productivity drive, the statement 'productivity is a marathon with no finish line' was used frequently by various personalities, including Lee Kuan Yew and Lee Hsien Loong in their capacity as Prime Minister almost 30 years apart. The message underlying this statement is that there should be dogged persistence and no let-up in the productivity drive. This message is important because productivity, stripped of its complexities, is really about making good use of all the resources available to produce goods and services that give maximum value to the economy. Regardless of Singapore's stage of development, productivity should therefore be a perennial concern.

Nevertheless, the reality is that in the last five decades, there was constant tension between the long-term requirement for a sustained productivity drive and the short-term need to seize growth opportunities to counter economic adversity. The latter was invariably accompanied by an increase in the inflow of low-skilled foreign workers into Singapore, which negated the productivity drive. Quantitative studies have thus concluded that Singapore's economic growth in the last 50 years was due largely to factor accumulation — labour, as well as capital — rather than TFP growth.

For good reasons, the Government is likely to continue taking a pragmatic, hard-nosed approach in tackling short-term problems. Hence, the tension between promoting productivity and seizing growth opportunities has to be addressed. The objective is to ensure that the short-term measures taken do not have lasting adverse effects on productivity improvement.

The tension can be managed if there is constancy in keeping the productivity torch burning even as the short-term economic needs are being taken care of. This was the case from the 1970s to the 1990s. In the 1970s, the Government turned its attention to the various crises, including two oil shocks, after it had declared the need to raise productivity. Nonetheless, the focus on productivity remained as NPB pushed ahead with its training, consultancy and promotion activities with assistance from UNDP. In the 1980s, NPB accelerated the productivity drive even as the Government tackled the first economic recession that hit post-independence Singapore in 1985. This was done under the ambit of NPC and with assistance from PDP. In the 1990s, when the Government focused its attention on the Asian Financial Crisis, PSB, under the aegis of the National Productivity and Quality Council (NPQC), pushed on with the total approach to productivity. In contrast, the productivity torch was all but extinguished in the 2000s as the Government tackled the different crises, including the dot.com crash in 2001 and the global financial crisis in 2007. This was due to the discontinuation of NPQC in 2001 and the change in the role of the Standards, Productivity and Innovation Board (SPRING) from the national productivity organisation to an enterprise development agency in 2004. While the productivity torch was rekindled in 2010, the challenge is to keep it aflame. Up till 2014, there appeared to be some semblance of the sustained productivity drive in the 1980s and 1990s. The series of activities undertaken culminated in the launch of the National Productivity Month in October 2014. However, the Way to Go campaign and the National Productivity Month appeared to be a one-off affair, as these were not continued.

There have also been changes to the council spearheading the productivity drive. In April 2010, NPCEC was set up to address both productivity and continuing education and training (CET). These two areas were split in November 2014, with productivity going under the ambit of a new NPC and CET under a separate SkillsFuture Council. In May 2016, CSIP was formed to take over and carry on what NPC and the SkillsFuture Council had done. Correspondingly, the productivity plans of NPC and the sectoral manpower plans of the SkillsFuture Council were folded under the Industry Transformation Maps (ITMs) overseen by CSIP.

These series of changes within a space of six years may give the impression of inconsistency in promoting productivity. First, the perception is that NPCEC was split into NPC and the SkillsFuture Council, and then the two entities were brought together again in the form of CSIP. While CSIP seems to cover more than NPCEC by including skills, innovation and internationalisation in addition to productivity, this is not necessarily the case. The three strategic areas and the narrow scope of productivity defined by CSIP are in fact factors that affect overall productivity.[2] These factors were also addressed by NPCEC, albeit not as well integrated in the sectoral productivity plans as they are in the ITMs. Second, the separation of the three factors from productivity may reinforce the view that they are distinct and unrelated (see 'Focusing on Particular Aspects of

---

[2] This is clear when one examines the determinants of productivity. See Amp-Box on *Productivity Primer* in Chapter 1.

Productivity at Any Point in Time' below). Third, with productivity being subsumed under the ITMs, together with skills, innovation and internationalisation, the productivity drive is no longer a separate movement. This could be detrimental to the long-term promotion of productivity, which enjoyed a high profile as the national Productivity Movement in the 1980s and 1990s.

The apparent downplaying of productivity from the mid-2010s came across most clearly in the *Report of the Committee on the Future Economy* and in the Budget 2017 Statement. In both cases, productivity receded into the background and was scarcely mentioned. Even though it could be argued that productivity is now embedded in the ITMs, it is no longer the focus as compared with the first half of the 2010s.

All such developments need to be carefully managed to dispel any impression that the Government is inconsistent in its productivity promotion effort. Equally important is the public communication of these developments. It cannot be assumed that the public is aware of the policy-makers' worldview.

Leading with a Single National Productivity Champion

The statement 'productivity is everybody's business' is often bandied about in speeches, publications and publicity material. The message is that everyone needs to have a stake in productivity and to be actively involved in productivity activities. For this to happen, there should be a leader or a champion that leads the way, provides guidance on what needs to be done, coordinates efforts, and galvanizes everyone to move in the same direction. The champion should also serve as the national productivity competency centre, with deep knowledge and expertise in productivity and working with other agencies to drive productivity improvement efforts at different levels of the economy.

From 1967 until the early 2000s, the productivity drive was spearheaded by a single agency — first, the National Productivity Centre and then its successors, NPB, PSB and SPRING. In addition, from 1981 till 2001, NPC and its successor, NPQC, provided the overall directions for the productivity drive. Between 2004 and 2009, there was a void as both the national productivity organisation and the national productivity council retreated from the scene. From 2010, with the setting up of NPCEC, the roles of the former NPC and NPQC were revived. Although NPCEC subsequently evolved into NPC and then CSIP, there is still a council that oversees the productivity drive in one form or another. The difference today is that there is no agency that has been designated the national productivity organisation or champion. On paper, in its Act, SPRING is still responsible for raising TFP. In reality, it is an enterprise development agency and it is not tasked by the Government to champion productivity. Even though the enterprise development work does cover productivity to some extent, SPRING is in effect no longer the national productivity organisation.

Recognising the need for an institution like the national productivity organisation of the past, the Economic Strategies Committee (ESC) recommended that a productivity and innovation centre be set up. Thereafter, it was put into effect by NPCEC. However, instead of a single national productivity organisation, three small productivity centres were set up — Singapore Innovation and Productivity Institute (SiPi) for the manufacturing sector, Singapore Productivity Centre (SPC) for the services sectors and Construction Productivity Centre (CPC) for the construction sector. SiPi and SPC are private entities while CPC is a unit within the Building and Construction Authority (BCA).

It is arguable whether this decentralised, multi-agency approach is more effective than the previous approach of a single national productivity organisation working with other agencies. First, there is duplication of resources and competition with one another since the different organisations have their own key performance indicators (KPIs) and are accountable to different Ministries. Second, there is sub-optimisation of size, which prevents economies of scale from being reaped. Third, a holistic approach is not taken to address productivity issues that cut across sectors, or to develop competencies and programmes that can be used in different sectors. Fourth, the lack of a single focal point for productivity confuses the

industry. Fifth, it is unrealistic to expect the national council overseeing the productivity drive, as well as its secretariat, to scrutinize
and coordinate the efforts of the different agencies since it is not
manned by full-time staff dedicated to the productivity drive.

Considering the small size of Singapore, a single national productivity organisation is likely to be more effective. There is no
doubt that the national productivity drive will involve various agencies. Hence, the national productivity organisation will have to work
closely with them. The first challenge is to build the competencies
of this organisation since these were dissipated when PSB divested
some of its core functions and when SPRING later became an enterprise development agency. Another challenge is to determine the
modus operandi of the organisation in relation to other agencies in
the current environment. One possibility is for the national productivity organisation to perform a similar role as that of NPB/PSB in
the past — serving as the secretariat, executing agency and competency centre of the national council driving productivity. In today's
context, the national productivity organisation will support and
work closely with CSIP and the lead agencies, and act as the competency centre, in developing and implementing the ITMs and any
other programmes.

Balancing National Approach and Sectoral Approach

For many of the economic programmes implemented, either a
broad-based national approach or a targeted sectoral approach can
be taken. A national approach enables a wide reach and uniformity
in messaging and application of policies, whereas a sectoral
approach allows for policies and programmes to be tailored to the
needs of the individual sectors.

In the 1980s and 1990s, an overarching national approach was
taken for the productivity drive. NPC/NPQC provided the overall
directions; NPB/PSB spearheaded the execution together with
other relevant agencies, and acted as the secretariat to the council;
and the national productivity campaign served as the glue, as it
were, binding the different parties together. This national approach

was complemented by a sectoral approach. For example, in the 1980s, NPC set up two committees, viz. Committee on Productivity in the Manufacturing Sector and Committee on Productivity in the Commerce Sector. There were also specific plans to boost the productivity of sectors such as retail, hotel and travel in the 1980s and 1990s. The feedback from many employers was that the national approach was useful since it created the right environment and gave them legitimacy in implementing productivity improvement programmes at the enterprise level.

When the productivity drive was revived in 2010, the approach taken was a sectoral one. Altogether, 16 sectors were identified by NPCEC for attention. The sectors were put under the charge of the relevant Government agencies, which were responsible for developing their respective productivity plans for approval by NPCEC and then implementing the programmes in the plans. This sectoral approach was subsequently reinforced by CSIP, with special attention given to the development and implementation of ITMs for 23 industries.

With the heavy emphasis on ITMs in both the *Report of the Committee on the Future Economy* and the Budget 2017 Statement, a sectoral approach is clearly preferred to a national approach. Overall, such a targeted approach is probably more effective than a broad-based approach. The relative inefficacy of a broad-based approach is epitomised by the two government assistance schemes of Productivity and Innovation Credit (PIC) and Innovation and Capability Voucher (ICV). While these two schemes are intended to encourage all companies, especially the small and medium enterprises (SMEs), to implement productivity initiatives, their impact on raising productivity has been limited. In fact, they might have inadvertently propped up some inefficient companies that would otherwise have closed down. It is thus not surprising that the Government has stated its intention to take a more targeted sectoral approach from now on.

Nonetheless, this does not mean that a national approach should be discarded completely. While a sectoral approach is intended to address the specific needs of the individual sectors, it begs the question of whether adequate attention and resources are given to cross-sector issues. An example is the structure of the economy, including the distribution of manpower resources among the sectors. As the sectoral approach attempts to raise the productivity of the individual sectors, it does not address the economic structure per se. Consequently, the number of new establishments in labour-intensive, low-value added sectors such as retail and food & beverage can continue to grow and absorb resources that could have been used more effectively elsewhere, and the more productive sectors may not grow fast enough due to constraint of resources. This in fact happened in the first half of the 2010s.

Thus, a considered decision needs to be taken on what should be done at the national level to complement the sectoral approach, so that the forest is not missed for the trees.

Understanding the Multiple Aspects of Productivity

Any attempt to address the issue of productivity must begin with good understanding of what it is, what determines it, and how it is measured.[3]

In the 1970s, productivity was associated with automation; in the 1980s, work attitudes and human relations held sway; in the 1990s, quality came onto the radar screen and the jargon of TFP emerged; in the 2000s, innovation overwhelmed productivity as if they were two distinct terms; and from the 2010s, productivity became just 'productivity.' With the formation of CSIP in 2016, productivity (narrowly defined) became distinct from skills, innovation and internationalisation even though all four are determinants of productivity (broadly defined).

Statistics-wise, labour productivity (value added per worker and, more recently, value added per hour worked) is the term that appeared most in the official publications, although other measures such as multifactor productivity (MFP) were subsequently included as well.

---

[3]The Amp-Box on *Productivity Primer* in Chapter 1 provides the basics to facilitate understanding.

How should productivity be best understood and measured today? What are the key determinants of productivity growth? How can the different aspects of productivity be given adequate attention and integrated with other economic and social issues? These questions have to be taken in the context of an economic structure, a populace and a digital age that are vastly different from the situation in the last 50 years.

While there is basic knowledge of what productivity is, the multiple aspects of productivity and how they are interlinked are not well known. It is not far-fetched to say that only a small minority of individuals understand the differences between all the terms, let alone the determinants, of productivity. This leads to three consequences.

First, without a good grasp of all the different terms and the multiple facets of productivity, there is the danger of making policy decisions that discard, or even destroy, what was done earlier because it does not seem important anymore. This could be one of the reasons for the turning point in the productivity drive in the 2000s. Because innovation was considered the critical engine of growth, the productivity drive was put on the back burner. This stems from a lack of understanding of innovation as the factor that can increase productivity by several orders of magnitude, compared with process improvements that may lead to only marginal increases in productivity.

Second, without clear understanding of the determinants of productivity at the different levels, the programmes implemented may be ineffective. At the enterprise level, productivity is determined by a host of factors that affect both the top-line and bottom-line of the productivity equation. Beyond the enterprise level, the productivity performances of sectors and the economy are affected by many other factors. The constant lament about a sector's low productivity despite intense enterprise upgrading efforts reflects a failure to differentiate the determinants of productivity at the various levels. Many of the factors beyond the enterprise level are structural factors that affect the productivity of individual sectors and the economy. Hence, no amount of enterprise-specific programmes, however important for companies, will be able to lift the low productivity of sectors such as retail and food & beverage unless the structural issues are addressed. These include the number and types of enterprises in the sector, employment share of the sector in relation to the more productive sectors, cost structure, and regulations governing the operating environment of the sector.

Third, at the enterprise-level, inadequate knowledge of the determinants and measurement of productivity leads to varying interpretations of what needs to be done to move the productivity needle. The widely-used measure of labour productivity is often misinterpreted to mean the productivity of the individual worker regardless of other factors. This may skew the types of programmes implemented to boost productivity, and workers take the blame when the company's productivity is low. When one realises that the labour productivity measure is based on value added per worker or hour worked, it becomes clear that many factors come into play besides the worker. This measure is as applicable to companies as it is to the economy. Yet, many companies do not think that it is useful to them, as evidenced by the productivity surveys conducted over the years. Invariably, they are more inclined to think of financial measures such as profit and sales revenue or operational indicators like sales per square foot, and fail to see their connection with value added. Compounding the problem is the fact that there are no comprehensive sets of lower-level measures that can be used by companies to track their performance, benchmark against others and link to the value added measure.

In the 1980s and 1990s, NPB and PSB did much to educate companies and workers on the meaning of productivity, the various measures of productivity, and the link between productivity and wages. Such efforts have since been discontinued. Clearly, there is a gap that needs to be filled. Since the environment has changed considerably, the exact manner in which the gap is to be plugged needs to be deliberated, planned and executed accordingly.

Focusing on Particular Aspects of Productivity at Any Point in Time

Related to the point about understanding the multiple aspects of productivity is the need for policy-makers to decide the focus at any point in time. This should be linked to the prevailing environment and the needs of the economy, which must therefore be well understood. The focus on work attitudes and human relations per se in the 1980s would seem unduly lopsided, but it made sense because work attitudes and labour-management relations then were not conducive to the push for capital-intensive industrialisation. Similarly, the promotion of quality and TFP in the 1990s and innovation in the 2000s was done in the context of what was considered important for overall productivity growth.

Whatever the focus is at any point in time, it must be backed by programmes that are both adequate for the circumstances and effective in their impact. Existing programmes will have to be reviewed and new ones may have to be implemented. For this reason, the programmes implemented in the productivity drive in each decade are listed in detail in the various chapters. Policy-makers, researchers and analysts can review them, analyse their adequacy and efficacy, and draw lessons for the future.

Besides a strong backing by programmes, the particular focus should be clearly linked to the overall productivity drive. The danger is that when different aspects or notions of productivity are being emphasised at different times, they may appear to be incoherent or inconsistent. A clear example is the promotion of productivity in general in the renewed Productivity Movement in the early 2010s, as opposed to the strong emphasis on TFP in the 1990s. What is worse is when a particular aspect is being promoted without reference to productivity or put forward as being distinct from productivity. This seemed to be the case when innovation was promoted in the 2000s. Similarly, beginning from 2015, innovation started hogging the headlines once again but outside the domain of productivity. With productivity and innovation being listed as two different strategic areas under CSIP, the risk of perceiving the two terms as different and unrelated becomes greater.

The reason sometimes given for not making an explicit link between a particular focus and productivity is that people are tired of the term 'productivity.' Such reasons are only detrimental to the long-term promotion of productivity. The link to productivity should not be severed at any time. Once a focus area has been decided upon, the overall communication strategy needs to be formulated to ensure that all the messages are presented as a coherent whole and that the link to productivity is clear (see 'Balancing Form and Substance in Productivity Drive' below).

Building the Productivity Culture

There are some areas that need to be sustained all the time even if the focus is on something else at any point in time. Building the productivity culture is one such area.

Culture is often considered the linchpin for the successful implementation of any programme, both productivity-related and non-productivity-related. An analogy that is aptly used is that of an iceberg. Typically, only about 10 per cent of the volume of an iceberg is above water, while the overwhelming 90 per cent is submerged and hidden from view. The large, invisible part that is below the water level is important as it supports and sustains what is above it. A culture that is conducive to productivity improvement is like the invisible part of the iceberg, while productivity programmes constitute the visible part. Without a strong productivity culture, it is unlikely that the programmes can be sustained.

In the 1980s and 1990s, the productivity culture was built largely through the productivity campaign and by getting workers to be directly involved in Quality Control Circles (QCCs). The directions taken were influenced much by the experience of Japan, where companies like Toyota were renowned for a corporate culture in which employees were engaged in various ways to improve the products and processes all the time. The campaign approach fitted snugly into the period when campaigns, slogans and mascots were common in Singapore.

No doubt, a productivity culture is just as important today as it was in the past. Recognising this, NPCEC stated 'foster a culture of productivity and continuous learning and upgrading in Singapore' as one of its aims. In recent years, though, it is an innovation culture that is being emphasised by different quarters but outside the domain of productivity. CSIP has stated that it aims to develop skills for the future and support productivity-led economic growth by 'fostering a culture of innovation and lifelong learning in Singapore.' This is a variant of NPCEC's aim, with culture of innovation replacing culture of productivity.

Several questions are pertinent. First, what constitutes a productivity culture in the current environment and how should innovation be factored in? Second, which countries or cities can be upheld as models for Singapore to emulate today? Third, is it possible to take the Singapore culture as it is and capitalise on it for the productivity drive? Fourth, if campaigns are no longer appropriate, what other ways are suitable to mould the desired culture? The directions taken to promote the productivity culture will depend on the answers to these questions.

Balancing Form and Substance in Productivity Drive

As in many other areas, form is as important as substance in the productivity drive. It is form that creates the image in the eyes of the beholder. That is why companies spend large sums of money to build their corporate image. Of course, form must be backed by substance but it should not take a backseat.

The productivity campaign in the 1980s and 1990s was intended to create a buzz to keep productivity alive. Fronted by Teamy the Bee as the productivity mascot, the productivity messages and programmes were publicised widely to sustain awareness and understanding and, ultimately, lead to action. The various surveys and feedback affirmed the strong impact of the productivity campaign. Besides generating interest in productivity, it made it more palatable for employers to implement productivity programmes as workers understood the need for them.

In conjunction with the renewed productivity drive in 2010, a national campaign was launched under the subtle banner of 'Way to Go.' As noted above on the issue of promoting productivity consistently, a National Productivity Month, reminiscing the Productivity Month of the 1980s, was designated in 2014 but it has since not been sustained. Compared with the 1980s and 1990s, the campaign and the Productivity Month were low-keyed, so much so that not much buzz and awareness was created.

The degree of emphasis to be placed on form in relation to substance ought to be reviewed regularly. If the Way to Go campaign and the National Productivity Month are deemed unsuitable, other ways to create the form should be conceived. Furthermore, with productivity being subsumed under the ITMs, and the fact that it is one of four strategic areas under CSIP, it is critical to keep the productivity drive above water. Only then can interest in productivity be sustained.

Learning from the Experience of Others

In contrast to the 1960s–1980s, there has been no large-scale learning or assistance like UNDP or PDP from the 1990s onwards. Today, learning takes place in other ways that were also used together with the UNDP and PDP assistance. These include study missions, engagement of individual experts, invitation of speakers to conferences, learning from other productivity-related organisations, and analysis of reports and publications. Learning is also facilitated through APO, particularly its Technical Expert Scheme (TES) and Bilateral Cooperation Between National Productivity Organizations (BCBN) programme.

Much of the learning that takes place is done by the individual Government agencies on their own. This raises several questions. First, what are the various forms of learning that should be institutionalised? Second, how are countries or cities in the forefront of productivity identified? Third, are there greenfields where Singapore should venture out on its own? Fourth, what coordination and sharing mechanism can be put in place to maximise learning effectively? Answers to these questions will determine the efficacy of knowledge management and learning that occurs.

The issue at stake is akin to what Paul Romer (1990), one of the most influential theorists of economic growth, has termed as 'excludability', i.e. the degree to which ideas and technologies are hindered from flowing from one organisation to another. The higher the excludability, the greater it is in hindering productivity and economic growth.

Journeying into the Next 50 Years

The journey in the last 50 years has taken Singapore from a Third World country to a First World country — a feat that is unmatched by most other countries. From a bird's-eye view, the policies taken to boost the nation's productivity have made a visible difference to the economic landscape. The points made in relation to the ten issues above certainly do not detract from the accomplishments in the last five decades.

As the journey into the next 50 years begins, the policies in place may have to be tweaked, revamped or even discarded to meet the needs of the day. In addition, some new policies may have to be formulated. Even as the old issues and challenges are resolved and the goals are achieved, new ones will crop up. Productivity is indeed a marathon without a finish line. As Prime Minister Lee Kuan Yew said fittingly in his speech at the Opening of Productivity Month in 1988:

> *"Productivity means to keep improving. We shall reach our goals, not next year, but in the next decade. When we get there, we shall discover that there will be further fields to conquer."*

Postscript

The cut-off date for writing this book was set as 2 March 2017, the date of the round-up of the Budget 2017 debate. This allowed inclusion of the salient points from the *Report of the Committee on the Future Economy* and the Government's response to it, while giving sufficient time to meet the publishing deadline.

Nevertheless, there are two significant developments after the cut-off date that warrant inclusion in the book to complete the account of Singapore's productivity journey in the last 50 years and to provide an insight into the future. Hence, this postscript has been added.

The first development is the formation of the Future Economy Council (FEC). This was announced by Prime Minister Lee Hsien Loong in his May Day Rally Speech on 1 May 2017. FEC has replaced the Council for Skills, Innovation and Productivity (CSIP), which was chaired by Deputy Prime Minister Tharman Shanmugaratnam. Chairing the new Council is Finance Minister Heng Swee Keat, who had earlier helmed the Committee on the Future Economy (CFE).

In his reply to a parliamentary question on the scope of FEC on 3 July 2017, he elaborated:[1]

> *"The Future Economy Council (FEC) will oversee the implementation of the CFE recommendations, and will build on the work of the earlier Council on Skills, Innovation and Productivity, which includes SkillsFuture initiatives and the Industry Transformation Maps. At its core, the scope and focus of the Future Economy Council is on growing and transforming Singapore's economy for the benefit of our people. This will be done at three levels — first, growing an economy that is vibrant, open and connected to the world, supporting the growth of new and existing industries; second, strengthening our enterprises through industry-specific transformations to help them grow, innovate and scale-up; and third, enabling Singaporeans acquire and utilise deep skills, so as to seize opportunities in the future economy."*

The second development is the setting up of a new government agency named Enterprise Singapore. This was announced by S. Iswaran, Minister for Trade and Industry (Industry), at the official opening of the Singapore Business Federation's new office on 5 September 2017. The new agency will be formed by second quarter 2018 through the merger of Standards, Productivity and Innovation Board (SPRING Singapore, or SPRING in short) and International Enterprise Singapore (IE Singapore). In its press release on 5 September 2017, the Ministry of Trade and Industry said[2]:

> *"Combining the strengths of the two agencies, Enterprise Singapore will be better-positioned to help our companies grow and seize international opportunities in the next phase of Singapore's economic development. Enterprise Singapore aims to build a thriving community of Singapore enterprises that are competitive and ready for the future economy. Building on the established capabilities and networks of IE Singapore and SPRING, Enterprise Singapore*

---

[1] Ministry of Finance (2017), *Scope of Future Economy Council,* Parliamentary Reply by Minister for Finance Heng Swee Keat to Parliamentary Question by Liang Eng Hwa, 3 July, Singapore.

[2] Ministry of Trade and Industry (2017), *Enterprise Singapore to Grow Stronger Singapore Enterprises,* Press Release, 5 September, Singapore.

will seek to deepen its knowledge of industries' and companies' needs, expand its networks within Singapore and overseas, as well as develop a more stream-lined and comprehensive suite of assistance programmes to enable enterprise growth."

These two developments have a direct bearing on the national productivity drive. The indications, both in form and substance, are that they will shift the course taken by the productivity drive in the last 50 years significantly.

The change in form is most glaring. For a large part of the past 50 years, there was no question about the drivers of productivity since the term 'productivity' was firmly ensconced in the names of the entities responsible for it. From 1981 to 2000, there was the National Productivity Council (NPC), which later became the National Productivity and Quality Council (NPQC). When NPQC was dissolved in 2001, the situation became ambiguous in the subsequent nine years. Thereafter, from 2010 till early 2017, there was the National Productivity and Continuing Education Council (NPCEC), which evolved into National Productivity Council (together with SkillsFuture Council) and then CSIP. Despite the transformation of the council over the years, the term 'productivity' was still prominent in its name. With the formation of FEC, 'productivity' ceased to be part of the name of the council.

The entrenchment of 'productivity' in the name of the executive body responsible for productivity has an even longer, as well as unbroken, history. This stretches all the way back to 1967 when the National Productivity Centre was formed. Subsequently, it morphed into the National Productivity Board (NPB), Singapore Productivity and Standards Board (PSB) and SPRING. Even though SPRING is effectively no longer the national productivity organisation since 2004, 'productivity' is still in its name. With the formation of Enterprise Singapore, 'productivity' will be obliterated.

Nevertheless, if the issue at hand is merely a change in form, the implication for the national productivity drive is at most inconsequential. The reality is that it is more than a name change. For both FEC and Enterprise Singapore, productivity will not be the centre of attention. FEC will focus on implementing the CFE recommendations, none of which is productivity-centric. At best, productivity is addressed as part of the Industry Transformation Maps (ITMs), which was already the case under CSIP. Similarly, Enterprise Singapore will drive enterprise development, not productivity per se. As both SPRING and IE Singapore are essentially enterprise development agencies, their merger into Enterprise Singapore will create an organisation that is well equipped with the capabilities to address the wide range of enterprise development issues. This is akin to the situation in 1996 in the domain of productivity. The formation of PSB that year, through the merger of NPB and the Singapore Institute of Standards and Industrial Research (SISIR), resulted in an organisation that was well able to address total factor productivity. With the formation of Enterprise Singapore, a strong enterprise development agency has taken the place of a strong national productivity organisation, which is, in any case, now an institution of the past after the divestment exercise in 2006.

From the national perspective, the two developments are likely to be positive for the economy — in particular, for the transformation of the key industries and the growth of Singapore enterprises. However, the same cannot be said of the national productivity drive since there is now no explicit focus on productivity and no institution (both in name and responsibility) that champions productivity. The signal is that productivity will no more be pursued separately from other economic objectives and plans, and hence there will no longer be a distinct productivity drive in the future.

After 50 years of the national productivity drive, what lies ahead is decidedly unclear. What is certain is that productivity will not be taken off the Government's radar screen altogether since it is a subject matter that is far too important to be dumped. What is uncertain is the level of attention that it will receive when there is no distinct national productivity drive.

Regardless, in charting the way ahead, three quotes are instructive and ought to be borne in mind. The first two are by Prime Minister Lee Kuan Yew, one at the start of the book and the other at the beginning of Chapter 1, and the third is by Finance Minister Dr

Goh Keng Swee at the beginning of Chapter 14. The worst state to avoid is groupthink driven by a penchant for what is in vogue without studying the historical facts to distinguish what is enduring from what is transient. The admonitory remark by Dr Goh Keng Swee, in his speech at the Fifth Dinner and Dance of the Democratic Socialist Club on 25 October 1970, is as pertinent today as it was nearly 50 years ago:

> *"We have in Singapore intellectual conformity in place of intellectual inquisitiveness. And the sum total of it all adds up to a depressing climate of intellectual sterility."*

This perverse outcome ought to be guarded against at all times.

Bibliography[1]

Chapter 1

1. Krugman, P. (1997), *The Age of Diminished Expectations: U.S. Economic Policy in the 1990s*, 3rd edition, The MIT Press, Cambridge, Massachusetts, pp. 11–20.
2. Solow, R. (1987), "We'd Better Watch Out," *The New York Times Book Review*, 12 July, p. 36.
3. Woon, K. C. and Loo, Y. L. (2017), *Prime.Pack — Lean Transformation and Competitive Advantage for Sustained Growth*, Publisher: Authors.

Chapter 2

1. National Productivity Board (1972), "National Productivity Centre — What It's All About", *Minimax*, April, Vol. 1 No. 1, pp. 2.
2. National Productivity Board (1987), *Our Story: 15 Years of NPB*, Singapore.
3. National Trades Union Congress, Singapore Manufacturers' Association and Singapore Employers Federation (1965), *The Charter for Industrial Progress and the Productivity Code of Practice*, Singapore.
4. Ng, J. (2001), "Singapore and the Asian Productivity Organisation (APO)," *Productivity Digest*, February, pp. 2–7.
5. Singapore Economic Development Board (1991), *Singapore Economic Development Board: Thirty Years of Economic Development*, Singapore.

---

[1] The bibliography excludes the Annual Reports of NPB, PSB and SPRING and the Acts of Parliament, which were referred to extensively for the various chapters of the book.

Chapter 3

1. Goh Keng Swee (1976), "A Socialist Economy that Works," in Nair, D. (ed.), *Socialism that Works...The Singapore Way*, Singapore, pp. 77–85.
2. National Productivity Board (1972), "We Have Become a Board," *Minimax*, June, Vol. 1 No. 3, pp. 1 and 3.
3. National Productivity Board (1975a), "National Productivity Campaign," *Minimax*, April, Vol. IV No. 4, pp. 1, 4 and 5.
4. National Productivity Board (1975b), "Productivity Committee Model Constitution", *Minimax*, April, Vol. IV No. 4, pp. 2, 3 and 6.
5. National Productivity Board (1978a), "NPB's Five-Year Plan — Our Achievements and Goals Ahead," *Minimax*, January, Vol. VII No. 1, pp. 3 and 5.
6. National Productivity Board (1978b), "NPB: The Next Five Years," *Minimax*, February, Vol. VII No. 2, pp. 5–6.
7. National Productivity Board (1978c), "Productivity Committees — the Total Approach Toward Higher Productivity," *Minimax*, August, Vol. VII No. 8, pp. 4–5.

Chapter 4

1. Chow, K. B., Chew M. L. and Su, E. (1989), *One Partnership in Development: UNDP and Singapore*, United Nations Association of Singapore, Singapore.
2. International Labour Organization (1983), *Assistance to the National Productivity Board, Singapore*, United Nations Development Programme, Geneva.
3. U.N. Commissioner for Technical Assistance, Department of Economic and Social Affairs (1963), *A Proposed Industrialization Programme for the State of Singapore*, Singapore.
4. Winsemius, A. (1984), "The Dynamics of a Developing Nation: Singapore," *Speech at General Electric International Personnel Council Meeting in Singapore*, 19 June, Singapore.

Chapter 5

1. Lee, K. Y. (2000), "Lessons from Japan," in *From Third World To First — The Singapore Story: 1965–2000, Memoirs of LEE KUAN YEW*, Times Publishing, pp. 579–589.

2. Ministry of Communications and Information (1986), *On the Transfer of the National Productivity Board (NPB) to the Ministry of Trade and Industry*, Press Release, 28 July, Singapore.

3. Ministry of Culture (1981), *Speech by Dr Wong Kwei Cheong, Minister of State (Labour) and Chairman, National Productivity Board, at the Inaugural Lunch/Meeting of the National Productivity Council, 25 September 1981*, Singapore.

4. Ministry of Trade and Industry (1986), *Report of the Economic Committee. The Singapore Economy: New Directions*, Singapore.

5. National Productivity Board (1981), *Report of the Committee on Productivity*, Singapore.

6. National Productivity Board (1987), *Our Story: 15 Years of NPB*, Singapore.

7. National Productivity Board (1990), *Productivity 2000*, Singapore.

8. National Productivity Council (1983), *National Productivity Council Progress Report: September 81–August 83*, Singapore.

9. National Productivity Council (1985), *National Productivity Council 2nd Progress Report (Sep 83–Aug 85)*, Singapore.

10. Ogilvy & Mather Public Relations (1986), *Towards Excellence: The Civil Service Productivity Campaign, 1981–1986*, Singapore.

11. Singapore Broadcasting Corporation (1982), *Readings in Productivity*, Singapore.

Chapter 6

1. National Productivity Board (undated), *Come on Singapore*, Singapore.

2. National Productivity Board (1982), *Observations and Recommendations on the Productivity Movement in Singapore by H. A. M. Cliteur*, Singapore.

3. National Productivity Board (1983), *Tomorrow Shall be Better than Today — A Productivity Action Plan*, Singapore.
4. National Productivity Board (1984), *Come On Singapore — Let's All Do a Little Bit More*, Singapore.
5. National Productivity Board (1986), *Coming on Stream: A Report on the Productivity Movement as at the End of 1986 by H. A. M. Cliteur*, Singapore.
6. National Productivity Board (1987), *Our Story: 15 Years of NPB*, Singapore.
7. National Productivity Board (1990), *Productivity 2000*, Singapore.
8. National Productivity Board (1991), *National Productivity Award*, Singapore.
9. National Productivity Board (1994), *Productivity: Working It Out with Teamy*, Singapore.
10. National Productivity Council (1983), *National Productivity Council Progress Report: September 81–August 83*, Singapore.
11. National Productivity Council (1985), *National Productivity Council 2nd Progress Report (Sep 83–Aug 85)*, Singapore.
12. National Productivity Council (1986–1993), *Productivity Statement*, Singapore.
13. National Productivity and Quality Council (1994), *Productivity & Quality Statement*, Singapore.
14. Ogilvy & Mather Public Relations (1986), *Towards Excellence: The Civil Service Productivity Campaign, 1981–1986*, Singapore.

Chapter 7

1. Japan International Cooperation Agency (2000), "Third-Party Evaluation: Singapore and Malaysia Industrial Projects," *JICA Annual Evaluation Report 2000*, Tokyo, Japan, pp. 299–302.
2. Japan International Cooperation Agency (2014), "The Kaizen Project — Laying the Groundwork for Singapore's Growth," *JICA's World*, Vol. 5, No. 4, pp. 4–5.
3. Japan International Cooperation Agency (2016), *History of Friendship and Cooperation: The 50th Anniversary of Japan-Singapore Diplomatic Relations*, Tokyo, Japan.

4. Lee, K. Y. and Lee, A. (1990), "The Transfer of Japanese Productivity Technology to Singapore — A Review of the Productivity Development Project," *Productivity Digest*, June, pp. 2–7.
5. Lee, K. Y. (2000), "Lessons from Japan," in *From Third World To First — The Singapore Story: 1965–2000, Memoirs of LEE KUAN YEW*, Times Publishing, pp. 579–589.
6. Ministry of Communications and Information (1990), *Welcome Address by Mr Mah Bow Tan, Minister of State (Communications & Information) and (Trade & industry), at the Productivity Development Project (PDP) Closing Ceremony, 25 May 1990*, Singapore.
7. Ministry of Culture (1983), *Speech by Prof Jayakumar, Acting Minister for Labour and Minister of State (Law and Home Affairs), at the Exchange of Notes for the Productivity Development Project, 7 December 1983*, Singapore.
8. National Productivity Board and Japan International Cooperation Agency (1990), *Further Fields to Conquer — A PDP Commemorative Publication*, Singapore.

Chapter 8

1. Krugman, P. (1994), "The Myth of Asia's Miracle," *Foreign Affairs*, Vol. 73, No. 6, pp. 62–78.
2. Ministry of Trade & Industry (1998), *Committee on Singapore's Competitiveness*, Singapore.
3. Ministry of Trade & Industry (1991), *The Strategic Economic Plan: Towards a Developed Nation*, Singapore.
4. National Productivity Board (1991), "Quality Work, Quality Life. 1991 Productivity Month Campaign", *Productivity Digest*, November, pp. 3–9.
5. National Productivity Board (1995a), *Report of Task Force on Institutional Reform for Productivity and Quality Improvements*, Singapore.
6. National Productivity Board (1995b), *Singapore's Productivity Movement: 1995–2000. Innovation & Quality*, Singapore.
7. National Productivity Council (1988), *Productivity Statement 1988*, Singapore.

8. National Productivity Council (1990), *Productivity 2000*, Singapore.

9. Tsao, Y. (1982), *Growth and Productivity in Singapore: A Supply Side Analysis*, PhD Dissertation in Economics, Harvard University, Cambridge, Massachusetts.

10. Tsao, Y. (1985), "Growth without Productivity: Singapore Manufacturing in the 1970s," *Journal of Development Economics*, 19 (1–2), pp. 25–38.

11. Young, A. (1992), "A Tale of Two Cities: Factor Accumulation and Technical Change in Hong Kong and Singapore," *NBER Macroeconomics Annual*, Vol. 7, pp. 13–54.

Chapter 9

1. National Productivity Board (1991), *A Tribute to the Singapore Workforce*, Singapore.

2. National Productivity Board (1994), *Productivity: Working It Out with Teamy*, Singapore.

3. National Productivity Board (1995), "Charting New Directions for Singapore's Productivity Movement 1995–2000," *Productivity Digest*, November, pp. 2–5.

4. National Productivity Council (1991), *The First 10 Years of the Productivity Movement in Singapore: A Review*, Singapore.

5. National Productivity Council (1996), *15 Years of the Productivity Movement, 81–96*, Singapore.

6. National Productivity and Quality Council (1999), *ProAct 21: from perfecting the known to imperfectly seizing the unknown*, Singapore.

7. Woon, K. C. and Loo, Y. L. (2017), *Prime.Pack — Lean Transformation and Competitive Advantage for Sustained Growth*, Publisher: Authors.

Chapter 10

1. EDB Society (2000), *Millennium Conference Report*, Singapore.

2. Hamel, G. (2000), *Leading the Revolution*, Harvard Business School Press, Boston, Massachusetts.

3. Koh, J. (2002), "SPRING is here!", *Productivity Digest*, May, pp. 2–9.
4. Ministry of Trade and Industry (2003), *Report of the Economic Review Committee. New Challenges, Fresh Goals — Towards a Dynamic Global City*, Singapore.
5. National Productivity and Quality Council (1999), *ProAct 21: from perfecting the known to imperfectly seizing the unknown*, Singapore.
6. Public Sector Divestment Committee (1987), *Report of the Public Sector Divestment Committee*, Singapore National Printers, Singapore.
7. Stern, S., Porter, M. and Furman, J. (2000), *The Determinants of National Innovative Capacity*, NBER Working Paper 7876, National Bureau of Economic Research, Cambridge, Massachusetts.
8. World Economic Forum (2002), *The Global Competitiveness Report 2001–2002*, Oxford University Press, New York.

Chapter 11

1. Abraham, M. (2001), "Commemorating 20 Years of Singapore's Productivity Movement," *Productivity Digest*, September, pp. 2–8.
2. National Productivity and Quality Council (1999), *ProAct 21: from perfecting the known to imperfectly seizing the unknown*, Singapore.
3. Singapore Productivity and Standards Board (2000), "Productivity 2000 Campaign Rally," *Productivity Digest*, April, pp. 7–8.
4. Ohno, I. and Kitaw, D. (2011), "Productivity Movement in Singapore," in Japan International Cooperation Agency (JICA) and GRIPS Development Forum, *Kaizen National Movement — A Study of Quality and Productivity Improvements in Asia and Africa*, GRIPS Development Forum, Tokyo, Japan, pp. 49–68.
5. Yap, J. (2001), "An Orchid for Productivity... An Orchid for Eternity," *Productivity Digest*, September, pp. 15–16.

Chapter 12

1. Committee on the Future Economy (2012), *Report of the Committee on the Future Economy*, Singapore.
2. Economic Strategies Committee (2010), *Report of the Economic Strategies Committee*, Singapore.

3. Lee Kuan Yew School of Public Policy (2016), *Singapore's Productivity Challenge: A Historical Perspective*, Singapore.
4. Ministry of Trade and Industry (2010), *The National Productivity and Continuing Education Council (NPCEC) Holds its First Meeting*, Press Release, 30 April, Singapore.
5. Ministry of Trade and Industry (2012), *"Way to Go, Singapore." Nationwide Movement Launched to Boost Productivity Efforts, 4 Additional Sectors Identified to Boost Productivity Drive*, Press Release, 3 January, Singapore.
6. Ministry of Trade and Industry (2015), *Committee on the Future Economy to Review Singapore's Economic Strategies and Position Us for the Future*, Press Release, 21 December, Singapore.
7. Ohno, I. and Kitaw, D. (2011), "Productivity Movement in Singapore," in Japan International Cooperation Agency (JICA) and GRIPS Development Forum, *Kaizen National Movement — A Study of Quality and Productivity Improvements in Asia and Africa*, GRIPS Development Forum, Tokyo, Japan, pp. 49–68.

Chapter 13

1. Goh, T.W. (2014), "Feature Article: A Shift-Share Analysis of Singapore's Labour Productivity Growth," *Economic Survey of Singapore 2013*, pp. 70–77.
2. Goh, T.W. and Fan, S.L. (2015), "Feature Article: Drivers of Labour Productivity Growth Trends in Singapore," *Economic Survey of Singapore 2014*, pp. 76–87.
3. McMillan, M. and Rodrik, D. (2012), *Globalization, Structural Change, and Productivity Growth*, IFPRI Discussion Paper 01160, February, International Food Policy Research Institute, Washington, D.C.
4. Ministry of Finance (2014), *Speech by Mr Tharman Shanmugaratnam, Deputy Prime Minister and Minister for Finance, at the 20th Business Excellence Awards and Inaugural Singapore Productivity Awards Ceremony*, 30 October, Singapore.
5. Ministry of Trade and Industry (2016a), *Understanding Our Productivity Performance*, June, https://www.mti.gov.sg/MTIInsights.

6. Ministry of Trade and Industry (2016b), *Industry Transformation Maps*, October, https://www.mti.gov.sg/NewsRoom.

7. Ministry of Trade and Industry (2016c), *Speech by Mr Tharman Shanmugaratnam, Deputy Prime Minister & Coordinating Minister for Economic and Social Policies, at the Opening of Select Group's Corporate Headquarters and Launch of the Food Services Industry Transformation Map on Thursday, 8 September 2016*, Singapore.

8. Prime Minister's Office (2014), *Speech by Prime Minister Lee Hsien Loong at Opening of National Productivity Month*, 7 October, Singapore.

9. Singapore Workforce Development Agency (2016), *Formation of the Council for Skills, Innovation and Productivity*, Press Release, 20 May, Singapore.

Chapter 14

1. Alesina, A., *et al.* (1992), "Political Instability and Economic Growth," *NBER Working Paper Series*, September, National Bureau of Economic Research, Cambridge, MA.

2. Pang, E. F. and Lim, L. Y. C. (2016), "Labor, Productivity and Singapore's Development Model," in Lim, L. Y. C. (ed.), *Singapore's Economic Development: Retrospection and Reflections*, World Scientific, Singapore, pp. 135–168.

3. Peebles, G. and Wilson, P. (2002), *Economic Growth and Development in Singapore: Past and Present*, Edward Elgar Publishing Limited, Cheltenham, UK.

4. Public Service Division (2010), *Speech by Deputy Prime Minister, Minister in Charge of the Civil Service and Minister for Defence Teo Chee Hean at the 2010 Administrative Service Dinner and Promotion Ceremony*, 30 March, Singapore.

5. Romer, P. (1990), "Endogenous Technological Change," *Journal of Political Economy*, Vol. 98, No. 5, pp. 71–102.

6. The World Bank (1993), *The East Asian Miracle: Economic Growth and Public Policy*, Oxford University Press, New York.

Index

Printed in the United States
By Bookmasters